THE CONCISE
USAGE AND ABUSAGE

A Modern Guide to Good English

THE CONCISE
USAGE AND ABUSAGE

A MODERN GUIDE TO GOOD ENGLISH

BY

ERIC PARTRIDGE

PHILOSOPHICAL LIBRARY
NEW YORK

Published, 1954, by Philosophical Library, Inc.
15 East 40th Street, New York 16, N.Y.

FOR

THE HEADMASTER AND MASTERS
OF COTTON COLLEGE:

WHERE I HAVE SPENT
SO MANY HAPPY AND PROFITABLE DAYS:
THIS AFFECTIONATE DEDICATION

PRINTED IN GREAT BRITAIN FOR PHILOSOPHICAL LIBRARY
BY WESTERN PRINTING SERVICES LTD., BRISTOL

21389

FOREWORD

It has occurred to others than the publishers and myself that a drastically shortened and mildly simplified *Usage and Abusage* would fill a too noticeable gap. Hence this book.

In the course of abridgement and simplification I have also brought the material up to date and have added a few entries that appeared to be advisable.

The 'square' parentheses at the end of certain entries indicate the valuable additions made by Professor W. Cabell Greet to *Usage and Abusage* in order to render it suitable for use in the United States of America. In the present work a few of those additions have been reduced in length.

ERIC PARTRIDGE

ACKNOWLEDGEMENTS

Grateful acknowledgement is made to the following publishers for their permission to quote from the works listed below:

The Appleton-Century Company, Inc.:
English Words and Their Background, by G. H. McKnight.
Modern English in the Making, by G. H. McKnight and Bert Emsley.
Jonathan Cape, Ltd:
American Speeches, by James Ramsay MacDonald.
Chatto & Windus, Ltd:
Seven Types of Ambiguity, by William Empson.
The Clarendon Press:
A Dictionary of Modern English Usage, and S.P.E. Tracts XIV and XV, by H. W. Fowler.
Logic and Grammar and *On Some Disputed Points in English Grammar*, by Otto Jespersen.
The Oxford Book of English Prose, edited by Arthur Quiller-Couch.
The Oxford English Dictionary and *The Concise Oxford English Dictionary*.
Constable & Co., Ltd:
Words and Idioms, by Logan Pearsall Smith.
The Thomas Y. Crowell Company:
Words Confused and Misused, by Maurice H. Weseen.
Curtis Brown, Ltd:
Slings and Arrows, by David Lloyd George.
Hamish Hamilton, Ltd:
The World of Words, by Eric Partridge.
Harcourt, Brace and Company, Inc.:
The Tyranny of Words, by Stuart Chase.
Harvard University Press:
Addresses on International Subjects, by Elihu Root; by permission of the President and Fellows of Harvard College.
D. C. Heath & Company:
A Grammar of the English Language, by George O. Curme.
Longmans, Green & Co.:
English Composition and Rhetoric, by Alexander Bain.
The Macmillan Company, New York:
The Elements of Logic, by W. S. Jevons and D. J. Hill.
Words and Their Ways in English Speech, by J. B. Greenough and G. L. Kittredge.
G. & C. Merriam Company:
Webster's New International Dictionary of the English Language, 2nd edition, 1934
Methuen & Co., Ltd:
What a Word!, by Sir Alan Herbert.
Sir John Murray:
The Growth of English and *A Short History of English*, by H. C. K. Wyld.

ACKNOWLEDGEMENTS

Dr C. T. Onions and Messrs Kegan Paul, Trench, Trubner & Co., Ltd:
An Advanced English Syntax.

Rand McNally & Company:
A Comprehensive Guide to Good English, by George Phillip Krapp.

Routledge & Kegan Paul, Ltd:
Slang To-day and Yesterday, by Eric Partridge.

Scott, Foresman and Company:
An Index to English, by P. G. Perrin.

ABBREVIATIONS USED IN THIS BOOK

adj., adjective
adv., adverb
ca. (*circa*), about
cf. (*confer*), compare
Con. O.D., The Concise Oxford Dictionary
e.g. (*exempli gratia*), for instance
esp., especially
fig., figuratively
ibid. (*ibidem*), in the same place
i.e. (*id est*), that is
L., Latin
lit., literally
n., noun
N.B. (*nota bene*), note well
O.E.D., The Oxford English Dictionary
op. cit. (*opus citatum*), the work cited
opp., opposed; opposite
p., page
q.v. (*quod vide*), which see
R.C., Roman Catholic
S.E., Standard English
S.O.E.D., The Shorter Oxford English Dictionary
S.P.E. Tract, Society for Pure English Tract
Times Lit. Sup., The Times (London) Literary Supplement
U & A, Usage and Abusage
v., verb
v.i., verb intransitive
v.t., verb transitive
Webster's, Webster's New International Dictionary (2nd ed.)

USAGE AND ABUSAGE

A

a, an. The indefinite article is often introduced, though quite superfluously, in such sentences as: 'No more signal a defeat was ever inflicted' (quoted by Fowler).
a- an- for 'not' or 'without' should be prefixed only to Greek stems, e.g. *anarchic*. 'Amoral' (says Fowler) 'being literary is inexcusable, and *non-moral* should be used instead.'
a for *an*. See AN.
A in titles. See TITLES OF BOOKS AND PERIODICALS.
a + noun + or two takes a plural verb. The formula obeys the general rule governing an example such as 'Either the head or the legs *are* injured'; thus: 'Another good yarn or two [i.e. two good yarns] *are* to be found in "The Moon Endureth".' Regarded in another way, *a good yarn or two* is synonymous with and tantamount to *several good yarns*.
Note that *a + noun + or so* must not be used as synonymous with *a + noun + or two*. *A pint or so = a pint or thereabouts = a pint (approximately)*; it takes a singular verb. If, however, you permit yourself to kill a duck or so, you must write *a duck or so are nothing to me*.
abdomen. See BELLY.
aberration is not a synonym of *absent-mindedness*, as in, 'Once, in a moment of temporary aberration, Mr Dorgan drew a huge, hook-bladed knife from a hidden sheath, felt its razor-like edge carefully with a black and calloused thumb, then returned it with every sign of satisfaction'.
abide ('can't abide him') is not strictly incorrect, but a low-class colloquialism. [In American usage it may have homely or half-humorous quality.]
ability and **capacity**. *Ability* is a power to do something, or skill in doing it, whether the something be physical or intellectual. 'Here, promotion is by ability, not by birth'; 'He has outstanding ability as a surgeon—a writer—a pugilist . . .'. *Capacity*, apart from its physical sense ('power to receive or to contain': capacity of 1,000 gallons), means either 'power to

absorb or learn knowledge as opposed to power-in-doing' or 'innate or native power as opposed to acquired power'. 'My capacity for mathematics is negligible.'
-able and **-ible**. See '-IBLE and -ABLE'.
ablution is now intolerably pedantic for 'the act of washing one's hands or face'; and *perform one's ablutions* is a sorry jest. *Ablution* should be reserved for its religious senses.
abnormal; subnormal; supra-normal. Any departure from the *normal* (or usual or standard) is *abnormal*. To distinguish further: Any such departure as is *below* the normal is *subnormal*; *above* the normal, *supra-normal*.
about should be avoided in such phrases as these: 'It is about 9 or 10 o'clock'; 'The boy is about 9 or 10 years old'; 'It happened about the 9th or 10th of October, 1939'. Correct thus:—'It is 9 or 10 o'clock' or 'It is about 9.30'; 'The boy is 9 or 10 years old' or 'The boy must be somewhere near 10 years old'; 'It happened on either the 9th or the 10th of October' or, less precisely, 'It happened about the 9th of June'.
above (adj.), common in business writing and reference works. Avoid it! 'The above facts' should be 'The preceding (or, foregoing) facts' or, better still, 'These (or, Those) facts'. 'The above statement' should be 'The foregoing statement' or 'The last statement' or 'This (or That) statement'. Especially to be condemned is 'The above subject': read 'This (or That) subject' or 'The matter already mentioned (or, referred to)'. *Above* (adv.), as in 'The matter mentioned above', has been grievously overworked.
above, misused for *more than*. 'Above a yard' and 'above a year' are loose for 'more than a yard, a year'.
above and **over**; **below** and **beneath** and **under**. (Prepositions.) *Above* is 'higher up a slope, nearer the summit of a mountain or the source of a river' (also, of time, 'earlier than'), as in 'Behind and above it the vale head rises into grandeur'.— 'Literally higher than; rising beyond (the level or reach of)', as in 'The citadel of Corinth towering high above all the land';

hence of sounds, as in 'His voice was audible above the din'.—Figuratively, 'superior to', as in 'He is above mere mundane considerations'.—'Higher in rank or position than; (set) in authority over', as in 'The conscience looks to a law above it'.—'In excess of, beyond; more than', as in 'But above all things, my brethren, swear not'.—'Surpassing in quality, amount, number; more than', as in 'Above a sixth part of the nation is crowded into provincial towns'.—'Besides', occurring in *over and above*, as in 'Over and above his salary, he receives commission'. (*O.E.D.*)

Over is 'higher up than', either of position or of motion within the space above, as in 'Flitting about like a petrel over those stormy isles'; hence (after *hang, lean, jut, project*, etc.) in relation to something beneath, as in 'The upper story projects over the street'. Also, fig., as in 'His speech was over the heads of his audience'. The spatial sense "above" passes into other notions: the literal notion is (*a*) combined with that of purpose or occupation, as in [to sit] *over the fire*, [to talk] *over a bowl, a glass*; (*b*) sunk in that of having something under treatment, observation, or consideration, as in *to watch* or *talk over*, and in *make merry over*.—In sense *on* or *upon*:—'On the upper or outer surface of', sometimes implying the notion of 'covering the surface of', as in 'Sitting with his hat low down over his eyes'. 'Upon', with verbs of motion, as in 'He threw a dressing gown over the recumbent man'. 'Upon', or 'down upon', as an influence, as in 'A great change came over him at this point of his life'. 'Everywhere on' or 'here and there upon', as in 'Cottages scattered over the moor' and 'Over his face there spread a seraphic smile'; cf. the sense 'to and fro upon; all about; throughout', with reference to motion, as in 'They travel all over the country', and the sense 'through every part of', as in 'He went over my proofs for me'.—In sense 'above in amount, number, degree, authority, preference', as in 'It cost him over £50', 'He has no command over himself'.—The general sense of 'across', whether 'indicating motion that passes over (something) on the way to the other side; or sometimes expressing only the latter part of this, as in *falling* or *jumping over a precipice*', e.g., 'The sun is peering over the roofs', 'She turned and spoke to him over her shoulder'; or indicating 'from side to side of' (a surface, a space),

'across; to the other side of' (a sea, a river), 'from end to end of; along', as in 'He fled over the plains', 'A free pass over this company's lines of railways'; or (of position) 'on the other side of; across', as in 'Our neighbours over the way'.—Of time: 'during; all through', as in 'Extending over a century'; or 'till the end of; for a period that includes', as in 'If you stay over Wednesday'. (*O.E.D.*)

'*Over* and *above* differ in that *over* implies vertically, while *above* may or may not. Thus, the entire second story of a building is *above*, but only a small part of it is directly *over*, one who stands *on* (*upon*) the ground floor. . . . *Over* and *above* agree in the idea of superiority but differ in the immediacy of reference. Thus, the rank of ambassador is *above* that of minister, but the British ambassador is not *over* the Chinese minister; he stands in that relation to his subordinates only. Similarly, *above* and *over* agree in the idea of excess, which *beyond* heightens by carrying with it the suggestion that the thing exceeded, itself goes far; as "One there is *above* all others well deserves the name of friend; His is love *beyond* a brother's" ' (*Webster's*).

In general, *over* is opposed to *under*; *above* to *below* (or *beneath*).

Below, beneath; under:—Beneath covers a narrower field than *below*; it has the following senses:—(*a*) 'Directly down from, overhung or surmounted by; under', as in 'To sleep beneath the same roof'; (*b*) 'immediately under, in contact with the under side of; covered by', as in 'The dust beneath your feet'; (*c*) 'lower than, in rank, dignity, excellence, etc.' (now usually *below*), as in 'Beings above and beneath us probably have no opinions at all'; (*d*) 'unbefitting the dignity of, undeserving of, lowering to', as in 'It's beneath his notice'. The *O.E.D.* thus summarizes the status and usefulness of *beneath*:—'In ordinary spoken English, *under* and *below* now cover the whole field (*below* tending naturally to overlap the territory of *under*), leaving *beneath* more or less as a literary and slightly archaic equivalent of both (in some senses), but especially of *under*. The only senses in which *beneath* is preferred' are (*d*) as in 'beneath contempt', and the fig. 'subject to', as in 'to fall beneath the assaults of temptation'.

What then of *below*? Primarily it = (*a*) 'at a less elevation than, i.e. lower than', as in 'below the level of the ocean', 'He hit his opponent below the knee', 'It is

possible to be below flattery as well as above it'; hence (b) 'lower on a slope than, farther down a valley or a stream than', also 'nearer the bottom of a room than', as in 'Below the village, the valley opens into a broad flat meadow'; (c) 'deeper than', as in 'Water was found about three feet below the surface', 'Language has to be studied both below the surface and superficially'; (d) of position in a graduated scale, e.g., that of a barometer, hence 'lower in amount, weight, degree, value, price, than', as in 'a rainfall below the average', also 'lower in quality or excellence than', as in 'One places Marlowe below Shakespeare', also fig., as in 'Unless he is sunk below a beast'. (O.E.D.)

The senses of under fall into four main groups:—(I) 'Senses denoting position beneath or below something, so as to have it above or overhead, or to be covered by it', as in 'Under a broiling sun, they toiled manfully', 'under the waves', 'under the American flag', 'a letter addressed under cover to a third party', 'Chance led him under an apple-tree'; (II) 'senses denoting subordination or subjection', as in 'Under the major was a captain', 'an office under government', 'He is under medical treatment', 'Sent under a strong guard to the Tower', under an obligation, 'He is under the impression that . . .'; (III) 'senses implying that one thing is covered by, or included in, another', as in 'Extreme vanity sometimes hides under the garb of modesty', 'Many matters that would come under this head are trivial', 'The word is explained under house', under my hand and seal; (IV) 'senses which imply falling below a certain standard or level', as in 'It was too great an honour for any man under a duke', 'The weight proved to be under 114,000 ounces', under age, (of spirit) under proof. (O.E.D.)

Of the relationship of below to under, Webster's writes thus: 'Below (opposed to above) applies to that which is anywhere in a lower plane than the object of reference; under (opposed to over), to that which is below in a relatively vertical line; under sometimes implies actual covering; as, below sea level, the valley far below us; under a tree, under the bed; the Whirlpool Rapids are below, the Cave of the Winds is under, Niagara Falls; the whole visible landscape is below, but only a small portion of it under, an observer in a balloon. . . . In their figurative senses, below and under agree in express-

ing inferiority, but differ (like above and over) in the immediacy of the relation expressed; thus, one officer may be below another in rank, without being under him in immediate subordination. Similarly, in reference to deficiency, below is commonly used in general, under in more specific, relations; as, a gold dollar weighing under 25.8 grains is below the standard; under six years of age, below the average.'

abridgement. See PRÉCIS WRITING, par. 2.

abrogate. See ARROGATE.

absence, misused for abstinence, as in 'Many schools allow absence from games to those who dislike them'. [This sentence with absence or with abstinence would not occur in American English. The idea might be expressed thus: 'Many schools excuse from sports students who don't like athletics.' Of course, 'Absences are not allowed immediately before or after holidays' is school jargon.]

absolute. See COMPARATIVES, FALSE.

abysmal; abyssal. Both = 'of the abyss', but whereas the former is figurative, as in 'abysmal ignorance', the latter is literal, with the specific sense, 'belonging to that belt of the ocean which is more than 300 fathoms down', as in 'abyssal zone'.

academic is a vogue word. Many words (and a few phrases) have acquired a power and an influence beyond those which they originally possessed; certain pedants say, Beyond what these terms have any right to mean or to imply. But like persons, words cannot always be taken for granted. It just cannot be assumed that they will for ever trudge along in the prescribed rut and for ever do the expected thing! Journalists, authors, and the public whim—sometimes, also, the force of great events, the compulsion of irresistible movements—have raised lowly words to high estate or invested humdrum terms with a picturesque and individual life or brought to the most depressing jargon a not unattractive general currency. Such words gain a momentum of their own, whatever the primary impulse may have been.

Examples: blueprint, complex (n.), fantastic, glamour, integrate, operative, pattern, reaction, rewarding, sublimation, urge (n.).

Acadia. See ARCADIA.

accelerate and **exhilarate** are more often confused, especially in the noun forms (acceleration; exhilaration), than one might expect. To accelerate is to quicken or speed up. To exhilarate is to arouse to mirth or raise to high spirits. 'An exhilarating conversation accelerates the mental faculties.'

accents. See DIACRITICS.

accept. See EXCEPT.

acceptance; acceptation. The former is used in all senses denoting or connoting the act of accepting and the state (or condition) of being received, as in 'the acceptance of a gift'; *acceptation* is reserved for 'the current sense of a word, the prevailing sense of a word', as in 'The acceptation of *imply* differs from that of *infer*'.

accessary and **accessory.** A minor participant in a crime is an *accessory*; the corresponding adjective is also *accessary*. [In American usage *accessory* is usual as noun and adjective.]

In the sense 'an adjunct, an accompaniment', *accessory* is now more general than *accessary*; as the corresponding adjective ('accompanying', 'adventitious') *accessory* is correct, *accessary* catachrestic.

accident is a mishap, a disaster. A fall from a horse is an accident; a broken leg, the result. Thus, 'He is suffering from an accident' is infelicitous for '. . . from the results of an accident'.

accidently for *accidentally*: a solecism occasionally encountered.

accompanied by. See PREPOSITIONS WRONGLY USED.

accompanist, not *accompanyist*, is usual for 'an accompanying musician'.

accomplish. See ATTAIN.

accountable should be confined to persons. 'This wretched nib is accountable for my scrawl' is catachrestic.

accounted for; in consequence of. See PREPOSITIONS WRONGLY USED.

accredit(ed). See CREDIT(ED).

accuse. See CHARGE.

ACCUSATIVE AND INFINITIVE. There is no difficulty with such sentences as 'I saw him fall' and 'Command the boy to appear'; or even with 'It is good for us to amuse ourselves sometimes'. 'I do not know where to go' and 'He is at a loss what to think' are simple enough. But 'Whom do men declare me to be?' is less obvious: it is the infinitive form of 'Who do men declare that I am?' (Onions.)

acknowledge, misused. 'His immediate departure had acknowledged the truth of that!' Things do not acknowledge, they constitute a proof.

acquirement; acquisition. The former denotes the power of acquiring; the latter, the thing acquired. 'His acquirements in music are greater than his acquisition of riches.'

act. See FUNCTION.

act on, misused for *react on*. 'The fear of losing his job acted on him in the performance of his duties and finally caused him to lose his precious job.'

actual and **actually** are unnecessary, in precisely the same way as *real* and *really* are, for the most part, excessive; *actual* is especially uncalled-for in collocation with *fact*, as in 'He is said to have died on a Monday; the actual fact is that he died on a Tuesday'.

adapt and **adopt** are often confused. To *adapt* a thing is to change it for one's own purpose; to *adopt* it is to accept it unchanged and then use it. Moreover, *adopt* must be distinguished from *assume*: one adopts a child, a religion, but one assumes a pose, an attitude—a debt, a task, a duty.

adapted for *suitable* is infelicitous. 'Ordinary language is not adapted to describe processes within the atom.'

add. See ANNEX.

addicted (to) is a pejorative. Do not, for instance, say, 'Addicted to benevolent action'—unless you're being facetious.

address should not be synonymized with *speech*, but reserved for 'a formal speech', 'a set discourse', a speech to celebrate an important occasion; thus 'The Queen's inaugural speech' is inferior to '. . . inaugural address'. An *address* in church is less formal than a *sermon*.

adduce is applied only to arguments, speeches, statements, or to persons, animals, objects as illustrations or samples, the sense being 'to bring forward (verbally) for consideration'. 'In proof of this they adduced many arguments', historian Robertson, 1765.

ADEQUACY. See SUITABILITY.

adequate enough is incorrect for 'sufficient' or 'suitable', and tautological for 'adequate'. The idea of 'enough' is contained within that of 'adequate'.

adherence; adhesion. In general, the former is figurative ('He was noted for his adherence to the principles of free thought'); the latter, literal ('The adhesion of this stamp to that envelope is in itself sufficiently remarkable'). It must, however, be borne in mind that in politics, *adhesion* = 'being a supporter or a partisan of a movement, a party', and that, in botany, *adhesion* is the opposite of *cohesion*.

adjacent; contiguous. The latter = 'touching', as in 'France and Spain are contiguous', 'France is contiguous to Belgium'; loosely, 'near but not touching'—a sense to be avoided. But *adjacent* has both of these senses.

ADJECTIVE FOR ADVERB. This is an illiteracy; but even a tolerably educated person may, in a slovenly moment, fall into such an error as this: 'The home team pressed *stronger* [for *more strongly*] towards the close of the game.' Some adverbs, however, may occur with or without the suffix '-ly'; e.g. *slow(ly)*, *quick(ly)*, *cheap(ly)*. The *-ly* forms are more polite, the root forms are more vigorous. Sometimes there is a difference in meaning: 'The ball went as *high* as the steeple'; 'I value it *highly*'.

adjectivally and **adjectively.** Both are correct, but the former is preferred, for the corresponding adjective is *adjectival*.

ADJECTIVES, POSITION OF. Make sure that the adjective immediately precedes the noun it qualifies; look out for group-words(*q.v.*) like *children's language, woman's college, men's shoes*. Harold Herd points out the absurdity of *stylish gentlemen's suits* for *gentlemen's stylish suits*. Is *an excellent woman's college* as clear as *an excellent college for women?*

ADJECTIVES,UNCOMPARABLE. See COMPARATIVES, FALSE.

administer (a blow) is not incorrect, but it is certainly infelicitous; one *gives* or, better, *delivers* a blow.

admissible. See ADMITTABLE.

admission. See ADMITTANCE.

admit, admit of; permit of; allow of. *Admit of* is a rather literary variation of one of the senses of *admit*, viz. 'to allow of the presence, or the coexistence, of; to be capable of; be compatible with', as in 'Sublimity admits not of mediocrity'.

Permit of is rather literary for *permit* in the sense, 'to give leave or opportunity to; to allow', as in 'Religion is reluctant to permit of idolatry', and is thus synonymous with *admit of* and *allow of.* (*O.E.D.*)

admittable is rare for *admissible*, except in the sense 'capable of being admitted to a place', as in 'Such a man is admittable to any society in London'.

admittance and **admission.** The former is physical ('No admittance here'); the latter, figurative and applied especially to 'reception or initiation into rights or privileges', as in 'The admission of immigrants into the United States of America has been much restricted of late years'; that example leads us to the fact that 'when physical entrance and access to privileges are combined, *admission* is the preferred form, as "admission to a concert, a play, a game" ' (Weseen).

adopt. See ADAPT.

advantage and **vantage.** The latter is 'the position or a condition that is above another, either literally or figuratively', as in 'He viewed the struggle from the *vantage* (or, the vantage point) of a safe job'. But 'He has an *advantage* over me, for he knows his subject'.

advent and **arrival.** The former connotes importance, deep significance, fate, the operation of natural law: 'The advent of summer had been preceded by the return to summer time'; 'The advent of death is of supreme importance to at least one person'. But 'His arrival at Marseilles took place on the first of June': *arrival* is neutral and it connotes comparative unimportance.

adventure; venture. 'In present use *venture* applies chiefly to business undertakings, especially such as involve chance, hazard, and speculation. *Adventure* applies chiefly to bold and daring experiences in the meeting of danger. Both words are used as verbs, but *venture* more commonly. It means to risk, hazard, take a chance, speculate, expose, and dare.' (Weseen.)

ADVERB, POSITION OF THE. See ORDER, towards end.

adverse to; averse to (or **from**). Respectively 'opposed to' and 'strongly disinclined to' or 'having a (strong) distaste for'. *Averse from*, though etymologically correct, is perhaps slightly pedantic.

advert; avert. Lit.,these respectively mean 'to turn to (something)' and 'to turn (something) away', or 'to prevent': 'He adverted to the plan that had been suggested'; 'He said that the danger had to be averted'.

advice is the noun, **advise** the verb.

advisedly ;intentionally. *Advisedly* = 'done judiciously, without haste, and after careful planning or consideration', whereas *intentionally* is much weaker, for it merely = 'done not by accident but *purposely*'.

aeriated, aeroplane, and **aerial.** See AIRIAL . . .

aeroplane. See AIRPLANE.

affect and **effect** as verbs are frequently confused. *Effect* is 'to bring about', 'to accomplish'; *affect* is 'to produce an effect on'; 'to attack, move, touch'. (*S.O.E.D.*) 'Mr Bell, Surgeon, deposed, that upon his examining the Body of the Deceased, he found several Bruises and Wounds upon it, but not of consequence enough to effect her life.' Possibly the surgeon had, when he commenced his deposition, intended to say 'effect her death'.

AFFECTATION. Affectation is a putting-on of literary airs and graces; artificiality of style, of phrasing, of words. 'The essence of affectation', said Carlyle, 'is that it be assumed.'

affirm. See ASSERT.

affirmative, reply in the. See CLICHÉ.

Africander (better than *Afrikander*) is not to be synonymized with *African* (n. and adj.). An *African* belongs to the African race, whereas an *Africander* is a white native of South Africa. (*O.E.D.*)

after. The senses 'on the analogy of' and 'according to' are Standard English, but they must be used with care, for they lead to ambiguity, as in 'This word (*exist*), after *be*, has come to possess many nuances' and 'This statement is after Darwin'.

aggravate, -tion. Already in 1896 John Davidson remarked that the use of *aggravate* was beyond cure. It is incorrectly used in the sense *to annoy* (a person); properly it means *to intensify*, usually for the worse. On the misuse of this word see especially *The King's English*, by H. W. and F. C. Fowler. Stylists avoid *aggravate* in the sense 'to annoy, to exasperate, to provoke'; but humdrum writers and hurried journalists may, if they wish, take heart of disgrace from the fact that *aggravate* has been used in these nuances since early in the 17th Century. *Aggravation* is likewise avoided by stylists, but pedants must cease from stigmatizing the word as bad English.

agnostic and **atheist.** Whereas the latter denies the existence of God, the former merely says that His existence cannot be proved; a liberal agnostic admits that His existence cannot be disproved.

agrarian for *agricultural* 'is still rather bookish'; in the main, it is confined to the *Agrarian Reforms* of Ancient Rome and the *agrarian* policies of political parties. As a noun, *agricultur(al)ist* is loose for 'a farmer', but it is justifiable when used as the opposite of *pastoralist* (a farmer of live stock); an *agrarian* is 'one who recommends an equitable division of land'.

AGREEMENT, FALSE. False Agreement affects two aspects of grammar.

A. NUMBER. Particularly verb with subject, as in 'He and I am going to Town'; but also in such a phenomenon as 'those kind of books'. Contrast 'that breed of horses', which, theoretically correct, is unidiomatic; as, idiomatically, we say 'that kind of book' (*not* 'that kind of books'), so idiomatically, we say 'that breed of horse'. (See KIND OF, ALL.)

Note that the verb *to be* agrees with its subject, not with its complement: thus, not 'A man *are* thousands of different persons' but 'A man is thousands of different persons' is correct. In 'The vividness of these delightful images *were* intensified by the desperateness of my own affairs', the subject is *vividness*, not *images*. In 'The rapidity of Lord Roberts's movements *are* deserving of the highest praise', the journalist has lost sight of the fact that it was the *rapidity* which deserved praise. See 'ONE, use of plural in v.

after' for a very common type of false agreement between subject and verb; here I note two further examples: 'Sorel's "Reflections on Violence" is one of the few works upon Socialism that can be, or *deserves* to be, read by the non-professional student'; 'Mr Yeats has written one of the simplest accounts of poetical composition that *has* ever appeared'. *What* sometimes causes confusion, as in 'I don't really see what my personal relationships *has* to do with the matter in hand, M. Poirot'.

B. POSITION. Theoretically, this kind of false agreement could be taken to include all wrong positions. And practically it is most convenient to treat first of (I) relative clauses (subordinate clauses beginning with *who*, *which*, *that*, *when*, *where*, and such rarities as *wherever*, *whereof*, *wherefore*, *whenever*) that have departed from positional agreement; and then consider (II) phrases and words that are out of position—that are in false agreement; and, finally, (III) several examples of pronominal errors.

(The position of adverbs, however, is discussed at ORDER and misrelated participles will be found at CONFUSED PARTICIPLES.)

1. *Relative Clauses out of position.* Relevant to this section is the misuse of the relative pronouns, *who* and *that*, *which* and *that*: see 'WHICH and THAT; WHO and THAT'. The importance of the correct use of the relatives may be gauged by such a sentence as, 'It is the question of the house that Jack built which is important in architecture'.

The danger of separating the relative from its antecedent should be obvious: that it isn't obvious may be guessed from the following examples:

'I had in the County of Northampton deposited my Heart in a Virgin's Breast, who failed in Credit and Sincerity', *The Life of Benjamin Stratford*, 1766: the writer's sense of position was as defective stylistically as it was cardially. A rearrangement is necessary; thus, 'I had . . . deposited my heart in the breast of a virgin, who failed . . .'.

'He stripped off the drunkard's covering (who never stirred)', Richard Hughes. Correct to: 'He stripped off the covering of the drunkard, who never stirred' (i.e., did not stir).

In 'There is room for a persistent, systematic, detailed inquiry into how words work that will take the place of the discredited subject which goes by the name of Rhetoric', the author has the excuse that if he attaches to 'words' its relative clause 'that will take the place of . . . Rhetoric', he thrusts 'work' to the end of the sentence; true, but why not recast the sentence, thus, 'There is room for a persistent . . . inquiry into the workability of words that will take the place of . . . Rhetoric'? One is not always obliged to knock down a brick wall; often it is easier—and occasionally it is much more effective—to go through the gate.

'C. E. M. Joad wrote a book to drive home the message of Radhakrishnan, in which he states flatly that his hero has attained to truth about the universe which is "from its nature incommunicable" ': 'such truth about the universe as is "from its nature incommunicable" '?

II. *In the agreement of words other than antecedent and relative*, we find that the implication of incorrect or foolish order is as strong as in the foregoing examples. Witness the following:

'What is the ultimate nature of matter? The question we know by now is meaningless.' Here the false agreement is flagrant. The writer means, 'By now, we know that this question is meaningless'.

'He arranges a meeting of his suspects to find out whether anyone reacts in any way peculiar to the sight of the body.' Obviously the author does not intend us to understand a 'way peculiar to the sight of the body'; he does mean, 'react to the sight of the body'. Therefore he should have written '. . . reacts in any peculiar way to the sight of the body'.

' "You'll like the Ole Man. . . . Treats you as if you was a human being—not a machine." '—Ten minutes later Meredith endorsed this opinion for himself. Alert, efficient, quiet both in manner and speech, he found the head of the borough police not only ready to condone his presence on the scene, but to thank him for his co-operation.' 'Alert, efficient, quiet both in manner and speech' does not, as it should, refer to Meredith but to

the head of the borough police ('the Ole Man').

'When they were gone, still carrying me, she sat down on a great smooth stone that was beside the well.' Who was carrying 'me'—'they' or 'she'? Presumably 'they'.

III. *Pronominal agreement, or lack of agreement*, has been exemplified in the section on relative pronouns. Here are two examples where other pronouns are involved:

'Left without a father at the age of three-and-a-half, her mother was her only guide.' It was not her mother who had, at the age of $3\frac{1}{2}$, been left without a father; it was the little girl. Recast thus: 'To the girl left without a father at the age of $3\frac{1}{2}$, the mother was the only guide.' Compare 'An only son, his mother had died when he was a child': his mother was not an only son; *he* was: therefore read, 'He was an only son, and his mother had died when he was a child'.

agricultural; agricultur(al)ist. See AGRARIAN. *Agriculturist* is gradually displacing the longer form.

ain't for *isn't* (colloquial) or *is not* (Standard English) is an error so illiterate that I blush to record it. As for *ain't* for *hasn't* (*has not*) or *haven't* (*have not*) . . .! More is to be said for *ain't* = *am not*, but it is now—and long has been—adjudged to be illiterate. [To Americans, G. P. Krapp's comment is of interest (*A Comprehensive Guide to Good English*, 1927): 'Although students of English and critical speakers would probably agree that *ain't* is low colloquial, it is true nevertheless that many educated persons permit themselves this habit, even though they reprehend it as careless. Only the enforcement of a strong academic authority prevents *ain't* from becoming universal colloquial use.']

airial, airiated and **airioplane** (phonetically spelt) are the frequent mispronunciations of persons unable to enunciate *aërial*, *aërated* and *aëroplane*. Usage now permits *aerial* and *aeroplane* as tri-syllabic; indeed it is thought pedantic to pronounce these two words as having four syllables. [Among American engineers *aerated* has commonly three syllables. *Webster's* allows for *aery* three syllables or two syllables.]

airplane is the usual American, **aeroplane** the usual English form. But the R.A.F. has adopted *aircraft*.

alarum is archaic for *alarm* (n.).

alibi is sometimes used, esp. in U.S.A.,

for an *excuse* or *pretext* of almost any kind, whereas, properly, it is only 'the plea that when an alleged act took place one was elsewhere' (*The Con. O.D.*). ' "I was too ill to write." "That's no alibi for failing to let me know; somebody could have 'phoned".'
alike, misplaced. 'For the moment it appeared quite convenient to regard myself as an executioner about to terminate a life alike forfeit to the laws of God and man', for 'a life forfeit to the laws of God and man alike', Eden Phillpotts, *Physician, Heal Thyself*, 1935.
alike . . . or for **alike . . . and.** '. . . He was taking, in colonial parlance, *a dry smoke*—that is, it was alike destitute of fire or tobacco.'
all, ambiguous. 'We have not always . . . sufficient means of distinguishing conveniently between the general and collective use of terms. In Latin [we have] *omnes* meaning *all* distributively, and *cuncti* [contracted from *coniuncti*, joined together] meaning all taken together. In English *all men* may mean *any man* or *all men together*. Even the more exact word *every* is sometimes misused, as in the old proverb, "Every mickle makes a muckle", where it is obvious that every little portion cannot by itself make much, [and that it can make much] only when joined to other little portions', Jevons and Hill, *The Elements of Logic*.
all alone is tautological for *alone*, but can be excused when 'all' is a genuine intensive.
all kind. Walking in London, W.C.2, on April 7, 1937, I saw a horse-driven cart bearing the legend, *All kind of old iron wanted*. Though 'all' should be followed by the plural 'kinds', it must be admitted that Swinburne, seldom at fault, has 'all kind of flowers', presumably to avoid the sibilant.
all right. See ALRIGHT.
all the lot. See LOT and WHOLE, THE.
allege commonly means 'to declare or assert on insufficient grounds' and it must not be made synonymous with *affirm*, *assert*, *declare*.
allegiance and **alliance**, often confused. The former is the loyalty that one owes to a person (e.g., one's queen), whereas the latter is a pact between two nations or states.
allergic. To *be allergic to* is being grossly misused—and in its incorrect senses, fatuously overused—for 'to dislike (intensely)', 'to be opposed to', 'to be antipathetic to', as in 'He is allergic to music,

you to noise'. Originally and usefully it is a medical word (the noun being *allergy*); its correct and—may I add?—its sensible use appears in this statement made, in 1926, by a medical man: 'Allergic hypersusceptibility is a special type of idiosyncrasy in which the patient reacts to special substances' (*O.E.D.*). *Allergy* is 'altered physiological reactivity': so don't go using it for 'dislike', 'antipathy', 'enmity or hostility', for it means nothing of the sort.
ALLITERATION. Apt alliteration's artful aid. Charles Churchill, *The Prophecy of Famine*, 1763.

In his *English Composition and Rhetoric*, Alexander Bain says:

'The term *Alliteration* is employed to signify the commencing of successive words with the same letter or syllable [as in *u-, ewe, yew, you*].Unless'—read *except* —'when carried out on a set purpose, it offends the ear: as *long live Lewis, come conqueror, convenient contrivance.*'

Alliteration is employed either stylistically or as a mnemonic device. It is frequent in advertisements: *Guinness is good for you, pink pills for pale people, the sunny South.*

The poets have made a happy use of it: for instance, Keats's 'the winnowing wind'; Swinburne's 'welling water's winsome word' and

Even the weariest river
Winds somewhere safe to sea,—

but then, of all poets writing the English language, Swinburne is the most frequent, versatile and felicitous alliterator.

Alliteration has been employed no less felicitously by the prose writers. The two great masters, in the present century, are G. K. Chesterton and Frank Binder.

Chesterton is the more pointed and epigrammatic manipulator of alliteration; Binder the more rhythmical and euphonious, the more sophisticated and yet the more profound.

Of Chesterton's works I choose one of the less famous, *The Paradoxes of Mr Pond*. It opens thus:—'The curious and sometimes creepy effect which Mr Pond produced upon me, despite his commonplace courtesy and dapper decorum, was possibly connected with some memories of childhood; and the vague verbal association of his name.' And here are three other examples:—'Paradox has been defended on the ground that so many fashionable fallacies still stand firmly on their feet, because they have no heads to stand on. But it must be admitted that writers, like other mendicants and mountebanks, frequently do try to attract attention'; (concerning Shakespeare's clowns and fools) 'The Fool is like a fantastic dancing flame lighting up the features and furniture of the dark house of death'; 'the trail of official fussing that crossed the track of the tragedy'.

Mr Frank Binder has, I believe, published only two books: *A Journey in England*, and *Dialectic; or, the Tactics of Thinking*. From the latter I take two brief passages. '. . . The seers and astrologers of long ago who, looking at nature as we look at a printed page, saw in fact phenomena, events, and beings, symbols of celestial significance and emblems of immanent meaning, types and figures in the splendid speech of all things where, from the quaint contingency of eclipses and calamities, comets and the comings of greater kings, planetary aspects and the collapse of kingdoms, the mystical mind might come to read the alliteration of life, the assonance of the soul, the far-off arpeggios in the concords of God.'

'Life in this embracing sense is not a fact but a faculty of nature, not a thing unique, discrete, and segregated with a poor and temporary place in our provincial bosoms, but a power both absolute and universal, a lasting possibility to which each atom has some trend and latent inclination. Each has a bias or bent to the spirit, a final predisposition, and allowing this, how shall we speak of men as being apart or as moving in a mystic remove from the world which holds us at one with itself? But not only are we so held, and not only the fabric of earth and sky is seen to fall into the bigger form and . . . personality of being, but all our aery estate of thoughts and dreams, of virtue and vice, of blessings and blasphemies, of purity and filth, of beauty and abomination, has, whether good or bad, its palpable part in the plan of things. For the world is an irrespective place, full, plenteous, and cosmopolitan, so free from prohibitions that he who seeks will find, who hopes will be sustained, who despairs will be left to despondency; a place so infinite in the forms of fact and fancy that men appear as everything and nothing, as the elect of heaven, as items of nature, or as poor parochial pawns in the one imperial purpose of God.'

allow. See ADMIT; ADMIT OF.

B*

allude, vaguer than *refer*, is applied to a mention either incidental (or casual) or indirect, whereas *refer* is specific and direct. 'She often alludes to her early life'; 'He refers to Clemenceau on page 89'.

allure (n.), 'attractiveness', is being overworked—and is inferior to *allurement*.

allure (v.) is 'to attract'(a person), favourably or neutrally; **lure** is 'to attract' (a person) to his disadvantage. 'Allured by the prospect of fame, he was lured into indiscretion by the purveyors of publicity.'

allusion. See ILLUDE; cf. ALLUDE.

almost for *virtual*, esp. in *almost certainty* for *virtual certainty* or *near certainty*. 'The almost certainty that the woman was by this time far away.' *Almost*, I believe, should not be used to qualify a *thing*, abstract or concrete; correct uses are, 'he was almost certain', 'he almost succeeded'. *Almost* for *virtual* has probably arisen on the analogy of *then* in, e.g., 'the then king'; but 'the then king' may be justified as a convenient brevity for 'the then reigning king' or as a shortened reversal of 'the king then reigning'.

almost never is feeble—so feeble as to be incorrect—for *hardly ever* or *very seldom*. 'He almost never visits me any more' = 'He rarely visits me (nowadays)'.

alone (adj.) is sometimes misused for the adv. *only*, as in 'It [the seizure of Kiaochau] was undertaken not alone without the knowledge of the Chancellor, but directly against his will'. See also LONELY.

along of for (1) *owing to* and (2) *with* is used only by the uneducated.

along with, in the sense of *beside* or *in company with*, is admissible.

already is an adverb; **all ready,** an adjective. 'Are they already all ready?' illustrates the usage.

already sometimes requires a progressive tense (*am doing, was doing, has been doing*, etc.) instead of a simple one (*do, did, shall do*, etc.). One cannot draw up a rule: here, as so often in the finer points of idiom, literary tact or grammatical intuition or, indeed, both are required. 'If the legacy gave him a motive' [in the past: complete], 'it's too late now to remove that motive. It operated, or it did operate[,] already.' Here I should, for 'operated . . . already', substitute, according to the precise time point required (only the author could tell us that), either 'was operating already' or, less probably (I feel), 'had been operating already'. (*Already* is badly placed.)

alright is an incorrect spelling of *all right* and an illogical form thereof. *All right* is an amplified form of *right* (correct; just, equitable; safe), as in 'He's all right: the fall did him no harm'. The exclamatory form (= Yes, I shall) is therefore *all right!*, not *alright!*, as in ' Will you attend to that little matter for me?" "All right!" '

altercation and **fight**.The former is verbal; the latter, physical. An *altercation* is a wrangle, a quarrelsome dispute, a heated controversy: 'Their altercation developed into a fight.'

alternate, alternately. See:

alternative and **choice.** The latter can be applied to any number, whereas *alternative* may be applied only to two courses of action—two possible decisions. 'The alternatives are death with honour and exile with dishonour'; 'He had the choice between fighting, running away, and capture'; 'The alternative is to . . .'; 'If you don't do that, you don't necessarily have to do this, for there are several choices'.

The adverb of *alternative* is *alternatively*, 'in a way that offers a choice between *two*'. The adjective *alternate* = 'arranged by terms', 1 and 2 being alternate numbers in 1,2,1,2,1,2,1,2 . . . In ordinary speech, 'He and I did the work on alternate days'—i.e., 'by turns of one day each', he one day, I the next; but 'The alternative days on which the work can be done are Monday and Wednesday'.

although is more dignified, more literary than *though*, except in *as though*, where *although* could not be used.

although . . . yet. To use both in a short sentence ('Although he returned only yesterday, yet he left again to-day') is unnecessary, but to imply that *although . . . yet* is always redundant is wrong, as can be seen from almost any long sentence. In long sentences, as also in short, (*al*)*though* posits a handicap, an obstacle, or an advantage, and *yet* emphasizes the result—the victory or the defeat. Of the two, *yet* is, in any sentence, the more safely omitted, for the omission of (*al*)*though* leaves the sense unresolved for too long, as in 'He came only yesterday, yet he departed this morning'.

altogether and **all together** are often confused: the former = 'entirely, on the whole'; the latter implies collocation or coincidence or unanimity of individuals. The misuse can lead to strange ambiguities; 'The house party came altogether' should read: '. . . came all together'.

always, improperly employed. 'I have

been a militant Communist and a constitutional Socialist and a Pacifist, and always there have been moments when I see all people . . . as frightened children.' Existence only in 'moments' is contradictory of 'always'.

a.m. = in the morning, **p.m.** in the afternoon and up to midnight. Avoid such phrases as '11 a.m. in the morning', '11 p.m. at night'.

am. Except in telegrams, diaries and in letters to intimate friends, *am* for *I am* should be avoided.

amatory and **amorous.** In current usage, *amorous* connotes concupiscence, the favourable adjective being *loving* (contrast 'a *loving* look' with 'an *amorous* look'). One speaks of *amatory* or *love-poems*; an *amorous* poem would be a love-poem that is sexually ardent.

amazement is 'overwhelming wonder, whether due to mere surprise or to admiration'. It must not be confused with the *surprise* (or the *wonder*) itself.

amazing means 'astounding'—capable of amazing a person. It should not be debased to mean *unusual* or *good* (or even *very good*) or *bad* (or even *very bad*). Many journalists and popular novelists have combined to make it a verbal counter—a 'rubber-stamp word', as Frank Whitaker has called it along with *ban, bid* (as noun), *chief* (as noun), *coup, drama, dream* (as adjective), *gang, gem, girl-wife, haul, pact, rail* (noun), *revelation, riddle, rush, thrill* (both noun, especially, and verb), *trek* and *wonder* (as adjective).

AMBIGUITY
'I have often been apprehensive, that the manner in which I express myself, may lead you into some mistakes of my meaning, the signification of words, in the language of men, being so unsettled, that it is scarce possible to convey a determinate sense . . .; for where different, or perhaps contrary meanings are signified by the same word, how easy is it for a mind, prone to error, to take the wrong one?' C. Johnston, *Chrysal*, 1768.

Ambiguity springs from woolly and muddled thinking; from a hasty fitting of words to the thought; from ignorance of the right uses of words; from the wrong order of words; from defective punctuation; and from numerous minor causes.

That ambiguity which springs from vague and muddled thinking is treated at WOOLLINESS, which is ambiguity on a large scale. Obscurity is treated at OBSCURITY. Ambiguity arising from defective punctuation is briefly treated at PUNCTUATION.

The relation of ambiguity to logic is so close that a chapter on ambiguity is to be found in every reputable treatise on logic. What follows is in parts an adoption, in parts an adaptation, of *The Elements of Logic*, by Jevons and Hill.

Of Logic, the most general practical part is that which treats of the ambiguity of terms—of the uncertainty and the variety of meaning possessed by words. Nothing can be of more importance to the attainment of correct habits of thinking and reasoning than a thorough acquaintance with the imperfections of language. Comparatively few terms have one single clear meaning and one meaning only; and whenever two or more meanings are confused, we inevitably commit a logical fallacy, darken counsel, render hazardous the way of communication. If, for instance, a person should argue that 'Punishment is an evil', and that, according to the principles of morality, 'No evil is to be allowed even with the purpose of doing good', we might not immediately see how to avoid the conclusion that 'No punishments should be allowed', because punishments cause evil. A little reflection will show that the word *evil* is here used in two totally different senses: in the first case it means 'physical evil', 'pain'; in the second, 'moral evil'. Because moral evil is never to be committed, it does not follow that physical evils are never to be inflicted.—The more a person studies the subtle variations in the meaning of common words, the more he will be convinced of the dangerous nature of the tools he has to use in all communications and arguments; the more careful should he therefore be in his use of words, and the more critical he will be of propagandist writings.

In Logic, terms are said to be *univocal* when they can suggest no more than one definite meaning; to be *equivocal* (or *ambiguous*) when they have two or more different meanings. The word *cathedral* is probably univocal or of one logical meaning only. *Church*, on the other hand, sometimes means the building in which religious worship is performed; sometimes the body of persons who belong to one sect and assemble in churches; and *the church* means the body of the clergy as distinguished from the laity. *Equivocal* itself is ambiguous: its meaning in logic, as in philology, has been defined above; but in common life, *equivocal* is applied to the statements or the terms of one who uses words consciously and deceitfully in a manner designed to produce a confusion of the true and apparent meanings; in the moral sphere, it means 'questionable', 'of suspect or dubious character or reputation'.

Equivocal words fall into three classes, according as they are equivocal

in sound only;
in spelling only;
in both sound and spelling.

Words equivocal in sound only or in spelling only give rise to trivial mistakes. When we hear them, we may confuse *right*, *rite*, *wright*, *write*; *rain*, *reign*; *might* and *mite*; but the context usually precludes misapprehension. Compare, too, *air* and *heir*, *hair* and *hare*. Words equivocal in spelling but not in pronunciation are a *tear*-(drop) and a *tear*, or rent, in cloth; *lead*, the metal, and the *lead* given by a person.

Much more important are the words equivocal in both spelling and pronunciation. These in their turn may be divided into three groups according as they arise:

(i) from the *accidental confusion* of different words;

(ii) from that *transference of meaning which is caused by an association of ideas*; and

(iii) from the *logical transference of meaning to analogous objects*.

(i) *Accidental Confusion*. In this class we have those odd and interesting, though comparatively unimportant, cases in which ambiguity has arisen from the confusion of entirely different words (whether from different languages or from different roots of the same language) that have in the course of—and from the rough usage by—time come to have the same sound and the same spelling. Thus *mean* signifies either 'medium', 'mediocre', from the Mediaeval French *moien* (Modern Fr. *moyen*), and 'base', 'vulgar', from Old English *gemæne*, 'belonging to the many'. The verb *mean* can hardly be confused with either of the adjectives *mean*, and it has, moreover, a distinct root.

(ii) *Transference of Meaning by Association of Ideas*. By far the largest proportion of equivocal words have become so by a transference of the meaning from the thing originally denoted by the word to some other thing so habitually connected with it as to be closely associated in thought. We have already seen the equivocality of *church*. In Parliamentary language, *the House* means either the chamber in which the members meet or the body of members that happen to be assembled in it at any time. Consider *foot*: the *foot* of a man; a *foot* measure; the *foot* (or base) of a mountain; those soldiers who fight on *foot*. Take *post*: that which is *posited* or *posted* firmly in the ground; a military *post*, the *post* of danger; *posts*, or horse-stages; the *post(s)*, or conveyance of news. *Man* is a male person, but it is also man or woman (*man* = mankind).

(iii) *Transference of Meaning by Analogy or by Real Resemblance.* A good example is afforded by *sweet*: a sweet taste, a sweet face, a sweet tune, a sweet poem. For *brilliant*, we have the original sense 'sparkling' or 'glittering'; a person who 'shines' is brilliant, perhaps because he has a brilliant or sparkling wit. It must, however, be admitted that in this group, there is little chance of confusion.

Ambiguity, however, is found not merely in single words but also and especially in phrases, clauses, and sentences. On ambiguity in general, the *locus classicus* is William Empson's *Seven Types of Ambiguity*.

In the course of summing up, Empson says that 'Of the increasing vagueness, compactness, and lack of logical distinctions in English, the most obvious example is the newspaper headline. I remember a very fine one that went

ITALIAN ASSASSIN BOMB PLOT DISASTER.'

He notes that the assassin was not an Italian and that therefore *Italian* must qualify the rest of the headline; that the dominant noun is *disaster*: hints that the adjective qualifying *disaster* is *bomb-plot*, that *assassin* should be *assassin's* and that *Italian* should be *in Italy*; and concludes that 'the main rhythm conveys: "This is a particularly exciting sort of disaster, the assassin-bomb-plot type they have in Italy"'. I suggest that the following rearrangement explains the headline:

ITALIAN DISASTER ASSASSIN'S BOMB-PLOT,

which = 'There has been in Italy a disaster caused by a bomb in an assassin's plot'. Empson's comment is delightful: 'Evidently this is a very effective piece of writing. . . It conveys [its point] with a compactness which gives the mind several

notions at one glance of the eye, with a unity like that of metaphor, with a force like that of its own favourite *bombs*': and he gently refrains from pointing out that it has one slight drawback, in that its meaning—even after an exasperating amount of cogitation by the reader—is far from clear.

This example caused Mr Frank Whitaker to speak as follows:—

'Headlines are a good starting point, not only because they offer the greatest temptation to the debaser owing to the stress under which they are often written, but also because they have created an important problem of another kind. They remind us every day, particularly in our more popular newspapers, that the grammatical sentence is no longer the only way of expressing a thought in modern English. We are, indeed, rapidly evolving a distinct headline language which bears little relation to everyday speech. That cannot be a good thing, because it means that we are approaching a stage, if we have not already reached it, at which a word will mean one thing when it is written and another when it is spoken.

ANTI-POSSESSIVE CRAZE

'In this headline language, logical distinctions in the meaning of words are being ruthlessly flattened out. It is a counterfeit language within a language, in which nouns are habitually made to do the work of adjectives, commas the work of heaven knows what, and from which the possessive case has almost disappeared. "Beware of the possessive", I read in one Fleet Street style sheet which in many respects is admirable—"beware of the possessive; it shows up a headline."

'What does that mean? I can quite understand the desire for action in headlines—the preference for lively, vigorous words—and there are no doubt many contexts in which the possessive case can be avoided without creating ambiguity. But this anti-possessive craze should be carefully watched. For example, I read in the "Star" last week the headline, "Question on Earl de la Warr speech", from which it was impossible to tell whether the speech was by Earl de la Warr or about Earl de la Warr. The distinction might be important, and it should be jealously preserved. Ambiguity is the enemy we have to watch, and our new headline language is full of it.'

After the felicities of Mr Empson and

Mr Whitaker, it is a sad decline to pass to some particular examples collected by myself; but they may serve as warnings. They fall roughly into five unequal and fortuitous groups of horrible examples: Wrong Adjective; Wrong Pronoun; *when* and *where*; Wrong Order; and Miscellaneous.

A good instance of wrong adjective occurs in Froude's *Henry the Eighth*: 'The Reformation . . . in the sixteenth century would have been left to fight its independent way unsupported by *the* moral corruption of the church from which it received the most powerful impetus': the *impetus* comes from corruption, not from *church*; if *that* had been written for *the*, there would have been no ambiguity. A very different example is this of double-pointedness (where only one point was intended) in a mid-Victorian's commencement of an article: 'We are all born idiots.'

Pronouns have to be handled with care; their misuse engenders some queer ambiguities, as in:— 'He put his feet upon the stove as *it* was cold.' Was the stove cold?—This example illustrates the potential ambiguity of the impersonal (or *it*) verbs—*it rains, it is raining*, etc.

'Such preparation may occupy six or seven stages. First of all *it* may be necessary to bleach the object, though *it* is by no means universal.' The first *it* appears to refer to *preparation*; reflection shows that *it* is part of the verbal phrase *it may be necessary*. The second *it* should refer to *object*, but it obviously doesn't: this *it* = 'this practice'.

'Although it [an estate] was not then specially laid out for shooting, a century and a half has, in fact, made it a very attractive *one*.' *One* refers to *shooting*, but in a sense not yet mentioned: 'a tract of country over which one has the exclusive right to shoot'.

'Jack and Florence met George and Lily at *his* place. I had told *them* to arrange something but *they* thought if *he* asked one of *them* to lunch *she* wouldn't come—*they* never quite hit it, perhaps *they* told you': a monstrous mass of ambiguity, cited by C. C. Boyd in his useful little book, *Grammar for Great and Small*.

When and *where* look innocent enough, but they are very far from being so innocent as they look. 'When did you arrange to meet him on Saturday night?' is a question that, when I read it, I took to mean 'On what date did you arrange that you should meet him on the Saturday night?'; I felt mildly annoyed when I saw that the reply was 'Somewhere about 7 o'clock, I think'. During the War of 1914–18, the constantly recurring 'Where were you wounded?' obviously admitted of two answers—locality (e.g., 'On the Somme'); part of the body ('In the arm').

Often the ambiguity springs from a careless arrangement of words. 'Smart men's suiting' and 'Stylish gentlemen's suits' are likely to be misunderstood.

'The flames . . . destroyed almost the last vestiges of past eras . . . vestiges which the ruthlessness of Henry VIII failed entirely to erase'; the context shows that 'failed to erase entirely' or 'failed to entirely erase', not 'entirely failed to erase', is intended.

'I was speaking to Miss Worsley of Holly Tye.' He was not speaking to a Miss Worsley that lived at Holly Tye, but of Holly Tye to Miss Worsley.

And here is a miscellaneous lot.

'Jewels of unimpeachable genuineness gleamed upon white arms and necks of a value enough [i.e., sufficient] to make up a king's ransom.'

'One remarks it as a defect only when judging the plan of the book apart from the contents,—a practice that leads one into illogical statements concerning things that are illogical only in appearance': for *a practice* read *the practice of thus judging books*.

' "You won't catch the flu germs walking in the open air", states a health enthusiast': ambiguity would have been removed if the statement had been written in the form, "You won't catch flu while you are walking"—or "Walking in the open air, you won't catch flu germs".

'Removers of distinction' is the proud slogan of a firm of carriers.

'Sullen, grey dawn crept over an equally sullen and grey lake, and Search watched its coming. But some time, from exhaustion, she slept.' But does 'some time' mean 'for some time—for some considerable time' or 'at a certain time (*or* hour)' or 'by a certain hour'?

ameliorate, misused for *appease*. 'How about taking advantage of Mrs Burleigh's invitation [to lunch] and ameliorating the more animal wants?'

amend, amendment; emend, emendation. To *amend* is 'to better; to improve' (something imperfect); politically, 'to make professed improvements in (a measure before Parliament)'. To *emend* = *emendate*, 'to remove errors from the text of (a document, a book)'. (*O.E.D.*)

America or **the States** for the United States of America. The former is commonly used, but obviously it is illogical, for it ignores the existence of Canada, Mexico, and the many nations of Central and South America. *American,* however, is the only convenient adjective for *U.S.A. The States* is not incorrect, but it is colloquial; in Australia, *the States* would, to a native-born Australian, refer rather to the various *States* of Australia than to the *States* of the U.S.A.

AMERICANISMS. See ENGLISH AND AMERICAN USAGE.

am finished for **have finished.** 'Je suis fini', said an Englishman in a French hotel when offered a second helping by the waiter, who looked at the 'finished' customer with sympathetic concern. *Be done with* is occasionally used!

amiable and **amicable.** *Amiable,* 'agreeable and good-natured', is applied to persons and their disposition: 'He was an amiable fellow', 'His was a most amiable nature'. *Amicable,* 'friendly', 'peaceable and pleasant', refers to relationships, attitudes (towards other persons), arrangements, conferences—in short, to the manner or process of doing: 'Amiable people generally have amicable relationships.'

amid, amidst. See 'AMONG and AMONGST'.

amn't. See A'N'T.

among and **amongst; amid, amidst; while, whilst.** The *st* forms are falling into disuse, partly because they are less easy to pronounce; partly because, when pronounced, they are less euphonious.

among other reasons; among other things. 'I am not . . . going to take you far into technical depths, because, among other reasons, I do not know enough.' If the author intends *along with other reasons,* why does he not say so? If *aside* (anglice *apart*) *from,* why not say so? If *in addition to,* then why not *in addition to*? *Among other things* is generally excused as an idiom: but even if it is an idiom, it is so blatantly self-contradictory and absurd that careful writers avoid it.

among(st) is occasionally misused for *amid(st),* as in '. . . Reveille, the voice of Western order amongst the babble of the East'. *Among* is used with separable objects and is usually followed by the plural; *amidst* means in the middle of, and 'that which surrounds may or may not consist of distinct and separable objects'. (*Webster's.*)

amoral = non-moral, not connected with morality; *immoral* = corrupt, licentious. 'A physiological text-book is amoral, but immoral persons may use such a text for immoral purposes'; 'The bright amoral virtue of courage'. (*O.E.D.*)

amorous. See AMATORY.

amount applies to mass or bulk, not to number. 'A large amount of animals' is absurd; 'a large amount of books' becomes ludicrous when juxtaposed to 'a large amount of paper'.

ample for *enough* (absolutely) is a colloquialism to be avoided in all self-respecting writing. 'Have you enough?' —'Yes, ample.' Probably short for the pretentious *an ample sufficiency.*

an; a. Before vowels and silent *h, an*; before consonants (other than silent *h*) and before *u* sounded *yoo, a.* Thus '*an* airy room', '*a* bad boy', '*a* use not known before'; '*a* horse'; '*an* hour ago'; '*an* honest fellow'; '*a* unique signature', '*a* eulogy as unexpected as it was flattering', '*a* union of two countries', '*an* hotel'. [Usually in America, '*a* hotel', '*a* historian'. (*After Webster's.*)]

analogous and **similar.** See 'SIMILAR and ANALOGOUS'.

ancient is opposed to *modern;* it refers to the remote past, especially to primitive languages and civilizations and to very early buildings, statues, writings, etc. Something that is no longer used—no longer in the style or the fashion, no longer handwrought or manufactured— is *antiquated:* but unless it is some hundreds of years old, it is not *ancient.* Words and phrases no longer used are *obsolete;* words used only in poetry or by very old people are *archaic, historical, obsolescent*—but the obsolescence of a word that has not long been in use cannot properly be called archaism.

and. In general, avoid beginning a sentence with *and*: its use is justified only when a very effective addition is desired or when an arresting accumulation is to be concluded.

and is unnecessary and incorrect in such a sentence as: 'But of all dwarfs none has bulked as largely in the public imagination . . . as "General Tom Thumb", and with whom all successors have had to stand invidious comparison'. Here 'and' should be omitted.

and etc. is a vulgarism for *and so forth, and so on, and other things, and the rest.*

and me with . . . This formula exemplifies the illiterate use of the accusative (or object) where there is no governing word.

'How could the room be cleaned, and me with my rheumatism?' (Onions, *An Advanced English Syntax*) is the illiterate equivalent of the standard nominative absolute used in

How can ye chant, ye little birds,
And I sae fu' o' care?

and moreover may occasionally be justified as an emphasized *and*—or an emphatic *moreover*. Usually it is a tautological form of *and*, as in 'And, moreover, when Big Tito had started a vicious fight, certainly for liberty if not for life . . .'.
and nor is occasionally found; all it means is 'nor'; literally ('and not . . . not') it is nonsense. 'But he did not move and nor did Julia.'
and/or is to be avoided, for it involves a typographical device. Use *either . . . or* or simply *or* or simply *and*; if none of these will serve, rewrite the sentence. See esp. 'Vigilans', *Chamber of Horrors*, 1952.
and which is permissible only when there is a preceding *which* clause, as in 'The house, which was empty and which was likely to remain empty, stood on the hill'. 'The house, situated on the hill and which was empty, was destroyed by fire' is inadmissible in English. The adjective + *and which* construction is a Gallicism.
and who is merely the personal counterpart of **and which**, *q.v.*
and whose. See WHOSE, AND.
and yet which is extremely clumsy for *which yet* or *and which yet*. In 'They were countryman's hands, which could break a rabbit's neck as scientifically as possible; and yet which could set a dog's leg . . . with as much kindness as any woman would show', change *and yet which could* to *which could, however, set*.
anent, 'about, concerning', is archaic and pretentious.
angle, 'point of view', is an Americanism (as is the slangy synonym, *slant*); not objectionable, but to be used sparingly.
angry at; angry with. The former of things and events; the latter of persons. 'He was angry *at* this incident—and *with* the policeman for having been too slow to prevent it.'
annex. In British usage this is the verb, the noun being either *annexe* (of a building) or *annexation* (acquisition—esp., political acquisition of territory). [In American usage *annexe* is a Gallicism, *annex* serving as verb and noun.]
    Do not misuse *annex* for *add*, or vice versa, for *annex* is not equivalent to *add*:

annex is 'to join as an additional part to existing possessions', as in Wellington's 'The whole country is permanently annexed to the British Empire'. (*O.E.D.*)
annunciation, 'announcement', is not to be confused with *enunciation,* 'degree of distinctness in pronouncing one's words'.
another . . . also is excessive for *another*, as in 'There was another idea also at the back of his mind'.
another, misused for *other*. Weseen gives the following examples of this misuse: 'Some kind or another'; 'one kind or another'; 'some way or another'.
another must not be used for *one other*. 'There is only another stile to cross before we reach the wood.'
another to is misused when made synonymous with *different from*. 'He wore another cap to mine.'
a'n't is the phonetically natural and the philologically logical shortening of *am not,* esp. in *a'n't I?*; *aren't*, though very common in print, is both illogical and illiterate, the more so as the *r* is not pronounced; *amn't* is ugly; *ain't* is illiterate and, on other grounds, inferior to *a'n't*.
    Note that *a'n't I* offers only two different stresses (of emphasis), whereas *am I not* affords three.
antagonist; opponent. An *opponent* is one who is on the opposite side, or one who opposes an idea, a measure; it is neutral —one's opponents in games are merely the other competitors or the opposing team. *Antagonist* is stronger; it connotes personal opposition in combat—duel, battle, war.
antagonize. 'To *antagonize*' is much stronger than 'to *oppose*'. To *oppose* is simply 'to be on the opposite side to', hence 'to resist'; to *antagonize* is to cause a strongly inimical reaction in another person by active opposition or by unfriendly behaviour, as in 'She antagonizes him by her personal remarks'.
ante = 'before' (in place or in time); *anti* = 'against; in opposition to'. See any good dictionary for examples. One of the commonest errors is *antichamber* for *antechamber*. Cf. *antedate* and *antidote*. But, exceptionally, in *anticipate, ante* has been changed into *anti*.
anticipate and expect. The former is incorrect both for the latter and for *await*, and its prevailing sense is 'to forestall' an action or a person. *The O.E.D.* registers, as blameless English, the senses, 'to take into consideration before the appropriate or due time' (e.g., 'to anticipate consequences and provide for the future')—'to

realize beforehand (a certain future event)', as in 'Some real lives . . . actually anticipate the happiness of heaven'—'to look forward to, look for (an uncertain event) as certain', as in 'Those not in the secret anticipated an acquittal'.

antimony; antinomy. The former, 'a hard white element used chiefly in alloys' (chemistry); the latter, 'an opposition or contradiction between two laws or principles' (philosophy).

ANTI-POSSESSIVE CRAZE, THE. See AMBIGUITY.

antiquated; antique. The former = 'out of use by reason of age; obsolete'; 'so old as to be unworthy to survive'; 'old-fashioned, whether as survival or as imitation', as in 'antiquated phraseology'; 'advanced in or incapacitated by age', as in 'His antiquated aunt was a sore trial to him'. (*O.E.D.*)

Antique = 'of the "good old times"'; antiquated; no longer extant', as in 'an antique courtesy'; 'of or after the manner of the ancients, esp. of Greece and Rome', and 'archaic', as in 'the antique mystery of the Sphinx'. (*O.E.D.*) Cf. ANCIENT.

ANTIQUES. See ARCHAISMS.

antisocial (or hyphenated). A vogue word—to be avoided.

anxious is not to be used as a synonym of *eager* ('He is anxious to go on this journey') or *desirous* ('She is rather anxious to paint'); but it is permissible for *solicitous* or *earnestly desirous*.

any, in a blended genitive. See GENITIVE, VAGARIES OF THE, last paragraph.

any, incorrectly used for *every, all*, etc.; *best of any* for *best of all*. 'James is the best schoolmaster of psychological manners of any novelist that has ever written.'

any, misused for **any other**. Examples: 'That winter was colder than any he had experienced' for '. . . any other'; better change to 'That winter was the coldest he had experienced'.—'It is a longer book than any he has yet written.'

any, misused for *at all*. 'It did not hurt him any.' A colloquialism, more common in the U.S.A. than elsewhere.

any, superfluous. *Any* is not needed in 'Such is indeed the fact, but it is a fact that does not help this Opus any, and so we disregard it in the argument'. This use of 'any' is an Americanism, not yet admitted into good English.

anybody's (or **anyone's**) **else; anybody's else's.** See ELSE'S.

any case, in. See CASE, IN ANY.

anyday; anyrate; anytime. Incorrect for *any day, any rate, any time*.

any more. See at almost never. As a synonym for *now*, it is, I believe, to be avoided. For 'I do not see him any more' read 'I do not see him now(adays)' or 'I no longer see him'.

any one; anyone. *Anyone* is synonymous with *anybody*; *any one* occurs, e.g., in 'He can beat any one of you'.

anyone is incorrect for either *any one* (*of* . . .) or *any* (pronoun); e.g., 'Mr Huitt . . . did not . . . summon anyone of the clients who were waiting to see him'.

anyone, anybody or **nobody (no one)** or **somebody (someone)** . . . **they.** The pronoun following these pronouns is *he* or *him* or *his* or *himself*, not *they* or *them* or *theirs* or *their own*; the same applies to the possessive adjectives, *anybody* (etc.) requiring *his*, not *their*. Thus, in Ruskin's 'Anyone may be a companion of St George who sincerely does what they can to make themselves useful', *they* should be *he*, and *themselves* should be *himself* (Onions); in 'Somebody came into the restaurant, ordered their meal, ate it; and then hurriedly they departed with a friend of theirs', *their* should be *his*, *they* should be *he*, and *theirs* should be *his*; 'Nobody cares what they do on holiday' is not only incorrect; it is ambiguous.

any place (anywhere); **anyways; anywheres.** Illiteracies.

any thing is justifiable when there is an opposition (whether explicit or implicit) to *any person*. Thus, 'He'll believe anything', but 'He is a fool to believe that any thing will ensure happiness'.

anyway, not *any way*, is correct for 'in any case'.

apart from ('in addition to'; 'without counting or considering') is English, the American equivalent being *aside from*.

apiary, a place for bee-hives; **aviary**, a place for captive birds.

apiece; a piece. The latter is a noun ('a portion'); the former is an adverb ('singly', 'each by itself'). 'Their pork pies cost sixpence apiece; a piece [i.e., the half of a pie] costs threepence.'

apology is too important to be used as a synonym of *excuse*. Nowadays an apology connotes recognition that one is in the wrong, whereas an *excuse* is a plea offered in extenuation or justification of a minor fault or neglect, or an explanation of such a fault or oversight. Further, *excuse* can be extended to the impersonal, as in 'The derailing of the train was the doctor's excuse for failing to attend his extremely important patient'. But do not, from that example, fall into the error of synonymizing *excuse* with *reason*.

appreciate is incorrectly used in 'Do you appreciate that something terrible may happen?' The correct uses of *appreciate* are these: To form (or make) an estimate of the worth, price, quality or quantity of (a person or things); to estimate correctly, or perceive the full force or significance of; to esteem adequately, esp. to esteem highly; to recognize the value or excellence of or in; (commercially) to raise the value of (opp. *depreciate*), or, v.i., to rise in value; to be aware of or sensitive to (a delicate impression, a nice distinction).

apprehensive. See TIMID.

appropriate (v.); **take.** These are not synonymous. To *appropriate* is 'to take to oneself, for oneself alone', but the prevailing sense is 'to set apart or to assign a sum of money for a specific purpose, especially by formal action'.

approximate (v.) for *resemble* is incorrect. 'Her murder was . . . skilfully arranged to approximate a suicide.'

approximately, misused for *almost* or *comparatively*. 'With . . . everything open it would be cool, or approximately cool, in the tropics.'

apt (to do something) = fit, suitable, or inclined to do it. Not to be identified with *likely*, as it is in 'He is not apt to gain that distinguished honour' when all that is meant is that he is unlikely to gain it. But *be apt to* (*do*) is good English in the following nuances:

(Of things) to be habitually likely, to be ready, to (do); (of persons) to be given, inclined, or prone to (do); to tend to (do).

arbiter; arbitrator. The former is general; the latter specific for one who has been appointed to settle a specific question.

arbour is sometimes confused with *harbour* and thought to be of the same derivation, but *arbour* derives from L. *herbarium*, and *harbour* (akin to German 'Herberge', French 'auberge', and Italian 'albergo') is otherwise derived. [American spellings are *arbor, harbor*.]

archaic. See ANCIENT.

ARCHAISMS or ANTIQUES. Archaisms are of two kinds: actual and potential. The potential antiques will be found at CLICHÉ and at SIMILES, BATTERED. Actual antiques—not all of them—are listed here.

The modern word (or phrase) is given in the second column; and when the antique is, in some special context, not an antique but a technicality, e.g., *whereas* in law and *morn* and *eve* in poetry, an indication is made parenthetically.

ANTIQUE	MODERN EQUIVALENT
abed (becoming an archaism)	in bed
abide (becoming an archaism)	
aforetime	formerly, previously
Afric (adj.: poetic)	African
albeit	although
Albion	England
amid(*st*)	among
an one	a one
anent	about, or concerning (preposition)
annoy (noun: poetic)	annoyance
Araby	Arabia
Arcady (poetic)	Arcadia
aright (only slightly archaic)	correctly
astonied	astonished
aught	anything
aye, for ever and	for all time; for ever
bale	evil; woe
Barbary	Saracen countries along North-African coast
behest; hest	an order
behoove or *behove* (vv.); *behoof; it behoves me*	to be an obligation on; an obligation; I ought . . .
benison	a blessing
betide	to happen to
betimes	early

ANTIQUE	MODERN EQUIVALENT
betrothal; betrothed	engagement (to be married); engaged. [*Betrothal* and *betrothed* are current in American newspaper-English.]
betwixt	between
bewray	to expose, reveal, indicate
blackamoor	Negro
bootless (adv.)	bootlessly
bounden	bound (except in *bounden duty*)
bridal	a wedding. [*Bridal* is American news-paperese.]
burgess	a citizen
burthen	burden
caitiff	a coward
Caledonia	Scotland
castor	a beaver
Cathay	China
chiefer; chiefest	more important; most important
Christmastide	Christmas time
citizenry	a body of citizens; citizens collectively
clang (preterite and past participle of *cling*)	clung
clime (poetic)	climate
clomb	climbed
clyster	an enema; a suppository
coal oil	kerosene. [*Coal oil*, still common in the U.S.A.]
coolth	coolness
cruse	an earthenware pot or jar
damosel (or *-zel*)	damsel (see ELEGANCIES), girl
date	limit, term, end
deceptious	deceptive
deem	to think or believe. [*Deem* in this sense is in American usage a false elegance.]
delicate (n.)	a delicacy or dainty
delve (not obsolete but obsolescent)	to dig
demesne; demesnes	domain; estates
despiteful	spiteful
destrier or *destrer*	war-horse
dight (ppl. adj.: poetic)	clad, clothed
doughty	brave; formidable
doxy	mistress; sweetheart; whore
drear (poetic)	dreary
drouth (poetic)	dryness; drought. [*Drouth* is current in parts of the U.S.A.]
durst	dared
dwell	to live (at a place)
eftsoon(s)	forthwith; often
eke	also
eld (poetic)	age
emprise	enterprise
engraven	engraved
ensample	an example, a sample
ere (poetic)	before
eremite	hermit
errant (adj.)	wandering
erst (poetic)	formerly; once upon a time
erstwhile (poetic)	formerly [improperly: former]; some while ago
essay	to attempt

ANTIQUE	MODERN EQUIVALENT
Ethiop; Ethiopia	Abyssinian; Abyssinia
eve (poetic)	evening
exceeding	exceedingly
faërie or *faëry*	fairy
fain (poetic adj. and adv.)	glad, gladly; ready, readily
fair, the (poetic)	beautiful, lovely or merely pretty woman
fare	to travel
fealty	fidelity, loyalty
foison	abundance
forgat (preterite)	forgot
forgot (past participle)	forgotten
forsooth!	truly!
fraught (poetic)	filled; laden
froward	haughty
Gaul	France
gentile	well-born
glad (v.); *glad oneself*	to make glad; to rejoice
goodly	good; attractive
gotten	(in England) got; [in the U.S.A. often *gotten*]; see entry at GOTTEN
grammatic	grammatical
habit; habits	clothing
haply (poetic)	by chance or accident
helpmeet	helpmate
hereof (legal)	of this
heretofore (legal)	before this; up to this time
hereunto (legal)	unto this
hest (poetic)	see *behest*
Hibernia	Ireland
hight (ppl. adj.)	called, named
hindermost	hindmost
howbeit	nevertheless
I wis	I know
illume	illuminate
Ind (poetic)	India
ken	knowledge
kin	relatives; one's family. [Old-fashioned but current in American usage.]
kine	cows
leal	loyal
leman (Romance)	sweetheart (either sex); lover or mistress
lief; I'd as lief	willing, glad; I'd gladly or willingly
liefer was to me, him, etc.	I (or he or . . .) had rather (do . . .)
liege	liege lord or liege man
mart	a market
maugre	despite (preposition)
meet	fitting, proper, seemly
meseems	it seems to me
methinks	I think
minion	a male favourite
moon	a month
monstrous	exceedingly
morn (poetic)	morning
mummer	actor in dumb show
Muscovy	Russia
natheless	nevertheless
nether; nethermost (poetic)	lower; lowest
nigh	near

ANTIQUE	MODERN EQUIVALENT
oft; ofttimes (both poetic)	often
olden (*times*)	the past, the distant past
Orient (adj.: poetic)	Oriental
orison (poetic)	prayer
otherwhile(*s*)	at times; at another time
pantaloon (whether as garment or as actor)	
pard	leopard
parlous	perilous, dangerous. [Dialectal in U.S.A.]
paynim	pagan, esp. Mohammedan
pecunious	wealthy
perchance (poetic; facetious); *peradventure* (facetious)	perhaps
plaint	a weeping; a complaint
plight	to pledge
price, of	precious; (of persons) excellent
proven (except in the legal *not proven*)	proved. [But *proven* is common in general American usage.]
psyche	cheval-glass
quick (except in 'the quick and the dead')	living; alive
quoth; quotha	said; said he
rufous	red
saith	says
sate	sat
save (poetic)	except
scarce (adv.)	scarcely
seigneur	lord
selfsame	(very) same
sideling	oblique(ly); sidelong
silvern	of silver; silvery
silly	simple; innocent
simples	herbs, or medicines therefrom
sire	father
something (adv.)	somewhat
spake	(he) spoke
span	(he) spun
speed (v.)	to thrive
spilth	a spilling; something spilled
stay	support
stoup (poetic; ecclesiastic)	a tankard; holy-water vessel
subtile	subtle
swoon (n. and v.: poetic)	faint
talesman (legal)	juror
tarry	linger
Tartary	the land of the Tatars
teen (poetic)	grief
tend (poetic)	attend to
testimony (legal)	an open attestation; a confession
thenceforth	from that time on(wards)
thereafter (legal)	after that time
thereof (legal)	of that
theretofore (legal)	up to that time
thrall	a slave
tilth	tillage
troth (also the verb)	truth; faith
troublous	troublesome, tiresome
trow	to believe
trusty (e.g., one's trusty sword)	trustworthy

ANTIQUE	MODERN EQUIVALENT
tryst (poetic)	a meeting, esp. a lovers' meeting
twain	two
umbrage, take	to take offence
unhand (v.), as in *unhand me, villain!*	to take one's hands off (a person)
unwitting	unknowing; ignorant
vagrom (adj.)	vagrant, vagabond; hence, erratic
Van Diemen's Land	Tasmania
varlet	a groom, a menial; a rogue
verily	truly
vicinage (legal)	neighbourhood, vicinity
void	empty
wax (v.i.)	to grow or increase
weal	welfare; the general good
ween	to think
whereas (legal)	since or because
whereat	at which
wherefore (legal)	for which reason
whereof (legal)	of which
whereon	on (or upon) which; immediately after which
whilom	once upon a time; some time before
whomso; whoso	whomever; whoever
whosesoever	of whatever person's
wight	a human being; gen. a man
wit, in *to wit*	namely
withal (except as an elegancy)	in addition, as well; nevertheless; therewith
wondrous (adv.)	wonderfully
wont	custom, habit
wot	know
woundy	extremely; excessively
writ (past participle)	written
yare	ready, alert, nimble
yclept	named; known by the name of
yon	yonder
yore, of	in ancient times; in the past
Yule; Yuletide	Christmas; Christmas-time
zany	a clown; a fool

aren't. See A'N'T.

are to + infinitive + preposition. See IS TO + infinitive + preposition.

Argentina; Argentine. It is best to retain *Argentina* as the name of the South American republic, *Argentine* (or *Argentinean*, preferably *-ian*) as that of a native of Argentina. *Argentine* is also the adjective, 'of or relating to Argentina', as in 'Argentine trade'. The modern tendency to speak of *the Argentine* instead of *Argentina* is to be resisted.

argot is misused when it is made equivalent to *jargon* (technical vocabulary or language; technicalities). 'Mathematics has been called the language of science. This is not quite accurate. Each branch of science has also an argot of its own.'

Aristarchus. See ZOILUS.

arise is now, in ordinary speech, used in preference to *rise* only in the transferred sense of a discussion (controversy, argument), a quarrel, a war arising. In formal writing, however, we may still *arise* from a sick bed or from a seat.

arrogate and abrogate. To *abrogate* a law is to repeal it; to *abrogate* a custom is to discontinue it. To *arrogate to oneself* (the simple verb is falling rapidly into disuse) is to claim or assume that to which one is not entitled, or to claim or assume unreasonably or arrogantly, as in 'They arrogated to themselves the right of approving or rejecting all that was done' and 'She arrogated to herself a certain importance'. (*O.E.D.*)

artist; artiste. The latter has been introduced into English 'in consequence of the modern tendency to restrict *artist* to those engaged in the fine arts, and especially painting (*O.E.D.*); an *artiste* being there defined as 'a public performer who appeals to the aesthetic faculties, as a professional singer, dancer, etc.' This derivative sense, 'one who makes a "fine art" of his employment, as an artistic cook, hairdresser', etc., is moribund—and soon, I hope, it will be dead.

artless; ignorant. The former is favourable (with a connotation of ingenuousness); the latter unfavourable.

Aryan. Until Hitler imposed upon the word a racial sense, *Aryan* was applied only to languages. Witness Professor Ernest Weekley, who says, 'From Sanskrit *arya*, noble. Hence also Greek *Areia*, Eastern Persia, and Persian *Iran*, Persia. Introduced by Max Muller, as generic name for inflected languages . . . Divided into West *Aryan*, i.e. most European languages (except Basque, Finnish, Hungarian, Turkish) and East *Aryan*, i.e. Persian, Sanskrit, and the Hindu vernaculars related to the latter. . . . Some use *Aryan* of the Asiatic group only.'

as for *because* is grossly overworked by many writers, who are apparently enamoured of its brevity; often *as* is ambiguous ('He could not work as he was ill in bed'). It is difficult to lay down rules for the use and discrimination of *as*, *because*, *for*, *since*, their correct employment being a matter of idiom. *As* is colloquial both for the objective, logical *because* and for the subjective *for*, either of which is to be preferred to *as* in good writing and dignified speech. In *since* there is a connotation of time: as a causal conjunction it derives from the temporal *since* (= after).

as for *that* (conjunction) is a solecism. 'He did not say as he liked it'; 'Not as I've heard or know of'. Read: 'He did not say that he liked it'; 'Not that I know of'—or 'Not so far as I know'.

as, unnecessary in such a sentence as: 'He expressed himself as anxious to do everything in his power to help.'

as, wrongly omitted, esp. after *such*. 'The only thing that spurred (annoyed) me was me being such a flat [as] to buy the home.' And it is better to retain the *as* introducing a simile; thus 'as dry as a bone' is preferable to 'dry as a bone'.

as, equally. 'It was accompanied by a hissing inbreath from Ferradi which was equally as vicious'; for 'equally vicious' or 'as vicious'. *Equally as* also = 'as much as' (no less than) in, e.g., 'He feels it equally as you do'. Both of these uses are abuses.

as a consequence of. See CONSEQUENCE OF.

as a rule . . . always. 'As a rule he was always in the drawing-room before the first gong sounded.' This is no less excessive than *generally . . . always*.

as . . . as. The second *as* should not be abandoned in such a sentence as 'The younger Pitt was as great and even greater than his father': read, 'The younger Pitt was as great and even greater than his father', or 'The younger Pitt was as great as his father or even greater'.

as . . . as and so . . . as. The former is neutral, colourless; the latter, emphatic. 'As soon as they were ready, they departed'; 'So soon as you are ready, we shall depart'. Where *to* + an infinitive follows, the formula is *so . . . as* (e.g., 'They were so clumsy as to be dangerous to their companions'), not because there is *to* + an infinitive but because there is considerable emphasis: here, there is—in addition to the idea of comparison—an unmistakable connotation of degree, so that *so . . . as* + infinitive has a different psychological origin from that of *as . . . as*. 'In negative assertions and questions implying a negative answer, *so . . . as* and *as . . . as* are now generally used interchangeably, but *so . . . as* is preferred by many writers and authorities . . .; as, he is not *so* cruel *as* the average boy.' (*Webster's*.)

as far as and so far as. In literal statements concerning distance, *as far as* is used in positive sentences ('I ran as far as I could and then walked'), *so far as* in negative sentences ('It was not so far as I expected'). In figurative statements, *so far as* is usual, as in 'So far as I can see, your idea is admirable'.

as follow is wrong for *as follows*. 'There were many articles in the room, as follow: a large table and a small one, a bookcase, six chairs, twelve maps, etc.' *As follows* is short for *as it follows* and, because it is impersonal, it is of the same order as the italicized words in 'I shall act *as seems* best', 'So far *as* in me *lies*'. (Onions.)

as if and as though are often synonymous, but should they not be differentiated? To define the difference is not easy: to exemplify is easy enough. 'Could you drive a ball four hundred yards?' 'As if I could!' —'Jack X. is an exponent of personal publicity, you know.' 'Oh yes, don't he lived aloud!' In short, *as though* connotes comparison, whereas *as if* stresses possibility or potentiality—or their opposite, impossibility. There has, since ca. 1940, arisen a belief, not yet quite usage, that *as if* should be used to the exclusion of *as though*. The latter cannot be analyzed; the former can.

as is (or **was** or **will be**) **the case with** is an intolerable tautology for *like*: 'As was the case with Bonnor, Bartlett is a mighty hitter'. Sometimes it is misused for *as for* or *as with*: 'As is the case with you, I fear the unknown less than I do the known.'

as many as is incorrect—for *such persons as* or *those who* (or *all those who*) in 'As many as require the book should order it before the edition (strictly limited) is exhausted'.

as per, 'in accordance with', is such horrible commercialese that even merchant princes are less than riotously happy when their secretaries wish it on them.

as to is sometimes introduced quite unnecessarily, as in: 'One can only guess as to how Mr Jaggers knew'. One would not insert *as to* before a 'why', so why insert it before a 'how'? A less reprehensible example is this, cited by Dr C. T. Onions: 'They could not agree as to whom they should elect', concerning which Dr Onions comments: ' "As to" may be omitted. It is not at all necessary, and is inserted in such cases probably in imitation of "They could not agree as to that".' *As to* is defensible when it synonymizes *in respect of* or *in the matter of*; it is defensible, too, though unnecessary, as a synonym of *about* or *concerning*.

as to whether is unnecessary for **whether.**

as too. In the following, 'As often happens with irresolute men, when they have once been fixed to a decision they are as too hasty as before they were too slow', *as too* is a very awkward construction, though perhaps not demonstrably ungrammatical; 'as much too hasty' or 'as over-hasty' would be better.

as well as is often ambiguous, as in 'The captain, as well as the sailors, suffered this bitter reverse', which may convey the fact that both the captain and his crew suffered it—or the different fact that the captain's power of endurance was equal to the crew's.

as what. See WHAT, AS.

as yet is unnecessary for *yet*. 'His mind . . . was not as yet completely ossified.'

ascribe and **attribute.** To *ascribe* something is to enter it in an account, to reckon or count it; to consider or allege as belonging *to*, to claim *for*. To *attribute* is to regard (something) as belonging *to* ('To attribute to a word a sense it does not possess'); to declare or impute as a

quality belonging or praper *to*, or inherent in ('A mystical character is apt to be attributed to the idea of moral obligation'); to reckon as a consequence of ('His shrivelled arm was attributed to witchcraft'); to declare to belong *to* an author ('A play attributed to Shakespeare'); to assign to its proper place or time ('This manuscript may be attributed to the 4th Century, A.D.'). (*O.E.D.*)

aside from. See APART FROM.

assemble together (v.i. or v.t.) is excessive for *assemble*. For 'The people assembled together' read 'The people assembled'.

assert is a strong word: do not debase it to equivalence with *say*.

assert, like *affirm* and *declare*, cannot be used with the infinitive unless a noun or a pronoun is put with that infinitive. 'I assert [or affirm or declare] you to be a thief' is correct, though less idiomatic than 'I assert [etc.] that you are a thief'. But one cannot say 'I affirm [etc.] to be a thief' instead of 'I declare [idiomatically; *not* 'affirm', nor 'assert'] myself to be a thief'. (Note that the first person requires, not *me* but *myself*.)

asset for *amenity* (of a place), or *valuable feature* or *factor*, is incorrect. *Assets* are the property of a person (or business) available for the discharge of his debts. Used loosely, says The Con. *O.D.*, for *any possession*; and improperly for any useful quality, as in 'Nearly everyone has graduated either through Surrey schoolboys' teams or the Surrey Wanderers, an asset which has played no small part in improving the county spirit, etc.'

assist to (do something) is incorrect for *assist in* (doing). We help a person to do, we *assist* in the action. Nesfield gives the example, 'He is looked upon as a great authority on these questions, and will assist to examine scientifically a number of these questions'. The first meaning of *assist* is *to be present at*; to *help* or *give aid* is subsidiary, and the word *help* is usually better.

assume. See 'ADAPT and ADOPT'.

assume and **presume.** *Presume* (v.i.), 'to be presumptuous', and *presume* (*up*)*on*, 'to take for granted', offer no difficulty: *assume* can never be substituted, here, for *presume*. As v.t., *presume* has the following extant senses: 'to take upon oneself, to undertake without premission or adequate authority', as in 'to presume to sit in judgment on the actions of kings'; 'to take for granted', as in 'to presume the death of the man that disappeared eight years before' or 'to presume that he who disappeared so long ago is dead'. To *assume* is 'to take unto oneself; to adopt', as in 'to assume a partner'; 'to take upon oneself, to put on', as in 'The Netherland revolt had . . . assumed world-wide proportions'; 'to take to oneself formally' (insignia of office; symbol of a vocation) and 'to undertake' (an office, a duty), as in 'He assumed the monastic habit'; 'to take as being one's own, to claim, to take for granted', as in 'That disposition . . . to assume . . . jurisdiction over other men's conduct'; 'to simulate or feign', as in 'scepticism, assumed or real'; 'to take for granted as the basis of an argument, a negotiation', as in 'William assumes the willingness of the assembly'. (*O.E.D.*)

assumption and **presumption** correspond exactly to *assume* and *presume*.

astonish, astonishment are stronger than *surprise* (n. and v.); *astound* and *astoundment* are even stronger. Note, however, that 'to *surprise*' basically = 'to take, come upon, unprepared, off guard, at unawares', senses that belong neither to *astonish* nor to *astound*. Cf. AMAZEMENT and AMAZING.

astray and **estray**. The former is adjective and adverb, as in 'The animal is astray' or 'The animal has gone astray'. *Estray* is a noun, as in 'That cow is an estray' (it has gone astray) and a legal verb, 'to roam, to wander, to stray'.

at about (six o'clock; halfway) is incorrect for *about* (six o'clock; halfway).

at and **in**. See IN and AT.

at is bad, if not absolutely ungrammatical, for *against*, in the following placard: 40,000 PROTEST AT FOOD PRICES.

at last. See LAST.

at length = *at last* but it also = 'fully' or 'in detail'.

ate, past tense of *eat* (*q.v.*).

atheist. See AGNOSTIC.

atmosphere, stratosphere, troposphere. See TROPOSPHERE.

attached hereto. Read *attached*.

attain; accomplish; attain to. To *attain* is 'to reach, to gain, to achieve'; to *accomplish* is 'to perform (a task), to succeed in (an undertaking)'. Weseen gives a useful example: 'He who wishes to attain success must accomplish something every day'. *Attain to* connotes either effort or a lofty ambition, as in 'He attained to fame only when he had been striving for thirty years'. (*O.E.D.*)

attended by. See PREPOSITIONS WRONGLY USED.

attitude. See REACTION.

attorney. See LAWYER.

attribute. See 'ASCRIBE and ATTRIBUTE'.

audience is properly a gathering of hearers or listeners. Otherwise, *spectators*, i.e. 'onlookers', is required.

aught, 'anything', is incorrectly used for the cypher, *nought*, which represents 'nothing'. 'For aught I know, he may be there' is correct, though slightly archaic; 'Put an *aught* (or *ought*) after 7 and you have 70' is incorrect—indeed, illiterate.

aura. 'McCarthy . . . lit his cigarette, holding the lighter so that it etched an aura upon its owner's face', exemplifies a not infrequent misconception, for the *aura* of person or thing is an *emanation from* him or it, *not shed* by something outside.

Aura is occasionally misused for figurative *air* (or *atmosphere*), as in 'In view of Lord Northcliffe's famous maxim, "When a dog bites a man, that's not news; but when a man bites a dog, that is news", it appears as if every happening of importance should be given an aura of drama'.

aural, 'of the ear', hence 'of hearing'; *oral*, 'of the mouth', hence 'spoken'.

AUSTRALIAN ENGLISH. See STANDARD ENGLISH, Section iv.

authentic has become a vogue word. Avoid it except in its literal senses.

author. See MAN OF LETTERS.

authoritive is wrong for *authoritative*.

auto for *automobile* is a colloquialism—hence, to be avoided in formal speech and writing. [In the U.S.A., *automobile* is now usually limited to attributive and adjectival uses, such as *the automobile business*. The noun is commonly *car*.]

autocracy and **autonomy** are occasionally confused. The meaning of *autocracy* is 'absolute government (by an individual or a paramount authority)'; of *autonomy*, 'the right of a state or institution to govern itself' (or the condition of a state possessing such right).

automaton has learnèd plural *automata*; ordinary — i.e., English — plural *automatons*.

AUXILIARY VERB (have, had, etc.), omission of. 'The preparation of a history of . . . reactionary movements which contributed towards shaping the course of political events for the past one hundred and fifty years' (for 'which have contributed'). [The substitution of the preterite and of *did* + inf. for the perfect is a distressing tendency in American speech.]

avail for *afford, provide*. 'Behind all variants and shades, there stands the absolute certainty that fingers are not the fonts of knowledge, and sucking them will avail no information.' *Avail* is here misused; a correct construction would be 'such action will not avail them'.

avenge and **revenge** (vv.); **vengeance** and **revenge** (nn.). The noun that corresponds to *avenge* is *vengeance*; that which pairs with *revenge* is—*revenge*. One *avenges* another or, less commonly, the wrong done to another, but one *revenges* oneself or the wrong done to oneself; *vengeance* is the exaction of justice (' "Vengeance is mine," saith the Lord') or, for oneself, what one deems to be justice (a 'getting even'), whereas *revenge* is satisfaction accorded to personal resentment ('He shall have his revenge the next time we meet'). The nn. are less often confused than the vv., and it is particularly to be noted that, in idiomatic English, one does not say 'I shall avenge—or, revenge—the person that does the wrong'. In short, *revenge* (n. and v.) is the more subjective or personal, *avenge* and *vengeance* the more objective and impersonal.

avenue, explore every. See EXPLORE EVERY AVENUE. Other strange uses of the word *avenue* have been noticed by Sir Alan Herbert, who quotes Mr J. H. Thomas's reported statement, '. . . I certainly did not shut the door to any avenue of peace'.

average = 'estimated by average' or 'equal to what would be the result of taking an average', hence 'of the prevalent (or, the usual) standard', as in 'A modern drawing of average merit', is permissible; but it is slovenly English to equate it with 'common' or 'typical'. (*O.E.D.*)

averse to (or from). See ADVERSE TO.

avert. See ADVERT.

avocation and **vocation.** One's *vocation* is one's occupation, one's work or employment; an *avocation* is that which calls one away from one's *vocation*—hence, a minor or subsidiary occupation, a by-work (or *parergon*), hence even a hobby. 'But as, in many cases, the business which called away was one of equal or greater importance . . . , the new meaning was improperly foisted upon the word: Ordinary employment, usual occupation . . .' (*O.E.D.*). Scrupulous writers observe the etymological and proper distinction, which, after all, makes for clarity.

await and **wait.** *Await* is used, (*a*) of persons, 'to wait for' (a coming event or person), as in 'I shall await your answer with the greatest eagerness'; and (*b*) of events, fate, honours, offices, duties, 'to be in store—or to reserve for', as in 'Honours and rewards which he little

deserved awaited him'. To *wait* is intransitive (with occasional transitive uses) and has a transitive form *wait for*: to *wait for* a person is to *await* him. (*O.E.D.*)

awake; **awaken.** The past tenses are *awoke* and *awakened*; the past participles *awaked* (or *awoke*) and *awakened*. As past tense of *awake*, *awaked* is archaic; as past participle of either *awake* or *awaken*, *awoken* is incorrect. 'I was awoken by that rather flashy young woman.' Moreover, the past tense of *wake* is *woke*; the past participle is *woken*. Of *waken*, both the past tense and the past participle are *wakened*.

award and **reward.** The latter is either a recompense or a recognition of merit; the former is 'a judicial sentence, esp. that of an arbitrator or umpire', hence 'that which is . . . assigned, as payment, penalty, etc., by the terms of the judge's sentence or arbitrator's decision'. (*O.E.D.*)

awhile for **a while** is catachrestic when *while* is a noun. 'I shall stay here for awhile' is incorrect for '. . . for a while'. Such a sentence as 'They followed it [an inlet] for awhile along the edge of the bank' brings one up with a jerk; *for a while* or, simply, *awhile* would have been correct.

AWKWARD PHRASING. The worst awkwardnesses are so idiosyncratic and so obvious that they require no comment; of the others, the majority will be found under such headings as False Agreement (*q.v.* at AGREEMENT, FALSE) and Order.

One cannot prescribe against awkward phrasing except in a general way: re-read everything you write, and do it as externally as you can by putting yourself in the place of the reader; any awkwardness will then manifest itself to you. Awkwardness is, if you like, the opposite of elegance; I prefer to call it the opposite of economy of words on the one hand, and on the other, the opposite of clarity.

Here is an example from a writer in whom such awkwardness is a rarity: '[There] stood, a slight, white-clad figure, in the bright circle of light cast by one of the lamps which was still alight, of the car from which she had been flung'.

awoke; **awoken.** See AWAKE.

ay and **aye.** In the sense 'ever', *ay* is to be preferred; in that of 'yes', *aye* is to be preferred, though *ay* is etymologically as correct as *aye*. *Ay(e)*, 'ever', is pronounced like the *ay* of *hay*; *ay(e)*, 'yes', is pronounced either 'eye' or like the 'ever' *ay(e)*.

B

baby. See INFANT.

back again is superfluous for *back* ('He gave me the coat back again'); also for *returned* ('I see you're back again').

bad (for *ill*), as in 'she was taken bad in the street', is a solecism. *Bad* is an adjective and correct in 'She feels bad'.

balance for *remainder* is catachrestic. 'The considerable balance of this list will be found in *Modern Criminal Investigation* . . . from which the above extract is taken.' Its use for *the rest* or *remainder* is described by *The O.E.D.* as 'commercial slang': it may have come from America.

baleful and **baneful.** *Baleful* is 'pernicious; destructive', also 'malignant'. *Baneful* is 'life-destroying; poisonous', also 'pernicious, injurious'. The points to note are that *baneful* does not mean 'malignant' and that *baleful* does not mean 'poisonous'. (*O.E.D.*)

baluster and **banister.** A *baluster* is a short, circular-sectioned, double-curved pillar or column, slender above and larger, pear-shaped below, 'usually applied in a series called a *balustrade*'; hence 'a slender upright post or pillar of any shape supporting a rail; in pl. a railing or balustrade'; hence, usually in plural, 'the upright posts or rails which support the handrail, and guard the side, of a staircase; often applied to the whole structure of uprights and handrail. Now more usually banister(s)'. (*O.E.D.*)

baptismal name. See CHRISTIAN NAME.

ban (v.) has since ca. 1930 been foully misused by journalists and by approximatists among writers. In current Standard English, it = 'to prohibit' (a thing) or 'to interdict or proscribe' (a person). The two chief journalistic senses are 'to dismiss', 'to deny the right of entry to': which, to put it bluntly, are as incorrect as they are unnecessary.

banister(s). See BALUSTER . . .

bank (n.). See SHORE.

Barbadoes is correct; but *Barbados* is now more usual for the British island in the West Indies. The river in Brazil: *Barbados*.

barbarian (adj.)='non-Hellenic' or 'non-Roman' (with reference to Classical times); as a synonym of *barbarous* (uncivilized), it is best avoided, and *barbarous* used in its place; *barbarous* also = 'cruelly harsh' and (of speech) 'harsh-sounding'. **Barbaric** = 'uncivilized', 'illiterate', 'non-Latin', 'outlandish'; it is well to reserve it for 'in the characteristic style of barbarians, as opposed to that of civilized countries or ages', as in 'Barbaric splendour of decoration' and 'barbaric art'.

To all of these adjectives, the corresponding agential noun is *barbarian*. (*O.E.D.*)

barely (or **hardly** or **scarcely**) **than** is catachrestic for *barely* (etc.) . . . *when.* 'Barely had her spirits fallen, leaving her to brood over the sea, than the pinch was repeated.' See also HARDLY . . . THAN.

barring. See CONJUNCTIONS, DISGUISED.

barrister. See LAWYER.

base or **basis.** In brief, *base* is literal for 'the lowest or supporting part', with various derivative technical senses, and *basis* is figurative, 'the main constituent, fundamental ingredient', 'foundation; ground-work', 'a principle, or a set of principles' as in 'Society rested on the basis of the family'. (*O.E.D.*)

basketfuls and **baskets full.** A *basketful* is a quantity that will fill a basket, whereas a *basket full* is a basket full of (e.g. potatoes).

bathos and **pathos.** (Adjectives **bathetic** and **pathetic.**) The former is a 'ludicrous descent from the elevated to the commonplace'; the latter, that artistic, musical or literary quality—hence, that quality in life—which excites either pity or sadness.

BATTERED SIMILES. See SIMILES, BATTERED.

bay-window; bow-window. The latter is segmentally *curved*; the former, rectangular or polygonal, though some writers make the term include curved windows, *bay* thus becoming generic and *bow* specific.

be (or **become**) + a single active verb. Ambiguity or awkwardness often results, as in 'They were not uncreative in their work, had to tackle new problems all the time, and so they were interested and worked with zest'.

beau ideal, as *The Con. O.D.* usefully points out, does not mean 'a beautiful ideal' but 'the ideal beauty', one's idea of the highest type of beauty.

be being + past participle. The progressive or expanded infinitive.

'He will not *be being* wounded every day but perhaps only once—possibly not at all—in the fighting.'

On asking one friend what he thought of this, I received the answer, 'There is no such construction'. Another friend said 'Yes, I've heard it, but it's obviously wrong'. I first wondered about it when I heard myself saying, 'I should not be being disturbed all the time by rushed jobs if I had independent means'. If I can say 'I am being disturbed all the time', why not 'I shall (or should or may or might) be being disturbed'? Is there a difference between 'I should not be disturbed all the time' and 'I should not be being disturbed all the time'? There is. In the former (and in all sensible variations of the same formula), the past participle has much the same force and function as an adjective (with *disturbed*, cf. *perturbed*): all past participles have become, or are in process of becoming, adjectives (*'Heard* melodies are sweet'): there we have the idea of *continuous* state. But in the latter—'I should not be being disturbed all the time'—we have the idea of a *continual* act or a recurring state of things.

Contrast 'He will be seen every day of the week' with 'He will *be being* seen every day of the week': in the former *seen* is virtually synonymous with *visible*.

Set 'He was not to be wounded in the War of 1914–18' over against 'He was not to *be being* wounded in the War'. In the former, the sense is 'He was not'—i.e., was not destined—'to receive a wound', whereas in the latter it is 'He was not (destined) to be wounded on numerous occasions'.

Now take the three forms of gerund (the verbal noun, the *-ing* noun): the active (*receiving wounds*), the neutral or intransitive (*becoming a casualty*), and the passive (*being wounded*). Put them within the frame of a sentence and we get:

'Receiving wounds is no fun';
'Becoming a casualty is no fun';
'Being wounded is no fun'.

Turn those sentences into *to be* equivalents:

'To receive wounds is no fun';
'To become a casualty is no fun';
'To be wounded is no fun':

crisp, clear-cut, single-action, time-limited connotations, as also are the gerundial variants. The continual, plural-action, time-extended (or expanded) forms corresponding to those gerunds and infinitival nouns are:

'To be (continually) receiving wounds is no fun';
'To be (continually) becoming a casualty is no fun';
'To *be* (continually) *being* wounded is no fun'.

In short, I firmly uphold the *be being* (*wounded*) construction because it expresses a shade of meaning not otherwise expressible: 'to be continually wounded or disturbed or perturbed or visited or captured or imprisoned or pursued or . . .' is ambiguous; but 'to be being constantly wounded or disturbed or perturbed or . . .' is unambiguous—and expressive.

PS. Having written the above, I thought, 'Perhaps I had better obtain outside opinion—the opinions of experts'. So I wrote to Professor Otto Jespersen and Dr C. T. Onions. Professor Jespersen referred me to his four-volumed *A Modern English Grammar on Historical Principles*, where the construction is given as a variety of the expanded tense; he cites 'There's no wedding. Who could be being married?' (Barrie, *Barbara's Wedding*) and 'I shall always be being pushed away' (Galsworthy). 'The difficulty is evaded in . . . " 'Nothing seemed to be getting done,' he complained" [H. G. Wells]' (He goes on to say, 'I have no examples of the perfect and pluperfect: *has (had) been being—d*'.) He adduces the comparable construction *being to be*, as in 'He had to think of everything familiar to him as being to be parted with'.

Dr Onions replied thus: 'There is no doubt that *be being —ed* is current and has a meaning. Thus, if one were not in the habit of shaving oneself, one might say, "This is the time I ought to be being shaved". It is, as you imply, usual with the modal or so called auxiliary verbs; I suppose some people include even *ought* among these!'

became + past participle. This construction is often ambiguous and always awkward or, at the least, infelicitous, as in 'Alan Kent became roused from sleep by the rattle of distant thunder'. That this construction is to be avoided will be the more readily perceived when we add another example: 'Her eyes became filled with tears'. Certain persons would suggest: 'Kent was roused from sleep by . . . distant thunder' and 'Her eyes were filled with tears': but both those sentences are time-ambiguous. I think that, in all such instances, the simple *active* tense is the best: 'Her eyes filled with tears'; 'The rattle of distant thunder roused Alan Kent from sleep'.

because is sometimes misused for *that*, as in 'The value of the book to civilized Europeans is because it is an anthology of

Chinese ideas and anecdotes'; cf. 'Because terms are muzzy . . . does not mean that nothing can be accomplished on the economic front'.

because and **for.** See 'FOR' and 'BECAUSE' and 'AS for BECAUSE'.

befall has a pejorative connotation; *happen to* is neutral; *fall out for* is favourable ('It might so fall out for anyone').

before for *until.* 'Not *until* I have passed that examination, shall I be able to go out to parties' is correct; 'Not *before* I have . . .' is catachrestic. Perhaps the reason is that *until* connotes inclusion in the following act or event, whereas *before* emphasizes not so much the ensuing act or event as the time or events preceding it.

begin. See COMMENCE.

beg leave (to say, etc.); **beg permission** (to differ, etc.). These forms are preferable to 'I beg to say' and 'I beg permission to depart'. Especially nauseating is 'I beg to advise you'; and 'I beg to remain Yours faithfully, ——' is insufferable.

begrudge and **grudge** are virtually synonymous: 'To give, grant, allow unwillingly; to be unwilling to give, grant or allow; to envy (a person) the possession of': but *begrudge* is the more formal word.

behalf of, in and **on.** Confusion leads to the loss of a very useful distinction. *On behalf of* = 'on the part of (another), in the name of, as the agent or representative of, on account of, instead of a person', often with the connotation of official agency, as in 'An application was made on behalf of the prosecutor for a remand'. *In behalf of* = 'in the interest of, as a friend or defender of, for the benefit of (a person)': 'Speak in my behalf, please' is 'Put in a good word for me, please'. (*O.E.D.*)

behind is the most serviceable of all the words for that portion of the anatomy on which one sits.

being to be. See BE BEING . . .

belief of. See PREPOSITIONS WRONGLY USED.

believable. See UNBELIEVABLE.

bellicose; belligerent. Respectively 'warlike' and 'occupied in waging war'.

belly is 'that part of the body which receives food', i.e., the stomach with its adjuncts; *stomach* is now more general than *belly* in this sense. The prevailing current sense of belly is 'that part of the human body which lies between the breast and the thighs, and contains the bowels', the medical term being *abdomen*,

which, by the euphemistic and the mealy-mouthed, is used in preference to the good English word.

below and **beneath.** See 'ABOVE and OVER'.

benefaction, misused for *benefit.* 'Gypsies were such a nuisance, they would say, that whoever had killed this man had probably conferred some benefaction upon the community at large.'

benevolence is occasionally misused for *beneficence,* as *maleficence* is for *malevolence*; and vice versa. *Beneficence* and *maleficence* are the doing of good and harm respectively; *benevolence* and *malevolence* are the corresponding sentiments. An instance of *beneficence* misused for *benevolence* occurs in 'Floating on a serene plane of airy beneficence, he suddenly discovered that people were not looking up to him among the stars, but somewhere on the ground near their feet.'

beside; besides. Mr Harold Herd, in *Watch Your English,* rightly insists on the distinction, giving examples of correct use: 'I first saw him beside the main entrance', and 'Have you any money besides this?'; also 'Besides, the season will not be over, etc.'

besides means 'in addition to', not *other than.* Clearly, then, it is misused in ' "Otherwise the wound must have been on the right side of the face—unless it was made by something besides the handle of the gear-lever" '.

best two (or **three** or . . .) and **two** (or **three** or . . .) **best.** Usage has tended to justify *two best,* probably on the ground that if we can say 'The most popular writers are X. and Y.', we can also say 'The two most popular writers are X. and Y.'—as we do. Contrast *first two* (etc.) which is correct, and *two first,* which is incorrect.

bête noir is a very frequent error for *bête noire.* Even *bête noire* is to be used with caution, for it is a cliché. What is wrong with *bugbear* that it should be supplanted by a Gallicism?

betray for *exhibit* or *disclose* is sometimes ambiguous. 'Only once . . . did I see J. W. H. T. Douglas betray his punishing powers [as a batsman]': cricketers know that the younger Douglas was a dour bat and that, here, *betray* must = 'exhibit'; but the uninformed might be pardoned for thinking that, on this occasion, he failed to do justice to an ability and habit of smiting the ball.

better and **bettor,** as the noun-agent of *bet* (v.). *The O.E.D.* admits the two forms.

better for *longer*. See BETTER THAN . . .
better for *rather*. 'On a May morning where should an Englishman be better than on Wenlock Edge?' The context shows that *better* does not signify 'morally better'; the reference is to choice.
better than for *more than* is not Standard English but dialect. 'Better than a mile' is a frequent example. *Better* in the sense of *longer* (in time)—' "When did he marry his mistress?" "About four weeks ago, or better" ' — is obsolete in Standard English.
between, misused. 'The Trades Union' as nickname of the 1st Dragoon Guards is derived, according to Frazer & Gibbons, 'from the K.D.G's being constantly employed in suppressing Trade Union disturbances in Lancashire and the Midlands between 1825–34'. It should be 'from 1825 to '34' or 'between 1825 and 1834'. *Between* is also misused for *among, amongst*, where more than two objects are referred to. 'Between her hair' was written by a poet who ought to have known better. Note too the error in 'In 1926 he returned to France, and since then has lived between there and the U.S.A.'
between each. See EACH, BETWEEN.
between [noun] **to** [noun] is incorrect—and silly—for *between . . . and . . .* as in 'Between London to Manchester, there are several large cities'; 'Between 9 a.m. to 6 p.m., I saw a battle'.
between you and I. *Between*, being a preposition, takes the accusative case equally with all other prepositions (*after me, after him and me, for you and me*): therefore, *between you and me. Between* and *betwixt* are, however, not, in function, parallel to *after, for, in, to*, where the preposition is governing single units: *for you and me* is *for you and for me; in him and me* (there is ambition) is *in him and in me . . .* But *between him and me, between you and me* do not equal *between him and between me, between you and between me*, the latter pair being nonsense. *He and I, you and I* may be regarded in phrasal units, of which only the first member (*he* and *you*) take the accusative, thus: *between him and I, between you and I.* Also, there are persons that, immediately detecting the grammatical error in *between him and I*, are blind to that in *between you and I*, for the reason that *you* is the same in the accusative (*for you*) as in the nominative (*you are here*), whereas it is *for him* and *he is here. Between you and I*, though in-

defensible grammatically, may be considered as a 'sense construction, and is often used by those who would never dream of saying *between he and I.*
biannual should be reserved for 'half-yearly'; **biennial** for 'two-yearly'. I myself, however, prefer *half-yearly* to *biannual.*
bibliography must not now be used—as before ca. 1925 it could be used—of a *list of authorities and/or sources, a list of books (and documents) read* (or *consulted*), a *list of books to read and study* (or a *reading list*); nor of a *catalogue raisonné*, which is a list of works, authorities, sources, with the addition of descriptive or critical details (e.g., 'Esp. valuable for the French influence on English drama'). A *bibliography* is properly, in general 'the' and in particular 'a', 'systematic description and history of books, their authorship, printing, publication, editions, etc.' (*O.E.D.*); that 'etc.' includes format, number of pages (e.g., viii + 288), type-fount (or *font*), number and kind of illustrations. The list of books by or on an author, or on a subject, becomes a bibliography only when the preceding particulars are noted against each book-title.
bid—preterite *bid* (archaic: *bad, bade*)—past participle *bid* (archaic: *bidden*).
bid. 'The sub-editor's worst crime is that he either takes a word with a simple meaning, and makes it stand for a vague, illogical mass of other meanings, or . . . applies strong, colourful words to unworthy ends, and so ruins their effectiveness when their use is appropriate.—To take a single instance, let me return to *bid*, which sub-editors have made me hate more than any other word in the language. According to my dictionary the verb *to bid* means to command, order, invite, announce, proclaim, or make an offer at a sale. The noun means an offer of a price. Now usage often leaves a dictionary behind, and for my part I am quite prepared to accept a new meaning of a word if there is anything to be gained by it. But the slavish way in which our sub-editors use *bid* to mean an attempt to do anything under the sun arouses my lowest instincts. "New bid for Europe pact", "Navy bid", "boxing bid", "desperate bid", "legitimisation bid",— I take them all from last week's papers' (Frank Whitaker, Dec. 13, 1938). It has, in short, become a journalistic fashion, which certain authors are mistaking for an intellectual necessity.

big for *important* or *leading* is a loose colloquialism, as in 'The big man in that firm is Smith'.

bimonthly and **semi-monthly** respectively = 'once every two months' and '(happening) twice a month'. **Biweekly** and **semi-weekly** = 'occurring every two weeks' and 'twice a week'. The spellings *bimonthly* and *bi-weekly* are preferable.

birth date, or **date of birth**; **birthday**. Respectively 'date on which one was born' and 'anniversary of one's birth'.

bison. See BUFFALO.

black (v.) is literal (e.g., to black one's shoes); **blacken** (v.t.) is figurative as in 'She blackened his character in the most unscrupulous manner'. But as an intransitive, *blacken* is used both lit. and fig.—as in 'I . . . believe that rain will fall when the air blackens'. (*O.E.D.*)

blame (something) **on** (a person) is colloquial—and unnecessary—for *blame* (a person) *for* (something).

blatant for *flagrant*, as in 'a blatant breach of good faith'.

blend into is incorrect for *blend with* and for the preferable *merge into* or *with*. 'Gardeners blend into their surroundings, and it is often possible to miss them completely in a walk around the garden.'

blend together is a foolish, redundant variation of *blend* (v.).

BLENDED GENITIVE. See GENITIVE, VAGARIES OF THE, last paragraph.

BLENDS. See PORTMANTEAU WORDS.

bloody 'is entirely without improper significance in America' (the U.S.A.), as H. L. Mencken has remarked in *The American Language.* But Americans writing for an English public and American visitors to Britain should remember that, in Great Britain, this word, despite its growing popularity there and its consequent weakening, is still regarded as unsuitable in dignified writing. (See 'The Word *Bloody*' in my *From Sanskrit to Brazil*, 1952.)

blue-print (or **blueprint**) is one of those vogue words which have been spawned by officialdom and journalism acting in unholy conjunction. Strictly a diagrammatic plan (white lines, etc., on blue paper), a technical scheme, it was already by 1941 in America—see, for example, John P. Marquand's sly hit at it in *So Little Time* (1943)—and by 1942 in Britain, the fashionable word for political, social, military plans, with a connotation of doctrinaire infallibility. 'A blueprint for invasion'—'a blueprint for victory'.

bluff, misused for *simulate*. 'To bluff intelligence is the easiest thing possible,' a crass Philistine once remarked: to simulate stupidity (or even to be stupid) is much easier.

bogey; bogie; bogy. These three spellings are interchangeable for the three meanings, 'the number of strokes a good golfer may be assumed to need for a hole or a course'—'an open railway freight-car' or 'a revolving undercarriage'—'a bogle, a goblin'. Writers would do well to attach the first meaning to *bogey*, the second to *bogie*, the third to *bogy*.

Bohemian is 'a native of Bohemia', hence 'a Gypsy'; **bohemian**, a transferred use, is 'a Gypsy of society', esp. 'a writer, artist, musician, actor that leads a vagabond or a free and irregular life'. (*O.E.D.*)

bona fide is occasionally misused for *bona fides*. 'Mussolini's *bona fide* has never been questioned.' *Bona fide* is a Latin ablative; it = 'with good faith'. In English *bona fide* is an adverb, and it = 'in good faith; sincerely; genuinely'; hence it is used as an adjective = 'acting, or done in good faith; sincere; genuine'. *Bona fides* is the Latin nominative, and in English it can be used both as nominative and as accusative. Properly it is a Law term = 'good faith; freedom from intent to deceive' (*O.E.D.*). *Bona fides* is singular, not plural as in '. . . As though Kingdom's *bona fides* were not accepted'.

book-learned and **bookish** are now uncomplimentary. The corresponding complimentaries are *erudite, learned, scholarly*. *Book-learned* and *bookish* connote 'ignorant of life, however much book-learning one may possess'.

born, borne. Correct uses are 'He was born on the first day of the New Year' and 'He was borne by his mother after three hours of labour'.

borrow (money) **of** (a person) is correct but slightly obsolescent; *borrow from* is now the usual construction.

boss (n.) is restricted by good writers to its political sense, 'a manager or dictator of a party organization in the U.S.A.'

both for *alike*. *Both* refers to two persons, things, groups, classes, kinds, etc., not to three or more thereof. '. . . A shrewd common sense, which kept her safe . . . from all the larger follies, whilst still permitting her to give full run to minor eccentricities, both in speech, deed and dress.' Cf. *both alike*, redundant for *alike*, in 'Both of the suits are alike'.

both for *each*. 'There is a garage on both sides of the street' should be 'There is a garage on each side of the street' unless the author means that a garage is partly on one, partly on the other side.

both the. This is catachrestic for *the two* ('The both bowlers were unsuccessful') and also for *both* (' "Good for the both of you", grinned Punch'.).

both + noun, misused for *the + noun + together*. 'Then *x* plus 650 is her share. Both shares equal $5,000' (read 'The shares together equal $5,000').

both . . . as well as is incorrect for *both . . . and*. See quotation at PERSONNEL.

both of us—**you**—**them** are correct; *we both* and *us both*—*you both* (whether nominative or accusative)—*they both* and *them both*—these are incorrect, though one often hears all of them except *they both*. That *they both* lags behind the others appears from the queer effect it produces in 'Estella threatening to kill herself—Jensen gripping her—they both struggling for the knife'.

both our fathers, both your husbands, both their books. These are the colloquial forms that correspond to Standard English *the fathers of both of us, the husbands of both of you, the books of both of them*. 'The need for a compact expression of this kind is often felt. We may sympathize with the little girl who, wishing to state that a certain pet was the common property of herself and her brother, said "It's both of our donkey"!' (Onions). The day may arrive when these colloquialisms will become good English: if they do, they will merely revert to Middle English practice. But although one can say *both our fathers*, what happens when the reference is to the father of two children? *Both our father* is (at present, anyway) impossible. *Both your husbands* is clear enough, at first sight; but it may refer to a young film star's two husbands (the present one and the divorced one). *Both their books* may, to the unthinking, appear innocuous: but there may be two persons, who have one book apiece, and therefore the reference could as well be to the entire book-stock of these two book-lovers ('*Both* their books are at the bindery') as to the thousands of books owned by a pair of bibliophiles. All in all, it looks as though we had better remain faithful to the accepted usage of the literate.

both the last is catachrestic for *the last two*. 'He could not have received both her last letters and not answered them.' *Both of her last two letters* and *her last two letters* are equally correct; the latter, the more idiomatic.

bounden. See ARCHAISMS.

bow-window. See BAY WINDOW.

bracket, singular, is not to be used for *brackets* (plural), better *square brackets*: []; for which, however, the correct name is *'square' parentheses. Round brackets,* an absurdity now happily obsolete, are properly called *parentheses:* ( ); and one of these round signs is a *parenthesis,* as also is the word, phrase or sentence within the pair of *parentheses.* To employ *bracket* for the *brace* used in coupling two lines of writing or printing, thus

$$\left\{ \begin{array}{l} \text{L. } vinculum \\ \text{Eng. } bond, \end{array} \right.$$

is a catachresis.

brand, a trademark, or the make of goods distinguished by such mark, can also be metaphorically applied when the intention is humorous; but it is inappropriate in the following: 'The Queen had her own brand of services in her own private chapel'.

bran-new; brand-new; brank-new. The third is incorrect, except in Scottish; the second is the original and best form; the first is etymologically senseless, and un-necessary, but—on the score of usage—is uncensoriously admitted by The *O.E.D.*

bravado and **bravery.** The former is never synonymous with the latter. *Bravado* is defined by The *O.E.D.* as 'ostentatious display of courage or boldness; bold or daring action intended to intimidate or to express defiance; often, an assumption of courage or hardihood to conceal felt timidity, or to carry one out of a doubtful or difficult position'.

brave new world. Overworked.

breadth; broadness. *Breadth* is the physical noun. It is also used in the transferred senses, *breadth of mind* (never *width of mind*), an extensive display of a quality ('breadth and accuracy of vision', Morley), and, in art, a broad effect. As the abstract noun corresponding to *broad,* 'coarse, indelicate', *broadness* (never *breadth*) is the correct term.

breath (*brĕth*) is the noun; **breathe** (*brēthe*) is the verb.

brethren is archaic for *brothers* except 'in reference to spiritual, ecclesiastical, or professional relationship'. (*O.E.D.*)

BREVITY.

Since brevity is the soul of wit . . .
I will be brief.—Shakespeare.

I labour to be brief and become obscure.
—Horace.

'On the principle of attaining ends at

the smallest cost, it is a virtue of language to be brief. If a thought can be properly expressed in five words, there is a waste of strength in employing ten.'—Bain, *English Composition and Rhetoric*.

In one sense, brevity is the enemy of TAUTOLOGY and the opposite of VERBOSITY. But to avoid tautology and verbosity 'is not all; there are direct means of attaining Brevity by the help of various devices of style' (Bain).

I. *The Choice of Words.* 'The extension of our vocabulary by classical and other foreign words has greatly enhanced the power of brief yet adequate expression. Many of the words thus acquired have in themselves a great fulness of meaning, the consequence of their being employed in the higher kinds of knowledge, and in the complicated operations of society. Such are—strategy, census, codification, autonomy, altruism, hedonism, correlation.' To which we may add such words as *adaptability, complex* (n.), *flair*.

'Take', continues Bain, 'a few quotations to illustrate this point:—

'Man is described by Pope as—

The *glory, jest,* and *riddle* of the world;

the words summing up very happily the substance of a preceding paragraph, which expatiates on the greatness of man's powers, the frequent absurdity of his conduct, and the mysteries of his nature. Again:—

And he, who now to sense, now nonsense leaning,
Means not, *but blunders round about a meaning*.

Thomson has the following, in reference to birds teaching their young to fly:—

The *surging* air receives
Its plumy burden; and their self-taught wings
Winnow the waving element.

The expressions here used bring before us in a few words the fan-like stroke of the wings on the one hand and the corresponding motion of the air, like that of waves, on the other.

But as along the river's edge
They went, and brown birds in the sedge
Twittered their *sweet* and *formless* tune.
(William Morris.)

Here, *twittered* describes the short, tremulous notes characteristic of the songs of the birds; *sweet* conveys the mental impression of the listener; while *formless*

gives in one word the idea that the song is not shaped after any fixed standard but is poured forth in endless variety.'

II. *Grammatical Forms and Syntactical Usages.*
(1) *Abstract Nouns.* 'His *refusal* justified my *adherence* to my plan' = *'The fact that he refused* justified me *in adhering* (or, *when I adhered*) to my plan'. Still more condensed is 'The passionate confidence of interested falsehood' (Adam Smith).
(2) *The attributive use of nouns,* i.e. *nouns used as adjectives* or as elements of compound nouns. E.g., 'a *bosom* friend', '*table* talk', 'an *earth* worm', 'a *birthday* present'.
(3) *Adjectives* are rather obviously short-cuts, as in—

Goodness and wit
In *seldom-meeting* harmony combined,

'The *mazy-running* soul of melody', 'The *astonished* mother finds a *vacant* nest'. So too the *adverb*, or the adverb and adjective, or the adverb and adjective and abstract noun, as in—

See nations *slowly wise* and *meanly just*
To *buried merit* raise the *tardy* bust.

(4) *Participial phrases for clauses.* An excellent example is this—

Vanished every fear, and every power
Roused into life and action, light in air
The *acquitted* parents see their *soaring* race,
And once *rejoicing* never know them more.

(5) *Prefixes and Suffixes; and Compounds.* Consider '*re*turn', '*re*unite', '*re*fund'; 'absentee*ism*' and 'admiss*ibility*'; 'forcible-feeble', 'semi-popish', 'little-minded'.
III. *Rhetorical Devices.* Perhaps a hint may be conveyed by the following examples:—

'He lives to build, not boast, a generous race.'

'And read their history in a nation's eyes.'

'Leave to the nightingale her woods;
A privacy of glorious light is thine.'

'A hand-to-mouth liar.'

'Murder will out.'

brief and **short.** *Brief* = 'of short duration, quickly passing away or ending', hence (of speeches, writings) 'concise or short'; it is virtually obsolete in reference ato extent in space.*Short*, on the other hand, refers to either time or space; but when it refers to the latter, it often has a connotation of curtailment or incompleteness, or sudden cessation, as in 'a short nap'.

BRITICISMS are such English words as are used in Great Britain and the British Empire (except Americanized Canada) but not, in the relevant senses, in the United States of America. See ENGLISH AND AMERICAN USAGE.

British Empire, the. See GREAT BRITAIN.

Brittania is a frequent misspelling of *Britannia* (as *Britany* is of *Brittany*).

broad and **wide.** See WIDE . . .

broadcast, to; he **broadcasted;** the news was broadcast or broadcasted.

broadness. See BREADTH.

Brobdignag, -ian are incorrect for *Brobdingnag, -ian.*

Brussel sprouts for *Brussels sprouts* is an astonishingly frequent error.

Bruxelles, Gand, Lyon, Marseille for *Brussels, Ghent, Lyons, Marseilles* are affectations in any English or American author writing for the English or American public. It is equally affected to pronounce *Lyons* or *Marseilles* or *Paris* as the French pronounce them.

bucket full; bucketful. Cf. BASKETFULS.

buffalo and **bison.** *Bison* originally was 'a species of Wild Ox . . . formerly prevalent in Europe' but now the term is applied properly to the North American species, which, therefore, is improperly called *buffalo. Buffalo* is that species of ox which was 'originally a native of India' (*O.E.D.*). [Nevertheless, in the U.S.A., the North American bison is generally known as the buffalo and under this name figures in the national stock of stories.]

Buhl (as in *Buhl table*) should be *Boule. Buhl,* says *The O.E.D.,* 'seems to be a modern Germanized spelling' and *Boule* is 'the more correct form of the word commonly spelt *Buhl*': but this is a far too lenient comment, for *Buhl* has no justification—not even that of universal error, *Boule* being, among the educated, an equally common spelling. 'Boule (André Charles) célèbre ébéniste, né à Paris en 1642, mort en 1732. Il éléva l'ébénisterie à la hauteur d'un art, et acquit une grande réputation' (Larousse).

bulk, the (never *a*). *Bulk* should be reserved for 'volume' or 'mass'. It is incorrect both for *the majority*, as in 'The bulk of slow bowlers prefer the eight-ball over, but the bulk of fast bowlers prefer the six-ball over', and for *the greater part*, as in 'the bulk of the book'.

BULLS. A *bull* is 'an expression containing a manifest contradiction in terms or involving a ludicrous inconsistency unperceived by the speaker' (*O.E.D.*). Often called *Irish bulls*: but *bull* was used in this sense long before it came to be associated with that people which has given us the best examples of felicitous incongruities.

Here are two bulls, said to be Irish:

the entrance out.

'If there was twelve cows lyin' down in a field and one of them was shtandin' up, that would be a bull.'

bumble-bee. See HUMBLE-BEE.

bunch. 'Good usage does not sanction the indiscriminate use of *bunch* for any and every group, and certainly not for groups of people' (Weseen).

burglarize is at all times inferior to *rob* (a house). In Great Britain it is regarded as journalese. *Burgle* is a facetious synonym.

burn down and **burn up** are excessive, unnecessary for *burn*—unless an intensive force is required. A house 'burnt *down*' connotes total destruction, a burning right to the ground; a letter 'burnt up' connotes total destruction, not a mere scorching.

bus (not *'bus*) is now Standard English for *omnibus.* The plural is *buses.*

BUSINESS ENGLISH. See 'OFFICIALESE, JOURNALESE, COMMERCIALESE'.

busyness, the state of being busy, is, according to *The O.E.D.,* a modern formation, made to distinguish it from *business,* which has come to have another meaning. It is a necessary word, and is found also in *Webster's.*

but (adv.) (= *only*) is tautological in 'There was but very little room for him in the small overcrowded cottage'.

Like the adv. *only,* the adv. *but* sometimes gets into a foolish or illogical position—as in 'A semantic analysis of economic theory would fill a book . . . Here, we have space but for a few examples— (read: 'space for but a few examples'). Also it can be ambiguous when it is used for *only,* as in 'Yes, but a portion of my tribe is with me, yet I cannot say that anyone is missing'. And 'We splashed out on to the lane . . . its mud was but less fathomless than the yard's', is very awkward if not entirely incorrect.

but (conjunction) is wrongly used in the following, quoted by C. C. Boyd (*Grammar for Grown-Ups*): 'A gale swept the roads, and his (Mr Cobham's) machine was unprotected. At midnight he attached a second anchor, *but* the machine weathered the gale undamaged'.

C

But must be used instead of *and*; the sentence should read: '. . . his machine was unprotected, but weathered the gale . . . because he had attached a second anchor'.

The conjunction *but* is also incorrect in the following: 'He will certainly say of Mallet that as a detective he was remarkable not so much for the questions he put but for those he avoided putting'; *not so much . . . as* is correct, but the sentence might also read: 'not for the questions he put, but for those, etc.'

but (preposition). The clearest exposition I have seen is the following, from Dr Onions's *An Advanced English Syntax.*

'*But* is a Preposition meaning "except", and, like other Prepositions, governs the Accusative [or Objective]:

' "No one would have thought of it *but him.*"

'If, however, a sentence like this is otherwise arranged, the Nominative is very commonly put instead of the Accusative:

' "No one *but he* would have thought of it."

The Accusative, in fact, is felt to be inelegant. *But* thus becomes a Conjunction, and the sentence must be regarded as equivalent to "No one would have thought of it, *but* he thought of it".

'Compare:

The boy stood on the burning deck,
Whence all *but he* had fled.'

but (preposition) does not equal *more than.* ' "I won't go into the house yet. Jut give it the once over. Won't take me but a few minutes." ' Equally bad is: 'It is not possible in a short article to mention but a few of the, etc.'

but, misused for *than.* 'The choice of war or peace is now in other hands but ours.'

but in *help but* and *cannot help but* (do something) is awkward and to be deprecated. 'Millions of hearts could not help but thrill in response.' Why not simply 'thrilled'? How does 'help' help?

but . . . however, used where either *but* or *however* (or *notwithstanding*) is needed, is incorrect; e.g., 'After judgment [in court], she pleaded her belly, and a jury of matrons being impanelled, they found her not quick with child; but, however, she was afterwards reprieved'. Trial of Mary Roberts in July, 1728.

but that after *doubt.* See DOUBT.

but that used, unnecessarily, for *that . . . not.* 'Brington was not yet so overgrown but that the unspoilt country was within easy reach of it.'

but what, in, e.g., 'I don't know but what . . .', is a clumsy alternative to *but that.*

but yet (cf. BUT . . . HOWEVER) is, at the least, infelicitous; *but* is strong, *yet* is mild, and *but yet* rings oddly. It is rather surprising to find it in so good a writer as R. B. Cunninghame Graham: 'Born when the echoes of the '45 were ringing (though faintly) through the land, he held the Stuarts in abhorrence, but yet hated the Hanoverians, whom he termed German Boors'.

by. I regret that *by* is being used more and more in place of the merely instrumental *with.* E.g., 'She moved him rather by her tears than by her appeal to his chivalry'.

by for *beside* can be dangerously (and indeed ridiculously) ambiguous. 'Two bottles which contained poison were found by the deceased': quoted by Nesfield.

by a long way is verbose for *far* or *much.* 'The starlings are by a long way the greediest.'

by the name of and **of the name of** are intolerably wordy for *named* (or *called*). And **go by the name of** is ambiguous in that it implies that the name is an assumed one.

C

cacao, coca, cocoa, coco(nut). Confusion is common. *Cacao* is a tropical American tree from the seed of which the beverages *cocoa* and chocolate are made; *coca* is a Bolivian shrub the leaves of which are chewed as a stimulant; the *coco* or *coker* is a tropical palm-tree bearing the *coconut* or *cokernut,* the usual spelling in commerce being *coker,* to avoid ambiguity. (*Con. O.D.*)

cache, for any hiding place whatsoever, is loose, and *cache* for 'to hide' anything anywhere is catachrestic. To *cache* is 'to put in a cache', 'to store (provisions) underground'. (*O.E.D.*)

calculate is an Americanism—and colloquial—for 'to think, opine, suppose . . .; to intend, purpose'. (*O.E.D.*)

caliber (American), **calibre** (English). Don't use it indiscriminately to = *order of merit, class, kind* and *type.* 'A poem of high calibre' and 'an artist of low calibre' are not wrong: they are merely ludicrous.

calix, calyx. *Calix,* a cup-like cavity or organ, is often confused with the botanical *calyx* (either $\bar{a}$ or $\check{a}$), the whorl of leaves forming outer case of bud.

calligraphy is frequently misused; i.e., it is a catachresis for 'handwriting'. 'The calligraphy expert'; 'A pointed irritable calligraphy'. Its correct sense is 'beautiful handwriting'.

calvary. See CAVALRY.

CANADIAN ENGLISH. See STANDARD ENGLISH, Section iv.

can and may. On Sept. 10, 1665, Pepys joined a party at Greenwich, where Sir John Minnes and Evelyn were the life of the company and full of mirth. 'Among other humours, Evelyn's repeating of some verses made up of nothing but the various acceptations of *may* and *can*, and doing it so aptly upon occasion of something of that nature, and so fast, did make us all die almost with laughing, and did so stop the mouth of Sir J. Minnes in the middle of all his mirth (and in a thing agreeing with his own manner of genius), that I never saw any man so outdone in all my life; and Sir J. Minnes' mirth too to see himself outdone, was the crown of all our mirth.'

Briefly, *can* is used of ability to do something; *may* of permission to do it. 'He who will not when he may, may not when he will' (wishes—and is able—to do so).

can for may. Child at table: 'Please, can I get down?' Mother: 'Yes, and you *may*.' —Admirer to pretty maiden: 'Phyllis, you can come and kiss me.' Phyllis: 'Oh, *can* I?'

[Many American teachers and writers will agree with Mr Perrin's statements on the use of *can* and *may* (*Index to Usage*, p. 108). After setting forth the usual distinctions as a guide for 'formal English', he boldly adds: 'In less formal usage *may* occurs rather rarely except in the sense of possibility: *It may be all right for her, but not for me. Can* is generally used for both permission and ability: *Can I go now? You can if you want to*. . . . This is in such general usage that it should be regarded as good English in speaking and in informal writing. *Can't* almost universally takes the place of the awkward *mayn't*: *Can't I go now? We can't have lights after twelve o'clock.*']

candidacy; candidateship; candidature. The first = 'the position or status of a candidate': *candidateship*, 'the position of a candidate'; *candidature* is the most 'active' of the three terms, for it = 'standing as a candidate'. (*O.E.D.*) [Only the first is commonly found in American usage.]

cannot help but. See 'BUT in *help but*'.

cannot seem to is misplacement of words = 'seem not to be able to'. 'I must be nervous this afternoon. I can't seem to settle down to anything.' Change to '. . . I seem unable to settle down . . .'. [American usage accepts *cannot seem to* as a useful colloquial idiom. *I seem unable to settle down* is, in comparison, awkward though logical.]

canon (ecclesiastic and textual), **cañon** (a chasm or ravine), **cannon** (warfare and billiards), **canyon** (the anglicized form of *cañon*).

CANT. The everyday sense of *cant* is 'an affected or unreal use of religious or pietistic phraseology; language implying the pretended assumption of goodness or piety', as in 'The whole spiritual atmosphere was saturated with cant'. (*O.E.D.*)

But in philology, *cant* is the technical term for the vocabulary peculiar to the underworld (criminals; tramps and beggars; prostitutes and 'ponces'; and such hangers on as 'fences'). It is to be hoped that the use of this short, convenient term will become more general.

Cant, in this sense, is often called 'thieves' (or underworld) slang'. It is true that the underworld employs a great deal of slang; nevertheless, when the underworld wishes to communicate in a manner incomprehensible to more respectable citizens, it employs what cannot accurately be designated 'slang', for it is a 'secret language': but even 'secret language' is slightly misleading, for only the key-words, the significant words, are 'secret'. The words for departure, escape, flight; for dying and killing; for thief, cheat, swindler, confidence man, professional tough, receiver of stolen property, prostitute, pathic; for policeman, detective, prison warder; for arrest and imprisonment; for begging, and professional tramping; for the victims of criminals and beggars; for means of conveyance; for money; for food and drink in general and for certain specific drinks and foods; for such buildings as banks and houses, hospitals, barns and casual wards; for doors, windows, stairs; for certain household effects; for jewellery and gems; for means of communication; for such animals as dogs and horses; for certain geographical and topographical features (e.g. roads); for the tools and devices used by criminals; for such weapons as a cudgel, a life-preserver, a revolver, a machine-gun; for such verbs as 'do' or 'make', 'unmake', 'destroy', 'hide', 'discover', 'place', 'forge', 'look', 'examine', 'handle', 'bungle'; for 'man', 'woman', 'child', 'father', 'mother', 'wife', 'husband'.

Cant terms leak out from time to time, with the result that many of them are ultimately included in some dictionary or other; nor always only there. Here are a few examples of such promotion in British English:—*Beak*, a magistrate; *bilk*, to cheat; *booze*, noun and verb, and *boozer* (drunkard and public-house); *cove* and *cull* (or *cully*); *doxy*; *duds* (clothes); *filch*; *hick* (a rustic); *jemmy*; *moll* (a woman); *nab*, to take, steal, arrest; *nob*, the head; *ponce*, a prostitute's bully; *prig*, to steal; *queer* and *rum* (odd, 'shady'); *ready* and *rhino*; *rig*, a swindle, to swindle; *scamp* (noun) and *scamper* (verb); *shicer*; *stow it!*; *tanner*, a sixpence, and *bob*, a shilling; *tip*, to give; *tout*, noun and verb; (to) *work* (a district, a street); *yokel*. In American English, *hobo*, *stool pigeon*, and *yegg* form excellent examples.

Many writers of 'thrillers' and especially 'deteccers' sprinkle their pages—chiefly their low-life dialogue—with cant words and phrases. Most of them, however, have but a slight knowledge of cant, and of the few words they know, some are obsolete; in one of the most popular crime-plays of recent years, a character was made to say *crack a crib*. Now, since 1900, to 'burgle a house (flat, etc.)' is not *crack a crib* but *screw a joint*. See esp. *A Dictionary of the Underworld, British and American*, by E. P.

can't seem to. See CANNOT SEEM TO.

canvas is a cloth material; **canvass** is 'to examine, discuss, solicit', as in 'to canvass votes'. As n., *canvass* = 'a solicitation of support [esp. at an election], custom, etc.'

canyon. See CANON.

CAPITALS IN GENERAL. See esp. my *You Have a Point There.*

CAPITALS IN TITLES. See TITLES OF BOOKS.

capacious in the sense of *spacious* is now so little used that it rings almost oddly enough to be designated a misuse, though admittedly it isn't one. ('Chewing hay in Don Angel's capacious stable.')

capacity. See ABILITY.

caption is often misused to mean a legend underneath (instead of above, as it should be) an illustration. [In the U.S.A., this usage to signify the letterpress accompanying an illustration is probably established.]

carburettor, -er. *The Con. O.D.*, giving

both, seems to prefer the latter, as does *Webster's*. *Webster's*, however, prefers—or seems to prefer—*carburetor* to *carburettor*. Britain knows not *carburetor*, -er.

care-free; careless. The former (also written as one word) = 'free from care or anxiety'. So does *careless*, which also = (of persons) 'inattentive, negligent, thoughtless', hence 'inaccurate', and (of things) 'artless', 'unstudied', 'done, caused, or said heedlessly, thoughtlessly, negligently'. (*O.E.D.*)

careful for; careful of (erroneously **with**). One is *careful for* (a person or thing) when one is full of care or concern for him or it; but one is *careful of* (a person or thing) when one is attentive to his or her interests, or when one takes good care of him or it. (*O.E.D.*) [In American usage *careful with* is as common as *careful of* in regard to things.]

cargo and **shipment**. The former is a ship-load, a lading, a freight; the latter has the same sense, but with the nuance 'a consignment of goods', and the active sense, 'an act of shipping (goods)'. On trains, *freight* or *load*; on lorries, in motor-cars, and in trucks (U.S.A.), generally *load*.

carousal (v.: *carouse*) is a carouse, a drinking bout, a drunken revelry; *carousel* (or *carrousel*) is a special kind of chivalric tournament, and it has no corresponding verb. [In American usage, *carrousel* is a merry-go-round.]

carping has occasionally been misused for *carking*, the former meaning 'fault-finding', the latter 'oppressive'.

case, in any, used in the sense *however you look at it*, is colloquial and ambiguous.

case (of), in the, is frequently misused for *in this* (or *that*) *connection*; also it is often quite unnecessarily used, as in 'There was a greater scarcity of crabs than in the case of herrings'. Despite Sir Arthur Quiller-Couch's furious and witty onslaught, *case* is still used with nauseating frequency.

cast = *dramatis personae*—the list, hence the personnel, of actors and actresses performing a play, whereas **caste** is an exclusive class (of persons); the term having originally been, as in India it still is, used of hereditary classes; hence, *caste* is applied to a rigid system of class-distinctions within a community.

caster; castor. The former is one who casts, e.g., a (metal-)founder; a certain type of wheel; a variant (indeed the original form) of *castor*, 'a vial', 'a cruet', for either of which it is the more sensible form. A *castor* is the unctuous substance also named castoreum; a hat; a heavy broadcloth; the mineral also known as castorite; and *castor(oil)*.

casualty, 'a fatal or serious accident or event' (*O.E.D.*), is often misapplied to the person to whom the accident happens; this misuse, 'to be or become a casualty', is rightly pilloried by Sir Alan Herbert. *Casuality* is an obsolete variant, now held to be an illiteracy. *Causality* is 'the principle of causal relationship'. [*Webster's*, concerning *casualty*, has this: '. . . a soldier unavailable for service, because of death, wounds, . . . or any cause.' This usage, for sailors as well as soldiers, is established in U.S.]

CATACHRESIS. A catachresis is a word misused (e.g., *anachronism* for *anomaly*, *to subject* for *to subordinate*); catachresis, as a fault in writing, is 'an improper use of words' (*O.E.D.*); etymologically, 'contrary-to-usage-ness'. Adjective: *catachrestic*.

This book deals with the commonest catachreses of the English language: to write at length on the nature of catachresis is therefore unnecessary.

cataclasm and **cataclysm**. *Cataclasm* means 'a break or disruption', as in 'The cataclasms of the moral and social world' and 'Any cataclasm, any violent disruption of what is the usual course of nature'; hence, in Geology, 'a breaking down, or crushing into fragments, of rocks', with adjective *cataclastic*. A *cataclysm* is 'a great and general flood of water', esp. the Noachian deluge; 'hence used vaguely for a sudden convulsion or alteration of physical conditions'; fig., 'a political or social upheaval that sweeps away the old order of things', e.g., the French Revolution of 1789. (*O.E.D.*)

Since the early 1930's, *cataclysm* has, among the intelligentsia and even among the intellectuals, been something of a *vogue word*.

catastrophic is occasionally misused, by violent writers, for *severe* or *drastic*; it affords an excellent example of 'sending a man on a boy's errand'.

catchup or **catsup**. See KETCHUP.

catholic, Catholic, Roman Catholic. See ROMAN CATHOLIC.

causality. See CASUALTY.

cause and reason. A *cause* is that which produces an effect; that which gives rise to any action, phenomenon, or condition. '*Cause* and *effect* are correlative terms' (*O.E.D.*). A *reason* is that which is advanced in order to explain the effect or result, or to justify it; the reason may or may not correspond to the facts; the reason one gives oneself may not be the true motive.'The reason of (or for) the seasons is physical' affords an obvious example of *reason* misused for *cause*.

cavalcade; procession. To use the former for the latter is not incorrect, but it is unnecessary and loose. Properly, *cavalcade* is 'a procession on horseback, esp. on a festive or solemn occasion'; hence 'a company of riders on the march or in procession' (*O.E.D.*). The recent theatrical and cinematic use of *cavalcade* for *pageant* is to be deprecated.

ceiling, the theoretical acme of an aircraft's flight, has become a bureaucratic counter or rubber-stamp word for 'limit' or 'maximum' or, as an adjective, 'highest', 'furthest', 'utmost'; e.g., 'the price ceiling of whiskey'—'the ceiling figure for demobilization'—'a new ceiling in exports'.

celebrity, 'fame', 'notoriety', is correct; correct, too, is the derivative sense, 'a celebrated (or distinguished) person', 'a famous person'; but it is overworked.

Celt and **celt**. Ackermann, *Popular Fallacies*,very concisely points out that '*Celt*, pronounced *kelt*, means the race (early inhabitants of parts of Britain); *celt*, pronounced *selt*, means a stone- or bronze-age implement of flint, stone or metal'. [In American usage, *Celt* and *Celtic* may be pronounced with *k*- or *s*-. The implement is pronounced 'selt'.]

cement and **concrete** are not synonymous. The latter is 'a composition of stone chippings, sand, gravel, pebbles, etc., formed into a mass with cement'. *Cement* is a substance—esp., a strong mortar—'used to bind the stones or bricks of a building firmly together, to cover floors, etc.'; hence, almost any cohesive, as, e.g., for stopping (or [American] filling) teeth. (*O.E.D.*)

censer (a vessel in which incense is or may be burnt) is not to be confused with *censor*.

censor (v.) and **censure** (v.). To *censor* is 'to act as censor to or of', 'to examine rigorously for moral or political fault, or for the untimely disclosure of official or military secrets', applied esp. to news, letters, plays, films. To *censure* is 'to criticize harshly or unfavourably; to condemn'. The corresponding nouns are *censure* and, to *censor*, the agential *censor* and the abstract *censorship*.

centre (American **center**) and **middle**. *Centre* is applied properly to a circle, a (literal) revolution,and centripetal attraction; in Geometry, it is the middle point of figures other than circles; it is the point of equilibrium; and in general use, it is 'the middle point or part, the middle or midst of anything', as in 'Full in the centre of the grove'. But one would not say 'in the centre of the road'. *Middle* applies to time, whereas *centre* does not; and spatially, *middle* 'applies to mere linear extension . . . but *centre* does not. *Centre* . . . is more precise than *middle*. The *centre* of the floor is a definite point; the middle of the floor is the indefinite space around or near the centre.' The line constituting the *middle* of any geometrical figure or physical space must run through its *centre*; but whereas there is only one centre, there are many middles—any point on the line stands in the middle—all according to the subject's position. (*O.E.D.*)

centre round for 'to gather, or to be arranged, around a centre' is ungrammatical, though sometimes used by statesmen and others. To *centre on* is correct. So are *centre in*, *be centred in*, but these imply an exact position or precise point. Also one may say that a thing is 'centred at' such and such a place, when the thing's *centre* is situated or has been placed in that locality. But one may not with grammatical propriety (nor with good sense) speak of *centre about* or (*a*)*round*, *be centred about* or (*a*)*round*.

century is not always synonymous with *hundred years*, as is seen in 'The connection between the law and medicine, although it has reached its fullest development only during the past century, is by no means new'. Here, obviously, 'past hundred years' would be better.

ceremonial (adj.); **ceremonious**. The former corresponds to the noun *ceremonial*, as in 'ceremonial dress'; it also = 'of the nature of a ceremony or rite; ritual, formal'; hence, 'relating to or involving the formalities of social intercourse'. Of sacrifices, shows, displays, *ceremonious* means 'full of ceremony; showy'; its prevailing current sense is (of persons) 'given to ceremony; punctilious'. *Ceremonial*, therefore, is now applied only to things; *ceremonious* to both persons and things. (*O.E.D.*)

certain. *A certain* is sometimes employed uselessly, as in 'Upon the other hand, the Inspector's feeling for "The Wallflower" was, perhaps, more than anything a certain admiration for an adversary who combined keen brain with utter fearlessness'.

cession (yielding, surrender) and **cessation** (end, ending) are occasionally confused. Do not confuse *cession* with *session*.

champagne is the drink; **champaign** is a plain, a level field. Without a plural and without *a* or *the*, it is 'a species of land or landscape: Flat open country, without hills, woods, or other impediments'. (*O.E.D.*)

chance, as well as being weak for *opportunity*, is sometimes misused for *possibility*, as in 'Not to mention the chance that Daisy had made it all up just to keep her brain occupied'.

change from and **change to** are often confused. 'A pleasant change *from* something *to* something else' is correct; 'Comfort is a pleasant change *to* discomfort' is incorrect.

chaperon is correct, **chaperone** incorrect. The careless are misled by the pronunciation(-*ōn*). [*Webster's:* 'The form *chaperone* is often used for a woman chaperon'.]

character is much wider than **reputation**; the former includes the latter term and may be used as a synonym for it, as in 'His character for sanctity'. (*O.E.D.*)

character of. See PREPOSITIONS WRONGLY USED.

charge. To *charge* a person *with* (a crime or even a fault) is to *accuse* him *of* it; *charge*, though synonymous with *accuse*, is more formal. Only the former can be used absolutely, as in 'It has been charged that Coleridge appropriated the ideas of Lessing'. (*O.E.D.*)

chart is obsolete in the general sense 'map'. In current use, it is short for *sea-chart*; it is used in certain technical senses, as in *magnetic chart, temperature chart, barometric chart*; where there is not a map but a graph, *graph* is displacing *chart*; hence it may be used for 'a sheet bearing information of any kind arranged in a tabular form'. (*O.E.D.*)

cheap price; dear price. Use *low price* and *high price*. To buy goods at a low price is to *buy* them *cheap*; *buy cheaply* is to do business at a low cost.

check is the American form of *cheque*.

cheery is rather trivial for *cheerful*.

chief. See COMPARATIVES, FALSE; *chiefest* is a literary antique.

child. See INFANT.

childbed and **childbirth**. The former, which is slightly obsolescent, stresses 'confinement' (the state of a woman in labour); the latter stresses 'parturition' (the action of bringing forth young). *Parturition* is technical.

childish; childlike. *Childlike* is 'like a

child'; (of qualities, actions) 'characteristic of a child', as in 'To place a childlike trust in Providence', 'childlike simplicity'; it is sometimes a neutral, sometimes (indeed, generally) a favourable adjective, whereas *childish* is unfavourable, with sense 'puerile', '*too* childlike', e.g. 'He's becoming childish', 'Don't be so childish!' (Based on *The O.E.D.*)

Chinese. See JAP.

choice (n.). See ALTERNATIVE. Avoid *choice* as an adjective, for it is commercialese.

choose, 'to want, to wish to have', is an illiteracy; but *not to choose* (to do something) is 'to forbear to do it' and excellent English.

chorography. See TOPOGRAPHY.

Christian name is inferior to *given name*, for what are non-Christians to make of *Christian*? FONT-NAME and BAPTISMAL NAME are synonyms.

Christmas. The abbreviation *Xmas* should not be used in formal contexts, and the pronunciation *Exmas* is an abomination.

chronic. As applied to diseases, *chronic* = 'lingering', 'inveterate', and is the opposite of *acute*; derivatively, then, it = 'continuous, constant'. The sense 'bad' is slangy.

cicada and **cicala.** The former is the usual English form; *cicala* is the Italian form. [The term *locust* is common in the U.S.A. for the cicada.]

Cilician and **Sicilian** are still often confused, as they have been since ca. 1600. *Cilicia* is a province of Asia Minor and *Sicily* the island divided from Italy by the Straits of Messina.

circumference. See RADIUS.

CIRCUMLOCUTION. See TAUTOLOGY.

circumlocution. See LOCUTION.

circumstances, in the and **under the.** Certain newspaper editors, in their style sheets, recommend the one and forbid the use of the other (*under the circumstances*). If one turns to *The O.E.D.*, one finds that both phrases are correct but that they have different functions: '*In the circumstances* is the phrase to use when mere situation is to be expressed; *under the circumstances* when one's action is affected by the circumstances'—and that is usually the sense to be conveyed.

cirrhous, cirrhus are incorrect for *cirrous* (adj.), *cirrus* (n.).

cite and **quote.** One may *cite* or *quote* a passage, a book, an author; for book and author, if only the title or the name is mentioned, it is better to use *refer to* or *mention* or *adduce*. It would be a con-

venience if *quote* were restricted to 'repeating the actual words', and *cite* to 'referring to the words (i.e., to the passage), the book, or the author': but usage has, so far, refused to yield to the need for precision.

city and **town.** *City* is correctly applied only to a town which has been created a city by charter; the presence of a cathedral does not, as often supposed, make a city, nor has every city a cathedral. In general, a *city* is larger, more important than a town; but usage differs in different countries. Idiom decrees that 'we go to town, but we go to *the* city. We live in town or live in *the* city. We leave town but leave *the* city' (Weseen). In England, *Town* = London, and *the City* (short for *the City of London*) is 'that part of London which is situated within the ancient boundaries' and esp. 'the business part . . . in the neighbourhood of the Exchange and Bank of England, the centre of financial and commercial activity'. (*O.E.D.*)

claim is catachrestic when used for *assert*, *contend*, or *maintain*, constructed with *that* . . . , as in 'He claims that he was absent', 'He claims that it would be better to . . .' . *Claim to be* is not wrong, but it is to be used with care; 'This book claims to be superior to the other' would read less oddly in the form, 'The author of this book contends that it is superior to the other'. (*O.E.D.*)

clang—*clanged*—*clanged*; **cling**—*clung* (obsoletely *clang*)—*clung*.

CLARITY. The opposite of OBSCURITY.

classic for 'important—or, the most important—event' is overdone by writers on sports and games.

Classical and **classic.** The former refers to the Greek and Latin Classics; the latter to the accepted literary works in other languages; or to the qualities thereof.

cleanly = 'habitually clean' and (of things) 'habitually kept clean'; *clean*, therefore, is not to be used in these senses, the only ones now possessed by *cleanly*. The same applies to *cleanliness* and *cleanness*.

cleanse should be reserved for moral, spiritual, religious (ritual) cleaning.

cleave. (1) 'to hew asunder, to split': preterite *cleaved* (archaic *clave, cleft, clove*): past ppl., *cleaved* (archaic *cleft, clove, cloven*): ppl. adj., *cleft* ('a cleft stick') and *cloven* ('the cloven hoof').

(2) 'To adhere *to*': preterite, *cleaved* (archaic *clave, clove*): past ppl., *cleaved*.

clench and **clinch.** *Clench* is 'to fix securely, make fast', but in reference to nails, *clinch* is more usual, as in 'to clinch the nails'. One either *clenches* or *clinches* a matter, affair, argument, bargain, but one *clenches* one's fist, fingers, jaw, lips, or, fig., one's nerves. In the sense 'to grip, to grasp firmly, to hold firmly in one's grasp', *clench* is used, as in 'Men who clench with one hand what they have grasped with the other' (Coleridge). *Clinch* is a later variant of *clench*. (*O.E.D.*)

clew and **clue.** As 'an indication, a "key" to a puzzle or a problem', *clew*, formerly common in English, is now an American spelling. This sense derives from *clew*, 'a ball of thread'—esp. as used in the legend of the Cretan Labyrinth. The nautical term is *clew*.

CLICHÉ. 'As to clichés, I daresay we are all in agreement. Haste encourages them, but more often they spring from mental laziness.'—Frank Whitaker in an address to the Institute of Journalists, Dec. 13, 1938.

'There is no bigger peril either to thinking or to education than the popular phrase.'—Frank Binder, *Dialectic*, 1932.

A cliché is an outworn commonplace; a phrase (or virtual phrase) that has become so hackneyed that scrupulous speakers and writers shrink from it because they feel that its use is an insult to the intelligence of their auditor or audience, reader or public; 'a coin so battered by use as to be defaced' (George Baker). They range from fly-blown phrases (*explore every avenue*), through sobriquets that have lost all point and freshness (*the Iron Duke*), to quotations that have become debased currency (*cups that cheer but not inebriate*), metaphors that are now pointless, and formulas that have become mere counters (*far be it from me to . . .*).

For the nature, kinds, origins of clichés—for a study and a glossary—see my *A Dictionary of Clichés*.

client and **customer.** *Client* = 'he who goes to a lawyer; he who has an advocate'; hence, 'he who employs the services of a professional man'. In relation to tradesmen, the correct term is *customer*: and what's wrong with *customer*, anyway?

climactic and **climatic; climacteric(al).** *Climactic* = 'of or pertaining to or resembling a climax' (an ascending series or scale); *climatic* = 'of or pertaining to climate'. *Climacteric*, less generally *-al*, is 'constituting or pertaining to a *climacter*

or a critical period in human life', as in 'climacteric period'; hence, 'constituting a crisis or an important epoch', as in 'This age is as climacteric as that in which he lived' (Southey). (*O.E.D.*)

climate, clime and **weather.** *Clime* is archaic and poetic for *climate*. *Climate* means 'a country's or region's weather and atmospheric conditions, *esp.* as these affect life—human, animal, vegetable'. *Climate* has been neatly defined as 'the sum and average of weather', *weather* as 'the atmospheric condition of a particular time and place'. Thus, 'In such a climate as that of Britain, there is no weather—only specimens of weather'. (Based on *The O.E.D.*)

climb up. (*Climb—climbed—climbed.*) In general, **climb up** is tautological for *climb* if *climb* is transitive; if it is intransitive, *up* is obviously necessary when the verb is not used absolutely.

clime. See CLIMATE.

clinch. See CLENCH.

close and **conclude.** See CONCLUDE and CLOSE.

close and **shut.** *Close* is the more general verb, '*shut* being properly only a way of closing; hence the former is generally used when the notion is that of the resulting state, rather than the process', the process demanding rather *shut* than *close*. Although one either *closes* or *shuts* a door, an eyelid, the distinction just made holds good: properly, therefore, one *shuts* the door and then it is *closed*; one *shuts* one's eyelids and then one's eyes are *closed*. To say that 'The British Museum library is shut in the first week of May every year' is loose for *is closed* (*to the public*). (*O.E.D.*) ['To *close* . . . (as compared with *shut*) is strictly to stop an opening; to *shut* is to close, esp. in such a way as to bar ingress or egress. *Close* is the more general, *shut*, the more direct, emphatic, and, often, strongly visualizing word.' (*Webster's.*)]

close down (a shop, a business); 'His shop closed down'. *Close* (*closed*) is sufficient, except nautically (of hatches). The same applies to *close up*, except in certain technical contexts—military, architectural, geographical. In short, make sure that *down* or *up* is necessary before you use it.

close proximity is tautological for *proximity*. For *in close proximity to*, say *close to* or *near*, according to the context.

clue. See CLEW.

co-respondent. See CORRESPONDENT.

cocoa-nut, coco(nut). See CACAO . . .

coker. See CACAO . . .

collect together is tautological for *collect*, for *collect* means 'gather together'. To apply *collect* to a single object is loose.

COLLECTIVE NOUNS: when singular and when plural. Such collective nouns as can be used either in the singular or in the plural (*family, clergy, committee, Parliament*), are singular when unity (a unit) is intended; plural, when the idea of plurality is predominant. Thus, 'As the clergy are or are not what they ought to be, so are the rest of the nation' (Jane Austen), where *clergy = members of the clergy*; 'Is the family at home?', i.e. the family as a whole, a unit, but 'The family are stricken with grief at father's death', where the various members are affected; 'The committee of public safety is to deal with this matter', but 'The Committee of Public Safety quarrel as to who its next chairman should be'; 'Parliament rises at the beginning of August', where M.P.'s are viewed as one body, but 'Parliament differ over the question of war', where the differences of opinion are emphasized; 'Our army was in a sad plight' but 'The military were called out'; 'The majority is thus resolved' but 'The majority are going home'.

Bain, in *A Companion to the Higher English Grammar*, draws attention to the 'convenience of a neutral number' and refers to the facilities there are in English 'for avoiding awkwardness and the committing oneself definitely to singular or plural in the use we can make of the forms common to both numbers, e.g., past tenses [except of *to be*], and the verbs *can, must, would, might,* and the like' (Onions); Bain illustrates his point thus:—

'But an *aggregate* [collective noun] of contemporary individuals of the same species *cannot* [good evasion of number] be properly said to form a generation, except by assuming that *they* and *their children are* all born, respectively at the same time' (*are* is especially wanted, there being an emphasis upon the separateness of the individuals).

[Perrin's notes are valuable for American students: 'There is often a temptation to use a collective noun and to keep it singular when the meaning really calls for a plural construction. . . . Obviously a collective should not be treated as *both* singular and plural in the same context.' *The family is well and send their regards* is clearly colloquial.]

COLLOQUIALISMS. 'The colloquial'— 'Colloquialisms'—is the name applied to that large tract of English which lies between Standard English and slang; it is of a status higher than that of slang, and, at its highest, it is scarcely distinguishable from Familiar English (informal Standard English). 'Every educated person has at least two ways of speaking his mother tongue. The first is that which he employs in his family, among his familiar friends, and on ordinary occasions. The second is that which he uses in discoursing on more complicated subjects, and in addressing persons with whom he is less intimately acquainted. . . . The difference between these two forms consists, in great measure, in a difference of vocabulary' (Greenough & Kittredge). Other and frequent features are a syntax so flexible as to become at times ungrammatical, a fondness for sentences with a single verb, the omission of *I* at the beginning of a sentence or a clause, a rapid leaping from one subject to another, and the use of words and phrases that, unintelligible or at best obscure in print, are made both clear and sometimes arresting by a tone or a gesture, a pause or an emphasis. 'The basis of familiar words must be the same in Standard as in colloquial English, but the vocabulary appropriate to the more formal occasion will include many terms which will be stilted or affected in ordinary talk. There is also considerable difference between familiar and dignified language in the manner of utterance'—in pronunciation and enunciation. 'In conversation, we habitually employ such contractions as *I'll, don't, won't, it's, we'd, he'd* . . . which we should never use in public speaking, unless with set purpose, to give a marked colloquial tinge to what one has to say' (Greenough & Kittredge).

Colloquialisms, like familiar and spoken English in general, vary tremendously from class to class, set to set, group to group, family to family, individual to individual, and even, according to the individual's mood or aspiration, from one *alter ego* to another. 'His social experience, traditions and general background, his ordinary tastes and pursuits, his intellectual and moral cultivation are all reflected in each man's conversation. . . . But the individual speaker is also affected by the character of those to whom he speaks. . . . There is naturally a large body of colloquial expressions which is common to all classes . . . but each class and interest has its own special way of expressing itself. The

c*

average colloquial speech of any age is . . . a compromise between a variety of [vocabularies]' (H. C. K. Wyld).

The colloquial is difficult to confine within practicable limits: and that difficulty is made none the easier by the fact that, as Henry Bradley once remarked, 'at no period . . . has the colloquial vocabulary and idiom of the English language been completely preserved in the literature' or even in the dictionaries. 'The homely expressions of everyday intercourse . . . have been but very imperfectly recorded in the writings of any age'; in the 20th Century, however, they have been far more fully and trustworthily recorded than in any earlier period. In the United States of America, the border-line between colloquialism and slang, like that between slang and cant, is less clearly marked than in Britain: but the general principles of differentiation remain the same.

[In American studies of usage, the term *colloquial* may include much of what Mr Partridge calls 'Familiar English (informal Standard English)'. *Webster's: 'colloquial.* . . . Of a word or a sense or use of a word or expression, acceptable and appropriate in ordinary conversational context, as in intimate speech among cultivated people, in familiar letters, in informal speeches or writings, but not in formal written discourse.']
COLONIAL ENGLISH. See STANDARD ENGLISH, Section iv.

colossal is an adjective that is overdone by indiscriminating writers (and speakers).

combat and contest. A *combat* is a fight, a struggle between enemies; a *contest* may be merely a competition, and is often between neutrals or friends.

come and go. Of their use, Alford writes: 'We say of a wrecked ship that she *went* to pieces; but of a broken jug that it *came* to pieces. Plants *come up, come* into flower, but *go* to seed. . . . The sun *goes* in behind a cloud and *comes* out from behind it. But we are not consistent in speaking of the sun. He is said to *go down* in the evening; but never to *come up* in the morning.' But what about Coleridge's

The sun came up upon the right, Out of the sea came he?

Idiom is paramount, as we see in *come loose* (cf. the slang *come unstuck*) and go *to pieces* (of a person); (of events) *come about,* but *so it went* (happened).

comic; comical. In current usage, only *comic* = 'belonging, or proper, to comedy'

(opposite to tragedy, in the dramatic sense); but *comical* is more usual in the nuances 'mirth-provoking, humorous, funny; laughable, ludicrous'. *Comical* alone has the colloquial sense, 'odd, strange; queer'; and *comic* that of 'comic actor', which in Standard English is *comedian.* (*O.E.D.*)

commence, in its ordinary meaning of *begin,* is a wholly unnecessary word. *Commence* is more formal, and it should be reserved as a continuation of Anglo-French use: in assocation with law, official procedure, ceremonial, church service, (grave) combat. See esp. *The O.E.D.* [*Commence* in circumstances where *begin* or *start* would be more suitable is not uncommon in American usage, especially in the South and West. Perhaps it was once a genteelism but it is idiomatic today.]
COMMERCIALESE. See OFFICIALESE.

common, basically 'belonging equally to more than one', 'possessed or shared alike by both or all (the persons or things in question)', as in 'The common ruin of king and people' (Burke); hence, 'belonging to all mankind alike', as in 'The higher attributes of our common humanity' (Nettleship); arising from or closely connected with those two senses are these others—'belonging to the community at large, or to a specific community; public', 'free to be used by all alike; public', 'of general application; general', as in 'common notions', and 'belonging to more than one as a result or sign of co-operation or agreement; joint, united', esp. *to make common cause with:*—All these are excellent English. Good English also are the following senses; but, as they tend to cause ambiguity, they should be displaced by: 'ordinary'; 'frequent'; 'undistinguished'; 'of low degree'; 'mean, of little value'; (of persons or their qualities) 'unrefined, vulgar'. (*O.E.D.*)
COMMONPLACES. See CLICHÉ.

comparative should not be used for *relative.* 'The argument that truth is comparative and not absolute is not valid.'
COMPARATIVE CLAUSES present few difficulties. There is often an ellipsis, as in 'You do not play cricket so (*or,* as) well as he', i.e., 'as he does'; 'It concerns you as much as me', i.e., 'as much as it does me'; 'He is shorter than I', i.e., 'than I am'. But, as Dr Onions points out in *An Advanced English Syntax,* a relative pronoun after *than* is always in the accusative.

'And then there is Woolley, than whom I have never seen a more gracious batsman';

'Beelzebub . . . than whom none higher sat' (Milton).

Note:—'He is as tall as me', 'She is as wise as him', and all other such *as* sentences are colloquial, not Standard English. [As C. C. Fries says, speakers of English have a feeling that when a verb does not have a pronoun, the pronoun is probably in an objective relationship.]

COMPARATIVES, FALSE, and False Superlatives. There are certain adjectives which are uncomparable: which do not admit of *more* or *most* before them, *-er* or *-est* tacked on to them. They are absolute and, in this respect, unmodifiable. One may perhaps, speak of *nearly* or *almost* or *not quite* 'infinite' or 'perfect' or 'simultaneous' or 'unique', but not of 'more infinite', 'more perfect', 'most simultaneous', 'most unique'.

Here is a short list of these uncomparable intransigents:

absolute
akin
all-powerful (see separate entry)
basic
certain (sure, convinced)
chief
city
comparative
complete
contemporary
country
crystal-clear
devoid
empty
entire
essential
eternal
everlasting
excellent (see separate entry)
fatal
final
full
fundamental
harmless
ideal (see separate entry)
immaculate
immortal
impossible
incessant
incomparable
indestructible
inevitable
inferior
infinite
innocuous
invaluable
invulnerable
irrefragable

} There are many such adjectives in *in-*

main
major and *minor*
manifest
meaningless
mortal (see separate entry)
obvious
omnipotent
omniscient
pellucid
perdurable
perfect
possible (see IMPOSSIBLE)
preliminary
primary
primordial
principal
pure
replete
rife
sacrosanct
senior and *junior*
simultaneous
sufficient
superior
supreme
superlative
sure (convinced)
town
ultimate
unanimous
uncomparable (see separate entry)
unendurable
uninhabitable
unique (see separate entry)
universal
untouchable
    and other *un-* adjectives
utter, uttermost, utmost (*q.v.* at UTMOST)
void
vital
whole
worthless

Note, too, that the corresponding nouns are likewise uncomparable: it is folly to speak of 'the utmost absolute', 'complete indestructibility', 'partial universality', and so forth. The same restriction applies to such nouns as *acme*. 'The utter acme of comfort' is not merely absurd but weak.

So too the adverbs corresponding to the adjectives listed above.

[Many of the best American grammarians are more tolerant that Mr Partridge of 'false comparatives and superlatives'. Some of these are illogical, some are not; almost all of them occur occasionally in the writings of the wise and judicious.]

compare and **contrast.** See 'CONTRAST and COMPARE'.

in a treatise; 'to sum up' (e.g., 'to comprise much in a short speech'); 'to comprehend or include *under* or *in* a class or denomination'; (of a thing) 'to contain, as parts forming the whole; to consist of (certain specified parts)', as in 'The house comprises box-room, nine bedrooms, bath-room, etc.'; and 'to embrace as its contents, matter, or subject', as in 'The word politics . . . comprises, in itself, a difficult study' (Dickens). (*O.E.D.*)

concensus. See CONSENSUS.

concerned about; concerned with. Respectively: anxious about; having an interest in or business with.

CONCESSIVE CLAUSES. Usually, the verb in concessive clauses is in the indicative; always, when the concessive verb implies a fact, as in '*Although you are poor*, you are happy'—or where there is less emphasis on the concession, 'You are happy, *although you are poor*'; '*Though he talks so much*, he never says anything worth saying'.

In such concessive clauses as refer to future time and in such others as show an action in prospect or under consideration, it is usual to employ the subjunctive mood (or its equivalent:—*may* or *should* + infinitive); present-day writers, it is true, often use the indicative, which is not incorrect but either crude or too matter-of-fact. 'Though everyone *deserts* you, I shall (or, will) not' seems second-rate beside 'Though everyone *desert* (or, *should desert*) you, I shall (or, will) not'; and 'Though your faults be many, he loves you' is preferable to 'Though your faults are many . . .'; and '(Al)though he die (or, should die) now, his name will live' is far superior to 'Though he dies now, his name will live'—indeed, there is a marked difference of nuance here.

In certain concessive clauses—'*Cost what it may* . . .', '*Be he* (or, *she*) *who he* (or, *she*) *may*, he must see me'—the verb comes at the beginning: but, these clauses being in the nature of formulas, there is little danger of one's going wrong.

The concession may be elliptical: 'Though [they are] outnumbered, they are fighting to the death'.

conclude and **close** (a speech). To *close it* may connote merely to end it, esp. if one has nothing more to say; to *conclude it* (a more formal phrase) is to bring it to a predetermined or rhetorical end.

conclude, misused for *decide*, as in 'The matter must wait, and Stone concluded to go to bed'. *To conclude,* to make a considered judgment, is followed by a clause: 'He concluded that resistance was futile'.

CONCORD, WRONG. See AGREEMENT, FALSE.

concrete. See CEMENT.

condition. (v.) See VOGUE WORDS.

CONDITIONAL CLAUSES have always caused trouble to the semi-educated and the demi-reflective; to the illiterate they give no trouble at all. Most well-educated persons have little difficulty.

The vast majority of conditional sentences fall into one or two classes, these being determined by the form (and meaning) of the principal clause, thus:—

Group I: Those sentences in which the principal clause speaks of what is, or was, or will certainly be (i.e., *not* of what would be or would have been), and in which the *if*-clause states, or implies, no fact and no fulfilment. This is what grammarians call Open Condition, as in 'If you are right, I am wrong', which does not imply that you actually are right. It does not matter whether the tenses are present or past ('If you did that, you were wrong') or future ('If you do this, you will be wrong')—or mixed, as in 'If he did it, he is a fool.' Nor does it matter what the mood of the principal clause: 'If I did that, forgive me!'

Group II: Those sentences in which the principal clause speaks of what would be or would have been, and in which the *if*-clause states, or implies, a negative. Grammarians call this: Rejected Condition, as in 'If wishes were horses, beggars would ride' (but wishes are not horses).

In this group, there is a special conditional form, as in 'If you were right, I should be wrong', to connote the remoteness of the supposition.

But most sentences in this group belong to two kinds:

(a) When the time referred to is the same in both clauses, we have:—
Present. 'If he did this, he would sin.'
Past. 'If he had done this, he would have sinned.'
Future. 'If he did this (or 'If he were to do this'), he would sin.'

(b) When the time is not the same in both clauses, we get the sentence-types, 'If he had not done this, he would be happier now' (or 'If I had not done this, I should be . . .') or 'I should (or 'He would') be happier now, if I (or, he) had not done this';

and 'If I were doing that now, I should not have been wounded' (or 'If he were doing that now, he would not . . .').

It is worth observing that in this group, the *if*-clause has its action thrown back in time and has its grammatical mood readjusted (subjunctive for indicative).

There is also a not unimportant Group III: Here, there are conditional sentences in which, as in Group I, the principal clause does not state, nor imply, what would be or would have been, but in which the *if*-clause not only indicates an action that is contemplated or planned but also connotes some degree of reserve on the part of the speaker. 'If this be true, we are all wrong' (but it is neither stated nor implied that the fact *is* known or even said to be true); 'If this were true, he was entirely wrong' (but it is neither stated nor known that this *was* true); 'Should this be true, we shall all be wrong' (but so far as our knowledge goes, we may be right).

In such sentences as '*Tell me a liar*, and I'll tell you a thief', '*Bid me discourse*, I will enchant thy ear' (Shakespeare), the italicized portions are virtual *if*-clauses, for they are disguised conditionals; but conditional clauses are generally introduced by *if* or *unless* (i.e., if not), as in 'I shall do as you ask, unless you countermand your instructions'.

Other disguised conditionals are those in which *were I* is used instead of *if I were*, and *had I* instead of *if I had*, and *should it* for *if it should*: 'Should it be wet, you had better remain in London'; 'Had I gone, I should have regretted it'; 'Were it possible, he would gladly do it'.

Semi-disguised conditionals are of the following kinds: '*Provided* (*that*) he leaves immediately, I agree to the plan'; '*Supposing* (*that*) it does not turn out as you say, what compensation shall I get?' 'They were always prepared for the worst *in case* the worst should happen'; 'So long as you hold fast to me, you'll be all right', where *so long as = if only*.

Elliptical are such conditional sentences as 'If inevitable, why complain?' = 'If it is (or, be) inevitable, why do you complain?'; 'Whether safe or unsafe, the bridge will have to be crossed' = 'Whether it is (or, be) safe or unsafe . . .'

The last example illustrates the rule that alternative clauses of condition are ushered-in by 'whether . . . or'. This 'whether . . . or' formula is simply a syntactical synonym of 'if . . . or if': 'If the bridge is safe or if it is unsafe, it'll have to be crossed' is less convenient, and unidiomatic, for 'Whether the bridge is safe or unsafe . . .'

(Based upon C. T. Onions, *An Advanced English Syntax*.)

conduct. See DECORUM.

conductive and **conducive**. *Conductive* is extant only in Physics: 'having the property of conducting heat, etc.; of or pertaining to conducting: esp. used of conductors of electricity'. *Conducive* (constructed with *to*) = 'having the property of conducting or tending to (a specified end, purpose, or result); fitted to promote or subserve', as in 'A treaty conducive to American interests'; also a noun, as in 'Walking is a great conducive to health'. The verb is *conduce to*. (*O.E.D.*)

conduit is pronounced 'kŭn′dit' or 'kŏn′-dit' (less fashionable); so is *Conduit* (*Street*). [In the U.S., the usual pronunciations are 'kŏn′dit' and 'kŏn′doo-it', the latter the pronunciation of the engineers and electricians who install *conduits*.]

confidant(e); confident. The latter is the adjective ('assured', 'trustful', 'bold'), the former the noun (feminine in *-e*)—'a person either trusted or being habitually or professionally trusted with secrets'.

CONFUSED METAPHORS. See METAPHOR, Part II.

CONFUSED PARTICIPLES. Here will be treated what are variously known as disconnected or misrelated or suspended participles, 'misrelated participles' being the commonest designation.

On this matter, Dr C. T. Onions is explicit. 'Avoid the error of using a Participle which has no subject of reference in the sentence, or which, if referred to its grammatical subject, makes nonsense. This mistake is not uncommonly made when a writer intends to use the Absolute construction [as in "*This done*, we went home"] . . . A sentence like the following is incorrect because the word to which the Participle refers grammatically is not that with which it is meant to be connected in sense: "*Born* in 1850, a part of his education was received at Eton". Correct thus: "*Born* in 1850, *he* received part of his education at Eton".'

Dr Onions cites these additional examples:—

Calling upon him last summer, he kindly

offered to give me his copy. [Say: *When I called.*]

Being stolen, the Bank of England refused to honour the note. [Say: *It being stolen*; or better: *The note being stolen*, the Bank of England refused to honour it.]

Looking out for a theme, several crossed his mind. [Who was looking out? Not "several".]

Being a long-headed gentlewoman, I am apt to imagine she has some further designs than you have yet penetrated.— *The Spectator*, 1711.

As Dr Onions points out, this sort of error is easy to fall into when one has such ellipses as 'while fighting' (while they were fighting), 'though fighting' (though he was fighting), where a conjunction (e.g., *while, though*) is coupled with a participle: 'While fighting, a mist rendered the combatants indistinguishable'; 'Though fighting bravely, his defeat was imminent'.

The error, however, will be avoided by all those who bear in mind the simple rule posited by that grammarian:—'The only case in which it is permissible to omit the subject in an Absolute Clause [or phrase], is when the unexpressed subject is indefinite (= one, people, French *on*)'. Here is an example:—

Taking everything into consideration, our lot is not a happy one. [*Taking* = one taking, i.e., if one takes.]

CONFUSION. See such headings as AMBIGUITY and CARELESSNESS.

confute. See 'REFUTE and DENY'.

congenial, 'to one's taste or liking' (as in 'a congenial task')—'suited to (the nature of a thing)', as in 'transplanted to a congenial soil, the hitherto sickly plant thrived wonderfully'—'kindred, sympathetic', as in 'We are congenial spirits', is not to be confused with *genial*, 'affable', 'cordial', 'kindly and easily accessible'. (*O.E.D.*)

CONJUNCTIONS, DISGUISED. These are *barring* ('Barring his weak heart, he was a healthy man'), *considering* ('Considering his opportunities, he was a failure'), *excepting, excluding* and *including, owing to* ('Owing to the flood, the bridge was impassable'), *providing* and its alternative, *provided, regarding, respecting* (synonymous with *in respect of*), *seeing* ('Seeing [that] he is ill, he had better stay here'), *touching*. These were originally participles, as one perceives immediately one considers such alternatives as, 'If one bars his weak heart . . .' and 'When you consider his oppor-

tunities . . .'. See C. T. Onions, *An Advanced English Syntax*.

connection and **connexion.** See '-ECTION and -EXION'.

connotation, connote are sometimes confused with *denotation, denote*. Make quite sure that you know the difference in meaning between these two pairs.

consciously, used loosely for *deliberately* or *purposely*. 'He was no conceited actor, consciously seeking applause even when he was off stage.'

consensus (not *concensus*) is 'agreement in opinion', esp. 'the collective unanimous opinion of a number of persons'; therefore *consensus of opinion* is, at the best, loose. One may, however, speak of a *consensus of MSS*, or *a consensus of evidence*.

consecutive for *successive*. 'Very few men have been in consecutive cabinets.'

consequence of, in; as a consequence of. These two phrases are occasionally misused for *by means of*. 'In consequence of their [certain swindlers'] address and conversation, they gain the esteem and confidence of some of the most opulent and respectable of their companions.'

consequent and **consequential.** The former adjective = 'resulting', 'as a result', 'in the result', as in 'He made a seditious speech in that stronghold of Toryism; the consequent uproar was tremendous, the subsequent proceedings, lively'. (*Subsequent* = 'after', 'following', 'ensuing'.) *Consequential* is obsolescent as a synonym of *consequent*; in Law, it = 'eventual', as in *consequential damages*; in general usage, it = 'self-important', as in the colloquial 'He's a cocky and consequential little blighter'. (*O.E.D.*)

consider for *to think, believe, hold the opinion* is not strictly incorrect, but, in these senses, it loses its proper meanings of *think over, ponder, meditate*.

considering. See CONJUNCTIONS, DISGUISED

consistently and **persistently.** The former = 'uniformly'; 'without absurdity', as in 'To act consistently, you must either admit Matter or reject Spirit' (Berkeley); 'compatibly', as in 'consistently with my aims'.

Persistently = 'perseveringly', 'enduringly' (esp. of physical processes and phenomena); 'with continuously repeated action', as in 'My frequent applications have been persistently ignored'. (*O.E.D.*)

consist in and **consist of.** *Consist in* is, in general, 'to have its being in'; specifically, 'to be comprised or contained in (actions, conditions, qualities', or other things non-material); 'to be constituted of', as in 'Moral government consists . . . in rewarding the righteous, and punishing the wicked', 'Not every one can tell in what the beauty of a figure consists'. *Consist of* is 'to be made up—or, composed—of; to have as its constituent parts, or as its substance', as in 'Newton considered light to consist of particles darted out from luminous bodies'. (*O.E.D.*)

consist of and **constitute**. 'A whole consists of parts; the parts constitute the whole', as Weseen has concisely noted.

constant, as applied to actions, processes, conditions, = 'perpetual, incessant, continuous; continual, but with only such intermissions as do not break the continuity': 'The supply of water may be either intermittent or constant', 'The constant ticking of a watch', 'Constant repetition of a phrase renders it nauseating'. (*O.E.D.*)

constitute. See COMPRISE and CONSIST OF.

constrain and **restrain**. To *constrain* a person is to compel or oblige him (to do it); it may be used with a simple object, as in 'The love of Christ constraineth us'; 'to confine forcibly', now only literary.—To *restrain* is 'to hold back' (oneself or another), 'Only fear restrained him'. (Based on *The O.E.D.*)

consume is to *use up*, not to *use*. The basic sense of *consume* is 'to destroy'. As Weseen has put it, 'A fire consumes a house, but does not use it; a man uses air, but without consuming it [unless he is in a hermetically sealed chamber]; a man both uses and consumes food'.

contact (v.). If you feel that without this American synonym for 'to establish contact with' or, more idiomatically, 'get in(to) touch with' [a person], life would be too unutterably bleak, do at least say or write 'to contact a person', not *contact with*, as in 'I've questioned every C.I.D. man I've contacted with'.

contagious. See INFECTIOUS.

contemporaneous and **contemporary** (erroneously *contempory*, both n. and adj.). Both = 'belonging to the same time or period; living, existing, or occurring at the same time', but the former is now applied mostly to things, the latter mostly to persons. There is, however, a further distinction that may—other things being equal—be held to overrule the preceding distinction: *contemporaneous* tends to refer to the past, *contemporary* to the present. Thus, 'Chatham and Johnson were contemporaneous, Attlee and Churchill are contemporary'; as a noun, *contemporary* has to do duty for both of these adjectives. In other words *contemporary* and *contemporaneous* might profitably be made, not synonyms but distinctions: it would help the cause of clarity if *contemporary* were confined to the actual present, *contemporaneous* to past periods that are under consideration as present times in those past periods, as in 'The novels contemporaneous with Fielding are more leisurely than contemporary novels (are)'.

contempt of and **contempt for** are, in general, synonymous; but the phrases *in contempt of* and *contempt of court* are invariable. With persons, however, we now prefer *for*, as in 'His contempt for John was immeasurable'.

contest. See COMBAT.

contiguous. See ADJACENT.

continual and **continuous** must not be confused. The former is defined as 'always going on', the latter as 'connected, unbroken; uninterrupted in time or sequence' (*Con. O.D.*). Cf. CONSTANT.

continuance; continuation; continuity. *Continuance* is the noun both of *continue* (v.t.), i.e., 'prolonging' or 'maintaining', as in 'The continuance of the unending task of human improvement', and of *continue* (v.i.), esp. as 'the going on (of an action or process), the lasting or duration (of a condition or state)', as in 'The sole cause of the continuance of the quarrel'. *Continuity* is lit. and fig. 'connectedness, unbrokenness, uninterruptedness'; hence, also, 'a continuous whole'. *Continuation* is 'continued maintenance; resumption', also, 'that by which or in which anything is maintained or prolonged': 'A continuation of fine weather' combines these two ideas. (*O.E.D.*)

contradictious and **contradictory**. *Contradictious* is extant only of persons, or their dispositions, 'inclined to contradict; disputations', a sense in which *contradictory* also is used, although it is generally applied to things that are diametrically opposed, or inconsistent in themselves.

contrary and **opposite**. *Opposite* is stronger than *contrary*, and in Logic there is a distinction. To adapt Fowler's admirable exposition, we notice that *All humans are mortal* has its contrary *Not all humans are mortal* (which is untrue); as its opposite, *No humans are mortal* (also untrue). The converse, by the way, is *All mortals are humans*. Likewise, *I hit him* has no opposite; but its contrary is *I* *did not hit him* and its converse is *He hit me*. See CONVERSE.

contrast and **compare**. To *compare* is to align the two (or more) sets of similarities and identities; to *contrast* is to align the two sets of differences and distinctions. In doing either, one is conscious of the other; whence the favourite type of examination question, 'Compare and contrast (e.g., Caesar and Napoleon)'.

conversation. See DIALOGUE.

converse, inverse, obverse, reverse. By far the most general of these terms is *reverse*, 'the opposite or contrary of something', as in 'His speech was the reverse of cheerful'; in coinage, *reverse* is the back of a coin, whereas *obverse* is the front (that side which bears the head or other principal design).

Except the last, these terms are technicalities of Logic: venturesome journalists and other writers should employ them with care. The corresponding abstract nouns are *conversion, inversion, obversion*; the verbs, *convert, invert, obvert*.

In general a *converse* is 'a thing or action that is the exact opposite of another'; in Rhetoric it is 'a phrase or sentence derived from another by the turning about or transposition of two important antithetical members', thus the converse of 'the possession of courage without discretion' is 'the possession of discretion without courage'; in Logic, *converse* is 'the transposition of the subject and predicate of a proposition . . . to form a new proposition by immediate inference', thus the converse of 'No A is B' is 'No B is A'.—For the relation of *converse* to *contrary* and *opposite*, see CONTRARY.

Inverse:—In general, it is 'an inverted state or condition; that which is in order or direction the direct opposite of something else': the inverse of ABC is CBA. In Logic, it is that form of immediate inference in which there is formed a new proposition whose subject is the negative of that of the original proposition.

Obverse:—In general, it is 'the counterpart of any fact or truth'; in Logic, 'that form of immediate inference in which, by changing the quality, from one proposition another is inferred, having a contradictory predicate'.

These definitions come from *The O.E.D.*

co-operation. See COLLUSION.

corporal and **corporeal**. *Corporal* = 'of or belonging to the human body', as in 'A favourite topic of ancient raillery was corporal defects' (Gibbon); *corporal punishment* is punishment inflicted on the body, esp. flogging. *Corporeal* is 'of the nature of the animal body as opposed to the spirit; physical, mortal', as in 'That which is corporeal dies at our death'; hence 'of the nature of matter as opposed to mind and spirit; material', as in 'The Devil is punished by a corporeal fire'. (*O.E.D.*)

corrective (n.) like *corrective* (adj.) takes *of*, not *for*. 'Mathematics is a powerful corrective for the spook-making of ordinary language'. [In American usage, *corrective for* instead of *corrective of* is not uncommon.]

CORRECTNESS or **CORRECTITUDE**. See STANDARD ENGLISH, Section iii.

correspond to and **with**. The question is often asked whether *to* or *with* is correct: both are correct, but their senses must be carefully distinguished. *Correspond to* = answer to in character or function, answer or agree in regard to position, amount, etc.; *correspond with* = communicate by interchange of letters. (*O.E.D.*)

correspondent is one who corresponds (writes letters); a **co-respondent** (or *corespondent*) is the external offending party in a divorce case.

cosmopolitan (n.) and **cosmopolite** are synonymous; the latter, obsolescent. [For American usage, *cosmopolite* has been revived by the 'sophisticated press'.]

costly and **dear**. Both = 'expensive' or 'too expensive'; but *costly* is preferred when the sense is 'of great price or value; sumptuous', as in 'a costly gown or jewel', 'a costly shrub', 'a costly palace', and in such transferred nuances as 'a costly emotion', 'a costly sacrifice'.

could for *can*. See PAST SUBJUNCTIVE . . .

could, misused for *might*. 'If there's no more need to sew your shirt on'—the reference is to the taking of risks—'you could just as well jump into the lake.'

council and **counsel** are often misused one for the other, the former being 'an advisory or deliberative assembly or body of persons', the latter meaning 'advice and opinion given or offered' (*O.E.D.*); *counsel* is also the correct spelling for a counsellor-at-law, a barrister, an advocate.

counterpart bears two senses almost startlingly different: (i) one of two persons or things that are complementary to each other ('Popular fury finds its counterpart in courtly servility', Hazlitt); (ii) 'a person or thing so answering to another as to appear a duplicate or exact copy of it', as in 'A portrait, the counterpart of her visitor'. (*O.E.D.*)

country man (or **woman**) and **countryman** (or **countrywoman**). Reserve the former for 'one who lives in the country and follows a rural occupation'; the latter is 'a native, an inhabitant', as in 'a *North-Countryman*', '*a fellow-countryman*', and also 'a compatriot'. 'The English avoid their countrymen when they are abroad.'

course. *Of course* is to be used sparingly.

courtesy. See CURTESY.

courts-martial is the correct plural of *court-martial*. [The plural *court-martials* has wide currency in the U.S.A., though *Webster's* allows only *courts-martial*.]

credible; creditable; credulous.(Negatives: *incredible*; *uncreditable* or, more generally, *discreditable*; *incredulous*.) *Credible* = believable; susceptible of belief. *Creditable* = worthy of praise or credit. *Credulous* = gullible.

credit and **accredit**. In no sense are these two terms interchangeable. The latter = 'to invest with authority', 'to vouch for'.

creole is a descendant of European (chiefly Spanish and French) settlers in the West Indies, Louisiana, Mauritius; not, as is often supposed, a half-breed of white and native races in those colonized countries. According to *Webster's*, *Creole* (with capital) has the first sense. It also means 'the French patois spoken in Louisiana'. Not capitalized it may mean 'a Negro born in America; a person of mixed Creole and Negro blood speaking a French or Spanish dialect; a half-breed'.

crevasse and **crevice**. A *crevice* is, in general, a cleft or rift, a small fissure, and in mining a crevice is 'a fissure in which a deposit of ore or metal is found', whereas a *crevasse* is a fissure, usually of great depth and sometimes very wide, in the ice of a glacier, and in the U.S.A., 'a breach in the bank of a river, canal, etc.; esp. a breach in the levée (or artificial bank) of the lower Mississippi'. (*O.E.D.*)

crime should not, except in jest, be debased to = 'an error, a minor fault or offence'. Cf. the misuse of *tragic*.

crisis. Shamefully overworked.

crossway, crossways, crosswise. *Crossway* is a noun ('by-way' or 'cross-road') and an adjective, 'placed, made, executed crossways', i.e., *crosswise*, which is only an adverb, with which, by the way, *The O.E.D.* makes *crossways* (here an adverb) exactly synonymous. *Crosswise* = 'in the

form of a cross' ('A church built cross-wise') or 'so as to intersect' ('Four of these streets are built crosswise'); 'across, athwart, transversely' ('A frame of logs placed cross-wise'; hence figuratively, 'wrongly' ('He seeks pleasure cross-wise').

ct and **x** as variants (*connection, connexion*). See '-ECTION and -EXION'.

cunning, 'amusing' or 'attractive', is an Americanism.

cupfuls and **cups full**. Cf. BASKETFULS.

curb and **kerb**. The latter is the usual spelling (in England but not in the U.S.A.) for the protective margin of a sidewalk.

curious. Subjectively it = 'desirous of seeing or knowing; eager to learn'; hence 'inquisitive', hence derogatory 'prying'. Hence objectively, 'deserving—or arousing—attention on account of novelty, peculiarity, oddity; exciting curiosity', hence 'rather surprising, strange, singular, or odd; queer'. (*O.E.D.*)

curtesy, courtesy; curts(e)y. *Curts(e)y* is an obeisance; *curtesy*, an obsolete form of *courtesy* in all its senses. In current usage, *courtesy* is limited to 'graceful politeness or considerateness in intercourse with others'; 'a courteous disposition'; 'a courteous act or expression'. *Of* (or *by*) *courtesy* = 'by favour or indulgence; by gracious permission'. A *courtesy title* is 'one that, without legal validity, is accorded by courtesy or social custom'; cf. *courtesy rank*.

customer. See CLIENT and cf. PATRON.

cute for *acute* is a colloquialism; for 'amusing' or 'attractive', an American colloquialism. Cf. CUNNING.

D

dam is incorrect for *damn* (n., v., and interjection); and *damn* ('It's damn cold') is incorrect for *damn'*, short for *damned* = *damnably*.

damaged is used of things (or, jocularly, of persons); *injured*, of persons and animal life. One should not, for instance, speak of one's teeth as being (or getting) *injured*.

'd and **'ld**. At present, *'d* is used both for *had* ('If I'd only known!') and for *would* ('If he'd only do it!') Would it not be better to reserve *'d* for *had* and set *'ld* aside for *would*? The adoption of this recommendation would at least serve to prevent an occasional ambiguity. According to certain authorities *should* has no shortened form. [American authorities regard '*d* as a colloquial contraction of *had, would* and *should.*]

dare, misused for *dared* or *dares.* ' "Did you touch the body?" "Oh, no sir—I daren't".' 'Fingleton *had* to find a background . . . He dare not appear on an empty stage. Background was essential.' 'If she dare, she dare'—for 'If she dare (*subjunctive*), she dares' (*indicative*). One would think that, like *must, dare* were single-tensed and single-numbered!

data is wrong when it is used for the correct singular, *datum.* 'For this data, much of it routine, it would be sensible to enlist the local authorities.' [In American English, *data* may be singular or plural. *Webster's,* Krapp, Perrin.]

date back to and **date back from.** Certain newspaper editors, on their style sheets, forbid the former and recommend the latter: actually, both usage and good sense tell us to prefer *date back to* to *date back from.* Style, prompted by economy of words, suggests that *date from* is preferable to either of the phrases under discussion.

daughters-in-law is the correct plural; so *sons-in-law, mothers-in-law, fathers-in-law.*
Day of Rest, the. See SABBATH.
deadly and **deathly.** Both = 'causing death, fatal, mortal', but *deathly* is obsolescent in this sense; as = 'of pertaining to death', *deathly* is poetical; indeed, the only general extant sense of *deathly* is 'death-like; as gloomy or still or silent or pale as death', as in 'a deathly silence, stillness, pallor'.

Deadly is more general. In addition to the sense noted above, it = (of things) 'poisonous, venomous, pestilential, esp. if to a fatal degree'; in Theology, 'mortal' as opposite to 'venial', as in 'the seven deadly sins'; 'aiming (or involving an aim) to kill or destroy; implacable; to the death', as in 'The contest . . . becomes sharp and deadly'; and 'death-like' ('a deadly faintness'), though in this nuance *deathly* is more usual. (*O.E.D.*)

deaf and **dumb** is the adjective; **deaf-mute** the noun.

deal, a, like a **good** (or **great**) **deal,** 'a large quantity or number', is a colloquialism.

deal in; deal with. Weseen neatly epitomizes the distinctions: 'In business we deal *in* commodities and *with* persons, as "They deal chiefly *in* iron products and deal *with* contractors in many cities". In discussion we deal *with* a subject, as "He dealt with all phases of the matter".'

dean and **doyen** are dignified words; therefore do not, as certain journalists use, speak of 'the dean (or doyen) of the caddies', 'the dean (or doyen) of polo-players', and so forth; as applied to a diplomatic corps, they are in place, though *doyen* is here the better term.

dear. See EXPENSIVE.
dear price. See CHEAP PRICE.
deathless, immortal, undying. 'We have not only *immortal,* but also *undying* and *deathless,* expressing different shades of meaning, e.g., we would not speak of *immortal* admiration or affection' (Weekley, *Something about Words*). Cf. the following examples of correct use from *The O.E.D.:* 'The faith that animals have immaterial and deathless souls', Tyler, 1871; 'The deathless name of Godwina', Freeman, 1876; 'The world itself probably is not immortal', Hume, 1752. For *deathless,* see also 'DEADLY and DEATHLY'.

deathlike. See DEADLY.
debate is misused when it is made synonymous with *doubt, pondering, question,* or *cogitation.* 'He wasted no debates on what had happened, but concentrated on how it happened, and attempted to guess how his own investigation might be involved.'

decease is the legal synonym of *to die,* which is preferable in every other context. The same applies to the noun.
decimate means only 'to take or destroy one in ten', but is loosely used for 'cut up, wipe out entirely, destroy'.
decisive(ly) for *decided(ly)*; the reverse is rare. A good example of this misuse is found in 'It being clear that the play was going to be a success, the party given after the show by Brooks-Carew was a decisively alcoholic affair'.
declare. See ASSERT.
decorum and **conduct.** The latter is neutral and it requires an adjective to determine it. *Decorum* is 'propriety of behaviour'; in plural it = 'proprieties', as in 'Hedged round by formalities and decorums'. (*O.E.D.*)
decrease over; decrease under. 'A 15% decrease over (or, under) the takings of last year': the former is absurd, the latter clumsy. Read 'A 15% decrease in the takings as compared with those of last year'. So too for *increase over.*
decumbent. See RECUMBENT.
definite and **definitive.** The difference is neatly given by Harold Herd, in *Watch Your English*: *Definite* implies that a thing is *precise, definitive* means that it is *final* (beyond criticism or refutation).

definitely. See REALLY.

deflection and **deflexion**. See '-ECTION and -EXION'.

deign for *see fit* or *consider fit* is infelicitous—not to say catachrestic. 'Dinah Lee testified that she saw a lady leave my house . . . at four o'clock [in the morning], when she [Dinah Lee] claims to have found the film which the prosecution deigns to hold as evidence of my guilt.'

delightful. See at GLORIOUS.

deliver. See ADMINISTER.

delude and **illude; delusion, illusion.** To *illude* is 'to trick', 'to deceive with false hopes', whereas *delude* is 'to befool the mind or judgement of (a person), so as to cause what is false to be accepted as true'. *Delusion* is 'believing—or causing another to believe—that the false is true'; 'a fixed false opinion', e.g., as a form of mental derangement. An *illusion* is 'a false conception or idea; a deceptive belief, statement, or appearance'. (*O.E.D.*) [Fortunately *illude* is rare in speech, for *elude* is commonly its homonym.]

demand is not 'to *order*', but to ask authoritatively or peremptorily for (a thing), or that something be done, as in 'Assent was categorically demanded', 'He demanded to be allowed to enter' or 'that he should be allowed . . .'; and 'to ask formally to know or be told', as in 'He demanded the cause' and 'All the members demanded who it was'. (*O.E.D.*)

demean is, by the prudent, used only in the v., *demean oneself*, 'to bear oneself', 'to comport oneself', 'to behave'. The v. *demean*, 'to lower', 'to make mean', shows signs of obsolescence, even in the once-stock 'I would not so demean myself'. To *demean oneself* is, commonly, to behave in a manner specified, as in 'He demeaned himself with courage'. *Demeanour* is 'bearing, (outward) behaviour'.

demi and **semi.** Both literally mean '(a) half'; the former, direct from French, the latter direct from Latin. In Heraldry, the term is *demi*; in armoury, *demi* = half-sized or smaller—so too in artillery, fortification, and military tactics; in weights and measures, music, geometry, *demi* = 'half'; in the names of fabrics and stuffs, it = 'inferior'; with class-nouns ('man', 'doctor', 'lady', etc.), it often = 'of equivocal character', as in 'demi-pagan', 'demi-priest'; with nouns of action or condition, it = 'partial', as in demi-toilet'.

Semi follows the same tendencies: in technicalities, it = 'half' (or, less generally, 'on a reduced scale'); with class-nouns and nouns of action, it = 'partial'.

In correlative pairs, only *semi* is used; as in 'semi-chemical, semi-mechanical'.

Word-coiners will, if they respect others as much as they respect themselves, reserve *demi* for words of French origin, *hemi* for words of Greek origin, *semi* for words of Latin origin, and *half* for those of Teutonic origin. (*O.E.D.*)

demise is a legal term, to be employed only in specific contexts; as a synonym of *death*, it is infelicitous and unnecessary, and as a euphemism it is deplorable.

demolish, less general than *destroy*, should, literally, be applied only to structures and, figuratively, be used only in the nuance 'put at end to', as in 'to demolish an argument, an objection, a doctrine, a theory; an etymology'. (*O.E.D.*)

denominate and **name** and **nominate.** To *denominate* is 'to name, to call by name, to give a name or appellation to', as in 'From him [Guelpho] they . . . were denominated Guelphs' (Fuller, 1639), 'This is what the world . . . denominates an itch for writing' (Cowper). It is, in current usage, constructed usually with a complement, i.e., as = 'to call' (witness the example from Cowper). The only general current sense of *nominate* is, 'to appoint (a person) by name to discharge some duty or to hold some office', as in 'The House of Commons was crowded with members nominated by the Royal Council' (J. R. Green), with the derivative sense, 'to propose, or formally enter, (a person) as a candidate for election', as in 'Any one may challenge the person nominated and start another candidate' (Jowett). (*O.E.D.*)

denote, misused for *show*. 'His turned-up shirt-sleeves and bare neck . . . denoted him to be one of the stage hands.' See also CONNOTATION.

dent and **dint.** In the literary sense, 'an indentation (in a material object)', *dent* is usual; in the figurative sense, 'an impairment, a shock or blow', almost 'a blemish', *dint* is usual, as in 'a dint in a reputation'. But whereas *dent* is never used figuratively, *dint* is often used literally.

deny, misused for *contradict*. 'I said that there were 101; he denied me and said there were 102.' See also REFUTE.

dependant; dependent. As also for *pendant, pendent*, the *-ant* form is preferred for the noun, the *-ent* for the adjective. [In American English, the final syllable of the adjective is *-ent*, of the noun, *-ent* or *-ant* (*Webster's*).]

deplete and **reduce**. The former is not synonymous with the latter, though almost so in the nuance 'to reduce the fulness of', as in 'to deplete a garrison'; even here, however, one speaks of a garrison's 'being depleted' as the result of, e.g., an attack, whereas 'to reduce a garrison, implies deliberation by its officers. In general usage, to *deplete* = 'to empty out, to exhaust', as in 'to deplete one's strength'.

deplore governs a thing or a quality, not a person. Thus the correct form of 'We may deplore him for his conceit' is either 'We may deplore his conceit' or 'We may condemn him for his conceit'.

depravation and **depravity**. *Depravation* is '(the act or fact of) making depraved or corrupt', whereas *depravity* is '(the process or fact of) becoming, or esp. having become, depraved, bad, corrupt': 'depravation of instincts and morals'; 'an unspeakable depravity caused him to be shunned by all decent people'. (*O.E.D.*)

deprecate for *depreciate* (and vice versa). *Depreciating, -ly*, are often misused for *deprecating, -ly*; *depreciation* is much less commonly misused for *deprecation*. (To) *depreciate* is the opposite of *appreciate* and is synonymous with *belittle*; to *deprecate* is to plead earnestly against, to express earnest disapproval of.

describe for *indicate* or *designate* or *denote* is catachrestic, slovenly, feeble, as in 'This blue print describes how the machine has been made'. As = 'to descry', it is a catachresis, as in 'The smallest blemish has not been described by . . . jealous . . . eyes'. (*O.E.D.*) [The second sentence does not offend American usage, though *describes* might well be *characterizes*. *Designate* in this sense is not usual, although one would say, 'The insignia on his shoulder designate his rank'.]

description (or **descriptive**) **about** is incorrect for *description* (or *descriptive*) *of*. The former is exemplified in 'Instead of a long description about studies into human communication and the meaning of language, we fill the gap with a new symbol—*semantics*'. Perhaps by confusion with *a discourse about* (something).

descry and **discern**. *Descry* is 'to catch sight of, esp. from a distance; to espy', as in 'To meet Albert, whom I descried coming towards us' (Queen Victoria,

1868). Hence, 'to discover by observation; to detect; to perceive'. 'To descry new lands, rivers or mountains in her spotty globe' (Milton).

To *discern* is, in current usage, 'to recognize or perceive distinctly' ('to discern the truth' or 'to discern that the truth is . . .'); 'to distinguish (an object) with the eyes', i.e., 'to descry', as in 'Good sight is necessary for one to be able to discern minute objects'. (*O.E.D.*)

designate should not be used as synonymous with *describe*, as in the butler's 'A suit which I should designate as on the loud side'. There is confusion here with the sense 'to point out by a name or by a descriptive appellation'.

desirable is 'worthy to be desired', 'to be wished for', whereas *desirous* is 'full of, or characterized by desire' and is always constructed with *of* ('desirous of doing something') or the infinitive ('desirous to learn all he could').

despatch. See DISPATCH.

despite, 'notwithstanding (an opponent, an obstacle)', is a shortening of *despite of*, itself a shortening of *in despite of*. The usual current form is *in spite of*; *spite of* is colloquial.

determinately and **determinedly** are occasionally confused. The latter = 'in a determined (i.e., resolute) manner', in which sense *determinately* is slightly obsolescent. As 'conclusively, finally', *determinately* is now rare; and as 'definitely, exactly, precisely' ('It was determinately discovered that . . .') it seems to be going out of use.

determine is, in Law, 'to put an end to (in time)' or 'to come to an end'; in general, it is 'to bring to an end (a dispute, controversy, or doubtful matter)', as in 'This ambiguity should be determined in one direction or in the other' (Mark Pattison); 'to decide upon (one of several)', as in 'It is the will which determines what is to be preferred or rejected' (McCosh); 'to ascertain definitely, to fix or know', as in 'Let us determine our route before we start on our journey'; 'to direct to some end or conclusion, or to come to a conclusion', as in 'It only determines or facilitates the action of chemical force' (Grove), '[She] took credit to herself for having determined Shelley to travel abroad' (Dowden).

To *be determined* is 'to be firmly resolved', as in 'He is determined to go whatever the danger'. (*O.E.D.*)

deterrent influence is an unnecessary elaboration of *deterrent* (noun and adjective) as in 'There cannot be too many methods of identification; the more certain a man is that he will be identified, the greater the deterrent influence to crime'.

detract and distract are sometimes confused. In current usage, *detract* is common only in *detract from*, as in 'Nothing detracts from one's virtue so much as too much boasting about it'; *distract* is 'to divert the attention of', hence 'to perplex, to agitate, perturb', as in 'Love distracts the student'. See also SUBSTRACT.

develop (preferable, by the way, to *develope*) is often used catachrestically for 'to arise', as in 'The totalitarian states, which have developed since the Great War [1914–1918], are opposed to the doctrines of democracy'. See also ENVELOP.

device; devise. As a noun, *devise* occurs only in Law. In general usage, *device* is a noun, *devise* a verb ('to plan, arrange, contrive'); *device* is a means whereby one is assisted in achieving one's purpose.— *Deviser* is general; *devisor*, legal.

devices should be used with caution as a synonym of *plans* or *activities*. 'Left to his own devices' is a cliché; but escape from that cliché and you fall into the pitfall of the unidiomatic, as in 'It was some hours later that the two men met, . . . because the Chief Inspector had been busy on his own devices'.

devilry; deviltry. The former is the Standard English word; *deviltry* is English dialect and an American variant. *Deviltry*, moreover, is less devilish and has a connotation of spirited mischievousness.

deviser; devisor. See DEVICE.

dexterous is usual, though **dextrous** is the sounder formation.

DIACRITICS is the erudite—and preferable—name of what most of us call accents, as in *fête*, *soigné*. See esp. *You Have a Point There* (2nd edition, 1953), Appendix II.

DIALECT. 'Dialect is essentially local; a dialect is [that] variety of a language which prevails in a district, with local peculiarities of vocabulary, pronunciation, and phrase' (H. W. Fowler); dialects, therefore, are languages *within* a language.

The peculiarities, especially if they are picturesque or forcible, are constantly being incorporated into general colloquial speech or into slang. At ordinary times, the incorporation is slow and inconsiderable, but on special occasions and during intense periods, as in a war (when countrymen mingle at close quarters with townsmen), numerous dialectal terms become part of the common stock and some few of them pass into formal speech and into the language of literature, whether prose or poetry. What we should like to see is a larger, more effectual contribution, for many effetenesses of Standard English would profitably be displaced by the picturesque and pithy words and phrases of much dialect. Those writers who deplore the outworn and senile-senseless character of many Standard English words and phrases and metaphors, would be better employed in rejuvenating the literary (and indeed the normal cultured) language by substituting dialectal freshness, force, pithiness, for Standard exhaustion, feebleness, long-windedness, than in attempting to rejuvenate it with Gallicisms, Germanicisms, Grecisms and Latinisms: and this holds for American Standard hardly less than for English Standard.

It is to be hoped that dialect-speakers will not be shamed out of their words, phrases, and pronunciations by 'cultured' visitors or near-visioned teachers or B.B.C. 'experts'. The influence of 'education' is already visible in the weakening of the local pronunciations of *Bodiam* (*Bodjum*), *Daventry* (*Danetree*), *Yealm* (*Yam*). It is time that the curb and snaffle of good sense should put a check to the nefarious teachings of the unimaginatively genteel. Country people should boldly preserve the traditional pronunciations.

dialectal and **dialectical** are often confused; the former refers to *dialect*, the second to *dialectics* (the art of argument).

dialogue, duologue, monologue; conversation. In their speech senses, *dialogue* is a conversation (between two or more persons); *duologue* is a conversation (esp. in a dramatic piece) between two persons; *monologue* is a speech delivered by one person when he is with others. *Conversation* is rather more dignified than *talk*, but it cannot be used, as *talk* is, for an informal address or short, familiar speech or discourse. [In American usage, *monologue* is often a synonym of *soliloquy*.]

dicta, '(noteworthy) sayings', is the plural of L. *dictum* and therefore it must not be used as a singular, as in ' "After all, speed is everything in our game!" With which dicta "Freddie the Fly" agreed' (John G. Brandon, *The Regent Street Raid*).

didn't ought. See OUGHT, DIDN'T . . .

dietician (or **dietitian**) is now much more common than the original *dietist*; *dietetic* is the adjective corresponding to *diet*, and *dietetics* is 'that part of medicine which relates to the regulation of diet'. (*O.E.D.*)

differ from; differ with. To *differ from* is 'to be not the same as; to hold an opinion different from that of another person', as in 'Milk differs from water', 'I differ from you in that matter'; the second sense ('to be at variance') may also be construed with *with* ('I differed with him in that matter'). (*O.E.D.*)

different is incorrectly followed by singular instead of plural in the following: 'Temple's basic mistake lay in failing to realise that the question had a completely different nature in France and in England', which should read 'had . . . different natures'.

different should not be used for *several* or *various*, as in 'Different actors performed for the occasion'; nor unnecessarily, as in 'Three different statesmen came to dinner'.

different to; different than. See THAN, DIFFERENT.

differently than is incorrect for *otherwise than*, as in 'I felt about it differently than I had ever felt about it before', Frank Tilsley, *I'd Hate to Be Dead*.

DIFFUSENESS. See TAUTOLOGY.

dig; past tense and past participle, *digged* or, now usually, *dug*.

dilemma, as 'a choice between more than two things or decisions' hence 'a predicament or "fix" ', is loose English.

dine is more formal—but also more economical—than *have dinner*.

dinner Parisienne, from a bill of fare in an Italian restaurant in Soho, is doubly wrong, (a) in confusion of two languages, (b) in feminine gender of adjective. 'Parisian dinner' would be English; 'dîner parisien', French.

dint. See DENT.

dipthong is incorrect for *diphthong*; **diptheria** for *diphtheria*. [*Webster's* lists *dipthong* as a variant of *diphthong*. The dissimilation whereby *-fth* becomes *-pth* in *diphthong* and *diphtheria* is very common in American speech. The spelling and the learned character of the words restrain but do not extirpate the tendency to dissimilate. In turn, the popular pronunciation creates a popular though erroneous spelling.]

dipsomania. See INEBRIETY.

direction, misused for *quarter*. ' "It's our duty to act." "Oh, very well," said West wearily. "I'll mention the matter in the right direction and see what can be done about it." '

directly for *immediately* is a colloquialism, as in 'The book was suppressed directly it appeared'.

disagree from is obsolete for *disagree with*.

disassemble is to break up an assembly, or to take (esp. a machine) apart; *dissemble* is to hide one's feelings or purpose.

disassociate. See DISSOCIATE.

disaster is a grave word: do not use it lightly. No more than *tragedy* is it to be made a synonym of a mere *misfortune*.

disbeliever is positive; *unbeliever* is neutral. 'He attacks *dis*believers, but has very little to say to mere *un*believers' (Whewell).

disc is a mere variant of *disk*, 'the earlier and better spelling' (*O.E.D.*). (Zoology and Botany employ the spelling 'disc'.)

discern. See DESCRY.

disclose (v.t.) is 'to reveal', *expose*, 'to unmask' or 'to place in a dangerous situation'.

discomfit; discomfort (v.). The latter is 'to make uncomfortable physically or uneasy mentally'; *discomfit* is both stronger and more general, for it = 'to defeat'; 'to thwart, to foil'; 'to throw into dejection, perplexity, confusion'. The noun is *discomfort*, 'lack of physical comfort', 'uneasiness whether physical or mental', and 'a hardship'. Its adjective is *discomfortable*. (*O.E.D.*)

discountenance is misused for *discount* or *counterbalance* by F. R. Burrow, *The Centre Court*, in 'Barrett and Dixon kept their title. The challengers were Rahé and Kleinschroth; but the English pair discountenanced all the Continental brilliance by adopting safety tactics throughout, and won by three sets to one.' The true sense of *discountenance* is 'to show disapprobation of, to disfavour'.

discourteous (noun: *discourtesy*) is 'rude', therefore stronger than *uncourteous* (noun: *uncourteousness*), 'wanting in courtesy'.

discover is archaic in the sense 'to reveal, make known'. Its prevailing current sense is 'to find out' (something already there).

discreet and **discrete.** The former is applied to tactful persons and circumspect behaviour; the latter means 'individually distinct', 'belonging to or consisting of distinct or individual parts', 'discontinuous'. The negatives are formed with *in-*.

disenfranchise is inferior to *disfranchise*.

DISGUISED CONJUNCTIONS. See CONJUNCTIONS, DISGUISED.

DISGUISED PREPOSITIONS. These are *during, pending*, and *notwithstanding*, as in 'during the week', 'pending these operations', 'notwithstanding his speeches'.

disillusionize. Pedantic for 'to *disillusion*'.

disinterested is incorrectly used for *uninterested* or *not interested*; its meaning is 'impartial; not studying one's own advantage'. I have seen it used also for *apathetic* (—a usage given by *Webster's*). The noun is *disinterestedness*.

disk. See DISC.

dislike to is incorrect for *dislike of*. 'It may be just a dislike to getting mixed up in such things', E. R. Punshon, *The Dusky Hour*. [In American English, *dislike for* is probably more common than *dislike of*.]

dislogistic is incorrect for *dyslogistic*, (of speech, words) unfavourable, opprobrious; *dyslogistic* is the opposite of *eulogistic*, as *dyslogism* is the opposite of *euphemism*.

dispatch and **despatch** (n., v.). '*Dispatch* is to be preferred, as at once historical, and in accordance with English analogy.' (*O.E.D.*)

dispense with is erroneously used for *dispose of*. 'The moment he had dispensed with all the formalities . . ., he was not long in starting.'

displace. See REPLACE.

dispose, depose. Ignorantly confused.

dissemble. See DISASSEMBLE.

dissimulate and **simulate.** One *dissimulates*—pretends not to have or be—that which one has or is; one *simulates*—pretends to have or be—that which one has not or is not. 'He dissimulated his cowardice, envy, suspicion, etc.'; 'He simulated drunkenness, interest, disinterest, etc.'

dissociate is now preferred to *disassociate*.

distinctive is often misused for *distinct* and *distinguished*. *Distinguished*, 'now almost always of persons', = 'remarkable, eminent, of high standing, famous'. *Distinctive* = 'characteristic; distinguishing'. *Distinct* = 'separate' ('Absolute as distinct from relative knowledge'); 'individual' (not identical); 'different in quality or kind' ('A distinct species of composition'); 'individually peculiar'; 'clear, plain, definite'; 'unmistakable'. ('A distinct change'.)

distract. See DETRACT.

disturb. See PERTURB.

diurnal. See DAILY.

divers and **diverse**, originally the same word and still frequently confused, now mean, (the former) *several* or *a certain number of*, (the latter) *of different natures*.

divolve for *devolve* merits inclusion, because it is committed by persons of some education.

divorcee is generic English for French *divorcé* (a divorced man) and *divorcée* (a divorced woman). But the distinction in the French terms is not to be lightly dismissed in deference to the Gallophobes.

do. As a makeshift, the verb *do* is colloquial rather than literary, except where it is obviously the best word to use. But be sure to put it in the same tense as the verb it represents. The present tense can be represented only by *do*; the progressive present by *am, is, are doing*, not by *do*; the preterite (simple past), only by *did*; the progressive past (or imperfect) by *was* or *were doing*, not by *did*, as in: 'Another company was making almost the same triangle story as you did'—properly, 'as you *were* [*making*, or *doing*]'; the simple future, by *shall* (or *will*) *do*; the progressive future by *shall* (or *will*) *be doing*.

dock does not = *pier* or *wharf*.

doctress is to be used only where sex is humorously emphasized.

domicile is in place as a legal term: otherwise, it is an affectation.

dominated with is incorrect in such a sentence as, 'They were enthusiasts dominated with one idea, but domination by one idea is often, if not usually, the equivalent of monomania'.

dominating, misused for *predominant*. The former = 'masterful'; the latter, 'principal' or 'outstanding'. Distinguish also *dominating* from *domineering* ('bullying').

DOMINIONS ENGLISH. See STANDARD ENGLISH, Section iv.

domino (cloak and mask; a piece in the game) has plural *dominoes*.

done with, be for *have done with*. See AM FINISHED.

don't is now a solecism for *doesn't*.

double entendre for *double entente* is a frequent curiosity; the French phrase is *d. entente*.

DOUBLE GENITIVE. See 'OF HER—OF HERS' and GENITIVE, VAGARIES OF THE.

DOUBLE SINGULAR. This device is at its simplest in the hyphenated form, e.g., 'The you-and-I that forms the

dominant chord in youthful love is not
wholly selfish'. The more general form is
that which sets two disparate things (or
actions) in a combination, as in 'The din
and smell was overpowering'. Apparently
a modification of the latter is 'The coming and going of passengers is variable';
but really it is a mere typographical
variant of the former, because one might
equally well write 'the coming-and-
going' (cf. the French *le va-et-vient*).
Occasionally we find the double singular
either misused or confused, as in 'The
heat and the jam'—i.e., crowd—'was so
oppressive that Iris was actually glad to
reach her own compartment'.

doubt (if, that, whether, etc.). *Doubt* may
be transitive or intransitive; no difficulty
arises in its transitive use ('I doubt the
man's honesty'). In its intransitive use,
the sentence following 'doubt' begins
with a conjunction, which in nearly
every case should be *that* or *whether*, in
spite of the employment by many
writers of *if*, *but*, *but that*. In the two
following examples *that* would be better
than *but* and *but that*: 'I do not doubt but
England is at present as polite a nation
as any in the world'; 'It never was
doubted but that one partner might bind
the rest'. It is, however, to be noted that
in negative and interrogative sentences,
doubt 'may take *but that* or (simply) *but*,
with the same meaning as the ordinary
that:

I do not doubt *but that you are surprised.*

Who doubted *but* [or *but that*] *the catastrophe was over?*',

as Dr Onions writes in *An Advanced English Syntax*. In the two following, *whether*
would be more correct than *that* and *if*:
'Schiller doubted that a poetic measure
would be formed capable of holding
Goethe's plan'; 'The master doubted if
all remedies were not barred'.—Haw-
thorne, 1858, 'I doubt whether English
cookery is not better', is correct. Some
ambiguity arises when 'doubt' is used in
the sense of *suspect* or *fear* (*that*).
Trollope's 'I doubt that Thackeray did
not write the Latin epitaph', and
Shelley's 'I doubt that they will not
contain the latest news', would have been
more clearly expressed, 'I doubt whether
Thackeray wrote—' and 'I doubt whether
they will contain—'. Pepys's 'Doubting
that all will break in pieces in the
kingdom' is an expression not of dubiety
but of fear. (*O.E.D.*) [American text-
books note that *doubt* (v.) is followed by

that when there is little or no doubt, and
by *whether* (formal usage) or *if* (informal
usage) when there is uncertainty. In a
sentence such as 'I doubt *whether* he will
come or not', *if* would be loose and
incorrect, because of the presence of
or not.]

dower and **dowry** should be kept distinct.
Dower is that 'portion of a deceased husband's estate which the law allows to his
widow for her life'; avoid it both in the
legal sense of *dowry* ('that money or property which the wife brings her husband')
and in the derivative sense of *dowry*
('gift or talent bestowed by nature or by
fortune'). (*O.E.D.*)

downward is adjective and adverb; *downwards* is adverb only, exactly synonymous
with *downward*: euphony is the criterion.

drama. Do not use this powerful word in
trivial contexts, as in 'Drama in the
monkey's compound'.

dramatic, misused for *drastic*. 'Lynch
will have to do something dramatic in the
last round if he is to win the fight.'

DRAMATIC IRONY. See IRONY, fourth
paragraph.

drank is the past tense; **drunk** the past
participle, of *drink*.

drastic means 'vigorous', 'vigorously
effective', 'violent', (of a medicine)
'acting strongly', or (of a person)
'acting severely'; it is incorrect to speak
of 'a drastic result'.

dream, as an adjective, is journalese;
e.g., 'his dream girl', 'my dream home'.

drunk (v.). See DRANK.

drunk (adj.); **drunken**. The former is predicative ('The man is drunk'); the latter,
attributive ('The drunken man'). *Drunken*,
however, is preferred in the nuance 'given
to drink, habitually drunk', whereas
'drunk on a given occasion' is *intoxicated*.
A person habitually drunk is a *drunkard*;
one ungovernably given to drink is a
dipsomaniac.

due to rings false in such a sentence as
this: 'Their masts, due to the sloping
effect given by the after legs of the tripod,
always looked from a distance to be
falling in towards each other'. We have the
authority of *The Con. O.D.* for saying
that 'the adverbial use for *owing*, *as I
came late due to an accident*, is incorrect'.
Owing to, used absolutely, like *considering*, is equivalent, by usage, to a preposition; *due to* may easily lead to
ambiguity. [For another opinion, founded
upon numerous and impressive quotations, see J. S. Kenyon's article on *due to* in
American Speech, vol. 6 (1930), pp. 61–70.]

duologue. See DIALOGUE.

DUPLICATED POSSESSIVE. See POS-
SESSIVE, DUPLICATED.

Dutch must not be used for *German*, nor
Dutchman for *a German*.

dyeing from to *dye*; **dying** from to *die*.

dynamic, misused for *tense*. 'He was cog-
nizant of the state of affairs behind, and
these were so dynamic, that it seemed an
explosion might occur at any moment.'

E

e, intrusive, as in *musheroom, umberella,
atheletic*; examples of the habit, frequent
among the illiterate, of introducing a
vowel sound to ease their way among the
clotted consonants. [Compare *ellum* and
fillum for *elm* and *film*.]

each as a plural. 'One thing, indeed, both
have in common, each are derived from a
correct normal use of language.' 'Both'
are and *have* but 'each' *is* and *has*. Mr
Wilfrid Whitten, in *Good and Bad English*,
justifies the plural verb in the sentence,
'Brown, Jones and Robinson each have
their plans', on the ground that the
writer 'refers to B., J. and R. as being of
one mind'. With due respect to Mr
Whitten, is it not clear that *each has his
own plan*? [General American practice
agrees with Mr Whitten.]

each, between. 'The crack way of running
over hurdles, in which just three strides
are taken mechanically between each
hurdle' is loose.

each and **every** are constantly used with a
plural pronoun in spite of the obvious in-
accuracy. 'Each of them was busy in
arranging their particular concerns.'—
Everyone must judge of their own
feelings.'—'Let each esteem other better
than themselves.'

Usually *each* or *every* can be changed
to *all* (or *both*) without injuring the sense.

each other. 'We know what each other are
doing' is cited by Henry Bradley, as instance of wrong use as a nominative; it
also illustrates the confusion of singular
and plural so often caused by the word
'each'. 'We know each what the other is
doing', is correct but stilted; 'Each of us
knows what the other is doing' over-
comes all difficulties.

each other and **one another.** 'Even the
atmospheres of Italy and Spain are quite
distinct from one another—or from each
other; I leave this point for grammarians
to decide; it leaves your humble preface-
writer gravelled', R. B. Cunninghame
Graham, Introduction to *Orvieto Dust*.

There is a rule—a very simple rule:
each other applies to two persons,
animals, or things; *one another* to three
or more. This constitutes, not a mere
grammarians' *ex cathedra* but a practical
utility; for instance, if the rule is observed, one can be in no doubt that 'They
hit each other' refers to two persons,
whereas 'They hit one another' refers to
three or more. Obviously, to follow the
rule is to ensure economy of words.

each other's, misused for *each other*.
' "We're both biassed . . . but perhaps
your bias and mine will correct each
other's" '—i.e., 'will correct each other'
or, better, 'will cancel each other'.

each, them, and **they each; we each** and **us
each; you each.** Here, the case of *each* is
parallel to that of *both* in *they* (or *them*)
both, we (or *us*) *both*, and *you both*.

'They each did something' should be
'Each of them did something'; 'You hit
them each' should be 'You hit each of
them' (or, better, 'both of them' if it's
two—'all of them', if it's more than
two). *We each* and *us each* should be *each
of us*: thus 'We each ate too much' should
be 'Each of us ate too much'; and 'The
bullet frightened us each' should be
'. . . frightened each of us '(but why not
'the bullet frightened both of us' or
'. . . all of us'?).

You each (whether nominative or
accusative) should be *each of you*. Thus,
'You each knew your lessons' should be
'Each of you knew your lessons' or, more
clearly, 'Both of you'—or 'all of you'—
'knew your lessons'; 'I taught you each'
should be 'I taught each of you' (or, to
make it clearer, 'both of you' or 'all of
you').

earlier on, popular with the B.B.C., is as
uneconomical as **later on.**

early date, at an. If it = 'soon', use *soon*;
otherwise it is too vague to be useful.

earthly is opposed to 'heavenly'; **earthy** is
'of earth or soil; like earth', and it is used
in *of the earth, earthy* for 'frail, human'.

easterly and **eastern.** In current use,
easterly is used mostly of winds, *eastern*
being the general adjective; *easterly*, however, is not incorrect in the sense 'situated
towards the east'.

eat has, in the past tense, either *ate* or *eat*;
both are correct, but the pronunciation of
the past *eat* is *ĕt*.

eatable; edible. Whether as noun or as
adjective, these two words are correct;
they are synonymous, but *edible* is the
more formal, esp. as the noun. As nouns,
they are mostly used in the plural. It is,

however, to be noted that *edible*, like *potable*, is generic, whereas *eatable* and *drinkable* tend to mean 'palatable'. Dr Harry C. Schnur writes: 'An edible fungus, if badly cooked, may be uneatable. Similarly coffee, as made in England, is potable but not always drinkable.'

echoism and **onomatopœia**; **echoic** and **onomatopœic**; **echo-words** and **echoic words.** *Onomatopœia* is the old name for 'the formation of names or words from sounds associated with the object or action to be named, or that seem naturally suggestive of its qualities' (*Con. O.D.*); Jespersen proposed *echoism* for this formation. Collectively, such words are now called *echo-words* (or *echoic words*), a better term than *onomatopœic words*. *Echoism* is preferable to *onomatopœia*. One says 'That word is echoic' and either '*Cuckoo* is an echoic word' or 'It is an echo-word'.

eclectic is occasionally misused, perhaps more frequently misunderstood, in the sense of *fastidious in choice of the best*, but has the opposite meaning (*Con. O.D.*), 'borrowing freely from various sources, *not exclusive* in opinion, taste, etc.'

economic corresponds to Political Economy, as in 'the economic factor'; *economical* is 'thrifty' or, of a thing, 'inexpensive'.

-ection and **-exion**. In the nouns: *connection, connexion*; *deflection, -exion*; *inflection, -exion*; *reflection, -exion*: the etymological spelling (with *x*) is preferred by *The O.E.D.*, which, however, allows that *reflection* is much commoner than *reflexion* in non-scientific terms, and implies that the same holds for *deflection* and *inflection*.

In non-scientific, non-technical senses, then, the *ct* form is the more usual but the less logical; *connexion*, however, is fast becoming predominant in all senses. [In American usage, *connexion, reflexion*, etc. are rare.]

-ed, termination of past participle. On the pronunciation of this we may quote *The O.E.D.*: 'The pronunciation *-èd* regularly occurs in ordinary speech only in the endings *-ted, -ded*; but it is frequently required by the metre of verse, and is still often used in the public reading of the Bible and the Liturgy. A few words such as *blessèd, cursèd,* [*accursèd*], *belovèd,* which are familiar chiefly in religious use, have escaped the general tendency to contraction when used as adjectives; and the adjectival use of *learnèd* is distinguished by its pronunciation from its use as simple participle (*learn'd*).'

edible. See EATABLE.

edifice = 'a building, a structure' or, derivatively, 'a large or imposing building'. Do not call a *house* an edifice.

educational; **educative**; **eductive.** The first is the general adjective corresponding to *education*. The second may be used in much the same way, but its specific sense is 'that has the power of educating, i.e., potentially educational; conducive to education'. The third corresponds to *eduction* and it = 'having the function of eliciting or developing', as in 'An eductive method of education'. (*O.E.D.*)

e'er and **ere** (both pronounced *air*), constantly met with in poetry, are sometimes misunderstood. The former is a contraction of *ever*, the latter is an old word meaning *before* (as in '*ere* long'). **effect, effection, effective.** See AFFECT.

effective; **effectual.** See EFFICIENT.

effeminate is not 'womanly', but 'womanish', 'unmanly', applied to men, their character, tendencies, habits, actions.

efficiency, misused for *proficiency*; **efficient** for *proficient*. 'If an amateur, through specialising, reaches a certain state [? stage] of efficiency and becomes a professional player, his motive for playing often changes with his status.'

efficient, effectual, effective, and efficacious are often confused. The *efficient* man (capable, *knowing his job*) is *effective* in action, and his action is *effectual* in achieving its purpose. An efficient doctor prescribes only such medicines as are *efficacious*.

effort for 'any kind of achievement', 'any result of activity', is trivial and it should be used only where the jocular is permissible. 'That drawing was a particularly good effort of the child's' is trivial; 'His greatest effort was to pull a cork out of a bottle' is—presumably—jocular.

egoism and **egotism.** The former is 'the habit of looking upon all questions chiefly in their relations to oneself', also, 'excessive exaltation of one's own opinion; self-opinionatedness': as in 'The egoism of man . . . can . . . read in the planets only prophecies of himself'. *Egotism* is 'too much *I* in conversation', 'the practice of talking about oneself or one's doings', as in 'the egotism of personal narrative'. Hence 'boastfulness', as in 'Without egotism, I can safely say . . .'

An egotistic man is not necessarily selfish; an egoistic one is. (*O.E.D.*)

Eiré. See GREAT BRITAIN.

either, often incorrectly used for *any* or *any one.* 'Did you notice anything peculiar about the manner of either of these three?' 'There have been three famous talkers in Great Britain, either of whom would illustrate what I say.'

either for *each.* 'When I was a child at an elementary school I was taught that it was incorrect to say "There are trees on either side of the road", as "either" means on one side or the other, but not both. Yet I find nearly all novelists, a famous thriller writer, and the daily Press making this mistake.' Cf. 'They never spoke about it: Edward would not, and she could not; but either knew what was in the other's thoughts'.

either or **either of,** (*neither* or *neither of*)+ n. with a pl. v.: these are incorrect; e.g., 'This was not to say that during those wearing days either of them were idle'. A similar error is made with *either . . . or*; e.g., 'Religious rites by which either Thebes or Eleusis were afterwards distinguished' (*O.E.D.*); 'Both poets are on the verge of mystical vision; neither actually seem to express it'; 'the requirements of parenthesis, neither of which are taken into account in the ordinary rule'. [When the whole thought has a plural character, such sentences 'have a natural if not a correct grammatical ring'. (Krapp.)]

either . . . nor for **either . . . or** is, one might say, the fantastic dream of a fanatical heresy-hunter: and yet it occurs. 'Its small and neat exterior gives to the unsuspecting client who tries it for the first time no indication either of the excellence of Mons. Laplanche's food, wines and cooking, nor of the preposterous charges made by Monsieur Laplanche.'

either of their sakes. See GENITIVE, VAGARIES OF THE, penultimate paragraph.

either . . . or, misused for *both . . . and.* 'Until then, I must ask you to preserve an open mind in your opinions, either of me or of what happened last night.'

elapse and **lapse** (vv.). Time *elapses* or slips away, passes, expires; *lapse* is (of men) 'to err', (of things) 'to fail, fall into disuse', as when a life-policy lapses because the insurance premiums have not been paid.

elder and **older.** The former is used only in family relationships or in reference to two specified persons: 'the elder brother', 'the elder partner'. *Older* is 'of greater age', 'longer established', as in 'an older

custom', 'He looks much older'. (*O.E.D.*)

electric; electrical. The former is now much the commoner. *Electrical* = 'connected with, dealing with electricity', as in 'There are very few electrical books in that library'; also *an electrical machine.* (*O.E.D.*) Figuratively, *electric* is now obligatory.

ELEGANCIES. Here is a short list of those words and phrases which the semi-literate and far too many of the literate believe to be more elegant than the terms they displace. Some are genteel; some euphemistic; some plain catachrestic. If in doubt, consult also ARCHAISMS and LITERARISMS.

ablutions, perform one's
abode (home)
al fresco
albeit (also an archaism)
anent
anno domini (age; old age)
anon
aroma
assemblage (collection; assortment)
assignation
at this juncture
au courant and *au fait*
bairn (except in Scotland)
bard
beauteous (except in poetry)
bereavement
boon (noun)
bosom
broidered
cachet (figuratively)
can but (can only)
charger (any horse)
charlady
City Fathers
collation
connubial rites
consume (to eat)
converse (as synonymous with *talk,* v.i.)
corpulent
countenance (n.)
crave (to beg; to ask)
cull (v.)
Cupid
damsel (except in verse or jocularity)
deboshed
deem
demise
denizen
develop (v.i. = to happen)
devotions, at one's
distrait(e)
divers (several, sundry)
divulge

dolorous (permissible in poetry and lofty prose)
domicile (noun, non-legally)
éclat
edifice; esp. *sacred edifice*
effluvium (smell); *effluvia* (scents)
elegant sufficiency, an
emanate (incorrectly used)
emolument
employ of, in the
emporium (shop)
epistle (any letter)
ere (also an archaism)
espousal
evince
expectorate
fain (also an archaism)
festive board, the (also a cliché)
floral tribute(s)
fraught
function (noun; used trivially)
garb (n.), *garbed*
garments
genus homo
goodly
gratis
habiliments
helpmeet
histrionic art
honorarium
Hymen (marriage, wedding)
imbibe
impecunious
implement (verb)
individual
instanter
interred; interment
Jehu (a coachman)
Jupiter Pluvius
lapsus calami
Leo (a lion)
liaison
libation (any potation)
liquid refreshment
lonely couch
luminary (e.g., a legal luminary)
magnum opus
menial (a servant)
mentor
mine host
misalliance
missive (any letter or note)
modicum
monarch
(to) *moot*
my Lady Nicotine
myrmidons
natal day
neophyte
non compos mentis
nuptials; nuptial couch

obsequies
of late (recently)
orb (sun, moon)
orient (or *O.*) *pearl*
ozone
panegyric (of any praise however trivial)
partake of (to eat)
paterfamilias
patronize (shop at; go to, visit)
peruse (to read)
petite
plight one's troth
post-prandial
posterior (backside); *posteriors* (buttocks)
prevaricate
purloin
raiment
redolent
remuneration
repast
repose (n. and v. in the senses: rest; sleep)
reside at
retire (go to bed)
Sabbath, the (Sunday)
sanctum (a study, a 'den')
satellite (a follower)
save (preposition; also an archaism)
soirée
sotto voce
spirituelle
spouse
steed
strand (shore)
sumptuous repast
swain
swoon (n. and v.)
tender one's apologies, condolences, etc.
Terpsichorean
terra firma
Thespian
thrice (except in poetry or lofty prose)
tiro (or *tyro*)
to the full (e.g., appreciate to the full)
transpire (to happen)
truly (as in 'truly great')
tryst (also an archaism)
twain (also an archaism)
umbrage (offence)
verily
veritable
verve
very (*heart-strings, life,* etc.)
viands (food)
victuals
visage
weal (also an archaism)
welkin
well nigh
wend one's way
withal

wont (custom; habit)
Yuletide (also an archaism)

elegant is not good English (nor yet good American) as a synonym for 'excellent' ('an elegant party') or 'first-rate' ('an elegant lawn-tennis player').

elemental, elementary. The former = 'of, connected with, like one or more of the four "elements" (earth, air, fire, water)'; 'pertaining to the powers, forces, agencies of the physical world,' as in 'elemental gods or spirits,' 'elemental religion', or 'like those powers' ('elemental grandeur'); 'of the nature of an ultimate constituent of physical substances' ('the elemental operations of Nature').

Elementary is 'rudimentary', as in 'an elementary book' or one that deals (simply) with first principles, 'elementary school' (one in which primary instruction is given). (*O.E.D.*)

elements, misused. See OFFICIALESE.

elicit and **illicit** are often confused in careless speech.

else but is still worse than:

else than is unfortunate; the sense should be rendered by *but* or *other than*. Nesfield, in his *Errors in English Composition*, commits it by saying 'The omission [of the Relative] can hardly be considered as anything else than a defect'.

else's. The following are correct although once they were colloquial and even now they are familiar S.E., and not full Standard:—

> *anybody* (or *anyone*) *else's*
> *everybody* (or *everyone*) *else's*
> *nobody* (or *no one*) *else's*
> *somebody* (or *someone*) *else's*
> *who* (or *whoever* or *whosoever*) *else's*.

What has happened is this: the *else* has, in essence, become incorporated with the pronoun (*anybody, someone, who*, etc.): although we do not write *anybodyelse, whoelse*, etc., yet we think of the combination as a unit. Therefore it is only *else* which takes the genitive form, *else's*.

Of the following sets, the first—regarded in England as incorrect—is acceptable in America, though only in a predicate position; the second set is wrong everywhere and in any position.

> *anybody's* (or *anyone's*) *else*
> *everybody's* (or *everyone's*) *else*
> *nobody's* (or *no one's*) *else*
> *somebody's* (or *someone's*) *else*
> *whose* (or *whosever* or *whosoever*) *else*

> *anybody's* (or *anyone's*) *else's*
> *everybody's* (or *everyone's*) *else's*
> *nobody's* (or *no one's*) *else's*
> *somebody's* (or *someone's*) *else's*
> *whose* (or *whosever* or *whosoever*) *else's*.

elude, delude, illude are often erroneously used one for another; their precise meanings are defined in dictionaries.

emanate, misused. 'The crime has astonished me. It's not the kind of thing I could ever imagine emanating from that house.' The writer means 'happening in that house'. *Emanating* is *flowing from*, immaterially.

emend. See AMEND.

emerge and **issue.** To *emerge* is 'to come forth into view from an enclosed and obscure place', as in 'The stream emerges from the lake, the moon from the clouds'; 'to rise into notice' and esp. 'to issue (come forth) from suffering, danger, embarrassment, etc.', as in 'France emerged triumphant from the great Revolution'; (of a fact, a principle) 'to come out as the result of investigation', as in 'At last there emerged Einstein's Theory of Relativity'.

To *issue*:—There is no difficulty about the transitive use. The v.i. is 'to go out or come out; come forth; flow out, sally out', as in 'A band of brigands issued from the stronghold', 'The river issued into the sea at a desolate point of the coast'; figuratively it is used in much the same way as *emerge*, i.e., 'to go out, or come out, of a state or a condition', as in 'He issued scatheless from that peril'; legally, 'to be born or descended' (cf. *'bodily issue'*) and, of revenue, income, etc., 'to accrue'; compare the more general sense, 'to take (its) origin; to spring; be derived', as in 'Can malevolence and misery issue from the bosom of infinite goodness?'; hence, 'to result', as in 'Excitement issuing from a stimulus'; hence, to *issue* (or end or result) *in*; to be published', as in 'Far too many books are issued nowadays'. (*O.E.D.*)

emigrant and **immigrant.** The same person may be both, but not at the same time: leaving his own for another country, he is an *emigrant*; arriving from another country, an *immigrant*.

employ is obsolescent for *employment*, even in *in the employ of*.

empty and **vacant.** Empty = 'containing nothing' (a jug without water, a room without furniture); 'carrying nothing' (*empty ship, empty hands*); of persons, 'frivolous'; of things, 'vain' (*empty plea-*

sures). But a *vacant* room or house is a room or house in which there are no people, i.e., 'unoccupied', as also in *a vacant post* (or *position*), *office*; (of time) 'free, leisure(d)', as in 'a hobby for one's vacant hours'; 'idle' (*a vacant life*); 'meaningless, expressionless, inane' (*vacant stare* or *look* or *smile*). (*O.E.D.*) **enclose, enclosure** are, by usage, preferred to *inclose, inclosure*.

end by. See PREPOSITIONS WRONGLY USED.

endless is 'without actual or readily discernible end'; it does not, in sober prose, = *innumerable*, as it is made to do in 'endless platitudes', 'endless examples'.

endorse; indorse. See INDORSE.

endways, endwise, are interchangeable.

engender for *cause* should be used with care. Primarily (esp. of the male), it = 'to produce (a child)'; its transferred senses are 'to give rise to, produce (a state of things), a disease, force, quality, feeling, etc.' (*O.E.D.*). 'Hate engenders strife' and 'Heat engendered by friction' are correct, whereas 'Coal is engendered by buried forests' is incorrect.

ENGLISH, STANDARD. See STANDARD ENGLISH.

ENGLISH AND AMERICAN USAGE. For those who wish to compare Americanisms and Briticisms, I list the four leading authorities:

> H. W. Horwill: *A Dictionary of American Usage*, 1935.
> G. P. Krapp: *The English Language in America*, 1925.
> H. L. Mencken: *The American Language*, 4th edition, 1936.
> A. W. Read: *Briticisms* (in preparation).

enjoy; enjoyed. 'Fortunately the Wages Tribunal disallowed this claim, although it virtually invited the applicants to make an application for some further improvement in the terms enjoyed'—i.e., to be had—'in the near future.' Another common misuse is the expression, 'He enjoys very poor health', and (almost as bad) 'does not enjoy good health', where there is no question of 'enjoyment', but of *having* good or bad health, or even of *suffering* from some complaint.

enormity; enormousness. The former is used of extreme wickedness, a gross offence; the latter only of great size.

enough, following an adjective, is equivalent to *sufficiently* preceding that adjective. Thus, *strange enough* = *sufficiently strange*, except that the former emphasizes *strange*, whereas the latter throws the emphasis on the adverb. (One does not say *enough strange*: usage forbids it.) But if we separate *strange* from *enough* by inserting a noun, we create at best a strangeness, at worst an ambiguity, as in 'Nature, that moves in us by strange courses enough if need be, . . .', where usage demands 'Nature, that moves in us by courses strange enough . . .'

Enough is never an adjective; *sufficient* is, in, e.g., 'That's not a sufficient reason'. 'Have you enough?' = the rather more formal 'Have you sufficient?'

enough that, enough so that. Incorrect for *enough to* (+ infinitive).

enquire is superseding **inquire; enquiry, inquiry.** See also the entry 'QUERY and INQUIRY'. [But *Webster's* maintains the opposite: "*Inquire*, etc., have for the most part superseded *enquire*, etc."] Certainly, *inquire, inquiry* are etymologically preferable.

ensure is to make sure or make sure of (a thing, or that . . .); **insure** is the more usual word in the field of *life-insurance*.

enthuse is to be avoided.

enthusiastic, misused for *excited*. 'The children are wildly enthusiastic as they push forward into the big tent (of the circus).'

entire. See 'COMPLETE, ENTIRE, WHOLE'.

entirely without being is very clumsy for *being without* or *being far from* or *although not at all*, as in 'Entirely without being distinguished, Meade had a brisk businesslike way'.

entity, misused. 'The medical profession, as a distinct entity, was afforded official recognition.' *Entity*, in its concrete sense, is 'something that has a real existence as opposed to a mere function'. (*O.E.D.*) 'Now a 'profession' has no concrete existence, but exists only by its 'function'.

entrance; entry. Both = 'the action of coming or going in', but *entrance* connotes the action, *entry* the result. *Entrance* = *right of entry* in 'Free entrance and safe egress'. Both nouns are used of 'that (whether open or closed) by which one enters', as a door or gate or passage; but only *entrance* is used attributively (*entrance-hall*). In seamanship and book-keeping, only *entry*. *Entry* is loose for *entrant* (in a competition or contest).

entrust. See INTRUST.

enumerable. See INNUMERABLE.

enunciation. See ANNUNCIATION.

envelop and **envelope** (nn.). The shorter form is preferable—as for *develop(e)*.

envelope (n.). Pronounce *enn-*, not *on-*. *On-* is the more absurd in that the French noun is *enveloppe*.

enviable, worthy of envy; **envious**, (of a person) feeling envy.

epistle and **letter**. Do not use the former as an exact synonym of the latter: an *epistle* is a formal or didactic or literary letter.

equal should not be used for *equable* as applied to mind or temper. One says 'an *equable* or tranquil mind' and 'an *equable* or even or unruffled temper'.

equal as. See PREPOSITIONS WRONGLY USED.

equally as. See AS, EQUALLY.

equate. One *equates* one thing either *to* or *with* another.

ere. See E'ER.

eruption is a bursting out, **irruption** a bursting in.

especial and **special**. As the opposite to *general*, *special* is preferred. But for 'preeminent, very distinguished', 'pertaining to one particular case' and also in the obsolescent phrase *in especial* (*for your especial benefit*), *especial* is used. The same applies to *especially* and *specially*.

essential ('absolutely necessary') should not be debased to mean merely *necessary*.

estray. See ASTRAY.

eternal. See COMPARATIVES, FALSE.

ethic and **ethical**, adjectives. Except occasionally in grammar (e.g., *ethic dative*), *ethical* is now the usual adjective corresponding to *ethics*.

ethic and **ethics**, nouns, are occasionally confused by those who should know better, for *ethic* is a word unknown to, or, at the least, unused by the great majority. *The O.E.D.* defines *ethics* as 'the science of morals', but a man's (or institution's) particular system of moral science may be called his *ethic*.

et cetera, etc., meaning 'and other things' (Latin plural neuter), is insulting when applied to persons. Publishers sometimes put *etc.* at the end of an incomplete list of authors. In formal writing, *etc.* should be avoided: use either *et cetera* or, better, an English euqivalent.

euphemism, confused with *euphuism*. A *euphemism* is a prudish evasion (*to go to his eternal rest* = to die); a *euphuism* is a stylistic excess (e.g., of antitheses) exemplified in and fathered by Lyly's *Euphues*, 1579, and *Euphues and His England*, 1580.

EUPHEMISMS. *Euphemism* comes from a Greek word meaning 'to speak favourably', and Greek provides what is per-

haps the most famous of all euphemisms: *Eumenides*, 'the Kindly Ones', for the Furies, the Avenging Gods.

In *The King's English*, the Fowlers define euphemism as the 'substitution of a mild or vague expression for a harsh or blunt one'. In *The Romance of Words*, Ernest Weekley speaks of euphemism as 'that form of speech which avoids calling things by their names' and observes that it results from 'various human instincts which range from religious reverence down to common decency'. Often, however, it springs from nothing so decent as either reverence or decency: too often it is an indication of prudery or an exaggerated genteelism.

Euphemism may be obtained by directing the thought in the desired direction, as in *honorarium* or *convey* (to plagiarize); by using an extremely vague phrase, as in *commit a nuisance*; by mentioning a significantly concomitant circumstance, as in *remove* (to murder); by being enigmatical or elusive, as in *lose the number of one's mess* (to die); by understatement, as in *have had a glass* (to be tipsy), or the negative litotes (*it's not too safe*); by irony; by employing another language (e.g., the Latin found in translations of *Daphnis and Chloe*); by reticence, as in *you know where to go* (to hell!); and by abbreviation, as in *w.c.* (itself euphemized to *w.*) and T.B.

See esp. 'Euphemism and Euphemisms' in my *Here, There and Everywhere*.

euphuism. See EUPHEMISM.

European requires *a* not *an*.

evacuate the wounded is a horrible variation of the dignified *remove the wounded*. Beginning as military officialese, it has become journalese—and far too general. I won't swear that I haven't used it myself.

even (like *actually*, *definitely*, and *really*) is often used where there is no need for it, with the result that, instead of the desired emphasis, there is weakness, as in 'That thoughtful, appraising look turned all the time upon himself, worried Granadi, rather; even hard-bitten as he was, and plausible, specious liar that he knew himself to be at a moment's pinch': 'hard-bitten though he was' would have served, with 'as' for 'that' as a further improvement.

event should not be made to do duty for *great event* or *important event*, for this use sometimes leads to ambiguity or obscurity.

eventuate. This bad, ugly and wholly un-

D

necessary word usually means no more than *to happen*, *to come to pass*. Sir Alan Herbert quotes a misuse supplied to him by a curate in the East End: 'If more people do not eventuate, the meeting will not be held.'

ever is often used unnecessarily, as in 'It remains doubtful whether any evidence against McCabe could ever have been collected by any methods other than those Smith used'.

ever expect, ever hope, illogically used for *expect ever, hope ever.* 'Do you *ever expect* to see him again?' is a loose substitute for 'Do you *expect ever* to see . . . ?' This appears even more clearly in 'Do you ever hope to see . . .' where *hope ever* is intended.

ever, seldom or. See SELDOM OR EVER.

everlasting. See COMPARATIVES, FALSE.

every. See ALL.

every, misused. 'We already possess four times as great a trade with China as every other nation put together' (*all other nations*).—' "We've got to have every possible information concerning him that we can get" ': *every* should be *all*, though *every piece of information* would also be correct.

every for ALL POSSIBLE. Weseen cites 'The court exercised every leniency' and asks, 'Does the writer mean each of various kinds of leniency?' [If he did, he should have written *every kind of leniency*.] 'No, he means all possible leniency in the fullest possible measure!'

Analogous are *every* for *ample* or *sufficient*, as in 'There is every reason for doing this', and *every* for *much* or *great*, as in 'He is deserving of every praise'; cf. also *every* for *complete, entire* or *perfect*, as in 'We have every confidence in him'.

every, tautological use of. See TAUTOLOGY.—Ambiguous: see 'ALL, ambiguous'.

every takes the singular. 'Every man must be at *their* desk' is incorrect. Cf. EACH.

every, misused for *everyone*. 'It [Stacy Aumonier's *Ups and Downs*] is for all and every', John Galsworthy's Preface, 1929.

every place for *everywhere* is loose, as in 'I looked every place for his book'.

every time for *always*. The former refers to separate occasions, *on each occasion*; the latter means *at all times*, or *all the time*.

everybody or **everyone** followed by *they*, etc. See THEIR.

everyone, misused for *every one*; e.g., 'Everyone of the things was in its right place'. *Everyone* is of persons, *every one*

of things; the former is self-contained, the latter sometimes not. So too *everything* for *every thing*.

everyone's (or **everybody's**) **else.** See ELSE'S.

everywhere means *in every place*, not *every place*, as is intended in 'Everywhere would be desolate'.

evidence and **testimony.** *Evidence* is 'an appearance from which inferences may be drawn; an indication'; hence, 'ground for belief', as in 'The weight of evidence appears strongly in favour of the claims of Cavendish'; whence the legal senses, 'information given in a legal investigation, to establish the fact or point in question', as in *to bear*, or *give*, or *give in evidence*: *the evidence* is 'the testimony which in any particular cause has been received by the court and entered on its records'; cf. *to turn King's* (or *Queen's*) or *State's evidence*.

It is best to reserve *testimony* for its set scriptural senses; one may, however, still speak of 'the *testimony* of the physical senses', though 'the *evidence* . . .' is now the general term. (*O.E.D.*)

evidence (v.). *To be evidenced*, for *to be shown* (or *indicated*), is ugly.

evince is used for *to show, exhibit, make manifest*, but it is a bad word and unnecessary.

ex-. See 'LATE and EX-'.

exactly for *precisely* is a loose colloquialism, not reprehensible in *exactly!*, 'quite so!', but to be avoided in such a sentence as 'He had not been exactly intimate with Sutton, but he had . . . developed a genuine liking and respect for him'.

exactly similar. See SIMILAR, EXACTLY.

EXAGGERATION. See HYPERBOLE.

examination paper for *script* is ambiguous, an 'exam. paper' being strictly the paper of questions set for examination, not the candidate's written answers (his *script*). [In American English, *script* is not current in this sense. Commonly, 'examination questions' are passed to the students, who write their '(examination) papers' or 'books'.]

example and **instance.** An *example* is a typical *instance*; but we may say either *for instance* or *for example*. Whereas *by way of example* is idiomatic, the phrase *ancient saws and modern instances* cannot be varied to . . . *modern examples*. We make an *example*, not an instance, of a person when, deterrently, we punish him; we set a good *example*; '*example* is better than precept'.

example where is incorrect for *example in*

which, as in 'This is an example where great care must be exercised'.

exceeding. See EXCESSIVE.

excellent. See COMPARATIVES, FALSE.

except and **accept** are often confused by the semi-literate: *except* is 'to make an exception of', *accept* is 'to take (a present, a dismissal, etc.)'.

except as a conjunction (= *unless*) is in the present century to be avoided: idiom has left it behind. 'I won't go except you do' is indefensible nowadays.

excepting. See CONJUNCTIONS, DISGUISED.

excepting and **except** as prepositions. In 20th-century usage, *excepting* is not an exact synonym of *except*: Mary Howitt's 'Nothing to be seen . . . excepting some blocks of marble' (1863) would now be '. . . except . . .'. *Excepting* is now virtually restricted to *not excepting*, as in 'Of all societies . . . not even excepting the Roman Republic, England has been the most emphatically political'. (*O.E.D.*)

exceptionable and **exceptional** are frequently confused. *Exceptionable* is that to which exception may be taken. *Exceptional* is that which is an exception.

excess, misused. See ACCESS.

excessive means 'beyond reason', as in 'excessive flattery'; *exceeding* means 'very great', as in 'We are grateful for your exceeding generosity'.

excluding. See CONJUNCTIONS, DISGUISED.

excuse me! is less strong and less formal than *pardon me!*

executor, executer; executioner. Only the illiterate confuse *executioner* (headsman, hangman) with either of the other two words. An *executor* is a legal term for 'a person appointed by a testator to execute his will after the testator's decease'; but an *executer* is a general term for one who, not in Law, carries out a plan, an order, a promise. (*O.E.D.*)

exemplary is not to be loosely used as a synonym of *excellent*. *Exemplary* = 'archetypal' and, as applied to persons or their attributes, 'fit to serve as an example or pattern for imitation', as in *exemplary conduct, an exemplary clergyman*; the latter sense is linked with that of 'serving as a specimen, a type', as in *exemplary drawings* (for pupils or students). (*O.E.D.*)

exert for *exercise* is a very common error —and a wholly useless synonym, productive also, at times, of ambiguity. 'This failure to identify exerted a depressing effect on the Chief of the Criminal Investigation Department which was not lessened by the garbled accounts pub-

lished in the evening papers.' Why not 'had'?

exhausting; exhaustive. *Exhaustive* (or very full; complete) instructions or information may, by the listeners, be found *exhausting*.

exhilarate. See ACCELERATE.

exist, 'to be', 'to have being', 'to possess reality', 'to live (on a low plane, or barely)', is a weak word when used for *subsist*, 'to support life', 'to find sustenance'.

exotic. Don't overdo this word, and make sure that you are using it correctly.

expect. See ANTICIPATE.

expensive is not to be used as exactly synonymous with *dear* or *costly*, for its connotation is either 'excessively dear (or costly)', as in 'an expensive lawsuit', or 'deliberately or intentionally costly', as in 'an expensive education'; moreover a thing 'comes *expensive*' when the expense is unexpectedly great. An experiment may be, or turn out, either costly or expensive.

experience is incorrect for *firm opinion* or *knowledge*. 'The *modus operandi*—which it is the police experience all the world over very few criminals ever vary.'

expertise, 'skill', should be used with caution, for it comes from French, where it means 'a survey', 'a valuation', 'an expert's assessment or report' (Chevalley).

explain does not mean 'show', 'indicate', 'prove'. 'In this glossary I have reached only *E*. This explains my rate of progress.'

explicit. See IMPLICIT.

explore every avenue, one of the common clichés of politicians, is a feeble and even contradictory expression. 'He'—an M.P. —'was tired of all the figures of speech about exploring every avenue, and leaving no stone unturned, and ploughing the sands, and so on' (John Ferguson, *Death of Mr Dodsley*).

expose. See DISCLOSE.

exposé for *exposition* (formal explanation) is a Gallicism—and unnecessary.

extant. See EXTENT.

extempore. See IMPROMPTU.

extemporize. See TEMPORIZE.

extempory is obsolete for *extempore*; illiterate for *extemporary*.

extend has been overworked in the sense of *offer* or *send*, as in 'I extended my deepest sympathy to him in his sorrow'.

extent is a noun; *extant* (surviving, still existing) is an adjective.

extra is colloquial when it is employed for *unusually*, as in 'extra good'.

extra, misused for *especial*. '[The new

hands], naturally, were the ones to be watched with extra vigour.'

F

fabulous, 'fabled, mythical, of the nature of a fable, belonging to a fable', hence 'astonishing, incredible'. (*O.E.D.*) This word is being grossly overworked. Use it with care.

face up to = to face (a situation) resolutely, whereas *face* merely = to have to deal with a situation, to *be faced with it*. The entry in *U. & A.* (p. 115) is incorrect.

FACILITY, or Extreme Readiness. In speech, the man that has 'the gift of the gab' usually elucidates his loosenesses by gesture and by emphasis or intonation. But in writing there is no equivalent to gestures, unless it be emphasis (with its concomitant risk of over-emphasis); none to intonation.

'Easy writing is hard reading' is true of everything but the most elementary and unsubtle writing.

I do not mean that, in writing, one should lose the thread and the verve by pacing the floor in search for the right word, the inevitable phrase: but all writing should be very carefully revised: at the back of one's mind should be the constant admonition, 'This may be clear in *my* mind, but it may not be clear to the reader'.

facility is often misused for *faculty*. Thus, 'He had a remarkable facility for flying'. The mistake seems to be caused by confusing such locutions as 'There were, he found, excellent facilities for flying' and 'He had a remarkable faculty in flying'.

fact, misused for *factor* (*q.v.*) is frequent in crime-novels since ca. 1920. 'Altogether she was a strange fact of the case.'

factitious and **fictitious** are occasionally confused. The former = artificial, not natural; not spontaneous. The latter = not genuine; arbitrarily devised; (of a name) not real; (of a character) deceptively assumed, simulated; imaginary, unreal; characteristic of fiction.

factor is often grossly misused to mean anything from *fact* to *feature* or from *causation* to *cause*; a 'factor' being correctly a contributory element in causation or the composition of anything. 'I am assured that the greatest income from any single factor in Switzerland is in connection with the League of Nations.' Especially frequent is the misuse of *factor* for *occurrence*, as in 'Sunburn and sand

in the food are usual factors of beach parties'. Frequent, too, is its misuse for *element* or *constituent*, as in 'If we did not have some other factor [than fat, starch, glycerine] in our make-up, we should all remain alike'.

faker ; fakir. The former (one who 'fakes', a swindler, an impostor) is incorrect for *fakir*, a Mohammedan religious mendicant, naked ascetic, wonder-worker.

fall (U.S.A.) is the English *autumn*; *fall* is the more Saxon, the more poetical word ('the fall of the leaf, the fall of the year').

FALSE AGREEMENT. See AGREEMENT, FALSE.

FALSE COMPARATIVES and **SUPER-LATIVES.** See COMPARATIVES, FALSE.

FALSE ILLITERACIES—false because the pronunciations are standard. E.g., *iz* for *is*, *duz* for *does*, *wot* for *what*.

falseness ; falsity. Both = 'contrariety to fact; want of truth'; both = 'duplicity, deceitfulness'; only *falseness* now = 'faithlessness, treachery', or an instance thereof; only *falsity* = 'error in general or a particular error, untrue proposition, statement, doctrine'. (*O.E.D.*)

familiar to. See PREPOSITIONS WRONGLY USED.

family. See FOLKS.

famous. See 'NOTORIOUS and FAMOUS'.

fantastic is being, has too long been, grossly overworked.

fantasy and **phantasy**. 'In modern use *fantasy* and *phantasy*, in spite of their identity in sound and in ultimate etymology, tend to be apprehended as separate words, the predominant sense of the former being "caprice, whim, fanciful invention", . . . that of the latter is "imagination, visionary notion".' (*O.E.D.*)

farther, farthest ; further, furthest. 'Thus far and no farther' is a quotation-become-formula; it is invariable. A rough distinction is this: *farther, farthest*, are applied to distance and nothing else; *further, furthest,* either to distance or to addition ('a *further* question').

farther to, misused for *farther from* or *opposite to*. 'On the farther side to that by which they entered.'

fascination of—for—by—with. Something has a fascination for a person, i.e., it fascinates him. 'The fascination of Elaine by Lancelot' is clear; but 'the fascination of Elaine' without a modifying 'by Lancelot' might have meant 'Elaine's fascinating qualities, or power of fascinating'. One is fascinated *by a person*, but *with a thing* (or a happening).

fashion is obsolescent for *manner* or *mode* of doing something, obsolescent for *method*. 'She has a strange fashion of speaking.'

fatal, 'deadly, mortal, resulting in death', should not be debased to mean *grave* or *serious*, as in 'He had a fatal motor accident last month, but has completely recovered now'. To debase it to synonymity with *unfortunate* is still worse.

FAULTY PRECISION. 'If the burglar had chosen Vanderlyn's room, it would almost certainly be he [Vanderlyn] and not the English maid, who would be lying dead at Bella-colline.' The correct form would be, 'it would almost certainly be Vanderlyn, and not the English maid, lying dead'.

favour, 'to regard with favour, to show favour to', even 'to have a liking or preference for' ('He favours Catholicism'), should not be used as a synonym of *prefer*. A good example of its misuse is, 'He favours a dog to a cat'.

favourable reception with. See PREPOSITIONS WRONGLY USED.

fearful; fearsome. In current English, both of these terms = 'causing or inspiring fear'; *fearsome* is rather literary.

feature for *achievement* is catachrestic. 'Until his retirement at 46, he retained his pace and accuracy in the field, a feature without parallel.'

feel (n.), 'feeling', is obsolescent for a mental sensation, as 'a feel of excitement'.

female as 'a mere synonym for "woman" ' is 'now commonly avoided by good writers, except with contemptuous implication' (*O.E.D.*) or with a facetious one.

femineity and femininity. The former is 'the quality or nature of the female sex', hence 'womanliness', hence 'womanishness'; *femininity* is used for 'womanliness' and also for 'womanishness'. Concretely, *femininity* is 'womankind'; and it has two applied senses, 'the *fact* of being a female' and 'a feminine peculiarity, especially in form'. (*O.E.D.*)

festal; festive. Both = 'of or pertaining to a feast or festivity', though the former is now more usual, as it also is in the senses (of a person) 'keeping holiday' and (of a place) 'given up to feasting or festivity'. Both = 'befitting a feast; hence, joyous, gay', but *festive* is now preferred in these nuances. *Festive occasion* and *festive season* are set phrases.

fetch and bring. Weseen excellently distinguishes them. 'Fetch implies that the [person] spoken to is some distance from the thing to be brought, . . . *bring* . . . that he is already near it. "Please bring me that paper you have"; "Please fetch my book from the library".' *Go* is redundant with *fetch*, 'as "Go and fetch the paper". *Fetch* means go to something, get it, and bring it here.'

few and a few. (Cf. the entry at GOOD FEW, A; GOOD MANY, A.)

The difference has been admirably determined by *The O.E.D.*:—'Without prefixed word, *few* usually implies antithesis with "many", [whereas] in *a few, some few* the antithesis is with "none at all". Cf. "few, or perhaps none", "a few, or perhaps many".'

The few now generally = 'the minority' and is opposed to *the many*, i.e., 'the majority'.

fictional, fictitious, fictive. *Fictional* is 'of, pertaining to, or of the nature of fiction', as in 'fictional literature', 'His fictional friends give him more pleasure than he gets from his real ones'. Both *fictitious* and *fictive* = 'counterfeit, feigned, not genuine', but the latter is obsolescent; *fictitious* in the sense 'of, in, or like fiction (literature)' is now less common than *fictional*; both *fictitious* and (the now rare) *fictive* are applied to assumed names; both of these adjectives, though the latter now rarely, = 'existing in or created by the imagination'. But *fictive* is the correct term for 'imaginatively creative', as in 'Having a . . . great fictive faculty'; *fictitious* alone is correct in the legal sense, 'a fictitious son', i.e., an adopted one, and in the general sense, 'arbitrarily devised', as in 'a fictitious measure of values'. (*O.E.D.*)

fiddle for *violin* is 'now only in familiar or contemptuous use' (*O.E.D.*). Unfortunately, the verb *fiddle* has gone the same way: we have to say, *play the violin*, and *violinist* rather than *fiddler*.

fiend is, in jocular usage, permissible for 'a person or agency causing mischief', as in 'an autograph fiend', but in the sense 'addict'—'fresh-air fiend'—it is slang.

figure is not synonymous with *number*, but only with 'a number expressed in figures', i.e., in numerical symbols. A *number* is expressed in *figures*; figures represent a number or numbers.

FIGURES OF SPEECH, as part of the equipment of prose style, are outmoded; felt to be artificial. If we use them, we use them, for the most part, subconsciously. For an admirable set of definitions and examples, see Fowler's *Modern English Usage*, at 'Technical Terms'; for a shorter

list, *English: A Course for Human Beings,*
Book II.

fill in ; fill out. These two phrases are not
interchangeable, as certain people seem
to think. *Fill in* is to complete (an outline); to insert (into speech or writing)
something that will occupy a vacancy, as
in 'He left the date blank for me to fill in'.
Fill out is to enlarge or extend to the
desired size or limit; it can be used of a
cheque, but *fill in* (or in England *fill up*) is
perhaps better.

final (adj.). See COMPARATIVES, FALSE.

final (n.). See FINALE.

FINAL CLAUSES. Final or purposive
clauses form one of the various kinds of
adverbial clause. They are introduced
either by *that* (usually preceded by *in
order* or *so* or—now only in literary
language—*to the* (*end*) or by *lest* (equivalent to *that . . . not*). The rule for the right
use of final clauses has nowhere been
more clearly stated than in Dr Onions's
An Advanced English Syntax.

'Final Clauses introduced by *that* take
may with the Infinite in present and
future time, *might* in past time.'

'I eat that I *may* live' is the literary
form of 'I eat in order that I may live' or
the idiomatic ' I eat in order to live'.

'I shall eat well in order that I *may* keep
fit.'

'They climbed higher that'—or *so that*
—'they *might* get a better view.'

'Conspirators are always secretive to
the end that their secrets *may* not be
divulged.'

'The conspirators were secretive to the
end that their secret *might* not be
divulged.'

Negative final clauses may be couched
in the *that . . . not* mode; so far as the
verbs are concerned, the sentences follow
the *that* mode.

'I eat that I may not die' or '. . . in
order that I may not die'.

'They climbed higher (in order) that
they *might* not fall.' But even now in
formal or literary language, as formerly
in nearly all cultured or educated speech,
that . . . not is less usual than *lest* in
negative final clauses. *Lest* takes *should*
(or, after the present or the future, *may*)
with the infinitive.

'I eat lest I *should* (or *may*) ⎫
die' ⎪ (*may* being
'I *shall* eat lest I *should* (or ⎬ obsolescent)
may) die' ⎪
'I *ate* lest I *should* die'. ⎭

The true subjunctive (*may* + infinitive,
might + infinitive, and *should* + infini-

tive being subjunctive-equivalents) is
now rare, except in poetry, poetic prose,
and prose that is either archaic or,
without being poetic, lofty or dignified
or vatic.

'He forgets not his viaticum lest he *fail*
to reach the happy shore.'

To act that each to-morrow
Find us farther than to-day.

'Relative Clauses with Final or Consecutive meaning sometimes take *shall*
(*should*), equivalent to the Latin Subjunctive.'

Build me straight a goodly vessel
That *shall* laugh at all disaster.
—Longfellow.

'An act might be passed which *should*
not entirely condemn the practice.' In
this latter sentence, *did* would have been
less formal than *should*.

finalize is not recognized by *The O.E.D.*;
Webster's admits it, but only by the back
door. As a synonym for *to complete* or *to
conclude* it is superfluous and ugly.

first for *at first* can lead only to ambiguity
or to that momentary check which is
more irritating though less dangerous.
'The murder might not be as commonplace in its occasion, nor its solution as
simple as he had first been inclined to
think.'

first for *just* (*after*) may be ambiguous, as
in 'When they were first married they
took several trips': better, 'Just after they
married, they . . .'.

first, two ; first, three ; first, four, etc., are
incorrect for *first two, first three,* etc. For
'the two first chapters in the book' read
'the first two chapters . . .' . This is the
English idiom; French has 'les deux pre-
miers chapitres . . .' .

firstly is inferior to *first*, even when
secondly, thirdly . . . follow it.

flair. Don't overdo this noun (which properly = 'instinctive discernment', 'unusually keen perceptiveness') in such
senses as 'inborn ability' ('He has a flair
for cricket') and—much worse—'liking'
('She has a flair for gimcracks'). (*O.E.D.*)

flaunt for *flout* seems to be a strange error
—and, some would say, a rare one. It
may be strange, but it is not rare. 'He
achieved strong local popularity, a priceless asset to a man who lives by flaunting
the law.'

flee and **fly.** The former has become literary; the latter, obsolescent, except in its
literal sense, 'to move through the air on
wings'. (*O.E.D.*)

fleshly is now used only in the senses (1) 'carnal', (2) 'lascivious, sensual': in which senses *fleshy* is catachrestic.

flier; flyer. Both are correct, the latter (esp. for 'an aviator') being the more common.

floor and **stor(e)y.** Usage prefers *stor(e)y* in relation to height, *floor* in relation to part of building; thus, 'The apartment is on the tenth floor of a fifteen-storey building'.

flow—*flowed*—*flowed*; **fly**—*flew*—*flown*.

fly. See FLEE.

flyer. See FLIER.

folks for *folk.* 'The old folks at home.' *Folk* is already plural, but the added *s*, though colloquial, modifies its meaning from the group or collective sense to that of the individuals composing the group.

follow. See SUCCEED.

follow behind is unnecessary for *follow.* 'I found certain men who had penetrated boldly into the heart of the subject . . . I follow behind them here.' If the gap is to be emphasized, why not 'follow from afar'? So too for *follow after.*

following, misused for *after.* 'For "following" . . . there is a quite satisfactory substitute, the simple preposition "after". What the luckless "after" has done to merit being quietly cold-shouldered out of the language I cannot conceive . . .

' "Following dinner, the band of the Guards played a selection of music in the blue drawing-room."

'One hopes that the band managed to overtake their dinner before the evening was out.

' "Following a chase half across Europe, a beautiful spy was captured at Bucarest." The lady was apparently following the chase that was following her. It sounds like a vicious circle.' (G. V. Carey, *Mind the Stop.*)

font-name. See CHRISTIAN NAME.

footpath. See PAVEMENT.

for. '*For* does not mean *against*' sounds like a fatuous truism, yet I have seen this sentence, 'The sentry was on guard for parachute troops', where the context made it clear that he was on guard *against* them.

for and **because.** The former is subjective ('Don't swear, for I dislike swearing'), the latter objective ('They did that, because events compelled them'); the former may represent the writer's own view, the latter the immediate and explicit cause.

for = *as understood by* is admirably brief; so brief as to lead to obscurity, as perhaps in '*Meaning for Scientists*'—one of the chapter headings in Stuart Chase's *The Tyranny of Words.*

for ever means 'for eternity', 'for one's life-time'; **forever** means 'constantly or continually', as in 'He's forever singing'.

for what? See WHAT . . . FOR?

for why, as in 'I'll tell you for why', is illiterate and verbose.

forbear. Incorrect for *forebear*, ancestor.

forceful; forcible. A *forceful* (not *forcible*) person is vigorous or strong or powerful; 'acting with force, impetuous, violent' is *forceful*; a writer, a painter, an orator that produces a powerful effect is *forcible*; a cogent, impressive or effective speech or style is either *forceful* or *forcible*; a weapon drawn with force is a *forceful* weapon; something done by force is *forcible* ('a forcible expulsion'), esp. in Law, as in *forcible entry, forcible dissolution* (of, e.g., Parliament). (*O.E.D.*)

forecast—preterite *forecast* or *forecasted* —past participle *forecast* or *forecasted.*

forego and **forgo.** The former means *to precede in time or place* (i.e., to go before); the latter, *to relinquish, to go without.*

foregoing. See ABOVE.

forgo. See FOREGO.

form. See SHAPE.

former for *first.* 'Jeffrey, Alexander and Sutton met in the former's office to discuss the situation.' 'In Jeffrey's office' would be the best phrase.

Former and *latter* are used only when there are two persons or things.

formula, plural of. See PLURALS . . .

forte is, in Music, dissyllabic; elsewhere it has only one syllable.

forward and **forwards.** *Forwards* is an adverb only; *forward*, both an adverb and an adjective. In Great Britain, the adverbs *forward* and *forwards* are used as in the masterly verdict of *The O.E.D.*: 'The . . . distinction . . . is that the latter expresses a definite direction viewed in contrast with other directions. In some contexts either form may be used without perceptible difference of meaning; the following are examples in which only one of them can be used: "The ratchet-wheel can move only *forwards*"; "the right side of the paper has the maker's name reading *forwards*"; "if you move at all it must be *forwards*"; "my companion has gone *forward*"; "to bring a matter *forward*"; "from this time *forward*".' [Of American usage, *Webster's* says: 'In general, *forward* tends to displace *forwards* in most or all contexts, although the latter is still often used to express the actual direction, as of a movement.' The military order is '(forward,) march'.]

fraction is infelicitous for *portion*; incorrect for *proportion*. 'A large fraction of what passes for human folly is failure of communication.'

frank. Do not overdo this word in its euphemistic sense, 'sexually outspoken'.

Frankenstein is frequently misused for *Frankenstein's monster*, which became dangerous to its inventive creator. Mary Wollstonecraft published, in 1818, her tale of terror, *Frankenstein*, which owed its inspiration to science.

free, gratis, and for nothing is a cliché, excusable only as a jocularity; **free gratis** and **free for nothing** are ludicrous tautologies.

freedman, an emancipated slave; **freeman**, one who is politically free, also one to whom the freedom of a city (or a borough or a company) has been granted.

freight. See CARGO.

FRENCH TAGS. See CLICHÉ.

FRENCH TERMS MISSPELT. A delightful correspondent writes, 'I rather wish you could have found a place in which to dismiss three misspellings that appear wrongly in nine out of ten English texts:

Folies Bergères for *Folies Bergère*;
hors d'œuvres for *hors d'œuvre*,

writers seeming to think that the former is a plural, but they are mistaken;

Mistinguette for *Mistinguett*.'

To that list, add: *crime passionel* for *crime passionnel*. The most common mistake of all, *bête noir* for *bête noire*, is treated separately.

frequent is now used only in the senses, 'happening at short intervals; often recurring; happening in close succession; (of a pause) faster than is normal', as in 'The crops suffered from frequent blights'; and (of an agent), 'constant or habitual', as in 'He was a frequent guest at the villa'. (*O.E.D.*)

friendlily is less frowned upon than it used to be, and when we become accustomed to the sound, we shall no longer find *friendlily* inferior to *in a friendly manner*.

friends with. 'I am friends with Bill' is as correct as 'We are friends of theirs'. As Dr Onions has remarked, this 'interesting case . . . is not so startling an anomaly as it seems; it is easy to see how (e.g.) "He and the Prime Minister are great friends", by assimilation to "He is very friendly with the Prime Minister", could give rise to "He is great friends with the Prime Minister" '. On the analogy of *friends with* is *shipmates with*: 'Captain Bolton of the *Caligula*, who tells me he was shipmates with you in the old *Indefatigable*'.

frightened of. Colloquial for *afraid of*.

Frisco for *San Francisco* is a colloquialism contemned by the cultured.

from hence is unnecessary; *hence* = from here, from this. The same applies to *from thence* and *from whence*.

from how, incorrect for *in comparison with* (*what*). 'I followed him into the room, which seemed oddly small, somehow, from how I had remembered it.' Better: 'in comparison with the room as I remembered it'.

front does not = *beginning*, as in 'the front of the book'; *at the front of the book*, however, is permissible in opposition to *at the back of the book*.(Weseen.)

froze, preterite; *frozen*, past participle.

FULL-STOPS, USELESS. See USELESS . . .

function, for *to act, to work*, should be used only of machinery or of an organ that works like a machine. It is pretentious for *informal* social gathering or festive meeting.

funds is permissible for money at one's disposal; but do not use it indiscriminately for *money* or *cash*.

funeral and **funereal.** Only the latter is used figuratively ('gloomy, dark, dismal, melancholy, mournful'), as in 'We marched at a funereal pace', 'funereal shades of night'. As 'of or pertaining to or appropriate to a funeral', *funereal* is now rare except in archaeology (e.g., *funereal papyri*), precisely as *funeral* is archaic in figurative usage. *Funeral*, therefore, is the correct current term for 'of or pertaining to the ceremonial burial (or cremation) of the dead; used, observed, delivered, etc., at a burial' (*O.E.D.*), as in *funeral rites, funeral urn, funeral pyre, funeral column*.

fungous is the adjective of *fungus*; the adjective *fungoid* is a botanical and a pathological technicality.

funny for *odd* or *strange* is a colloquialism. Also it tends to produce ambiguity: one is too often constrained to ask, '*Funny*, "strange", or *funny*, "ha! ha!"?'

further, furthest. See FARTHER.

further to that is a commercialized and verbose elaboration of *further* or *furthermore*.

fuschia, a very frequent error for *fuchsia*.
FUSED PARTICIPLES. 'Fused Participle', says H. W. Fowler, at the beginning of his spirited article thereon in *A Dictionary of Modern English Usage*, 'is a name given to the construction exemplified in its simplest form by "I like you pleading poverty", and in its higher development by "The collision was owing to *the signalling instructions* laid down by the international regulations for use by ships at anchor in a fog *not having been properly followed*" '; it was, by the way, Fowler who invented the name. An example midway between the two extremes is this, 'Y.Y.'s distillation of fun . . . has done much to make up for *that paper having spoiled* other Christmas dinners besides his and the Professor's' (from a letter in *The New Statesman and Nation*, early in 1938).

The fused participle has caused much heartburning. There are two main schools of thought: The Fowlerites, who consider it the abomination of abominations; the Onions men and the Jespersenites, who, on certain points, oppose the Fowlerites.

Let us consider the pronouncements of the judicious Dr C. T. Onions in *An Advanced English Syntax*; the inadequately appreciated H. W. Fowler; the luminously sensible Professor Otto Jespersen. In that order.

'Notice', says Dr Onions, 'the following alternative constructions, the first involving the use of the Gerund, the second that of the Verb Adjective in -ing (Active Participle):

What is the use of *his coming?*—of *him coming?*

He spoke of *its being* cold—*it being* cold.

We hear every day of *the Emperor's dying*—*the Emperor dying*.

Forts were erected to prevent *their landing*—*them landing*.'

To those I should like to add:

What is the use of *his having come*—of *him having come?*

He spoke of *its having been cold*—*it having been cold*, &c., &c.

'Some people', continues Dr Onions, 'insist that the first of these constructions should always be used.' 'If', he remarks in a footnote, 'this rule were pressed, we should have to say: "His premature death prevented *anything's coming* of the scheme"—which can hardly be called English'; i.e., it is unidiomatic. 'But the second is the older use, and, moreover,

D*

involves nothing illogical or inconsistent with other uses of the Participle, which may generally be paraphrased by "in the act of -ing". We find a good instance in Clarendon of the Gerund qualified by a possessive: "Sunday passed without *any man's taking* notice of *the keeper's being* absent".'

H. W. Fowler deemed the fused participle to be 'a usage . . . rapidly corrupting modern style': but Dr Onions's statement of the historical facts has shown that the fused participle was formerly the general usage; the inference is that the apostrophized form (*Jack's coming*) is a modern improvement,—for Onions, Jespersen and other authorities fully admit that, in many instances, the apostrophized (or possessive adjective + gerund) form is an improvement, a very useful distinction, but do not enforce its application so widely, nor so rigidly, as does the tonic author of *Modern English Usage*. Fowler takes three sentences—(1) 'Women having the vote share political power with men', (2) 'Women's having the vote reduces men's political power', and (3) 'Women having the vote reduces men's political power'. He proceeds thus:—'In the first the subject of the sentence is *women*, and *having* (*the vote*) is a true participle attached to women.' Agreed; but would not the construction and the sense have been clearer if the sentence had been written either 'Women, having the vote, share political power with men' or (stylistically preferable) 'Having the vote, women share political power with men'? For if there is much virtue in an *if*, there is much value in a comma. In this matter, my advice is: Before you decide on a possessive + gerund construction or, if you are not sure of your ground, a fused participle, examine whether a participle construction, *duly punctuated*, does not make a more elegant as well as a more logical sentence. And I submit, for your consideration, two sentences:—

'All of you shouting at once confuse me': if the emphasis indicates, and the context connotes, that the sense is 'Shouting all at once, you confuse me', then *shouting* is an ordinary participle and the sentence is correct. But is not the sense 'Your (collective) shouting confuses me', with the emphasis on the noise of the shouting? The proposed alteration, however, is drastic. Let us, then, see what happens if we apply the possessive + gerund construction: 'All of your' or 'all your'—'shouting at once confuses me'. But 'all of your shouting at once' makes *all* the subject—and that is not the sense intended; 'all your shouting at once' provides the right sense, but strikes one as being unidiomatic. The general opinion is that in 'all of you shouting at once confuse me', *shouting* is a true participle, and that the sentence is therefore correct; and Fowler would have added, 'Well, anyway, " All of you shouting at once *confuses* me" is an example of the fused participle and the sentence is wrong'. But both forms ('all of you shouting at once confuse me' and '. . . confuses me') are heard, and *in both there is, I think, a fused participle*. And, assuming that the writer or speaker is using the form that conveys his meaning the better, are not both forms correct? In 'All of you shouting at once confuse me', there is a sense construction; in 'All of you shouting at once confuses me' one may postulate an ellipsis. In the latter, you may supply 'the fact of' before 'all of you . . .'; the subject would be 'the fact' and the verb, therefore, singular. In the former there is, subconsciously, the apposition: 'all of you', which naturally will take a plural verb, and 'shouting at once' (i.e., simultaneously),—or, in other words, there are, according as one regards the sentence subjectively or objectively, two ideas, cumulative ideas, or two facts, cumulative facts: 'all of you' (i.e., 'your plurality', connoting 'mere weight of numbers') and 'shouting at once' (i.e., 'collective shouting', hence 'the din you make'): psychologically, the speaker is confused not only by the noise but also by the fact that he realizes that the noise is made, not by one person (who may be a lunatic) but by many (some of whom may be sensible men): considered together but *not* identified, the noise and his numerical inferiority confuse him. 'All of you shouting at once confuse me' I defend as containing, in grammar, an apposition of two subjects and as being, in reality, a juxtaposition (hence, a cumulation) of two facts.—This, however, is not to defend either form of the sentence stylistically ('By shouting all at once, you confuse me' would be preferable), but merely to defend my opinion that both forms of the sentence are idiomatic and psychologically coherent.

The second example is:

'In the moments of that reflection, George telling the story of Brenda quite obliterated the picture of George done in the eye and foaming at the mouth' (Richard Blaker). Concerning this sentence two preliminary observations may be made:—We can safely omit 'in the moments of that reflection'; we must take 'George telling the story of Brenda' as equivalent to 'the picture [i.e., the visual memory] of George telling the story of Brenda'. We may reduce the sentence to a terser form,

'George telling the story of Brenda obliterated George done in the eye and foaming at the mouth',

provided we remember that there are two contrasted memories ('George telling the story of Brenda' and 'George done in the eye and foaming at the mouth'), both sharply visualized. Fowler, I think, would have said that this should read: '*George's telling* the story of Brenda obliterated *George's being* (or *having been*) *done* in the eye and [on that account] foaming at the mouth', which, on first thoughts, may seem not merely feasible but preferable to the original. But is it equally convincing when we restore the sentence to its fuller form, 'The picture of George's telling the story of Brenda obliterated the picture of George's being (or having been) done in the eye and foaming at the mouth'? Does not the possessive + gerund construction destroy the vividness of the two pictures? Does it not even change two memory-*pictures* into two mental *ideas*? Both aesthetics and logic require the retention of 'George telling the story of Brenda', and 'George done in the eye and foaming at the mouth'. If *telling* and *done* and *foaming* are ordinary participles, no alteration of the sense will result from putting the sentence into the participial mode, thus: '[The picture of] George, telling the truth, obliterated the picture of George, done in the eye and foaming at the mouth'. It may be advanced that this is shorter than, but grammatically equivalent to, 'The first picture of George (a George telling the story of Brenda) obliterated the second picture of George (a George done in the eye and foaming at the mouth)'. If that is so, the fused participle is not involved.

In Fowler's second example,

'Women's having the vote reduces men's political power', the subject is the gerund (or verbal noun, as some people prefer to designate it), *having* (*the vote*), and *women's* is the possessive case, i.e., an adjective-equivalent, attached to that verbal noun. About this type of sentence, there is no argument: all the authorities are agreed both on its correctness and on its convenience.

In his third example,

'Women having the vote reduces men's political power', the subject of the sentence is obviously, not *women* (for if *women* were the subject, the verb would be *reduce*), 'nor *having* (for if so, *women* would be left in the air without grammatical construction), but a compound notion formed by fusion of the noun *women* with the participle *having*. 'Participles so constructed, then, are called fused participles, as opposed to the true participle of No. 1 and the gerund of No. 2' (Fowler).

Probably one feels that 'Women's having the vote reduces men's political power' is preferable to 'Women having the vote reduces men's political power', but how far is that feeling the result of intellectual conviction and how far is it caused by the fact that here we have '*women* having the vote' and not '*woman* having the vote'? Most fair-minded citizens will readily admit that 'Woman having the vote reduces men's political power' rings much less oddly than 'Women having the vote reduces men's political power', especially if we balance the sense by changing 'men's' to 'man's'. Fowler would have done better to omit any reference to the grammatical number, for it is irrelevant to the discussion; to introduce it at all is to obscure the issue. Let us, then, take the revised sentence, 'Woman having the vote reduces man's political power', and see whether it will stand the various tests. 'Woman, having the vote, reduces man's political power' —the participial mode—makes poor sense; 'Woman's having the vote reduces man's political power'—the gerundial mode—is correct. But the correctness of the gerundial mode does not necessarily involve the incorrectness of the fused-participle mode. Grammar has its alternatives: the rightness of one construction does not preclude the rightness of the alternative.

If one compares '*Woman having* the vote reduces man's political power' with Dr Onions's example, 'His premature death prevented *anything's coming* of the scheme', one may, if one is an aesthete, be tempted to exclaim, 'Oh, but "anything's coming of the scheme" is so ugly that one simply couldn't use it! Only "anything coming of the scheme" is possible. "Woman's having the vote" is not so disgusting, so let it pass.' But is euphony the only—is it even the most important— reason why 'His premature death prevented anything coming of the scheme' is preferable to '. . . anything's coming . . .'? Dr Onions implies (for he does not actually state) that '. . . anything coming . . .' is idiomatic, for he goes almost so far as to say that '. . . anything's coming . . .' is unidiomatic—is, in short, un-English.

Now, in the idiomatic there is usually a basis of good sense. Obviously, the fused participle has historical precedent strongly behind it. Has it also reason, sense, necessity to support it? Dr Onions maintains that it is at least not illogical, nor inconsistent with other participial usages.

Let us return to 'Woman having the vote reduces man's political power'. This is equivalent to 'The female vote (or woman's vote) reduces man's political power' or 'Voting by women reduces man's political power' or even 'Woman's voting reduces . . .' But as 'woman's voting' = 'female voting', might not 'woman-voting' be so used? It is true that we speak of 'child-murder', not of 'child-murdering', but we do speak of 'pig-sticking'. Here 'child' and 'pig' are, as it were, accusatives after 'murdering' and 'sticking'. We could, however, use nominatives in the same way; primitive and savage peoples do; compare 'We hear of *it being* cold'. Moreover, *woman* (or, for that matter, *women*) *having the vote* may be regarded as a unit, with the two simple ideas *woman* and *having the vote*, which appears less odd if we write it *woman-having-the-vote* (= *female suffrage* or German *Frauenstimmrecht*). It seems likely that this unit-formation is, psychologically, at the back of Dr Onions's non-gerundial examples and that we need not rack our brains to find compounds.

This seems even more likely when we are confronted with such an example as 'For the first time the possibility of something serious having happened entered Jeffrey's mind'. According to Fowler, this should be '. . . the possibility of something serious's having happened . . .', which can hardly be called English. Consider, too, the following examples from Jespersen's 'On ING' in his masterly paper, *Some Disputed Points in English Grammar*, evoked in stern opposition to Fowler's article in *Modern English Usage* and based mainly on usage and partly on convenience:

'I cannot understand no *rain falling*', i.e., (the fact) that no rain falls or has fallen.

'Journeys end in *lovers meeting*' (Shakespeare).

'She had calculated on her *daughters remaining* at N.' (Jane Austen).

Note: 'He had every day a chance of *this happening*' (Fielding), 'He wouldn't hear of *that being* possible' (Dickens), 'We are mortified at the news of *the French taking* the town from the Portuguese' (Swift), 'I am not surprised at *young or old falling* in love with her' (Thackeray), 'No fear had they of *bad becoming* worse' (Wordsworth), 'Besides the fact of *those three being* there, the drawbridge is kept up' (A. Hope). Here we have instances of words that cannot form a genitive; 'but are they therefore to be excluded from being used as the subject of an ing-combination?' as Jespersen pertinently asks.

In many groups of words, it is difficult to form a genitive, and so the fused participle is preferred: 'The danger of *the chair and its occupant being* dashed against the rugged face of the precipice' (Scott)—not *the chair's and its occupant's* nor *the chair and its occupant's*; 'Laughing at *Sir John Walter and me falling* out' (Swift)—not *Sir John Walter's and my*, nor *Sir John Walter and my*; 'What is the good of *mother and me economising*?' (Hardy); 'We were talking about getting away. *Me and you getting* away' (Kipling) and 'There is the less fear of *you and me finding* one' (Conan Doyle),—'*I and your* or *All and your* or *my and your* getting away' being as unnatural as '*you and my* or *your and my* finding out'; *mine and yours* (for '*me and you* getting away') being even more absurd.

Jespersen calls the construction of '*woman having the vote* (reduces man's political power)' a nexus. This nexus arises from the feeling, or the subconscious understanding, that *woman having the vote* is a unit. Not merely is it a psychological unit. It is also a speech-unit; it is indivisible.

Such speech-units are in keeping with English idiom: witness the group genitive and the relative pronouns *that*, *which*, *who*, which can refer to a phrase or even a sentence as naturally as to a single word.

The final position is this:

When the participial construction (rightly used in 'Women, having the vote, share political power with men') fails to convey the sense intended *and* when the possessive + gerund (neat enough in 'Women's having the vote reduces men's political power') would be either clumsy

or ambiguous, then the fused participle is, to guard against clumsiness, preferable, and to guard against ambiguity, inevitable; and it can be used without departing from English usage and without offending English good sense.

But this is not equivalent to saying that the *ing*-construction is not extremely clumsy at times. 'When it is clumsy, turn the sentence differently' is the safe and obvious practice to observe. It is, however, to be remarked that, even here, the fused participle is frequently less clumsy than is the possessive + gerund, as some of Jespersen's examples have shown.

And, whatever you do, avoid a mixture —unless there is an imperative reason for using the two different constructions. Sometimes a writer falls between two stools, as in 'For my own part, I have no great objection to *Cockney being described* as vulgar or even to *its being denied* officially the status of a dialect' ('being officially denied' would have been preferable).

future refers to something that has not yet happened; do not, therefore, use it for *subsequent* or *after*, as in 'We do not know her future manoeuvres when she made the decision'.

G

game. 'Game in England—Hare, pheasant, partridge, grouse and moor fowl. Game in Ireland—Same as [for] England, with the addition of deer, landrail, quail, black game, and bustard. Game in Scotland— Same as [for] England, with the addition of ptarmigan.' (*Diary*, issued by Hay & Son, Ltd., Sheffield.) [*Webster's*: 'The various animals (chiefly birds and mammals) which are considered worthy of pursuit by sportsmen. Among birds the order Galliformes, and the duck, plover, snipe, and rail families, contain the majority of those ordinarily considered game.']

Gand for *Ghent*. See BRUXELLES . . .

gantlet is in England an obsolete form of *gauntlet*, whether independently or in the phrase, *run the gauntlet*. In U.S.A., the phrase is written *run the gantlet*, in order to distinguish *gantlet* from *gauntlet* (glove), for the *ga(u)ntlet* of the phrase is a corruption of *gantlope*, a totally different word.

gaol, gaoler; jail, jailer. The former pair is the earlier, but the latter is the usual one: *gaol, gaoler* are archaic.

gargantuan, misused. 'The water was alive

with traffic, Lilliputian tugs were performing gargantuan towing feats.' The author means *gigantic* or, better, *Brobdingnagian*.

gasolene and **gasoline** (likewise pronounced *-ene*) are equally correct. *Gas* is a colloquial abbreviation, originally American, and is in Britain used mostly in *step on the gas*, 'to make haste'.

gem for *something greatly prized* (a 'treasure') is colloquial and therefore to be avoided in dignified contexts; it can easily be overdone in any kind of context.

gender refers to words only.

general. See UNIVERSAL(LY).

generally for *usually* (as a general rule; in most instances) is not incorrect, but it may lead to ambiguity, as in 'It is generally wet and cold in S.W. New Zealand'.

generally always. The two adverbs used together are contradictory.

GENITIVE, GROUP. See GROUP GENITIVE.

GENITIVE, MUTILATED. Avoid 'Dickens' novels' for 'Dickens's novels' and 'St James' Park' for 'St James's Park' and esp. 'St James' ' for 'St James's' (the London district). For the genitive, see *English: A Course*, Book I, pp. 50-51, and for finer points:

GENITIVE,* VAGARIES OF THE. The basis from which we arrive at vagaries of the genitive (or possessive) case is the general rule that a singular *boy* takes apostrophe *s*: *boy's*; the plural *boys* takes apostrophe: *boys'*. The main exceptions are that those words whose interior changes take apostrophe *s* in both the singular and the plural: *man's*, plural *men's*; *woman's*, plural *women's*; *child's*, *children's*; *cow's*, *kine's*; *pig's*, *swine's*: and that nouns that remain unchanged also take apostrophe *s* in both numbers: *one sheep's* (*wool*), *two sheep's* (*wool*).

Other exceptions are these: nouns ending in *-nce* take, in the singular, an apostrophe, as in *for patience' sake, for conscience' sake*, but in the plural they take *s'*, as in *for their consciences' sake*, in accordance with the general rule for the plural; *for goodness' sake* is a formula,—contrast *for mercy's sake*; nouns ending in *s*, followed immediately by a noun beginning with *s*, and nouns ending in *ses*, or *sess* or *sses* or *ssess*,or in *sis* or *siss* or *ssis* or *ssiss*, or in *-xes* (as in *Xerxes' army*), take in the singular an apostrophe, as in *Pears' Soap* (the three consecutive *s*'es in 'Pears's

---

* For a brilliant account of the genitive in general, see Geo. O. Curme, *Syntax*. The ensuing article is, in several places, a précis of Curme.

soap' being felt to be excessive) and in 'the *oasis*' verge', '*molasses*' attraction for children'.

In the past it was a very general, as it is now a not infrequent, practice to form the genitive singular of all nouns ending in *s* and especially those ending in *ss* (*hostess*) by adding an apostrophe to both the nominative singular (*a hostess' duties*, *your Highness' pleasure*) and of course in the plural ('The *three hostesses' houses* were in Park Lane'); but now it is usual to form the singular genitive by adding *'s* (*a hostess's duties, your Highness's pleasure*) —which seems to be a sensible idea, for if you can say *three hostesses' houses*, you can easily say *a hostess's duties*. There is, however, a strong tendency to retain *Jesus'* and *Demosthenes'*, *Socrates'*, and other such genitives of Greek proper names.

In those three paragraphs, there are no vagaries properly so called, at least in the rules enunciated, although it is true that certain idiosyncratic writers fall into vagaries when, in defiance of rule and clarity, they depart from those rules. [American readers may wish to consult *Webster's* entry for '*possessive*', Perrin's discussion of *Jones*, and *A Manual of Style* (University of Chicago Press).]

In the group genitive (*the King of England's power*), a group of words is made to conform to the rule that governs single words. See GROUP GENITIVE.

The same principle determines the genitive ending of two or even three nouns in apposition. Thus, *John Williamson, the aforementioned tenant* becomes in the genitive *John Williamson, the aforementioned tenant's house*, or, for legal clarity, *John Williamson's (the aforementioned tenant's) house*; *Albert, the Prince Consort* becomes *Albert, the Prince Consort's home*; *Arthur Wellesley, Duke of Wellington, the Field Marshal* becomes *Arthur Wellesley, Duke of Wellington, the Field Marshal's victory at Waterloo.*

'If two names are connected by *and* and represent persons that are joined together in authorship, business, or a common activity, the second name alone assumes the genitive ending: "*Stevens and Malone's* Shakespeare", "in *William and Mary's* reign", but of course "*Steele's and Addison's* [work or] works" when we are speaking of the separate sets of two different authors' (Curme), and 'Elizabeth's and Victoria's reign [or, better, reigns]' when we are dealing with two separate reigns. In the same way, 'if two or more names connected by *and* represent persons that are joined together in possession, the second or [the] last name alone assumes the genitive ending: "*John and William's* uncle", "*John, William and Mary's* uncle". "We paid a visit to *Messrs Pike and White's* works." "My *father and mother's* Bible."—But we must give each genitive its genitive -*s* if there is no joint possession: "*My father's and my mother's* birthdays both fall in June, two days apart" ' (Curme).

Two pronouns (*You and I*) or three pronouns (*he, you and I*) need careful handling: '*Your and my contract* (or *contracts*) has (or have) been signed'; '*His, your and my contract* (or *contracts*) has (or have) been signed'. An alternative to *your and my contracts*, where the contracts are separate, is *your contract(s) and mine*.

Noun and pronoun (*John and you*) or pronoun and noun (*you and John*) follow the same rule: *John's and your contract(s)*, *your and John's contract(s)*.

There are to be noted several rules of a different order. 'First [the] use [of the genitive case] is now in ordinary prose almost restricted to personal beings [and animals], and even such phrases as "society's hard-drilled soldiery" (Meredith), where *society* is personified, are felt as poetical; still more so, . . . "thou knowst not gold's effect" (Shakespeare) or "setting out upon life's journey" (Stevenson). But in some set phrases the genitive is [well] established, e.g., "out of *harm's* way"; "he is at his *wits*' (or *wit's*) end"; so also in the stock quotation from *Hamlet*, "in my *mind's* eye", etc. Then to indicate measure, etc.: "at a *boat's* length from the ship", and especially time: "an *hour's* walk", "a good *night's* rest", "*yesterday's* post"; and this even extended to such prepositional combinations as "*to-day's* adventures", "*to-morrow's* papers".

'Secondly, . . . the subjective genitive . . . is in great vigour, for instance in "the King's arrival", "the Duke's invitation", "the Duke's inviting him [gave him much pleasure]", "Mrs Poyser's repulse of the squire" (G. Eliot). Still there is, in quite recent times a tendency towards expressing the subject by means of the preposition *by*, just as in the passive voice, for instance in "the accidental discovery by Miss Knag of some correspondence" (Dickens); "the appropriation by a settled community of lands on the other side of the ocean" (Seeley), "the

massacre of Christians by Chinese". "Forster's Life of Dickens" is the same thing as "Dickens's Life, by Forster". — The objective genitive, — where the genitival noun or pronoun is affected by the following noun instead of affecting that following noun (*his defeat* = *the defeat of him*, not *the defeat by him*), —was formerly much more common than now, the ambiguity of [this] genitive being probably the reason for its decline. Still, we find, for instance, "his expulsion from power by the Tories" (Thackeray)', where, however, 'by the Tories' dispels all ambiguity, ' "What was thy pity's recompence ? " (Byron). " England's wrongs" generally mean the wrongs done to England. . . . In "my sceptre's awe" (Shakespeare, *Richard the Second*, I, i, 118] we have an objective, but in "thy free awe pays homage to us" (*Hamlet*, IV, iii, 63) a subjective genitive. But on the whole, such obscurity will occur less frequently in English than in other languages, where the genitive is more fully used' (Jespersen, *Growth and Structure of the English Language*). The same ambiguity attaches to *of* + noun, as in *the love of God*, which only the context can—yet sometimes does not—make clear, for by itself it may = 'the love felt by God' or 'the love felt for God'.

Stylistically, the '*s* and the *of* forms of the possessive are often varied or mingled. Thus Elizabeth Barrett Browning's 'all the hoofs of King Saul's father's asses' would probably, in good prose, become 'all the hoofs of the asses of King Saul's father' or, better, 'all the hoofs of the asses owned by King Saul's father'; and Pinero's 'He is my wife's first husband's only child's godfather' might be rendered a little less monotonous by a change to 'He is the godfather of the only child of my wife's first husband'.

Note the place of the genitive in 'The desire *of my heart* for peace', *of my heart* being less important than *for peace*; to stress the genitive, put it last, as in 'the desire for peace *of every man, woman and child in that great nation*'. (Curme.)

Then there is the double genitive case, exemplified in such phrases as 'a friend of my *father's*', 'three friends of *mine*', 'that hat of *his*', 'and dress of *Jane's*'. For the pronominal type of this strange genitive, see OF HER—OF HERS.

These pronominal examples are much less likely to lead to trouble than are the others: *that hat of his, that football of theirs, this pain of mine* are unambiguous;

but what are we to say of *this beauty of my sister's* and *this famed beauty of my famous sisters'*? To the reader, they are clear; the listener does not know whether one or two or several sisters are concerned. Scrupulous writers remember the sound rule that everything should be as clear to a listener as to a reader; especially do they avoid the double genitive with nouns in the plural, as in *in some retreat of his or his friends'*, where the apostrophe after *friends* clarifies the thought of the author: listeners, unfortunately, do not hear an apostrophe. But nouns in the singular are often equally susceptible to misapprehension by a listener, as in ('It was no fault *of the doctor's*'). 'The *of*-genitive ['of the doctor'] is here, as often elsewhere [e.g., to distinguish between objective and subjective genitive], a clearer form, and is often preferred', remarks George O. Curme. The same authority has smilingly noticed that 'although the double genitive with nouns is in general subject to ambiguity, many [writers and speakers], desirous of its lively effect, take their chances with it, trusting to the [context or the] situation to help them out'.

'In the case of personal pronouns', Curme remarks, 'there has long been a tendency to differentiate . . . form and meaning, namely, to employ *his, her*, etc., in the possessive relation and *of him, of her*, etc., in the partitive relation, stressing the idea of an integral part . . . : "*His hair, his eyes*", etc., but "She was the daughter of a lumberjack and woodcraft was bred into the very fiber *of her*" (*Saturday Evening Post*, July 29, 1916). "The man had something in the *look of him*" (Browning, *An Epistle*). "I don't do it for the honour *of it*." As this differentiation has not become thoroughly established, we still more commonly employ here the old undifferentiated forms *his, her*, etc., for either the possessive or the partitive relation: "his eyes" and "The man had something in *his* look". But we now always use the form of when the pronoun is modified by a relative clause: "Then first I heard the voice *of her* to whom . . . the Gods Rise up for reverence" (Tennyson, *Œnone*, 1.105)', it being loose English to write such a sentence as 'I put the money into *his* hand *who* needed it'.

In general, the 'very fiber *of her*', 'something in the look *of him*' form is poetic, literary; Carlyle says, 'The chief quality of Burns is *the sincerity of him*';

Jack London, in *White Fang*, has 'They were moulding *the clay of him*'. These examples are cited by Curme, who then adds:—'In a number of expressions the partitive genitive of personal pronouns is also common in plain prose, usually, however, without the poetic [connotation] of the preceding examples, [but] merely stressing the idea of an integral part: "That will be the end *of it*, the last *of it*". In a vague way we feel life and death as parts of us, vital parts of our human experience: "I couldn't do it for *the life of me*". "That will be *the death of you*".'

Worth noting, though it presents few difficulties, is the genitive absolute: that genitive in which the governing noun is omitted and which applies especially to residences and to places of business, as in 'Buy a loaf at the baker's in the next street', 'I spent a pleasant hour at Smith's [house, flat, etc.], after an unpleasant half-hour at Robinson & Smith's [office or shop or factory]'; 'John has asked whether he might go for part of his holiday to his *uncle and aunt's*'; but if the uncle and the aunt occupy separate residences, the sentence must end: 'go . . . to his *uncle's and* (his) *aunt's*'. Now, 'the governing noun is regularly omitted when the possessive genitive points forward or backward to a preceding or following governing noun, for the genitive here is now felt as a possessive pronoun, like *mine, hers*, etc. . . . "John's auto is larger than *William's and* mine" ' (Curme).

Finally we come to what Curme calls the Unclear Genitive and the Blended Genitive.

Unclear Genitives: 'The loss of distinctive genitive form . . . in a number of pronouns and limiting adjectives has weakened English expression.' Fielding wrote: '*Both their several talents* were excessive', whereas a Middle English author would have written *bother their* (or *their bother*) *talents*, where *bother*, in either *bother their* or *their bother*, is a distinctive genitive form—*bother* as distinctive from the nominative *both*. Fielding's *both their several talents* would, in correct Modern English, be *the several talents of both of them*, which is weak and wordy in comparison with the Middle English *bother their* (or *their bother*) *several talents*. 'This older usage', as Curme points out, 'is best preserved in the subjective genitive category in connection with the gerund: "Your mother will feel *your both* going away" (Mrs Gaskell, *Wives and Daughters*, Ch. xiv.) "Isn't it dreadful to think of *their all* being wrong!" (Sir Harry Johnston, *The Man Who Did the Right Thing*, Ch. ii).—It is also well preserved in the possessive category in such expressions as *both our lives* [are at stake], *both our minds* [are made up], but we now feel the old genitives as plural limiting adjectives. . . . This old usage survives in popular speech: "She is *both their mothers*, i.e., "the mother of both of them". "It is *both their faults*" [i.e., the faults of both of them]. In the literary language it lingers on in *for both their sakes, for both our sakes* [for the sake(s) of both of them—of us]. Similarly, when *of* is inserted after *all, both, none*, etc., to give expression to the partitive idea: "I'm taking the trouble of writing this true history *for all your benefits*" (Hughes, *Tom Brown's School-Days*, I, vi), instead of the correct *for the benefit of all of you.* "A painful circumstance which is attributable to *none of our faults*" (Thackeray, *Pendennis*, II, Ch. xxxv), instead of the correct *the fault of none of us.*' This difficulty affects also *each* and *either* (and *neither*): 'for each of our sakes' should be 'for the sake of each [or, all] of us'; 'It was neither of our faults' should be 'It was the fault of neither of us'. Note, however, that *neither of their faults*, like *both of their faults, all of their faults*, etc., is correct in such sentences as 'Smith's fault was gluttony; Robinson's avarice. But *both of their faults* paled into respectability in comparison with Jones's, for that was a tendency to murder those who contradicted him' and '*Neither of their faults* seems of much account when set beside Jones's. . . .'

Blended Genitives: These are more subtle: they constitute a nice test of the correctitude of even the best writers. 'In the partitive category', writes Curme, 'there is a tendency, once much more common than now, to blend the genitive with some other construction, resulting in illogical expression: "His versification is by far the most perfect *of any English poet*" (Saintsbury, *Nineteenth Century Literature*, 268), a blending of "His versification is far the most perfect *of all English poets*" and "His versification is more perfect that that *of any other English poet*" ',—but should not the former sentence read '. . . *of all English poets*'? Such 'omission of the word *other* after *any* . . . is a form of blending still common. In comparisons where there is present the idea of a group

or class, the superlative represents the group as complete, while the comparative represents the separation of one or more from all the others in the group. Hence we should say "[His versification] is [by far] the most perfect *of all English poets*" ' —more logically, *of all English poets*'— 'or "is more perfect [by far] than that *of any other English poet*" ' (Curme). Curme, however, should add that Saintsbury could also have written: 'He, of all English poets, has by far the most perfect versification' or 'Of all English poets', his is by far the most perfect versification', or even 'Of all English versifications, his is by far the most perfect'. (For the further infelicity, *the most perfect*, see COMPARATIVES, FALSE.)

genius, 'native intellectual power of an exalted type; instinctive and extraordinary capacity for imaginative creation, original thought, invention or discovery. Often contrasted with *talent*' (*O.E.D.*), must not be debased to = *talent*, which should be confined to 'a special natural ability or aptitude; a natural capacity for success in some department of mental or physical activity' (*O.E.D.*), but without inspiration or ultimate power.—Do not confuse *genius* with *genus*, class, category, kind.

gent, 'gentleman', is an illiteracy except when it applies to such a man as might be expected to use the word.

genteel; gentle; Gentile. The last = 'non-Jewish'; the second is now confined to the senses 'mild, not savage, not cruel, not rough'; *genteel*, in Standard English, is now pejorative or, at best, playful.

gentleman. See LADY and MISTER.

geography, chorography, topography. See TOPOGRAPHY . . .

GERUND. A very clear treatment of the subject is to be found in Dr C. T. Onions's *An Advanced English Syntax*. Here are various examples of correct usage:

'The *digging* of the foundations was hard work';

'The train will be long in *coming*';

'Now cease *complaining* and start work'.

With constructions dependent:

'He spoke of there *being a danger*';

'Your *being friends* will ease the situation';

'There are more ways of killing a cat . . .' .

With adverbial modifications:

'*Staring about aimlessly* will do no good';

'There is no *getting to the borders of space*'.

With adjectives:

'There's *no refuting* so cogent an argument'.

Note that when the gerund governs—i.e., is followed by—an objective (or accusative), there are, in 20th Century English, two constructions:

'Much diffidence was felt about *demanding money*';

'*The demanding of money* was the cause of much diffidence'.

Demanding money is the more general usage when the gerund depends on a preposition. *The demanding money* is now obsolete: a good thing too, for it led to ambiguity: *the electing councillors* could either mean 'the election of councillors' (to the Town Council) or 'those Councillors who elect' (the Chairman).

The gerund governed (i.e., preceded) by *a* or *a-* (i.e., *on*), as in 'I went a-buying', is archaic—when, at least, it is not dialectal. There is, however, a literal survival, with the preposition omitted:

'The church is *building*' (a-building, or in the course of building—or being built).

A purely syntactic difficulty occurs in such sentences as these:

'What a long time you are *dressing*!';

'He was too much occupied *watching* the passers-by to notice what was being discussed';

'They continued *eating* until they could eat no more'.

Thus:—'What a long time you are *a-dressing*' or '. . . in dressing';

'He was too much occupied, *a-watching* (or, in watching) . . .' or 'Watching, he was too much occupied . . .';

'They continued their eating . . .' or 'eating, they continued until . . .'.

Precisely as there are misrelated participles, so there are misrelated gerunds. 'The gerund', Dr Onions remarks, 'must be handled carefully with respect to its reference to the rest of the sentence. Do not write, e.g.:—"After *fighting* the flames for several hours the ship was abandoned." Here, *fighting* refers grammatically to "the ship", which makes nonsense; say: "After they (the crew . . .) had been fighting" or "After fighting the flames . . . the crew abandoned the ship".'

GERUND AND PARTICIPLE CONFUSED. (See also preceding article, last paragraph.) This example shows the error

and affords material for the correction of the error. 'He describes . . . how Smith rang him up at my place. But he does not realise how very odd it is that Smith should ring him there . . . McCabe *goes on telling* us how he went back to the studio, how Smith took him up to Robertson's room, how Robertson . . ., and how Smith suggested that . . .' Written as printed here, *goes on telling* connotes that McCabe had already begun to tell how he went back to the studio etc.; the context shows that not the gerund but the present participle is required, thus: 'McCabe *goes on, telling* how he went back . . .'.

gesture is inappropriately used for speech or behaviour indicative of intention, good- or ill-will. 'The United States Cabinet to-day sat . . . to consider a world-gesture which is intended, etc.'; 'The right gesture in jewellery'. (*O.E.D.*)

get. This verb always implies *to obtain*, *procure*, *acquire*, *attain* (to), *receive*; its use, especially in the past tense, *got*, to imply the mere fact of possession is the commonest of colloquialisms, but unnecessary and incorrect. See GOT.

gibberish. See JABBER.

gigantic, misused for *abundant*, *copious*, *heavy*. 'The waterfalls would have been a great nuisance if we had not been wet through, for the spray was so gigantic we couldn't have escaped a soaking.'

gilded and **gilt** are both correct as preterites and past participles, though *gilded* is now much the commoner. As adjective, *gilt* is now confined to the literal sense.

gipsy—gypsy; Gipsy—Gypsy. The word being a corrupted form of *Egyptian*, there is good ground for preserving the latter spelling; the former is, however, much more generally used; perhaps, as *The O.E.D.* suggests, because of the awkward appearance of the two *y*'s; the absence of this objection in the plural may account for the more frequent *Gypsies*. The capital *G* should be used when the people or language is meant (as *English, French*, etc.), but not when *gipsy, gypsy*, is adjectival.

girl-wife for a (*very*) *young wife* is shamefully overworked by those who write for the sensational section of the Press.

give for *form* or *constitute*, as in 'Language gives a guide to national character', is not only misleading but also a most damning indication of poverty of vocabulary.

given name. See CHRISTIAN NAME.

glamour. The noun of:

glamorous for *romantic* or (of a scene, a

night, etc.) *lovely* or (of a woman) *beautiful and attractive* or (of a way of life) *exciting* or *adventurous* or (of a love-affair or a flirtation) *amorous* belongs to advertising.

globe. See EARTH.

glycerine, glycerin. See '-ILE and -INE'.

goanna is popularly used in Australia for the monitor lizards (Varanidae); it is a corruption of the word *iguana*, though the true iguana is not found in that country.

go by the name of. See BY THE NAME OF.

good few, a; a good many. What is the difference? Cf. the entry at 'FEW and A FEW'. *A good few* is 'a fair number', but it is a dialectism and a colloquialism. *A good many* is also a colloquialism; its sense is 'a very fair number'. Both phrases are vague, but *a good many* represents a slightly larger number than *a good few*.

The American *quite a few* = 'a considerable number'.

got and have got. The too frequent slovenly substitution of *got* for other verbs expressive of *possession, acquiring, attainment, arrival, achievement*, etc., was noted as early as 1789 by the author of *Aristarchus; or, The Principles of Composition.*

'I GOT on Horseback within ten Minutes after I received your letter. When I GOT to Canterbury, I GOT a Chaise for Town. But I GOT wet through before I GOT to Canterbury, and I HAVE GOT such a Cold as I shall not be able to GET rid of in a Hurry. I GOT to the Treasury about Noon, but first of all I GOT shaved and drest. I soon GOT into the Secret of GETTING a Memorial before the Board, but I could not GET an Answer then, however I GOT Intelligence from the Messenger that I should most likely GET one the next Morning. As soon as I GOT back to my Inn, I GOT my supper, and GOT to Bed, it was not long before I GOT to Sleep. When I GOT up in the Morning, I GOT my Breakfast, and then GOT myself drest, that I might GET out in Time, to GET an Answer to my Memorial. As soon as I GOT it I GOT into the Chaise, and GOT to Canterbury by three: and about Tea Time, I GOT home. I have GOT Nothing particular for you, and so Adieu.'

'Every phrase in this Extract,' says the author, 'is in popular and perpetual Use; and it is far from my Wish to deprive the Vulgar, and the wealthy illiterate of so convenient an Abridgement of Terms.

On the Contrary, I recommend it to the pious care of Dr —— to compose a History of the World, on this elegant Plan of Abbreviation. All the Events, from the Birth of Time to his Majesty's Journey to Cheltenham may be detailed without the Aid of a single Verb in the English Language, the omnipotent GET excepted.

'This Verb is of Saxon Origin; *Arrival* at the Place of Destination, the primitive Idea; hence *Acquisition*; and hence *possession*. With the latter Idea, the Illiterate use it in Construction with *Have* —*I have* HAVE; in other Words, *I have* GOT. E.g., *I have got* a Father ninety Years old.

'For obvious reasons, *I have got a Father* must be restricted to *I possess*; consequently, it is absurd to prefix HAVE—*I have* POSSESS!!

'It may, therefore, be advanced as a general Rule,—when *Possession* is implied, it is vulgar to use HAVE in Construction with GOT.

'Permit me to add, our Ancestors have furnished us with innumerable Terms to express all the Ideas which the Vulgar affix to their FACTOTUM—GOT.

'Are you in Quest of any Thing? Do not exclaim with the Illiterate—I HAVE GOT it. But say—I have FOUND it or I HAVE it, HERE IT IS, etc.

'Again. "I *mounted* my Horse, or I *was on Horseback* within ten Minutes after I *received* your Letter: as soon as I *arrived* at Canterbury, I *engaged* (or *hired* or *stept into*) a Post Chaise for Town. I *was* wet through before I *reached* Canterbury, and I *have* (or *I have taken*) such a Cold as I shall not easily *remove* (or *cure*). I *arrived* at the Treasury about Noon, having previously shaved and drest. I soon *discovered* the Secret of *introducing* a Memorial to the Board; I could not, however, *obtain* an immediate Answer, but the Messenger told me, that I should probably *receive* one, next Morning. I *returned* to my Inn, *Supt, Went* to Bed, and *Slept* well. I *rose* early, and *drest* immediately, after *Breakfast* that I might be in Time for the Answer to my Memorial. As soon as I *received* it, I *took* Post Chaise, *reached* Canterbury by three, and my home about Tea Time. I *have* nothing particular to add."

'It was not my Design to paraphrase the Extract in Terms of Elegance, I only wished to prove, that Men of common Education might express the usual Occurrences of Life, without the Aid of GET and GOT and I HAVE GOT, etc.'

gotten is obsolete in Great Britain, except in the cliché, *ill-gotten gains*; but in the U.S.A., *gotten* (past participle) is preferred to *got*.

graduate is 'to admit (a candidate) to a university degree' or (of the candidate) 'to take a university degree'; *to be graduated* expresses a single nuance—that of 'to be admitted to a university degree'.

GRAMMAR. This is no place for a general discussion of grammar, for in this book a knowledge of the essentials of accidence and the simplicities of syntax has been assumed. Perhaps see Books I and II of my *English: A Course for Human Beings.*

For those who desire to examine 'the heart and soul' of grammar, there is one book that stands high above the rest: *The Philosophy of Grammar,* by Otto Jespersen. Jespersen is the author of *A Modern English Grammar on Historical Principles,* a masterly work, though less consecutively written than the warmly to be recommended *A Grammar of the English Language,* by George O. Curme and Hans Kurath.

Syntax has been admirably treated by Dr C. T. Onions in *An Advanced English Syntax.*

Of short grammars, Jespersen's *Essentials of English Grammar* is the best. A suggestive and entertaining little book is C. C. Boyd's *Grammar for Grown-Ups.*

A bird's-eye view of comparative grammar is afforded by E. A. Sonnenschein's *The Soul of Grammar*: 'to the advanced student grammar is a fascinating subject, just because he knows that he is dealing with an organic writing'. But however far advanced he is, the student must beware of falling into the error of supposing that there is such a thing as a universal grammar, applicable to every language. Grammar is based on language—the particular language concerned—and has no existence apart from language; grammar is a set of rules codifying usage, not a code superimposed on language and predetermining usage; in short, grammar must modify itself as language changes, grammar being made for man, not man for grammar.

Nevertheless, where grammatical rules make for a clarity that would disappear with the disappearance of the rules, it is better to preserve and maintain the rules, —until, at least, a simpler or more satisfactory rule is devised or evolved. For instance, to ignore the useful distinctions between *shall* and *will*, *that* and *who* (or *which*), is to set up ambiguity without any fully compensating gain.

grand as a passe-partout of admiration is to be avoided, not merely because it is a colloquialism (the adverb *grand*, 'He's doing grand', is, by the way, an illiteracy) but also and especially because it is not a precise term but a lazy man's substitute for thought. See also GRANDIOSE.

grandiloquent, magniloquent and **eloquent.** *Eloquent* is a favourable term; the other two are pejorative. *Magniloquent* means 'ambitious in expression'. *Grandiloquent* is applied to a person, his speech, his style, and it = 'characterized by swollen or pompous expression'. (*O.E.D.*)

grandiose is more particular, more specific than *grand*. *Grandiose* = 'producing an effect or impression of grandeur or greatness; characterized by largeness of plan or nobility of design', as in 'The simple and grandiose taste of the Hellenic architects'; also it = 'characterized by formal stateliness', a sense that is disparaging, as in 'Mr Urquiza entered first, with a strut more than usually grandiose', where the nuance is that of 'pompous' or 'aiming at grandeur'. (*O.E.D.*)

grateful and **gratified.** *Grateful* = 'feeling gratitude' and (only of things) 'pleasing to the mind or the senses' (a literarism); but *gratified* = 'pleased; 'satisfied, humoured, indulged', as in 'a gratified tone of voice', 'gratified acknowledgements', 'His vanity was gratified by the homage . . . paid him'. (*O.E.D.*)

gray—grey. Both are correct, and they are without real distinction of meaning, though certain writers have fancied a suggestion of lighter tint in *grey*, of darker in *gray*. [Webster prefers *gray*.]

great is an infelicity for *much* in such a context as the following: 'During the last few years great publicity has been given to the Physical Fitness Campaign'.

greater part. See MAJOR PORTION.

greatly for *largely* or *mainly* is catachrestic. 'There is little doubt that hatred borne by one nation towards another is greatly due to a lack of understanding of their respective racial characteristics.'

Grecian and **Greek.** *Grecian* is gradually being superseded by *Greek* in almost every sense of both the adjective and the noun. As adj., it survives only in *Grecian bend* and *Grecian knot, Grecian bather* and *Grecian netting,* all in specialized senses. In short, the adjective is now rare 'except with reference to style of architecture and facial outline'. As a noun, *Grecian* is extant in only three senses: (*a*) a person learned in the Greek language, a Greek scholar; (*b*) such a Jew of the Dispersion as spoke Greek, a Greek Jew; and (*c*) a boy in the highest form at Christ's Hospital, 'the Blue-Coat School'. (Based on *The O.E.D.*) *The Greeks* is now obligatory.

GREEK AND LATIN. To refrain from using Greek and Latin words when they are the best available, when indeed no others will perform the work that the Classical words will do, is childish. In science, philosophy, medicine, technology, they are inevitable.

On the immense number of current Latin words and phrases that an educated person must be familiar with, Sir Alan Herbert has eleven very useful pages, in *What a Word!*

grey. See GRAY.

grisly; grizzly; grizzled. *Grisly* = 'causing horror or terror', hence 'causing uncanny or extremely unpleasant feeling', 'grim', 'ghastly'; *grizzly* and *grizzled* = 'grey', esp. 'grey-haired'.

GROUP GENITIVE. The rule governing the use of the genitive (*boy's, boys'*; *woman's, women's*) is extended to any phrase that can be regarded as a unit and that is not of an inordinate length.

'The position of the genitive now', says Jespersen, 'is always immediately before the governing word, and this in [conjunction] with the regularity of the formation of the [genitive] case has been instrumental in bringing about the modern group-genitive, where the *s* is tacked on to the end of a word-group with no regard to the logic of the older grammar: *the King of England's power* (formerly 'the kinges power of England'), *the bride and bridegroom's return, somebody else's hat*, etc.' Dr Onions adduces *A quarter of an hour's ride* and continues with the necessary caution:—' [The group genitive] must not be extended beyond reasonable limits; such ludicrous phrasings as the following will be avoided: "*the father of the child's* remonstrances" (instead of "the remonstrances of the child's father"), "that's *the man I saw yesterday's son*", "that's *the passenger that missed the train's luggage*" ': with which it is interesting and instructive to compare Shakespeare's 'I do dine to-day at the father's of a certain pupil of mine' (cited by Onions).

grudge. See BEGRUDGE.

guarantee is noun and verb; **guaranty** is noun only. The former noun is general, legal and commercial; the latter, legal and commercial, is the more usual for 'the act of guaranteeing or giving a security' and 'something given or already existing as security'. Avoid *guarantee* and *guaranty* in the sense 'a guaranteeing party', i.e., a *guarantor*; the person to whom the guarantee (or guaranty) is given is the *guarantee*. Cf. WARRANT and WARRANTY.

guarantee for is catachrestic for *guarantee*, or for *vouch for*. 'Who could guarantee for Mr McCabe?'

guess is colloquial in the senses 'believe, think, suppose, expect'. In current Standard English its predominant senses are 'to estimate' (to guess a weight, a direction, a value, etc.) and 'to form an opinion or hypothesis respecting (some unknown state of facts), either at random or from indications admittedly uncertain; to conjecture', as in 'we may guess when its growth began' and *as I guess, so I guess, one may guess*.

gypsy. See GIPSY.

H

habitable, inhabit, inhabitable, uninhabitable. Respectively 'liveable-in', 'to live in', 'liveable-in', 'not liveable-in'. *Habitable* is nowadays applied mostly to houses or flats, *inhabitable* to countries.

hacienda. See RANCH.

had. See WOULD HAVE.

had is improperly used by Eric Partridge (*French Romantics' Knowledge of English Literature*, 1924) in the following: 'At the former date, A. de Pontmartin's father had a prefect of police say to him, etc'. The idiom is common in America, where a man introducing a friend may say: 'I'd like to have you shake hands with Mr So and So'; here *have* means *cause to*. The *O.E.D.* confirms this definition: 'To cause, procure, or oblige (a person to do something)', and extends it thus: 'To wish, will, require that something be done', and gives examples: 'I would have you make an essay to accomplish it'; 'I would not have it spoken about'. Now 'A. de Pontmartin's father' did not *will* or *cause* 'the prefect of police' to say something to him, but happened to be spoken to by that official. (W.B.) [*Webster's* does not discriminate against this usage and cites (under HAVE, 18) 'He had his leg broken'.]

had best ; had better. See WOULD BEST and WOULD BETTER.

had have ('If you had have come'). Redundant *have*; an error by no means confined to the illiterate. This construction, in which the *have* is intrusive and which has the still more illiterate variant *had of*, is not an error I should have signalized here, had it not been for the following sentence met with in a very good novelist, 'But then, thought Rome [an educated woman], should I have been any more understanding if I hadn't have happened to have been there that afternoon when Mark's name was mentioned'.

had rather. See WOULD RATHER.

had used to be for *had been* or *used to be*, or for preterite + *formerly* (before or after the verb), seems an odd mistake; but it is not so infrequent as the paragons would have us think. 'To Basil Woolrich, sitting in the room at the top of Rynox House which had used to be that of F.X., came the clerk Harris.'

hail and **hale** (v.). The former is 'to salute with "hail!"; to greet; to welcome'; hence, 'to call to (a ship, a person) from a distance in order to attract attention', but *hale* is 'to draw or pull', 'to drag or bring violently', as in 'He was haled to prison'. (*O.E.D.*)

half. See DEMI.

half a dozen and **half-dozen** in British usage are the better ways of writing these phrases. *The O.E.D.* gives them as equally good English. Whereas one says *a half-dozen*, one does not say *a half a dozen*, and *the half-dozen* is more idiomatic than *the half a dozen*. [*Webster's* hyphenates the adj. *half-dozen*, but not the noun phrase.]

half after (8 o'clock), **a**, is less usual than *half-past* (eight). The same applies to *a quarter after* (for *a quarter past*).

hallelujah. See ALLELUIA.

handfuls and **hands full.** Cf. BASKETFULS.

handicap is not to be used loosely as a perfect synonym for *hindrance*. *The O.E.D.* accepts as Standard English the figurative sense, 'any encumbrance or disability that weighs upon effort and makes success more difficult'.

hangar ; hanger. The former is used in only one sense, 'a shed for sheltering aircraft'.

hanged is used of capital punishment only ('He was hanged'—not *hung*—'yesterday'; 'The executioner hanged the criminal'). *Hung*, preterite and past participle, is applied to things, as in 'The picture was hung too low', and 'I hung the picture as high as I could'.

happiness should not be debased to the sense, 'pleasure'.

hardly and **scarcely** are virtual negatives. 'Hardly a man was there' and 'Scarcely a run was scored' are correct, but 'I didn't hardly (or, scarcely) know him' is incorrect. 'Touring arrangements have been made. Why? Nobody hardly tours in that country now' is another example of an error that is an illiteracy—a solecism—a damning social lapse.

hardly . . . than, like *scarcely . . . than*, is a frequent misconstruction. 'Hardly was Edward dead than a struggle began for the possession of the reins of power', Ransome, *History of England* (Nesfield); substitute *when* for *than*.—Cf. BARELY . . . THAN.

hari-kari is a misspelling and mispronunciation of the Japanese *hara-kiri*, a method of suicide sometimes practised in Japan.

harmless. See COMPARATIVES, FALSE.—Cf. the synonymous INNOCUOUS.

haste ; hasten. Keep the former as a noun, the latter as a verb.

hate is much stronger than *dislike*: do not, therefore, use them synonymously.

have. See POSSESS.

have a right to is catachrestic when = *ought to*. Herd happily cites the ludicrous 'He has a right to be hanged'. *Have a right to do* connotes privilege, not penalty.

have dinner. See DINE.

have got for *have*. 'I can truthfully say that I have not got an enemy in the world.'

he. See at 'THEY . . . HE'.

healthful, archaic for *healthy*, should be reserved for 'promoting or conducive to bodily health'—hence, '. . . to spiritual health'. (*O.E.D.*)

Heaven (capital *H*) is 'the habitation of God and his angels'; *the heavens* (small *h*) are 'that expanse in which the sun, moon, and stars are seen'. (*O.E.D.*)

heavenward is the adjective and preferable adverb, *heavenwards* a variant of the adverb.

Hebraic ; Hebrew. See SEMITIC.

hectic (adj.) 'applied to that kind of fever which accompanies consumption' (*O.E.D.*), is, because of the flush which it causes, misapplied to any state of excitement, as in 'We had a hectic time'.

help (it), with **can** or **could.** *Not*, though necessary to the sense, is often erroneously omitted, as in Newman, *Apologia*. 'Your name shall occur again as little as I can help, in these pages', the sense being

'—shall occur only when I cannot help (or prevent) it'.

help but, cannot. See BUT.

helpmate and **helpmeet.** Both of these words are applied especially to a wife or a husband; the latter is archaic.

hemi-. See DEMI-, fourth paragraph.

hence is sufficient; *from hence* is tautological. *Hence* is redundant in 'It won't be a long time hence, before we sail'.

henceforth and **thenceforth.** The former = 'from this time or point'; both have the connotation of *onwards*. Except in legal and formal contexts, they are obsolescent.

her, of and **of hers.** See 'OF HER—OF HERS'.

her's for *hers*, a frequent illiteracy. Cf. *it's* for *its*, *their's* for *theirs*, *your's* for *yours*, *our's* for *ours*.

hereabout; hereabouts. Both = 'in this neighbourhood'; usage appears to be adopting the latter.

heretofore and **theretofore.** See ARCHAISMS.

herself. See MYSELF.

hew—preterite, *hewed*—past participle, *hewn*: these are the correct forms.

hide—**hid**—**hidden** (or, now obsolescent, (**hid**). See also CACHE.

him, of. See GENITIVE, VAGARIES OF THE.

himself. See MYSELF.

Hindi and **Hindustani.** *Hindi*, the chief vernacular of northern India, is an Indo-Aryan language; it is divided into two groups, the Eastern Hindi dialects and the Western Hindi dialects. The most important Western Hindi dialect is Hindustani, which, containing—especially in its sub-dialect, Urdu—many words adopted from Arabic and Persian, is 'current as a lingua franca over nearly all India' (*Webster's*).

hindsight (or *hind-sight*) should be confined to the contrast of *hindsight* with *foresight*.

hire and **lease** and **let** and **rent.** Of these four verbs, only *let* (or *let out*) is univocal ('to grant the temporary possession and use of [property] to another in consideration of payments of money', i.e., of rent). The other three have opposite senses: (1) to *let*; (2) 'to pay rent for, to take or occupy by payment of rent'. In England *rent*, however, is now used mostly in the second sense: it is the usual opposite of *let*. *Hire* is now little used of land or houses, and it is applied mostly in sense 2. *Lease* is a formal term; the one who lets is the *lessor*, he who pays rent is the *lessee*.

historic; historical. The latter = 'of the nature of history' (*historical novel*); the

former = 'famous or important in history'.

hold up and **uphold.** Reserve the former for literal, the latter for figurative contexts.

holily is obviously much more economical than *in a holy manner*.

holocaust is 'destruction by fire': do not synonymize it with *disaster*. Moreover, it is properly an ecclesiastical technicality.

home is the residence of a family, a household; it should not be used as a synonym for *house*, as in 'Homes for Sale'.

home, be. To say that a person 'is home' for 'is at home' is slovenly and ambiguous.

homicide. See MURDER.

honester is equally acceptable with *more honest*, but most of us avoid *honestest* as being difficult to pronounce with dignity.

honorarium (plural, -*iums*; pedantically, -*ia*) is not synonymous with *salary*. Originally (as still) it was an honorary reward; thence it came to be, and predominantly it is, a fee for services rendered, esp. services rendered by a professional person (barrister, architect, doctor). Sometimes it is a complimentary fee paid to one who is not entitled to either salary or fee, as, e.g., to a non-professional club secretary.

honorary; hono(u)rable. The latter is applied to that which is worthy of honour; the former, apart from legal phrases, has these two allied senses: 'holding a title or position conferred as an honour either without emolument and without the usual duties or obligations on the one hand, the usual privileges on the other', as in *honorary colonel, honorary magistrate*, and 'rendered or conferred merely for the sake of honour', as in *honorary colonelcy*; the oldest sense is that of 'denoting—or bringing—honour; conferred (or rendered) in honour', as in 'The simple crown of olive, an honorary reward'. (*O.E.D.*)

hooves as plural of *hoof*. See SPOOF.

horrible, like *awful, dreadful, terrible*, is overdone. Don't. Above all, do not so shear it of its value that it becomes a mere equivalent of *disagreeable*.

host for *large quantity*. 'Frank had arranged for a host of provisions to be laid up in the larder here.' *Host* is properly a large number of individuals.

hot cup of cocoa, coffee, tea (etc.), is condemned by purists, who uphold *cup of hot cocoa* (etc.). The latter is more logical; but only at first sight.

how for *that* should be avoided except in indirect questions. Thus, 'He does not realise how very odd it is that Smith should ring him there' is correct and clear; but '[He] goes on telling me how he went back to the studio' is ambiguous for the intended meaning, which is 'that he went back to the studio', not 'in what manner' nor 'in what conveyance he went back to the studio'.—'I do not know how you contrive to make ends meet' is correct; but 'I told him how I had spent four years in France' is ambiguous, for it may mean either plain fact or coloured manner.

how, as, is vulgarly used for *that* or *whether*, e.g., 'He said as how he would be late tonight'.

however comes, not at the end of a sentence or clause ('He refused further refreshment, however'), but after the first significant unit, as in, 'He, however, did not think so' (emphasis on 'He'), 'He flinched, however, when the gun went off' (although he had shown himself calm up to that point), 'In the morning, however, nothing was done' (in contrast to the preceding afternoon), and 'Germane to my subject, however, is the misplacing of *but, however, though*'.

human, 'belonging to or characteristic of mankind'; **humane,** 'kind' or (of knowledge) 'Classical'.

humble-bee and **bumble-bee** have caused a 'big-end, little-end' and a century-old discussion among the inexpert. Both are correct.

humorous; humoristic. The latter should never be used in any sense or nuance of the former: *humoristic* = 'of or like a humorist', as in 'He had a remarkable humoristic talent', 'humoristic cynicism'. Note the difference in spelling; *humorist*, by the way, is preferable to *humourist*.

hurricane. See CYCLONE.

HYPERBOLE. *The O.E.D.* defines it as 'A figure of speech consisting in exaggerated or extravagant statement, used to express strong feeling or to produce a strong impression, and not intended to be understood literally'.

Here are two examples of good hyperbole:

Not in the regions
Of horrid hell can come a devil more
    damn'd
In evils, to top Macbeth;

I was all ear
And took in strains that might create a
    soul
Under the ribs of death.

But hyperbole may be incongruous or ludicrous; in this form, it has a

second name—Exaggeration or Over-Emphasis.

'Crime, shielded beneath the garb of outward apparent virtue, stalks abroad unblushingly at noon-day, in the midst of society, or riots under cover of darkness, in its secretly guarded haunts of infamy. No community is free from its contamination': Geo. P. Burnham, *Memoirs of the United States Secret Service.*

hypercritical (excessively or finically critical) is occasionally confused with *hypocritical.*

HYPHENATION. In the life of compound words there are three stages: (1) two separate words (*cat bird*); (2) a hyphenated compound (*cat-bird*); (3) a single word (*catbird*).

Apart from that general process of language, there are (*a*) many instances in which the hyphen is necessary; and (*b*) others in which there is an important distinction between a hyphenated compound and two separate words; and others (*c*) in which the hyphen, by being misplaced, sets up an error or an ambiguity.

(*a*) *The hyphen that is necessary—or, at least, advisable.*

'They were using it to mark straight lines for relaying some flagstones.' *Relaying* is intended.

That the hyphen is especially useful in objective combinations—i.e., combinations in which the first noun is the virtual object of the action denoted or connoted by the second noun—may be indicated by 'General Curley . . . known as "the Indian-fighter" ': one who fights the Indians; General Curley is obviously not 'the Indian fighter', an Indian that is a fighter.

In *Grammar for Grown-Ups,* C. C. Boyd quotes, 'Every dog loving man should buy a ticket for this show', and remarks that 'without a hyphen between *dog* and *loving* it looks as if the editor had expected the dogs to buy the tickets'.

(*b*) *Hyphenated compound and two separate words.*

Compare 'The author's tense-sequence' (sequence of tenses) 'is defective in this passage' with 'A tense sequence of events'—a sequence of tense events—'succeeded a dull sequence'.

Compare also *bull's-eye* (a sweetmeat) with *bull's eye* (the animal's eye), as in 'He hit the bull's eye with a bull's-eye'.

(*c*) *Hyphen misplaced.*

'I am an old cloathes-man' (*The*

Sessions Papers of the Old Bailey, 1773). The reporter should have written, '. . . an old-cloathes man', the reference being not to his age but to his profession.

In *The Times Literary Supplement* of April 8, 1939, appeared this very pertinent letter from Dr R. W. Chapman:—HYPHENS.

'Sir,—All students of typographical practice must have noticed the awkwardness which results when a hyphen is used to connect compounds not themselves hyphenated. Thus "The Chipping Norton-Stony Stratford road" might be thought by a stranger to mean the road that leads from Chipping to Stratford by way of Norton Stony. The example which follows is extreme in my experience because the expression is tripartite. A writer in the American *Publishers' Weekly* (Feb. 11, 1939) explains that Mr Stanley Morison believes that early printing types were influenced not only by manuscript but also by engraved or carved letters. "He would like to replace our present concept of a dual relationship calligrapher-typecutter with a new calligrapher-letter engraver-typecutter triangle." It needs an effort to realize that the three sides of this triangle are (1) calligrapher, (2) letter engraver, (3) typecutter.'

Here I have merely skimmed the surface of Hyphenation. In the Fowlers' *The King's English*, there is an excellent short account; in *Modern English Usage*, an admirable long account. See also a long, systematic chapter in my *You Have a Point There: A Guide to Punctuation and Its Allies*, 1953. [American readers may wish to consult *Webster's* dictionary at the entry *compound*, n.]

hyphenize is inferior both to *hyphenate* and to *hyphen*; one would do well to adopt *hyphen*.

I

I easily becomes egotistical, but it is preferable to 'your humble servant', 'the undersigned', 'your uncle', and all other such puerilities.

-ible and **-able**. The former represents Latin *-ibilis*, as in *audible, flexible, legible, permissible, possible, terrible, visible*. It is often displaced by *-able* in such Latin words as have come through French, also in such words as are regarded as having been formed immediately on an English verb: *convertable* for the usual *convertible, dividable, readmittable, referable, tenable*.

In phrases, only *-able* is permissible: *come-at-able, get-at-able*.

-ic and **-ical**. In general, the *-ical* form is obsolescent: except in certain formulas, *-ic* is fast dispossessing *-ical*, as in *comic(al), terrific(al), fantastic(al)*. There is, however, often a nuance involved, as in *ethic, ethical*; *economic, economical*; *historic, historical*.

ice coffee, ice tea. Incorrect for *iced coffee, iced tea*. Cf. the following entry.

ice-water; iced water. The former is correct only in the sense 'water formed by melting a piece or block of ice'.

idea, misused for *principle* or *assumption*. 'Four kinds of explanations which people give to justify their beliefs: 1. *The impulsive*: Much used by primitive man in the idea that any explanation was better than none.'

idea of (or **notion of)** for *idea* (etc.) *that* is occasionally ambiguous, as in 'This ties in with Korzybski's central idea of knowledge as structural'.

ideal (adj.) does not admit of comparison. 'I think it is one of the most ideal spots in the whole of Scotland.' Moreover, *ideal* is catachrestic when it is used as a synonym of 'favourite', as in 'My ideal type of house is a bungalow'.

identification. See IDENTITY.

identify for *connect*; a gross catachresis: as in, 'He has been identified with church work for many years'.

identity, 'a person's personality and individuality', must not be confused with *identification*, 'the establishment of a person's name and individuality'.

ideology. A vogue word.

IDIOM AND IDIOMS.

'If there is one thing more than another that I have learnt in Fleet Street it is never to underrate the importance of usage. It is blind and often illogical, but when it makes its mind up nothing can withstand it; and whatever else may be said of it, it has done much to make our language the richest in the world.' Frank Whitaker.

The best account of idioms is that in Dr Pearsall Smith's *English Idioms*.

Generically, *idiom* is 'used . . . to describe the form of speech peculiar to a people or nation'. Particularly, *idioms* are 'those forms of expression, of grammatical construction, or of phrasing, which are peculiar to a language, and approved by its usage, although the meanings they convey are often different from their grammatical or logical signification' (L. P. Smith).

'The idiosyncrasy of English, like that

of other languages, is perhaps most strikingly exemplified in the use of prepositions. Prepositional usage in all languages contains . . . much that is peculiar and arbitrary; the relations to be expressed by prepositions are often so vague and indefinite, that many times one might seem logically just as right as another, and it is only "that tyrannical, capricious, utterly incalculable thing, idiomatic usage", which has decreed that this preposition must be used in this case, and that in another' (Jespersen, *Progress in Language*). For instance, 'we tamper *with*, but we tinker *at*; we find fault *in* a person, but find fault *with* him; we act *on* the spur of the moment, but *at* a moment's notice; we are insensible *to*, but are unconscious *of*; we say *for* long, but *at* length. . . . Americans speak of getting *on* or *off* a train, in England of getting *in* or *out of* it; "*up to* time" is the English idiom, "*on* time" the American. The difference is one of usage; either is correct from the point of view of grammar.' Compare such terse prepositional phrases as *by fits, for ever, for good, in fact, in general.*

A large class of English idioms consists of phrases 'in which two words are habitually used together for the sake of emphasis', e.g., *hue and cry, fits and starts, free and easy, hard and fast; by and by, over and over, round and round; bag and baggage, safe and sound, spick and span; high and dry, fair and square; as bold as brass, as large as life, as thick as thieves.*

Perhaps the most interesting class of idioms is that in which metaphor renders the idiom more telling, more effective. Originally confined to that trade or profession, sport or game, which originated them, these idioms 'are found to be capable of a wider use; . . . and little by little the most vivid and useful of these phrases make their way into the common vocabulary and come to be understood by all'. From sailors we get *take in a reef, turn adrift, cut the painter, on the rocks, when one's ship comes home,* and a host of others; soldiers have passed on to us such phrases as *take alarm, pass muster, at close quarters, on the qui vive, to hang fire,* and *lock, stock and barrel*; from hunting come *to hunt down, to give tongue, to lead a dog's life, to have a hair of the dog that bit you, a run for one's money, out of hand, with a heavy hand,* etc.; domesticity yields *to get on like a house on fire, next door to, on the shelf, a drop in the bucket, as stiff as a poker, to boil over, to butter up.*

if, omission of. 'And yet, come to the rights of it, he'd no business there at all'; this abbreviation of *if you come* is slovenly.

if for *whether* is always wrong and often ambiguous, but the mixture of the two is wrong, ambiguous—and amusing. 'She was wondering if Rupert would like an heir, and whether it was time that they moved from the doll's house in Bourdon Street into a house of more sensible proportions, and if Makepeace would keep a supply of records from *Private Lives* and the best honey and produce them placidly on a tray whenever they were needed.' A particularly illuminating example is afforded by the second *if* in 'Rex was still speaking in an absent fashion, as if he were working round to a point and wondering if to make it'. [Many American grammarians grant the use of *if* for *whether* in informal style if the tag *or not* is omitted.]

if is often misused by competent but hasty writers, where the right word is *and* or *but* (as though I should have written 'by competent *if* hasty writers'); thus, 'Which picture . . . is likely to be nearest the truth?—that neat, simplified one which our descendants will master from their text-book histories, or that more complicated affair with which we are so painfully, if confusedly, familiar'. *If*, in such a sentence, implies a contrast between qualities unexpectedly found together, whereas no such contrast is seen in 'painfully' and 'confusedly'.

if and when is usually tautological for *when* (or *if*), as in 'I'll pay when I see you', 'I'll shout if it's necessary'.

if need be is correct with Present ('He always does that, if need be') or Future ('He will always do that, if need be'); but with Past, the correct form is *if need were* ('He always did that, if need were'). Those who feel that, whereas *if need be* is literary, *if need were* is both literary and archaic (although it is not archaic), may, if they wish, use *if necessary*, which does away with the verb in the conditional, in all tenses.

When *if* = 'when', the indicative (*if need is, if need was,* etc.), not the subjunctive, is required.

if not, ambiguity of. An example is quoted by Sir Alan Herbert (*What a Word!*): 'England's Captain . . . played one of the greatest, if not the most attractive innings of his career . . .' (*The Observer*). He invites us to think this over: 'Was the innings "the most attractive" (as well as "one of the greatest") or not? Honestly, I do not know.'

-ify is incorrect for *-efy, -ifaction* incorrect for *-efaction*, in the following verbs and their corresponding abstract nouns:
    liquefy, putrefy, rarefy, stupefy, torrefy, and in certain other scientific terms.

ignoramus. See PLURALS, UN-ENGLISH.

ignorant. See ARTLESS and ILLITERATE.

ilk, of that. *Of that ilk* means 'of the same (estate)'; thus *Guthrie of that ilk* means 'Guthrie of Guthrie' (Ackermann). Often erroneously used in journalism for 'of that family, clan, class or kind'.

ill and **sick**, as applied to persons. Both are used predicatively; the former, rarely otherwise: 'He is ill, or sick'. But 'He is a sick man'—not, in current usage, 'He is an ill man'. As applied to other than living things, *sick* has special reference to nausea, as 'a sick headache'. Cf. 'SICK and SICKLY'.

ill of. See PREPOSITIONS WRONGLY USED.

iilegible. See UNREADABLE.

illicit and **elicit.** See ELICIT.

ILLITERACIES, FALSE. See FALSE ILLITERACIES.

illiterate and **ignorant.** The former = 'not knowing how to read or write', the latter = 'markedly deficient in knowledge'. An illiterate person is not necessarily ignorant.

illude, illusion, confused with *allude, allusion,* and *elude, elusiveness.* The indiscriminate fall into these errors. To *allude* is to 'refer casually' (to); to *elude* is 'to evade', and *illude* is 'to trick'. See also DELUDE.

illustration and **example.** *Illustration,* in one of its derivative senses, does = *example* or *instance;* but it is more dignified than *example* and has a subconnotation of 'image or picture', as in 'An illustration of the principle which runs throughout nature', 'Charles James Fox afforded an excellent illustration of bohemianism-cum-integrity'. (*O.E.D.*)

imaginary; imaginative. Respectively 'imagined', esp. in the sense 'unreal'; and 'endowed with (a powerful) imagination', 'pertaining to the imagination as a mental faculty', 'bearing evidence of high creative force' (e.g., *an imaginative poem*). (*O.E.D.*)

imagine for *to suppose* is not bad, but rather familiar English.

imbue, misused for *instil.* One is *imbued* or *inspired with*: one *instils* something *into* a person. Incorrect is 'The courage he imbued into his men'; equally incorrect is

'The address instilled every citizen with fresh confidence'.

immanent, imminent, eminent. These and their corresponding nouns and adverbs are often interconfused; for their different meanings, see any good dictionary.

immigrant and **emigrant.** See EMIGRANT . . .

immoral. See AMORAL.

immortal. See DEATHLESS.

immunity and **impunity.** Apart from its technical senses in Law, Ecclesiasticism, Medicine, *immunity* = 'exemption from any usual liability; freedom from anything evil or harmful', as in 'immunity from pain'. *Impunity* is less extensive: it = 'exemption from penalty (e.g., a fine) or a punishment (e.g., imprisonment)', and, in a weakened sense, 'exemption from loss or injury, security': 'In England, one can't commit murder with impunity'. (*O.E.D.*)

impecunious is 'penniless, in want of money'; not 'unthrifty'.

imperative and **imperious.** In 1794, Gouverneur Morris wrote the useful words, 'Subject to the imperative, and too often the imperious, mandates of a committee'. The basic sense of *imperative* is 'of or like or expressing a command', hence 'peremptory' ('He spoke in an imperative tone'); hence 'urgent' or 'obligatory', as in 'The condition of the sick and wounded made it imperative to ship them to Egypt'. The predominant current sense of *imperious* is 'overbearing, domineering, dictatorial', as in 'A proud, imperious aristocrat, contemptuous . . . of popular rights'. (*O.E.D.*)

implement, 'to complete, to fulfil' a contract, a promise, a condition, has been so much used by the cultured since ca. 1925, that it has acquired the stamp of a literarism. Avoid it.

implicit and **explicit.** *Implicit* is 'implied though not expressly stated; naturally or necessarily involved in, or inferable from, something else', as in 'Proofs are either implicit and indirect, or explicit and direct'; hence 'virtually or potentially contained *in*', as in 'The blessing implicit in all heaven's chastenings'. *Explicit* is '(of utterances) distinctly expressing *all* that is meant' (*explicit promises*); hence '(of persons) saying all that one means'. (*O.E.D.*)

imply for **infer.** See INFER.

important must not be used as though it were a mere synonym of *chief, main, principal.* 'The important differences between Association football and Rugby football are in the number of players who compose a team, the shape of the ball, the size of the pitch, the method of scoring, the carrying of the ball in Rugby football, the heading of the ball in Association football.'

impossible. A thing is either possible or impossible; therefore 'more possible' is catachrestic for 'more feasible' or 'more practicable'.

impracticable and **impractical.** The former = 'that cannot be effected or dealt with; unmanageable, unserviceable', as in 'an impracticable road', 'an impracticable plan'; the latter = 'unpractical', as in 'He was a great poet but an impractical man' (but see also UNPRACTICABLE).

impressible and **impressive** are occasionally confused; so are the adverbs *impressibly* and *impressively*. *Impressible* = 'easily impressed'; *impressive* = 'likely or sure to impress others'.

impromptu; extempore. Both are adverbs = 'without preparation or premeditation'; only *impromptu* is a noun; both are adjectives, *impromptu* being 'improvised', as in 'an impromptu speech', hence 'makeshift', as in 'an impromptu raft'. An *extempore* speech may have been prepared, but not to the extent of being written down or memorized: it is not read, nor has the speaker any notes. *Extempore* is more usual than *extemporary*.

impunity. See IMMUNITY.

in and **at.** Concerning prepositional idioms, Pearsall Smith has posed the distinction better than I've seen it put anywhere else: 'More interesting are the cases where the difference of usage is not really arbitrary, but may express a shade of meaning which we are ourselves perhaps unconscious of. A curious instance of this is the way we use the prepositions *in* and *at* with the names of places. We say some one is *in* London, *in* Rome, *in* Paris, but usually *at* Oxford, *at* Rouen. The general rule is that we use *in* for large cities and capitals, *at* for smaller places'; (in a footnote) 'Shakespeare used *at* London, . . . when London was a smaller place than it is now'. He continues with the caution that, 'we commonly use *in* rather than *at* even for a small place if we ourselves are there, probably because then it bulks more largely in our imagination'.

in- and **un-** in adjectives; **in** and **un** as prefixes. In general, **in** is the prefix that goes with words of Latin origin or with such words of French origin as spring from Latin; *un* is the prefix that goes with the words from Old English, Scandinavian,

German. Thus, *infelicitous*, but *unhappy*. But the influence of *un* is so strong that it is attached to many words of Latin origin: *unfortunate*.

in for *into*. 'Plane dives in reservoir'; 'I went in the Perla [a café], and sat down at a table'. Cf. the opposite error (*into* for *in*).

in for *within* causes ambiguity; e.g., 'I can get up in five minutes'.

in as much as, in so much as, in so far as may be written *inasmuch as, insofar as, insomuch as*, but not *in asmuch as, in somuch as, in sofar as*. The usual modern forms are *inasmuch as* and *insomuch as*; but *in so far as. In so far as* = 'in such measure or degree as', 'to such extent that'; *insomuch as* (slightly obsolescent) is virtually co-extensive with *inasmuch as*, which = *in so far as* (as here defined), but also = 'in proportion as' or 'according as', hence, 'in that', 'considering that', 'since', 'because'.—Nor can *in so far* (etc.) be made equivalent to *in so far as* (etc.): 'Winning this election meant nothing to me except in so far it was a fight'.

in behalf of. See BEHALF OF.

in comparison of. See PREPOSITIONS WRONGLY USED.

in consequence of. See CONSEQUENCE OF.

in despite of. See at DESPITE.

in excess of is not to be used indiscriminately for *more than*, as in 'The fee was in excess of £5'.

in my opinion. See OPINION.

in respect to. See PREPOSITIONS WRONGLY USED.

in spite of. See at DESPITE.

in the circumstances. See CIRCUMSTANCES.

in the nature of for *about* or *approximately*. 'We are communicating with the Company to ascertain what rate of interest they charge and the amount they would be prepared to advance which we imagine would be in the nature of £450 if required.'

in view of the fact that is not quite the same as *in that*: to confuse them is to destroy a useful distinction. How oddly sounds this sentence: 'Both games are good for character in view of the fact that they both call for team work.'

inapt, 'inappropriate', hence 'unskilful, awkward', is preferable to *unapt*; *inept* is the word to use for inappropriate speech, tone, allusions, and for absurd or foolish actions, consequences, as in *inept interference*. The corresponding nouns are *inaptitude, ineptitude*.

inasmuch as. See IN AS MUCH AS.

inaugurate, 'to begin formally or ceremonially', is grandiose for *begin*.

incapable connotes innate or permanent lack of ability: *unable* connotes inability 'in a specific situation or at a specific time': 'He is incapable of doing such a thing' and 'He is unable to do it'.

incessant, 'unceasing, ceaseless' (actions; persons), is not to be used for *everlasting*.

incident (adj.) and **incidental**. *Incident* is 'likely or tending to befall or affect; hence, naturally appertaining or attached *to*', either with *to* ('The physical weaknesses incident to human nature'), or absolutely ('The Puerto Rico expedition, and the incident aggressive steps taken in the campaign'). Do not use it in the senses of *incidental*, which = 'casual, fortuitous', as in 'Even corruptness may produce some incidental good', and (of a charge or expense) 'incurred apart from the primary disbursement', as in 'The house rent, and the incidental charges of a family'. Do not use *incidental* in the senses attaching to *incident*. (*O.E.D.*)

incidently for *incidentally* is commoner than one might think.

inclined for *likely* (or *apt*), when it is applied to things, is a usage to be avoided, as in 'They wrote the truth, which, though interesting, is inclined to shock us'.

inclosure. See ENCLOSE, ENCLOSURE.

including. See CONJUNCTIONS, DISGUISED.

incom'parable and **uncompa'rable**. See UNCOMPARABLE; also COMPARATIVES, FALSE.

INCOMPLETE INFINITIVE. See 'TO for *to* + infinitive'.

inconsequent; inconsequential. The two senses of *inconsequential*, 'characterized by inconsequence of reasoning, thought, or speech', hence 'of no consequence or importance', are covered by *inconsequent*, which is to be preferred in the former sense but is rare in the second—but then, so is *inconsequential*.

increase over. See DECREASE OVER.

incredible, incredulous, uncreditable. See CREDIBLE . . .

incumbent. See RECUMBENT.

indestructible. See COMPARATIVES, FALSE.

indexes. See INDICES.

indicated, be, is not good English for *advisable* or *that has been advised*, as in 'Prompt action is indicated'.

indices; indexes. The former is obligatory in Mathematics and Science; *indexes* is correct for 'an index of names, subjects, etc.'; in all other senses, *indices* is now the more usual plural.

indict and **indite** are pronounced alike, but the former = 'to accuse', whereas the latter = 'to write'.

indigestible and **indigestion**, but **undigested**.

INDIRECT SPEECH. See REPORTED SPEECH.

indiscreet and **indiscrete**. See DISCREET . . .

indiscriminate. See 'UNDISCRIMINATING and INDISCRIMINATE'.

indite. See INDICT . . .

individual is not synonymous with *person*; it connotes a person as an entity—as distinct from a class.

individually is often used unnecessarily.

indoor is the adjective, **indoors** the adverb.

indorse and **approve**. The former is not to be used for the latter.

indorse and **endorse**. The form *endorse* is preferred in English commerce, *indorse* in English legal and statutory use; in the U.S.A., *indorse* is used—and recommended—to the exclusion of *endorse*.

indulge, misused for *satisfy*. 'Amateur theatricals indulge my real bent.'

indulge in; engage in. The former is catachrestic when used for the latter.

industrial; industrious. Respectively 'connected with industry' and 'diligent'.

inebriety is 'now chiefly applied to habitual drunkenness'. *Dipsomania* (violent or persistent drunkenness) is a stronger word.

inept. See INAPT.

inevitable has come to have what philologists term a pejorative connotation and what others call an unfavourable sense. It is, therefore, out of place in the following sentence: 'The most dramatic event was [Lord] Hawke's intrepidity in dropping Peel . . . when it would certainly rob Yorkshire of almost inevitable championship': substitute *certain* for *inevitable*.

inexplainable; inexplicable. Both mean 'that cannot be explained'; but the latter has what the former has not, an additional nuance, 'unaccountable'.

infant, child; baby (poetic and archaic: **babe**). In general use, an *infant* is a child in arms (*babe in arms* is the set phrase); in law, a minor (a person under 21). A *child*, in general use, is under fourteen or, more logically, below the age of puberty; in law, (one of) the offspring; a *baby* is a child still at the breast or on the bottle.

infectious and **contagious**. A *contagious* disease is one that is spread by actual contact, either with the person or with some object that has been in contact with him; an *infectious* disease is spread by germs, in the air or in water.

infer for *imply*. *Infer* is 'to deduce'; *imply* is 'to include in reality, to express indirectly: to mean'; also 'to hint'. ' "I had a detailed report from Penfold Travers. ... Very terse indeed. ... He inferred we were all blockheads in Bombay" ', exemplifies the misuse.

inferior (or **superior**) **than** is a gross, yet alarmingly frequent error for *inferior* (or *superior*) *to*. Nesfield quotes 'A man of far inferior abilities than Bismarck'.

inferiority complex. See COMPLEX.

infinite is a dignified word; an uncomparable adjective: do not debase it to equality with '(very) great' or 'vast', as in 'His infinite worries caused him to become a victim of insomnia'.

infinitely small is loose, infelicitous English. *Infinitesimal* is the word required.

INFINITIVE, SPLIT. See SPLIT INFINITIVE.

inflammable and **inflammatory.** The former is applied to that which (fig., that person who) is combustible (or can easily be set fire to); the latter, to that which causes the fire; especially if it is particularly likely to cause it; hence, to 'stimulating' (liquors).

inflection and **inflexion.** See '-ECTION and -EXION'.

informant; informer. Respectively, anyone who gives information on a stated occasion, and one who lays information against another.

-ing for **-ed.** Of this misuse ('I want my hair cutting', 'Do you want your car washing?'), 'Jackdaw' in *John o' London's Weekly*, Jan. 6, 1939, remarks that the examples (and the practice) 'seem to halt somewhere between idiom and idiocy; I leave them there'. There is confusion with 'My hair needs cutting' and 'Does your car need washing?', where *cutting* and *washing* are gerunds, and perhaps also with 'The cathedral was building', i.e., a-building. [Unknown in America.]

ingenuous, 'innocent, artless', is often confused with *ingenious*, 'clever at contrivance'.

inhabitable. See HABITABLE.

inherent and **innate.** The latter (properly 'inborn', hence 'native' to a person, 'natural') is no longer used for the former. *Inherent* = 'existing in something as a permanent attribute; belonging to the intrinsic nature of that which is spoken of'; hence, 'intrinsic, indwelling'; hence 'essential', hence 'vested (*in*)', as in 'The supreme authority is inherent in the legislative assembly'. (*O.E.D.*)

inhibit and **prohibit.** In Ecclesiastical Law, *inhibit* is to forbid or interdict; in general use, it is to restrain, check, prevent, stop, as in 'The reflex actions of the spinal cord may, by appropriate means, be inhibited'; in modern psychology, an *inhibition* is 'a (or the) restraining or checking of a thought or an action by the (unconscious) will'. *Prohibit*, in general use, is to forbid, as in 'The law prohibits larceny': cf. 'Fear can inhibit a man from action'. (*O.E.D.*)

inhibition; (less) inhibited. Thanks to the Freudians, we have, since about 1910 in scientific and since about 1918 in cultured circles, heard almost too much about the over-inhibited person and about his (and other people's) inhibitions. An *inhibition* is one's shrinking, whether instinctive or habit-produced, from a forbidden action; nowadays it is often, by the devotees of the cult of self-expression and self-realization, applied to the dictates and the promptings of a natural modesty and a decent self-restraint.

initial for *primary* is feeble.

initiate, 'to begin, to introduce, to originate', is a dignified word. Do not use it as an easy synonym for *begin*. Its predominant sense is, 'to admit (a person) with due rites to a society, etc.', hence, 'to instruct in the elements of a subject, a practice', as in 'to initiate into freemasonry'.

injured. See DAMAGED.

inmost; innermost. The latter = 'furthest within', as in 'The third and innermost barrier' and 'innermost thoughts'; but both spatially and figuratively ('most intimate or secret'), *inmost* is preferable and more usual. (*O.E.D.*)

innate. See 'INHERENT and INNATE'.

inquire, inquiry. See ENQUIRE; also QUERY.

inquisitor is now rare except in its historical connexion with the Spanish Inquisition.

insensible, like *insensitive*, is now constructed with *to*.

insert in; insert into. The former emphasizes the general idea of the verb, the latter the inthrusting. *Insert in* = 'place in', whereas *insert into* rather = 'introduce into'. The former, in short, is static rather than dynamic; the latter is indubitably dynamic.

inside of. See OUTSIDE OF.

insignia is a plural.

insignificant does not mean 'small', but 'unimportant'.

insinuate, now a pejorative, should not be flattened to equivalence with *to suggest.*

insipid. See VAPID . . .

insofar as; insomuch as. See IN AS MUCH AS.

insoluble and **insolvable.** The former is much the more general.

inspect is 'to look closely into or at; to examine', not merely 'to see', as in 'Many citizens wish to inspect the new pool'.

instance (n.). See EXAMPLE.—As a verb, it is not rare in the sense, 'to cite as an instance or example', as in 'I may instance olive oil, which is mischievous to all plants'.

instance where ('This is an instance where a doctor is powerless') is incorrect for *instance in which.* Cf. EXAMPLE WHERE.

instant (n.). See 'MINUTE and MOMENT'.

instanter (instantly) is properly a legal term; its use in other contexts is—except perhaps as a humorous term—to be discouraged. Some good people employ it as an elegancy.

instead of for *than for* or *than with* is a strange error—not at all rare. 'The poor chap would probably be fifty times better off with a thousand pounds now instead of a lot more an unknown number of years hence.'

instil. See IMBUE.

instructional and **instructive.** Both = 'educational' and 'conveying instruction or information', but the former stresses the teaching, the latter the information imparted. 'An instructional course for young officers may be instructive' or informative, interestingly educative.

insuccess. See UNSUCCESS.

insurance. See ASSURANCE.

insure. See ENSURE.

integrate; integration. 'Integration of personality' has long been a commonplace among psychologists; in politics and sociology, *integrate* and *integration* appeared, as counters, early in 1942 and have done much damage since those dark days. On June 29, 1942, 'Peterborough' (literally a multiple personality) of *The Daily Telegraph* delivered himself of this now-as-then timely and satiric verdict. 'After a noteworthy career of some seven years the word "co-ordination" is fast becoming demoded in the best political quarters. Any M.P. who wants to keep abreast of the times is now careful to speak of "integration". So much is the word to the fore in Ministerial statements and Whitehall announcements that I suspect a co-ordinated—I mean integrated—move to secure its adoption. It has obvious advantages. It saves a hyphen, to say nothing of a letter.'

intelligent (of persons), 'having the faculty of understanding', especially in a high degree, or (of things) 'displaying that faculty'; *intelligible*, (of either persons or things) 'easily understood; comprehensible'; *intellectual*, 'relating to the intellect'. *Intellectual* should not be used as a synonym of 'learned'. The old gag that 'An intellectual is not necessarily intelligent' is made possible only by this catachresis.

intensely for *very* must be used cautiously. One may say 'intensely hot (or cold)', even 'intensely unpleasant', but not 'intensely wealthy'.

intentionally. See ADVISEDLY.

intently is sometimes misused for *intensely*, as in ' "Don't push your face so close to mine", Nigel begged. "I dislike your moustache intently" '.

inter = 'between' or 'among', as in *intercede, intersection*; *intra* = 'within', as in *intramural, intravenous.*

intercalate. See 'INTERJECT and INTERPOLATE'.

interest. See INTRIGUE.

interesting. This passe-partout adjective is to be used very sparingly and, even when used, it must be only after much thought. If you mean 'puzzling', say so; if 'dramatic', say *dramatic*; if 'unusual', then *unusual*; if 'important', then *important*; if 'full of character or incident or implication(s)', then, for the sake of the right word, use the right words!

interject and **interpolate.** The former, intransitive, is to interrupt a conversation; the latter, transitive, is to insert something in a script or a publication—or indeed in a conversation, but without the abruptness or rudeness connoted by *interject*. To *intercalate* is to insert (a day) in a calendar or—a transferred use —to insert, in a series, something extraneous.

into for *in*. 'A far larger number [of compositions], cast (so to speak) into the same mould, have wearied the public.' The error arises from the two meanings of 'cast' and from some ambiguity in the use of 'mould'. Another good example is 'He had understood at the beginning but failed to understand now as the threads ran away, on their own, into various directions'.

intolerable, 'unbearable' (hence, 'excessive'); **intolerant**, 'unwilling—or unable —to endure (something specified)', 'dis-

posed to persecute those who differ'.
(*O.E.D.*)

intoxicated. See 'DRUNK (adj.); DRUNKEN'.

intra. See INTER.

intrigue and **intriguing**, 'to interest', 'to
arrest the attention' and 'interesting' or
'arresting', are to be avoided: not only
are they unnecessary, but they are
wrongly derived from the French, for in
that language *intriguer* means 'to puzzle',
'to exercise the wits (of a person)';
intrigue and *intriguing* became vogue
words in Britain in 1934 or 1935. They
came from the U.S.A., as two quotations
may serve to indicate. 'I should hate
to think,' writes Maurice Acklom in *The*
(American) *Bookman* of April, 1919, 'we
are all of us being baffled or intrigued
(*intrigued*—that is indeed a word which
Sophia Kerr might well have added to
her "detestable" list in the February number)'; and 'This little flurry in crime has
proved rather interestin', or, as the
magazine writers say, intriguing—beastly
word' (S. S. Van Dine, *The Benson
Murder Case*, 1926).

intrude, misused for *obtrude* (to which the
adjective is *obtrusive*). 'She was . . . a perfect companion, docile and admiring,
never intruding her own personality.'

invalid; invalidated; invalided. *Inval'id* =
'not valid'; and *in' valid* = '(a person) that
is ill', whence the pun 'An invalid
invalid'; *invalidated*, 'rendered not valid;
null and void' (e.g. *invalidated evidence*);
invalided = 'rendered—or accounted—
an invalid; disabled by illness or injury',
as in 'Invalided out of the Army'.

invaluable, like *priceless*, now means
'valuable to a high degree'; the senses
'without value', 'having no (high) price'
are obsolete. The opposite of *invaluable*
is *valueless*; that of *priceless*, is *worthless*.

invective. See SATIRE.

invent. See DISCOVER.

inverse. See CONVERSE.

Inverted Commas to Indicate Slang. See
SLANG, Section III, last paragraph.

invite for (an) *invitation* is incorrect and
ill-bred and far too common.

involved by. See PREPOSITIONS WRONGLY
USED.

invulnerable, like *absolute* and *perfect* (see
COMPARATIVES, FALSE), is a superlative:
one can say 'almost (or, virtually) invulnerable' 'well nigh absolute', 'almost
perfect', but, as one cannot say 'more
absolute' or 'rather (or, more) perfect',
so one cannot say 'rather invulnerable'.

inward, inwards. The latter is adverb only
('with scales turned inwards', 'duties paid

inwards'); the former, both adverb (less
usual than *inwardly* and *inwards*) and adjective ('inward vitality').

IRISH BULLS. See BULLS.

IRONY. 'Irony consists in stating the
contrary of what is meant, there being
something in the tone or the manner to
show the speaker's real drift', Alexander
Bain.

Bain gives many examples; several will
suffice.

Job's address to his friends, 'No doubt
but ye are the people, and wisdom shall
die with you'; the Mark Antony oration
('honourable men') in *Julius Caesar*;
Swift's *The Tale of a Tub, The Battle of the
Books*, and *Gulliver's Travels*, all three for
sustained irony; Bentham's constant
references to English law as a 'matchless
institution'; in such commonplaces as
'a superior person', '*too* charming!', 'It
never entered his wise head'.

Dramatic irony is that which consists
in a situation—not in words; or rather,
not in words alone, but in words plus
situation; when an audience or reader
perceives a point that the characters concerned do not perceive.

Irony must not be confused with sarcasm, which is direct: sarcasm means
precisely what it says, but in a sharp or
bitter manner: it is the instrument of
indignation, a weapon of offence, whereas irony is one of the vehicles of wit. In
Locke's 'If ideas were innate, it would
save much trouble to many worthy
persons', *worthy* is ironical; the principal
clause as a whole is sarcastic—as also is
the complete sentence. Both are instruments of satire.

irreligious. See UNRELIGIOUS.

irrespective of; irrespectively of. Usage
tends to prefer the former, where, probably, *irrespective* has adverbial force.
Where there is no *of*, *irrespectively* is
obligatory.

irruption and **eruption** are often confused.
A safe rule in such words is that the
initial *ir* signifies *in*; the *e, out.*—Cf.
IMMIGRANT, EMIGRANT.

is (or are) to—like *was* (or *were*) *to*—
followed by an infinitive, is an ambiguous
construction. Take 'He is to set a high
standard, I believe': the context may or
may not remove the ambiguity, but the
sentence as it stands means either 'He is
destined to set a high standard—such is
my belief', or 'He has been instructed to
set a high standard—or so I've been told',
or 'It is planned (or, ardently desired) by
others—he perhaps unknowing—that he

shall set a high standard', or even 'He intends, I understand, to set a high standard'. Consider also 'He was to have departed yesterday', which may mean 'He intended to depart yesterday' or 'According to instructions, he should have departed yesterday' or 'It was planned (or, ardently desired) by others—he perhaps unknowing—that he should depart yesterday'. A good writer will take care to convey the exact sense he intends.

is when is a stupid beginning for a definition, as in 'Quadratics is when the highest power of the unknown is a square'.

-ise and **-ize** (verb endings). See -IZE . . .

issue is misused in a dozen contradictory and confusing senses, especially by politicians and leader-writers. See Sir Alan Herbert's *What a Word!* for examples and comments.

it, misapplied. 'He put his feet up on the stove as it was very cold', meaning the weather, not the stove.—'Londonderry Corporation decided to reconsider the decision to ban jazz on the Guildhall organ as it was injurious to the instrument.'

it is me for *it is I* 'is a form of speech frequent in current English and is used even by educated speakers, who would not, however, say "it's *him*", "it's *her*", "it's *us*", or "it's *them*", these being generally regarded as vulgar or dialectal. The sound-analogy of [*it is*] *he*, [*it is*] *she*, and [*it is*] *we* has no doubt furthered the use of *me* as a regular and natural form of expression in such cases', which is not to say that Dr Onions (*An Advanced English Syntax*) recommends its use. It is to be noticed that those educated speakers who say 'it's me' or 'it is me' would not say 'It is me who wrote that essay'. *It is me* (or *It's me*) is defensible, however, when the statement is exclamatory: likewise *it's her* (or *him* or *us* or *them*) is justifiable when its use is exclamatory. [In America, *it's me* is acceptable colloquial English; that is, it is used in good speech. There is no occasion to write it. *Us, him, her, them* are less common after *to be*, and their acceptableness is disputed. However, when a pronominal subject is not followed by its verb, the pronoun often appears in the objective case. That is, the habits of word-order are stronger than the habits of inflection. We expect subject + verb + object.]

ITALICS. Italics should, in good writing, be used with caution and in moderation; their most legitimate purpose is to indicate emphasis in dialogue, and, everywhere else (but there too), to indicate foreign words and phrases and titles. See also TITLES OF BOOKS.

See G. V. Carey, *Mind the Stop*, the Fowlers' *The King's English*, and esp. E. P., *You Have a Point There*.

it was as if . . . This is a stylistic cliché, as in 'It was as if the world stood still' or 'It was as if he had only then begun to live'.

item for *affair* or *matter* or *subject*, or *fact* or *incident*, is not merely slovenly but misleading; it is almost as bad as falling weakly back on *you know what I mean* when one is too lazy to remember.

item for (specific) *object* is of the same order as the preceding error, but is perhaps more objectionable, for some particular object should be named. It is certainly less justifiable than *gadget* or *thingummy*, the tools-for-all-occasions of the incurably slothful and the unashamedly woolly.

item is often misused in non-commercial writing; e.g., 'The bed . . ., a table and a chair, were its only items of furniture'.

its is the genitive of *it*; **it's** = *it is*.

it's me. See IT IS ME.

itself. See MYSELF.

-ization, -isation. These noun-endings, like the participle-adjective endings -*ized*, -*ised*, correspond to:

-ize and -ise, verb-endings. The following summary rule is based on *The O.E.D.'s* article (at -*ize*): With very few exceptions, you will be safe if you make every verb, every derivative noun or participial adjective, conform to the -*z* type, for this suffix comes, whether direct or via Latin or French, from the Greek -*izein*: to employ -*ise* is to flout etymology and logic. Moreover, whether the spelling be -*ise*, or -*ize*, the pronunciation is -*ize*: another reason for using it. Where there are, in dictionaries, the alternatives -*ise* (etc.) and -*ize* (etc.), use -IZE.

Although -*ize* is the normal form, there are certain verbs that, not derived from Greek, always take -*ise*. The most important of these, according to H. W. Fowler's valuable list, are: *advertise, apprise, chastise, circumcise, comprise, compromise, demise, despise, devise, disfranchise, disguise, enfranchise, enterprise, excise, exercise, improvise, incise, premise, supervise, surmise, surprise*; to which add *televise, revise*. The verb for 'to force open' is spelt either *prise* or *prize*: I suggest that, to differentiate it from *prize*, 'to value highly', *prise* be used in the 'forcible' sense.

J

jabber is an excellent term for 'incoherent, inarticulate, or unintelligible speech', a sense for which *gibberish* is also used. But as a synonym of 'chatter', 'prattle', 'voluble talk', *jabber* is somewhat discourteous.

Jack or **Jack Tar**, like *Middy* (*q.v.*), is now used only by the ignorant landsman. A similar ban affects *Tommy* (*Atkins*).

jail; jailer. See GAOL, GAOLER.

Jap (n. and adj.) is a colloquialism—not to be employed in the society of a Japanese, any more than *Chinee* or *Chinaman* is respectful to a Chinese.

JARGON. 'The pure research chemist will say, "Chlorophyll makes food by photo-synthesis". The practical engineer does not know what he—the scientist—is talking about. But if the statement is rephrased, "Green leaves build up food with the help of light", anyone can understand it. So, says [C. F.] Kettering, if we are going to surmount the boundaries between different kinds of technical men: "The first thing to do is to get them to speak the same language".'— Stuart Chase.

In his masterly preface to *The Oxford English Dictionary*, Sir James Murray sets the stage thus:—'The English Vocabulary contains a nucleus or central mass of many thousand words whose "Anglicity" is unquestioned; some of them only literary, some of them colloquial [i.e., "used in speech": not in my sense], the great majority at once literary and colloquial—they are the *Common Words* of the language. But they are linked on every side with words that are less and less entitled to this appellation, and which pertain ever more and more distinctly to the domain of local dialect, the slang and [peculiar expressions] of "sets" and classes, of the popular technicalities of trades and processes, of the scientific terminology common to all civilized nations, of the actual languages of other lands and peoples. And there is absolutely no defining line in any direction: the circle of the English language has a well-defined centre but no discernable circumference. The centre is occupied by the "common" words, in which literary and colloquial [i.e., spoken] usage meet. "Scientific" and "foreign" words enter the common language mainly through literature; "slang" words ascend through colloquial usage; the "technical" terms of crafts and processes, and the "dialect"

E

words, blend with the common language both in speech and literature. Slang also touches on one side the technical terminology of trades and occupations, as in "nautical slang", "Public School slang", "the slang of the Stock Exchange", and on another passes into true dialect. Dialects similarly pass into foreign languages. Scientific language passes on one side into purely foreign words, on another it blends with the technical vocabulary of art and manufactures.'

Jargon, originally the warbling of birds, has been loosely employed for cant, slang, pidgin English, gibberish: it should be reserved for the technicalities of science, the professions, the Services, trades, crafts, sports and games, art and Art.

Anyone desirous of going further into the question of jargon should read the chapter entitled 'Technical Words' in Professor G. H. McKnight's *English Words and Their Background*. Certain aspects of the subject are briefly treated in Stuart Chase's *The Tyranny of Words*.

Jehu, 'a coachman', is outworn. Don't shred the tatters.

jerrymander is incorrect for *gerrymander*.

Jew; Jewish. See SEMITIC.

jim-jams; jitters. The former is now a colloquialism, the latter is still a slang term: neither, therefore, has yet qualified to appear in serious writing.

JINGLES; UNINTENTIONAL RHYMES. Avoid these unsought, infelicitous solicitors of sense. 'In most *prose*, and more than we ordinarily *suppose*, the opening words have to wait for *those* that follow' affords an excellent example of how *not* to write prose that is intended to be either effective or melodious.

This is the fault noticed by Alexander Bain when, in *English Composition and Rhetoric*, he says, 'Unpleasing are iterations within words or at the end of words: *indulgent parent, uniform formality, instead of a steady . . ., he is tempted to attempt.*

'Even a short interval is not enough to allow the repetition of very marked sounds: as "I confess with humility, the sterility of my fancy, and the debility of my judgment".'

job for one's profession, trade, vocation is a colloquialism; *job of work* is Standard English, dating from the 16th Century.

JOHNSONESE. *Johnsonian* is defined by *The O.E.D.* as 'a style in English abounding in words derived or made up from

Latin, such as that of Dr Johnson'; but, in current usage, it is applied to 'stilted or pompous style, affecting polysyllabic classical words' (*Webster's*).

Jespersen has written, 'I can find no better example to illustrate the effect of extreme "Johnsonese" than the following:—

' "The proverbial oracles of our parsimonious ancestors have informed us, that the fatal waste of our fortune is by small expenses, by the profusion of sums too little singly to alarm our caution, and which we never suffer ourselves to consider together. Of the same kind is the prodigality of life; he that hopes to look back hereafter with satisfaction upon past years, must learn to know the present value of single minutes, and endeavour to let no particle of time fall useless to the ground." William Minto, in *A Manual of English Prose Literature*, translates that passage as follows:— "Take care of the pennies", says the thrifty old proverb, "and the pounds will take care of themselves." In like manner we might say, "Take care of the minutes, and the years will take care of themselves".'

In short, do not use a heavily Latinized style unless you wish to obtain an effect that can be obtained thus and only thus; an effect, maybe, of extreme formality or majestic impressiveness or sonorous euphony. *He died poor* is always preferable to *he expired in indigent circumstances*, but a *disastrous conflagration* might, in certain circumstances, be preferable to *a great fire*—especially if the results and not the extent are being referred to.

JOURNALESE. See OFFICIALESE.

journey. See TRIP.

judged as to whether it is (or was or will be) + adjective is a clumsy variation of *adjudged* + that adjective. Thus 'No word can be judged as to whether it is good or bad, correct or incorrect, beautiful or ugly, or anything else that matters to a writer, in isolation' would be more effective if the author had written, 'No word can be adjudged good or bad . . .'.

judgement and **judgment**. Although the latter has come to be the commonly accepted spelling there does not appear to be any reason for the omission of the *e*; many of the best writers retain the *e*, and many scholars have, since ca. 1920, recommended *judgement* as the more sensible and also as the more practical form.

judicial and **judicious** are frequently confused. The former = 'connected with, pertaining to, or proper to a court of law or a legal tribunal; belonging to or characteristic of a judge'. *Judicious* = 'having sound judgement; wise in thought or behaviour; prudent; showing sound judgement'.

juncture, at this. Physically, 'at this joint or junction'; hence, 'at this crisis'. Even the sense 'at this particular point of time' is not incorrect, but its usage has been so debased that *at this juncture* is now avoided by self-respecting writers.

junior. See 'SECUNDUS and JUNIOR'.

just is sometimes misused for *quite*. 'That forgetfulness had been well done, but not just well enough.'

just means either *precisely* or *only*: obviously, therefore, it is to be used with care. Moreover, it has, in time-contexts, the sense of 'at, but certainly not later than'; sometimes, in this sense, it is preceded by *only*, as in ' "Was it so late as 11 o'clock?" "Yes, but just"—or only just—"11" '. Hence, avoid *just* = 'precisely' except in time-contexts; and even there, *precisely* (or *exactly*) is preferable.

just as is catachrestic for *according as*. 'Liberty to individuals may be a good or a bad thing, just as they act, but liberty means power when men are in a body.'

just exactly. This combination of almost synonymous terms is justly—and exactly —described by Fowler as 'bad tautology'.

just going to (do something) 'has been much criticized. *Just about to* is preferable, as "I am just about to leave home".'

just the same does not equal *just as well*, as it is sometimes made to do. 'There is no need for grandeur in life to give happiness. The simple things provide it just the same.'

justify, 'to excuse, to exonerate', is occasionally confused with *rectify*, 'to correct', 'to redress': one can *justify an error*, but that is different from *rectifying an error*.

juvenile and **puerile.** Cf. *childlike* and *childish*. *Juvenile* is 'young', as in 'juvenile messengers', 'juvenile attendants'; hence 'belonging to, suited to, intended for youth', as in 'juvenile books'. *Puerile* is now confined to the sense 'childish'. Cf. 'YOUNG and YOUTHFUL'.

K

kerb. See CURB.

ketchup, catchup, catsup. The earliest is *catchup*; the prevalent 20th-Century form is *ketchup*, the least used is *catsup*. [*Catchup* is the common form in American English.]

key. See OPERATIVE.

kind . . . are for *kind . . . is*. 'Kittens and good scientists tend to let new experience pour in until some kind of workable relationships with past experience are established.'

kind of (e.g., rare) for *rather* (rare) is a solecism.

kind of, all. Not a serious solecism; according to *The O.E.D.*, 'still common colloquially, though considered grammatically incorrect'. (But *all manner of* is an established usage.) Similarly, *these* or *those kind of things*, pedantically judged incorrect, is a justifiable English idiom; Dean Alford (*The Queen's English*, 1870) is worth quoting on this point: '. . . it is evident that this tendency, to draw the less important word into similarity to the more important one, is suffered to prevail over strict grammatical exactness. We are speaking of "things" in the plural. Our pronoun "this" really has reference to "kind", not to "things"; but the fact of "things" being plural, gives a plural complexion to the whole, and we are tempted to put "this" into the plural. That this is the account to be given, appears still more plainly from the fact that not unfrequently we find a rival attraction prevails, and the clause takes a *singular* complexion from the other substantive, "kind". We often hear people say "this kind of thing", "that sort of thing". It must be confessed that the phrases, "this kind of things", "that sort of things", have a very awkward sound; and we find that our best writers have the popular expression, *These kind, those sort*. Thus we have in Shakespeare, *King Lear*, "These kind of knaves I know"; *Twelfth Night*, "that crow so at these set kind of fools"; in Pope: "The next objection is, that these sort of authors are poor".'—In a gardening article in a daily paper, we find 'The newer kind (of aubrietia) spread rapidly', which is certainly incorrect and should be 'The newer kinds'.

kind of a for *kind of* is excessive, for 'What kind of a house do you live in?' means no more than 'What kind of house . . .?'

kindred to is wrongly used for *akin to* in the following: 'We need to know that other planets are inhabited by beings fulfilled and moved by a fire and spirit kindred to our own—otherwise what a dreadful loneliness oppresses us!'

kinema, kinematic(al), kinematics, kinematograph, kinematographic, kineograph: these are etymologically correct, but usage is discarding them for the *cine*-forms.

kingly, royal, regal. 'Who is able', asks Jespersen, 'to tell exactly how these adjectives differ in signification? And might not English like other languages (*royal* in French, *kongelig* in Danish, *königlich* in German) have been content with one word instead of three?' But only *kingly* can be used as the masculine counterpart to *queenly*. *Regal* is the least used of the three, and is usually confined to the figurative or transferred senses, 'stately', 'splendid', as in 'She is a most regal woman', 'He wore his robes with a regal air'. *Royal* is the most general: 'of or pertaining to the sovereign; belonging to the royal prerogative', as in 'the Royal Family', 'royal power'; hence 'belonging to, or devoted to the service of the sovereign', as in 'the royal forest'; hence 'befitting a sovereign; princely; munificent', as in 'royal splendour', 'royal hospitality',—being in this nuance of 'splendid, magnificent', a synonym of *regal*. (*Webster's*.)

kneeled and knelt are equally correct as the preterite and past participle of *kneel*.

knit and knitted. Both are correct as the preterite and past participle of *knit*.

L

laded; laden; ladened; loaded; loaden. *Laded* is the preterite and the past participle of *lade*, 'to put the cargo on board (a ship)'; but *laden* is the more usual past participle. *Ladened* is the preterite and past participle of *laden*, a Scottish variant of *lade*. *Loaded* is the preterite and past participle of *load*; *loaden* is dialectal. (*O.E.D.*)

lading. See CARGO.

lady, which has a social—almost a Society—connotation, should not be used as a synonym for *woman*, any more than *gentleman* should be used as a synonym for *man*. Only those men who are not gentlemen speak of their women friends as *lady friends*, and only those women who are not ladies speak of themselves as *ladies* and their men friends as *gentlemen friends*.

laid; lain. See 'LAY and LIE'.

lama, a Tibetan or Mongolian Buddhist

priest, is sometimes confused with *llama*, a South American animal.

lapse. See ELAPSE.

large is not—whereas *great* is—the adjective that should go with *breadth* (or *width*), *depth, distance, height, length*.

large-scale is correctly used of maps, in opposition to *small-scale*; but as a synonym for *large* it is both long-winded and unnecessary. It smacks, too, of 'big business', where the phrase 'large-scale operations' is not unknown.

large-size ('a large-size apple') is incorrect for *large-sized*, which many (myself included) would say is excessive for *large*.

last for *end*. Incorrect, as in 'Towards the last of the chapter'.

last for *latest* is incorrect for the sense 'most recent'. 'The last arrival' for 'the latest arrival', is not only incorrect but extremely ambiguous. Cf. 'LATTER for *last*'.

last, misused for *preceding*. 'The pioneers of semantics whose work we have attempted to summarize in the last four chapters have not . . .'

last, two ; three last ; four last, etc. English idiom demands *last two, three, four*, etc. For 'the three last chapters of the book' read 'the last three chapters . . .'; French idiom has 'les trois derniers chapitres'.

last but one in such a phrase as 'in the last but one sentence' is top-heavy. Better 'in the last sentence but one'; or perhaps, 'in the penultimate sentence'; *last but one*, unchanged, should be used only in a predicate, as in 'In the sentence that comes last but one', 'It is the sentence last but one'.

last-mentioned. See 'LATTER and LAST-MENTIONED'.

late and **ex-.** 'The late President' is dead; 'the ex-President' is alive, *ex-* meaning 'former' but excluding death.

lately. See 'LATTERLY and LATELY'.

later and **latter.** *Later* is the comparative of *late* (in time), superlative *latest*; *latter*, the second of two things mentioned, has also the special sense 'near the end' of a period of time, as in 'the latter part of the year'.

later on for *later* (adv.) is an uneconomical colloquialism. Compare EARLIER ON.

LATIN ADJECTIVES, USELESS. See USELESS LATIN ADJECTIVES.

LATIN TAGS. See CLICHÉ.

LATINISMS. See GREEK AND LATIN and JOHNSONESE.

latter, misused for *last*. 'Over all, was an aura of life, and youth, and happiness. But . . . there were others in that room

whose countenances and general demeanour suggested anything but the latter emotion.' 'Latter' should be 'last' (of three). But *life* and *youth* are not *emotions*, and it is very doubtful whether *happiness* (except when *joy*) is one.

latter and **last-mentioned** (or **named**) should be applied, respectively, to the second of two things, and to the last of three or more: in 'Tennis and squash are good exercise but the last-mentioned is too strenuous', *last-mentioned* should be *latter*.

latterly and **lately.** Both refer to time; the former is rather literary in the sense 'of late' (*lately*), but is preferable to *lately* in the sense 'at the latter end' (of a period).

launder (preterite *laundered*) is the verb corresponding to *laundry*; in good English the latter is not used as a verb.

lawyer ; attorney ; notary ; solicitor, barrister. A *barrister* pleads in the courts; a *solicitor* does not,—he advises barristers in their cases and clients before, during and after cases, originally in equity only. An *attorney* performs the same work as a solicitor, but only in Common Law, and he is properly a *public attorney* (as opposite to a *private attorney* or *attorney in fact*, one who has *power of attorney* to act for another in business and legal affairs) or *attorney-at-law*; in current English, *solicitors* include *attorneys*. A *notary* (in full: *notary public* or *public notary*) is 'a person publicly authorized to draw up or attest contracts or similar documents, to protest bills of exchange, etc., and discharge other duties of a formal character' (*O.E.D.*). *Lawyer* is generic: 'a member of the legal profession; one whose business it is to conduct suits in the courts, or to advise clients, in the widest sense embracing every branch of the profession, though in colloquial use often limited to attorneys and solicitors' (*ibid.*). [The American terms are *lawyer* and, occasionally in certain phrases, *attorney* (*-at-law*), nowadays without difference in meaning. *Barrister* and *solicitor* are not current. *Notary* (*public*) is as defined above.]

lay and **lie,** verbs active and passive, in the infinitive and present and past tenses, are continually misused and confused with each other, sometimes even in good literature; e.g., Byron, *Childe Harold*, iv. 7-9.

And send'st him . . . to his Gods, where
   haply lies
His petty hope in some near port or bay,

And dashest him again to earth:—there let him lay.

in which 'lies' is correct, but 'lay' incorrect. 'Eddy went forward and laid down'. *Lie—lay—lain*; *lay—laid—laid*: these are the correct forms. (*Lie*, to tell a falsehood, takes *lied* both in the preterite and in the past participle.)

'ld. See "D and 'LD'.

leading question does not mean an unfair question but simply 'one that suggests the proper or expected answer', especially (in Law) 'a question which suggests to a witness the answer which he is to make'. (*O.E.D.*)

learn has preterite and past participle *learned* and *learnt*. *Learnt* is disappearing from general use, but some discriminating writers and speakers retain it as past participle. Cf. LEAN and LEAP.—*Learn* for *teach* is a solecism.—The participial adjective *learned* is pronounced with two syllables.

lease (v.). See HIRE.

least for *lesser* (the smaller) is unfortunate; it destroys a valuable distinction.

leave, in *leave* a person *alone*, *leave me be*, *leave go of*, is a solecism for *let*. To *leave a person alone* is to allow him to remain in solitude; to *let him alone* is to cease from bothering him. [Those Americans who know that to *leave a person alone* often means to allow him to remain in peace, undisturbed, will find authority in *Webster's*, LEAVE, 3. *Leave me be* is rustic or dialect; *leave go of* is vulgar.]

legionary; **légionnaire** (properly: written in italics). The latter is, in English, noun only: 'a member of the French Foreign Legion', for which *legionary* is better, for *legionary* is 'a soldier of a legion, whether ancient (especially Roman) or modern (especially French)'. As an adjective, *legionary* = 'of or belonging to or characteristic of a legion'. Note, however, that *Legionary* or *Légionnaire* (or *Legionnaire*) also, since 1918, means 'a member of the British or the American Legion'. (*O.E.D.*) [*Legionnaire* is much more common than *legionary* for a member of the American Legion.]

lengthways and **lengthwise**. Both are adverbs, with sense 'in the direction of the length' ('A hollow tube split lengthways', 'downward lengthwise'); the latter seems to be gaining the ascendant. Only *lengthwise* is an adjective. (*O.E.D.*)

less for *fewer*, *not so many*, is incorrect in 'There were less people at the match than I expected'.—In the correct 'the number of people was less', *less* qualifies *number*, not *people*. [But *less* frequently occurs in place of *fewer* with collectives, as 'to wear less clothes' (*Webster's*); 'less people' is defensible, but not 'less persons'.]

less and **lesser**. *Less*, adjective, is the comparative of *little*, with superlative *least*; it is also an adverb, the comparative of (the adverbial) *a little*. *Lesser* is adjective only. *Less* (adj.) is both attributive (as in 'in a less degree') and predicative ('And then the signs he would suppress . . . grew less and less'; 'It is less'); *lesser* is attributive only ('The lights of lesser craft dipped by'). With reference to material dimension, *less* has given way to *smaller*, but it has been retained with reference to number or degree ('19 is less than 20'). (*O.E.D.*)

lessee; **lessor**. See HIRE.

lest, misused. 'Walking to the *wagon restaurant* she looked enviously into each sleeping-car lest one would prove empty, and spare her the embarrassment of the couchette.' For *lest one would* read *in case one should*: she hoped, not feared, to find one.

let takes the accusative, not the nominative; 'Let you and I go' is incorrect for 'Let you and me go'.—For *hire*, *let*, *rent*, see HIRE.

LETTER-WRITING does not fall within the scope of this book. See the relevant chapter in *English: A Course for Human Beings*, Book I.

lexicon is often restricted to a dictionary of Greek, Hebrew, Syriac, or Arabic.

liable (to do) for *likely* (to do), as in 'he is liable to make that mistake', is incorrect; but it is correct to say 'he is liable (i.e., subject) to error'.

libel is printed (or written), whereas *slander* is spoken; to prove *slander*, an independent witness is required.

licence is the n., **license** the v. [According to *Webster's*, the preferred spelling of both noun and verb is *license*.]

lie. See 'LAY and LIE'.

lifelong and **livelong**. The former is literal, 'lasting or continuing for a lifetime', as in 'The lifelong disability of deaf-mutism'; *livelong* is an intensive of *long*, as in 'Throughout the livelong day he had a presentiment of misfortune' and has come to have the connotation of 'tedious'.

ligature. See DIPHTHONGS.

light, 'to dismount, to descend', is being displaced by *alight*.—The v. *light*, 'to give light; to set fire to', has preterite and past participle *lighted* or *lit*. As an attributive adjective, *lighted* is the more usual: *a lighted cigarette*.

lightening and **lightning**. The former = '(a) making lighter or less heavy'; *lightning* is the visible discharge of electricity in the sky.

like for *as* is incorrect in: e.g., *to do like I do* (correctly *to do as I do*). It would appear to be going too far to call it an illiteracy; but it is at least 'a loose colloquialism . . . avoided by careful speakers and writers' (Onions). [For comment on American use, see Perrin, *An Index to English*.]

like for *as if* is incorrect. 'Carted her out limp—looked like a chloroform-pad had been at work.'

like as if is illiterate. 'The troop have set out with four days' supplies, so it looks like as if we were going no further than Ladybrand.'

like that, 'in that way', is not absolutely wrong, but it is vague; and often it is slightly ambiguous. 'Does he care for you like that' does not impress one as either vigorous or precise.

limited 'is not', Weseen pertinently remarks, 'in good use as a substitute for *small* or one of its synonyms. "A man of limited (meagre) education and limited (inadequate) capital is likely to be limited to a limited (scant) income." ' Properly it = 'restricted, narrow, closely circumscribed'.

linage, less happily spelt *lineage*, is the number of lines of printed (or written) matter, or payment according to the number of lines; *lineage* is ancestry or pedigree. The former has long *i* and only two syllables; the latter, short *i* and three syllables.

line, 'a profession or trade, an occupation', has been so overdone that one would be wise to avoid it—in good writing, at least.

lineament, 'a facial feature', is occasionally confused with *liniment*, 'an embrocation'.

linguistics is rather 'the science of languages' and *philology* 'the science of a specific language or of language-as-communication'; the latter, however, is often used synonymously with the former. Meillet & Cohen's *Les Langues du Monde* is linguistics, but the history of the English vowels is philology.

liquidate, liquidation. Vogue words.

lit; lighted. See LIGHT.

literal. See LITERATE.—Do not confuse with *littoral*, 'adjacent to the shore'.

literally, when used, as it often is, as a mere intensive, is a slovenly colloquialism, its only correct use being to characterize *exactness to the letter*. 'William Hickie' once overheard the following: 'He literally turned the house upside down.'

LITERARISMS are either the journalese of the literary or such unusual words as are used only by the literary or the learned.

And both kinds are to be distinguished from Elegancies (*q.v.*); for elegancies are the 'literary or cultured English' of those who are neither literary nor cultured.

If in doubt consult ELEGANCIES and also ARCHAISMS.

acerb
acolyte (non-ecclesiastically)
adumbrate
alchemy (figuratively)
alembicated
amplitude (non-scientifically)
arcana
aura
autochthonous
avid
avocation

balm
beatific
bedizened
bucolic

catharsis
certitude
cerulean
chieftain
chivalric
cognoscenti
confrère
continuum (used figuratively or non-technically)
converse (conversation)
couched (expressed)
crepuscular
crux

daedalian
darkling
deft and *deftly*
delectable and *delectation*
denigrate
derogate from
descant
discrete
dolorous

ebon (as in 'ebon night')
effete

emanate (correctly used)
empyrean
encomium
envoy (of a poem)
epicene
esurient
eternize
ethereal
etiolated
exacerbate; exacerbation
excerpt (v.)
exemplar

feral
firmament
flee
fleece (to cheat)
fount
froward (also an archaism)
fulvid and *fulvous*

gelid
gilded youth
glabrous
grateful (of things: pleasing, acceptable)
gubernatorial

haste (v.)
heaven (sky)
helot
homo sapiens
hymeneal

immarcescible
implement (to fulfil)
in very truth
ineluctable
inexpugnable
imbrue (v.)
infinitude
intrinsic
inwardness
irrefragable
iteration and *iterate*

jocose

lassitude
laud (n. and v.)
lave (v.)
Lethe
liege-lord (non-feudally; non-facetiously)
literati
longanimity
lustrum

mantle (figuratively)
meretricious
metempsychosis
mulct (*of*: to deprive of)

neophyte
nepenthe (or *N.*)
nimbus
no other, be able to do

obloquy
olden
opuscule
ordonnance
ordure
otherwhere

paramount
paramour
parergon
paucity
penumbra
perdurable
peripatetic
perspicacious; perspicacity
perspicuity
pestilence
plenitude
plenteous
plethora
polity
polymath
pother
prescience; prescient
proem
provenance
pusillanimous

quietude

regimen
Renascence, the
respire
retirement (see RETIRACY)
r(h)odomontade

scabrous
sempiternal(ly)
significant (important)
similitude
smite
something (somewhat or rather)
straightway
supererogatory
supernal
superimpose
surcease (n.)
suspire
susurrus
suzerainty
swart

Tartarean (or *-ian*)
tantamount
thrasonical
toper

transpire (used correctly)
turpitude

umbrageous
unobtrusive(ly)
untoward

vacant (of persons: idle)
vault (to leap)
verdant
verisimilitude
verities, the
virtuoso (pl. *virtuosi*)
visitant

wain
warranty (but not as a legal term)
what time (while; when)
whence
whither
wilderness
wondrous (adj.) and *wondrously*
writ (written)
wroth

LITERARY STANDARD. See STANDARD ENGLISH, Section ii.
literate means 'able to read and write'; the opposite of *illiterate*. For a confusion with *literal*, see the passage quoted at MALAPROPISMS.
literature for printed matter of any kind, e.g., for advertising matter, is a colloquialism—an extremely silly and unfortunate one, for it tends to degrade a good word.
littoral. See LITERAL.
livelong. See LIFELONG.
llama for *lama*. See LAMA.
load. See CARGO.
loaded; loaden. See LADED.
loan as a verb for *lend* is good American, but it is not yet good English.
loath; loathe; loth. *Loth* is an alternative form of *loath*, 'disinclined', 'reluctant', as in 'I am loath (or loth) to believe it' or in *nothing loath* ('not at all unwillingly'). *Loathe* is a verb, 'to feel dislike or aversion for', e.g. for food: 'To dictate their terms to statesmen who loathe the necessity of submission'; 'Your stomach soon must loathe all drink and meat'. (*O.E.D.*)
locality and **location.** A *locality* is the situation or position of an object, or the place in which it is to be found; it is applied especially to geographical position or place; also a district, a place, regarded either as the site occupied by certain persons or things or as the scene of certain activities. 'A blind man . . .

feeling all round him with his cane, so as to find out his locality'; 'The tremendous rainfall of the Khasi Hills, amounting in some localities . . . to 559 inches of annual rainfall'. *Location* is local or definite position, as in 'location in space'; the two senses, 'a tract of land marked out or surveyed', e.g., a mining claim, and 'place of settlement or residence', are American, as also is the cinematic *location* ('on location'). (*O.E.D.*)
locate, meaning *to place*, is misused for *to find*; as the maid said about some articles lost by the laundry, 'I expect they'll be able to locate them'.
located. *To be located*, 'to reside'; 'to live (in a place)', is an Americanism.
locution and **circumlocution.** The predominant sense of *locution* is 'a form of expression; a phrase; an expression', as in 'The introduction of new words and locutions'. A *circumlocution* is a roundabout, esp. if wordy, phrase or expression —e.g., *in respect of* and *with regard to* for *about* or *concerning*. (*O.E.D.*)
lonely; alone. *Lonely* is solitary; *alone*, by oneself. One may be alone in a wood, yet by no means lonely; or one may be walking in a crowded street, yet be intolerably lonely.
look over. See OVERLOOK.
look well and **look good.** To *look good* is to appear good; to *look well* is to be well ('She looks well'), hence to be attractive ('He looks well in that suit').
loose and **loosen.** The former is usual in the sense, 'to undo, to unbind, set free from material bonds', as in 'He loosed the dog'. The latter is more general in the sense 'to relax or slacken', as in, 'loosen one's joints', 'loosen discipline'; hence 'to unfix or detach; to render less firm or cohesive', as in 'to loosen the stones in a wall', 'to loosen the soil'. (*O.E.D.*)
loose for *lose* is a misspelling not infrequently met with; inexcusable, for the two words are pronounced differently.
Lord's Day, the. See SABBATH.
lot. *A lot* for a large number or quantity; *the lot* for the whole number or quantity; are too common in our speech to be condemned as incorrect, but their use where any refinement or elevation of language is required is impossible, for they are not Standard English. *All the lot* is almost a vulgarism.
louring. See LOWERING.
love, in good English (whether spoken or written), is not to be debased to equivalence with *to like*, however amusing it may be in conversation ('He just loves cricket').

lovelily is good English and it means 'beautifully', as in 'Lovelily shines the moon'. Where it is cacophonous, use *in a lovely manner*.

low. See LOWLY.

LOW LANGUAGE. See VULGARISMS.

lowering (n. and adj.) = 'depression' or 'depressing' ('Fever is very lowering') and 'frowning; gloom or gloomy' (*lowering looks, lowering sky*); *louring* is used only in the second sense. The O.E.D. prefers the *lour* form for the 'frowning, gloomy' sense.

lowly should be avoided as the adverb of *lowly*, 'humble', for it is often ambiguous, as in 'The preacher spoke lowly': for 'in a low voice', use *low*; for 'in a lowly manner', use either *in a lowly manner* or *lowlily*. There is an adverb *lowly*, and it occurs in both of these senses: but avoid it!

luncheon is a formal (e.g., a civic) *lunch*.

lure (v.). See ALLURE (v.).

lustful; lusty. The former = 'pertaining to or full of sexual desire', with adverb *lustfully*; the latter (with adverb *lustily*) = 'vigorous', as in 'He's a fine, lusty fellow', 'He dealt the bully a lusty blow'.

luxuriant for *luxurious*. The former, 'producing abundantly, growing profusely', is an adj. of active properties; the latter, 'given to luxury or self-indulgence, of or pertaining to, or characterized by luxury' (*O.E.D.*), is passive. Often confused in application, as are the adverbs *luxuriantly* and *luxuriously*.

Lyon for *Lyons*. See BRUXELLES.

M

macintosh, not *mackintosh*, is the strictly correct name of the rain coat, for it was called after one Charles Macintosh; but the *ck* form has been so widely used that one feels pedantic in even mentioning the *c* form.

mad for *angry* is a colloquialism.

Madam is the correct English form of the French *Madame*; the plural, however, is as in French: *Mesdames*.

magisterial and **magistral.** In current usage, *magistral* = 'masterly' as in 'a magistral arrangement of complex facts'.

The predominant sense of *magisterial* is 'of, belonging to, proper to a magistrate; holding the office of a magistrate', as in 'a magisterial inquiry', 'magisterial duties'. A useful sense is that of 'assuming authority, schoolteacher-like', hence 'dictatorial', as in 'He delivered his

E*

instructions in a magisterial voice'. (*O.E.D.*)

mail. See POST.

main. See COMPARATIVES, FALSE.

maintain, misused for the intransitive *obtain* ('to exist; be practised, be habitual') as in 'Does that puerile practice still maintain?'

major. See COMPARATIVES, FALSE. A thing or fact is either *major* or *minor*—and that is all there is to it.

major portion and **greater part.** The latter would be preferable in 'He devotes the major portion of his time to gardening'.

majority, misused for *larger part* of a thing; e.g., 'The majority of the book is instructive'. *Majority* applies only to numbers; it = 'the greater number'.

MALAPROPISMS. A malapropism—the adjective, by the way, is *malapropian*—is a 'ludicrous misuse of [a] word, especially in mistake for one resembling it (e.g., *a nice derangement of epitaphs* for *arrangement of epithets*)', to quote The Con. O.D. With this, compare the pleasing example perpetrated at the Old Bailey in 1851, 'He struck me . . . he called me all the *epitaphs* he could'. The term derives from Mrs Malaprop in Sheridan's *The Rivals*, produced in 1775; she was noted for her ability to misapply long words, e.g., 'as headstrong as an allegory on the banks of the Nile'. This kind of mistake has been felicitously used by many writers. In an English paper set in a School Certificate examination, there occurred this question:

'Point out and correct any mistakes in word usage and idiom in the following passage:

'Mary entered the luxuriantly [*luxuriously*] furnished room and was welcomed by the baroness. She was indeed surprised by the warmth and pleasantry [*pleasantness*] of her reception considering all she had heard of her hostesses masterly [*hostess's masterful*] ways. It would not be difficult now, she thought, to explain her purport [*purpose*] in coming to the castle. Suddenly her eye was attracted by a small picture which hung [better, *was hanging*] between the tall French-windows, and the baroness interrupted [*intercepted*] her glance. "My dear, you are perspicuous [*perceptive*, or *observant*]; I see you have already noticed my Orozzi. It is indeed quite unique [see UNIQUE] and priceless, though some people find the colours crude and the drawing primary [*primitive*: better *elementary*] and are worried [better, *perplexed*] because they find no allusion [*illusion*] of perspective in the background." "Ah yes," said Mary, "but these kind [*this* (or *that*) *kind*] of people always look for a literate [*literal*] meaning in a work of art, and nothing else." "I see you are by no means *ingenious* [*ingenuous*: better, *ignorant*] in these matters," observed the baroness, and Mary smiled, well pleased with the complement [*compliment*].'

See especially the chapter in Book II of my *English: A Course for Human Beings*. **malapropos** is the correct English way of writing the adopted French phrase, *mal à propos*. *Malapropos*, originally an adverb, has become an adjective and even a noun.

Malay, used as the name of the country *Malaya*, is a frequent error. A *Malay* is a native of that country, *the Malay* (adj.) *Peninsula*.

male. See MANLIKE.

maleficence; malevolence. See BENEFICENCE.

Mall and **Pall Mall**. Uncertainty as to the pronunciation of these names is often shown and conclusive authority is wanting. In the Mall it may be *Mawl* or *Măl*, but *Měl* is deemed incorrect, whereas in Pall Mall the pronunciation *Pěl Měl*, usual in the 17th Century when the game from which it is derived was fashionable, has been retained and is correct, as is also *Păl Măl*, but not *Pawl Mawl*.

man-like. See MANLIKE; MANLY; . . .

man of letters; writer; author. Whatever the nuances may have been in 1900, the differentiation now prevalent is this:— The term *author* is applied to a writer of *fiction*; *writer* to a writer of *fiction*, *history, biography, belles-lettres*; *man of letters* to such a writer of any or all of these, plus poetry, plus works of scholarship,—but if his fiction is preponderant, he is usually relegated to the rank of *writer*, precisely as a *writer* that produces very little except fiction becomes an *author*. Note that a person that writes only—or mostly—poetry is generally called a *poet*, seldom a *writer*, never an *author*. A person that writes plays—or mostly plays—is generally called a *dramatist* (serious plays) or *playwright* (any kind, all kinds), not an *author* (despite the call 'Author! Author!'). One who writes reviews is a *reviewer*; if he writes a novel or two, he is usually spoken of as 'reviewer turned author', and all those novelists whom he has slated (and not a few others) rend him limb from limb—though not in the open; if he writes very well, he may become a

writer, and if he not only writes very well but is a scholar, he may, by his friends, be described as a *man of letters*.

Man of letters, however, is, even among those who merit that designation, avoided by the modest, for it has a slight taint of highbrowism and, if used by themselves, more than a tinge of pretentiousness; they prefer to be called *writers*. *Author* has also a generic sense, as in 'The Society of Authors' and in legal and official documents and in semi-official publications (e.g., *Who's Who*); in its restricted sense (a writer of fiction), *author* is a useful welder of *novelists* and *short-story writers*—a combination that calls for some such neologism as *fictionist*. *Writer* is probably the most useful of these three terms; t is certainly the least invidious; underwriters and copy-writers may generally be trusted not to usurp the more general term.

manifold; multifarious; multiform; multiple. For *manifold*, see the remarks at -FOLD; but it does also = 'consisting of many of one kind combined; operating many of one kind of object', as in 'a *manifold* bell-pull'; further, it = 'numerous and varied', as in 'O Lord how *manifold* are thy works!'

Multifarious emphasizes 'the diversity, sometimes even the incongruity, of the elements involved', as in 'The *multifarious* complexities of human character'.

Multiform = 'having many forms, shapes, or appearances', as in 'A plastic and multiform unit'.

Multiple (see also -PLE) = 'containing (something) more than once, or containing more than one (of a thing); consisting of more than one', as in *multiple stores, a multiple vote, multiple solutions* (of a problem).

mankind should be followed by *it*, not by *he*. 'By [the middle of the 15th Century], through the application of science and invention, new possibilities were available to mankind which were likely to have an even larger effect on his future than those of agriculture and the techniques of early civilization.' Probably the confusion is caused by taking *mankind* to be a synonym of *man*, as of course it is—but of *man* generically, not of *man*, the male human being.

manlike (or **man-like**); **manly**; **mannish**; **male**; **masculine**. *Manly* (falling into disuse in the sense 'mannish') is favourable, connoting the good qualities of a man; *mannish* is unfavourable if it is applied to a woman, and it means 'resembling a man', but as a synonym of *manly* and *manlike*, it is obsolescent; of *manlike* the predominant sense is, 'characteristic of a man as opposite to a woman or a child', but when applied to an animal, it = 'resembling a human being'; *male* is 'of the masculine sex, *qua* sex, as opposite to the feminine sex'; and *masculine*, the grammatical opposite of *feminine* (*gender*), is in general use in the senses 'peculiar to or assigned to males; consisting of males', as in *masculine attire*, and 'virile; vigorous; appropriate to (excellences of) the male sex', as in *masculine licence, masculine force, masculine style.* (*O.E.D.*)

manslaughter. See MURDER.

manuscript means 'written by hand' and *manuscripts* should be reserved for handwritten copies of, e.g., a book; that which is typed is a *typescript*. But *manuscript* is often used for *typescript* (whether noun or adjective): which seems a pity!

map. See CHART.

marionette. See PUPPET.

Marseille for *Marseilles*. See BRUXELLES.

mart is slightly archaic for *market*.

martyr (to) for *victim (of)* or *one suffering (from)* is hyperbolical; *a martyr to epilepsy* is admissible, *a martyr to colds* is absurd.

marvel and **miracle** are overworked—and too often used hyperbolically.

masculine. See MANLIKE . . .

masochism. See SADISM.

mass is sometimes used for *majority*, as in 'The mass of the people gained their enjoyment as spectators'.

massacre (n. and v.) refers to wholesale killing, mass-slaughter, not to the murder of one person. 'He swore the most dreadful oaths that he would "massacre her".'

masseur, masculine; **masseuse**, feminine. They may now be regarded as English words; do not, therefore, italicize them.

masterful; masterly. In current usage, they are distinguished thus:—*Masterful* is 'imperious' or (of actions) 'highhanded, despotic', as in 'She was proud and masterful', 'This masterful disregard of logical thought'; 'qualified to command; powerful or vigorous in command or in rule', as in 'Henry VIII was a masterful King'. *Masterly* is applied either to persons or their actions or abilities, and it = 'resembling or characteristic of a master or skilled workman; skilfully performed, done, exercised', as in 'The thought is masculine and the expression masterly'; 'a masterly stroke'. (*O.E.D.*)

materialize, 'to become visible or perceptible; to become real, actual, actual fact; against general opinion or serious obstacles to succeed, make its way', is overdone, as in 'There were doubts of his ability to come at all, but he materialized'.

materially is not incorrect in the sense 'to an important extent; substantially; considerably, greatly', as in 'Short cuts, by . . . which the road was materially shortened', but there is, especially among journalists, a tendency to overdo it.

maximum and **minimum**, meaning the absolute *most* and *least*, are abused.

may and can. See 'CAN and MAY'.

may and might. See SUBJUNCTIVE.

maybe is to be preferred to the original *may be* as a colloquial synonym of 'perhaps'. ' "You'll say it's likely enough that there was money and may be jewellery sent over to him from France".' It is permissible to write '. . . money and (it may be) jewellery'.

me for *I*. See IT IS ME.

me with . . . See AND ME WITH . . .

mean time and **meantime.** *Meantime*, adverb, is short for *in the meantime* (originally *in the mean time*), 'during a specified interval'. In current usage, *mean time* is, by discriminating writers, confined to the sense *mean solar time*.

means, 'an instrument, agency, method, or course of action, by the employment of which some object is or may be attained, or which is concerned in bringing about some result' (*O.E.D.*), is plural in form but singular in sense and construction, as in 'I was the means of this being done'.

Mecca, being the birthplace of the Prophet, is a place of religious pilgrimage for Mohammedans, but to say that 'Ryde Pier is a Mecca for anglers' is to debase metaphor from the sublime to the piscatorial.

media. See MEDIUMS.

medium-size (adj.) is incorrect for *medium-sized*; and often *medium-sized* is unnecessary for *medium* or *average*.

mediums are spiritualistic or, (of persons) 'intermediaries' or 'mediators', or absolute as in 'The large hats are ugly, the mediums are tolerable, the small ones are pretty'; in all other senses, the plural is *media*, although *mediums* is gaining ground.

memoranda is the plural of *memorandum*; and because the plural is more often used than the singular it is occasionally taken for and construed as a singular (cf. STRATA). The English plural, *memorandums*, is gaining ground: and there is no reason why you should not use it. The unforgivable sin is to form the plural in *-as*.

menace, 'a threat', should not be overdone. That Kenneth Farnes was a better bowler than writer appears from: 'McCabe is a good second-string to the Bradman menace', *Lyons' Sports Sheet*, May 8, 1938.

mental to describe a mentally disordered person is a modern slang term.

mere is often unnecessary. Properly it is a strong word and therefore should not be used weakly, as in 'Sometimes this "frankness" is mere vulgarity', where the simple *vulgarity* would be stronger.— *Merely* also is misused. See PURE and ONLY.

mesdames. See MADAM.

Messrs should be confined to commerce; elsewhere *Messieurs*. The best abbreviation, in English as in French, is *MM*.

metal has been displaced by *mettle* for ' "the stuff" of which a man is made, with reference to character'. (*O.E.D.*)

METAPHOR. I. *General.*

Metaphor, as defined by *The O.E.D.*, is that 'figure of speech in which a name or descriptive term is transferred to some object different from, but analogous to, that to which it is properly applicable'; derivatively, an instance of this, i.e. a metaphorical expression—a transference or transferred usage.

Aristotle, in *The Poetics*, went so far as to declare that 'the greatest thing by far is to have a command of metaphor' and added that, 'to employ metaphors happily and effectively', it was necessary to have 'an eye for resemblances'.

II. *Confused or Mixed Metaphors.*

In Bain's *English Composition and Rhetoric*, there is a sound, though unimaginative, section on mixed metaphor.

Bain introduces the section with the sibyllic words,'The brevity of the Metaphor renders it liable to the vice called Mixing Metaphors': is it not rather the confused thinking of the perpetrator?

'This arises', Bain says, 'when metaphors from different sources are combined in the same subject: as "to *kindle* a *seed*". We may *sow* a *seed* or *kindle* a *flame*; but kindling a seed is incongruous and confusing to the mind.

'The following example from Addison is familiar—

I *bridle* in my struggling muse with pain
That longs to *launch* into a bolder *strain*.

Three different figures'—horse, ship, music—'are conjoined in one action.

' "The very *hinge* and *centre* of an immense system": "hinge" is out of place': but is it? Here we have not a mixing but an adding or a collocation of metaphors, for 'centre' is as much a metaphor as a 'hinge'.

' "All my pretty *chickens* and their *dam*" is the mixing of two metaphors. . . .

' "Physiology and psychology thus become united, and the study of man passes from the uncertain *light* of mere opinion to the *region* of science."

' "The very recognition of these by the jurisprudence of a nation is a *mortal wound* to the very *keystone* upon which the whole vast arch of morality reposes." '

After citing other examples, Bain goes on to say, 'There is no objection to different metaphors being successively applied to the same subject, provided they are kept distinct. Thus: "They admire the profundity of what is mystical and obscure, mistaking the *muddiness of water* for *depth* (1), and *magnifying* in their imaginations what is *viewed through a fog* (2)." '

Nor do we now subscribe to the dictum that 'the mixture of the metaphorical and the plain or literal is also objectionable. Dryden, speaking of the aids he had in his translations, says, "I was sailing in a vast ocean without other help than the *pole-star* of the ancients, and *the rules of the French* stage among the moderns" ': *rules* itself is naught but a metaphor—originally.

Let me now adduce an instance of a more glaring kind. Sir Boyle Roche, Irish politician, is reported to have said:

'Mr Speaker, I smell a rat; I see him forming in the air and darkening the sky; but I'll nip him in the bud.'

But some 19th-Century wit elaborated the original, and the form in which most of us know this delightful mixture is:

'Mr Speaker, I smell a rat. I see it floating in the air; and if it is not nipped in the bud, it will burst forth into a terrible conflagration that will deluge the world.'

meticulous is erroneously used to mean 'careful of detail in a praiseworthy manner'; properly, it implies excess of care and an overscrupulousness caused by timidity. It is also misused in the sense of *neat* and *tidy*, e.g., 'He was ushered into a small, meticulous inner office of white enamel'. Here the writer means *carefully tended*. To be meticulous is a quality possible only to a conscientious person.

METRES, POETICAL. Fascinating; but none of my business. For a first-class exposition, see Fowler's *Modern English Usage*, at 'Technical Terms'; for a shorter account, my *English: A Course for Human Beings*, Book II.

mid, preposition, is—except in traditional and scientific phrases—rather literary (and poetic). Write *mid*, not *'mid*.

middle. See CENTRE.

Middle East, Far East, Near East. The Near East (Egypt, Palestine, Syria, etc.) has unfortunately become the Middle East; apparently the Far East (Japan, China, Siam, Malaya) remains the Far East, and what used to be the Middle East is now simply the East.

Middle West; Middle Western. See MID-WEST.

middy. 'Taffrail' writes: 'We read in newspaper articles and boys' books of adventure of "middies". We sometimes even hear the term used in conversation round tea-tables ashore, but to call a present-day midshipman a "middy" to his face would make him squirm.'

'midst is inferior to *midst*; now rather literary than spoken English, it has, for the most part, been superseded by *among* or *in the midst of.*

Midwest, Midwestern; Middle West, Middle Western. As applied to the central United States. 'Usage', remarks Weseen, 'seems to favour *Midwest* and *Midwestern* as adjectives and . . . *Middle West* as the noun. But *Midwest* [not *Midwestern*] is sometimes used as a noun and *Middle West* and [less often] *Middle Western* are often used as adjectives.'

might for *would*. See SUBJUNCTIVE (near end).—*Might* for *may*. See PAST SUB-JUNCTIVE . . .—For the correct use of *may* and *might*, see the same article.

mind, 'to remind', is obsolescent; *mind*, 'to remember' (v.t.) is archaic.

miniature should, as an adjective, be used with care. It is not a synonym of *small* or *little* or *dainty.*

minimize: 'to reduce to the smallest possible size, amount, or degree', as in 'Clerical vestments are minimized', and 'to estimate at the smallest possible amount (or value)' as in 'Jesus did not minimize sin': is not to be degraded to equivalence with to *decrease, diminish, lessen,* as in 'Why seek to minimize the danger?' (*O.E.D.*)

minor. 'Of very minor importance' is ludicrous. Cf. MAJOR, *q.v.*

minute (n.) and **moment.** A *minute* is an objective, precise period or measure of time; a *moment* is a subjective, imprecise period (not a measure) of time. Do not, therefore, exclaim impatiently, 'Oh, tell him I'll see him in a minute' if all you mean is 'in a moment'.

miracle. See MARVEL.

MISPRONUNCIATIONS. For an excellent list, see pp. 263–298 of Whitten & Whitaker's *Good and Bad English.*

MISQUOTATIONS. ' "Similarity of style. . . . Two or three times the fellow tried to disguise it . . .". "Oh, but there was more than that!" cried the other. . . . ". . . Now, look at this. The Minister of Imperial Finance, in his efforts for advancement of self, would do well to remember that hackneyed line of Pope: 'A little learning is a dangerous thing'. Did you see that?"—Anthony opened his eyes. "I did. And thought how refreshing it was to see the quotation given right. They nearly all get it wrong, though you'd think anyone could see that Pope couldn't have been such a fool as to say a little knowledge was dangerous. Knowledge is always useful; learning isn't, until you've got plenty. But go on . . ."—Masterson was searching feverishly. ". . . here we are! Listen . . . 'when Greek joins Greek then comes the tug of war!' . . . How many times d'you see that given right?"—"Never," said Anthony. "They all say 'meets'."—"There you are then. . . . Style—similarity of style, I mean—isn't proof; but this orgy of correctitude *plus* that similarity is. . . . There are plenty more instances . . . There's one I remember well . . . It said . . . : *'facilis descensus Averno'.* What about that?"—Anthony sat up. " *'Averno'* is very rare", he said slowly. "But it's a better reading . . ." ' (Philip MacDonald's *The Rasp,* 1924).

As this entry is not intended to cover even the commonest of the many misquotations, I shall note only a few others.

That he who runs may read should be '[Write the vision, and make it plain upon tables] that he may run that readeth it' (*Habakkuk*, ii, 2); the meaning was that 'he who reads the information may run away and act upon it' (Ackermann, *Popular Fallacies*).

Fresh fields and pastures new should be 'Fresh woods and pastures new' (Milton).

A parting shot was originally 'a Parthian shot'; and *All that glitters is not gold* was 'All that glisters . . .'.

Water, water everywhere, and not a

drop to drink should be 'Water, water
everywhere, nor any drop to drink'
(Coleridge).

Of the making of books there is no end
is properly 'Of making many books there
is no end', which occurs in the Bible.—In:

To die: to sleep;
No more; and, by a sleep to say we end
The heart-ache and the thousand natural
    shocks
That flesh is heir to, 'tis a consummation
Devoutly to be wish'd (Shakespeare)

shocks is frequently misquoted as *ills*.

Prunes and prisms is incorrect for
prunes and prism; and *leather and
prunella* for *leather or prunella*.

Cribbed, cabined and confined is incorrect for Shakespeare's '[Now am I]
cabin'd, crib'd, confin'd, bound in'
(*Macbeth*, III, iv. 24).

Flat, stale and unprofitable is a mis-
quotation of Shakespeare's 'How weary,
stale, flat, and unprofitable, Seem to me
all the uses of this world'.

MISRELATED GERUND. See GERUND,
last paragraph.

MISRELATED PARTICIPLE. See
CONFUSED PARTICIPLES.

misremember is correct in the sense 'to
remember incorrectly or incompletely';
dialectal in the sense 'to forget'.

miss for *escape* (*the notice of*). 'The mere
sight of Osaki du Channe is enough to
give any C.I.D. man the idea that I'm
somewhere about. But, if you're travelling entirely alone, the fact may miss
them.'

Miss and **Misses.** The formally correct
plural of *Miss Hume* is *the Misses Hume*;
but *the Miss Humes* is permissible.

missis (or **missus**), **the,** is at best a colloquialism for '(one's) wife' and (also without *the*) 'the mistress' of the house.

mistaken; misunderstood. 'I was *mistaken*' = 'I was wrong, in error'; 'I was
misunderstood' = 'Somebody (or some
persons) failed to understand me'.

MIXED METAPHORS. See META-
PHORS.

MM. See MESSRS.

mob is a dangerous or at least a potentially disorderly crowd; do not use it of
any crowd, nor of companies of animals.
The mob is the populace, the masses.

model is a pattern or a representation in
scale or proportion; do not use it where
copy, reproduction, or, esp., *replica* is the
precise word. See, above all, *The O.E.D.*

modest is often misused for *moderate*.
The former is defined by *The O.E.D.* as
'unobtrusive, retiring, bashful; decorous
in manner and conduct; scrupulously
chaste in feeling, language and conduct';
the latter as 'avoiding extremes; of
medium or middling size, quality, price,
etc.'—As applied to persons, the two
terms have a kindred, though not the
same meaning; a 'modest' man is
naturally of 'moderate' language and
behaviour, but one has no right to
speak of, e.g., 'a modest rate of interest'.

MODIFIED STANDARD. See STAN-
DARD ENGLISH, Section ii.

Mohammed, Mohammedan are the correct and accepted forms, though *Maho-
met, -an,* are frequently found.

moment. See MINUTE.

momentary is 'transitory'. But *momentous*
is 'important' of events, and 'weighty' of
statements or decisions.

monies is incorrect for *moneys*; after all,
the singular is *money*, not *mony*.

monologue. See DIALOGUE.

Mons., whether written or spoken, is
regarded by Frenchmen as a gratuitous
insult. Say or write *Monsieur*; write *M*.

monstrous, even when it means *enormous*,
has a connotation either of abnormality
or of ugliness. Subjectively, it means
'horrible, atrocious' or 'outrageously
wrong; contemptibly absurd'.

MOOD IN SYNTAX; right use of
mood: See esp. SUBJUNCTIVE and TENSE-
SEQUENCE but also CONCESSIVE and
CONDITIONAL and FINAL.

moonlight, adjective, except in *moonlight
flit*(*ting*), *moonlight dancing,* and deriva-
tives, is now less used than *moonlit*.

moral and **morale.** Mr Frank Whitaker
once wrote: 'Take the word "moral",
meaning "of good morals". We had used
it for centuries in that sense when somebody discovered that the French used it
to mean "the spirit of the troops".
"Ah", said this person, "a useful word.
We must bag that." So we took it, added
an "e" to distinguish it both in spelling
and [in] pronunciation from "moral",
and made it our own. It didn't matter a
pin to Mr Usage that the French have
the two words, and use them in precisely
the reverse sense. But although this
happened years ago, it still matters to
The Times . . . It still spells it without an
"e" to remind us that we mustn't play
tricks with other people's words. It might
as well talk to the moon. The distinction
is useful, and because it is useful it has
established itself.'

Fowler upholds *morale*; so do I.

more for *other* is to be avoided; it leads

to ambiguity, as in 'Most people have heard of Shaftesbury, Southwood Smith and Chadwick, but there were many more ardent reformers who are now forgotten'.

more -er (e.g., *more brighter*). Now a solecism, though in Middle and Early Modern English it was common and permissible.

more often. See OFTENER.

more or less certain, though illogical (see COMPARATIVES, FALSE), is idiomatic English. 'It expresses a valuable shade of meaning, and has earned its keep over and over again', Frank Whitaker, 1939.

more perfect, like *more inferior, more superior, more unique, more universal,* is an absurdity. See COMPARATIVES, FALSE.

moron is properly 'one of the highest class of feeble-minded; an adult having an intelligence comparable to that of a normal average child between eight and twelve years of age'; hence, as a colloquialism, 'a stupid person; a fool'. (*O.E.D.*)

mortal, whether 'human' ('mere mortal man') or 'death-causing', is an uncomparable adjective. See COMPARATIVES, FALSE.

mortar. See CEMENT.

Moslemin, the plural of *Moslem,* is sometimes ignorantly used as the singular. It is safer to treat *Moslem* as English and to say *Moslems.*

most is pleonastic before superlative of adjj. and advv. Shakespeare's 'This was the most unkindest cut of all', effective in its emphasis, affords no excuse.

most should not be used of comparison between two; 'Of those two men, Jack is the most intelligent' should be '. . . more . . .'

most and mostly. See MOSTLY.

most and the most are occasionally confused, with resultant ambiguity. 'What I should most like to do would be to die without knowing I was even in danger of dying'; but 'Which do you like the most —cricket, lawn tennis, or golf?' In other words, *most* is absolute, whereas *the most* is relative.

most all, properly '*most all,* for *almost all,* is an illiteracy. [In American usage, *most* for *almost* is dialectal or colloquial.]

most part is incorrect for *greater* (or *greatest*) *part* or *main part* except in the phrase *for the most part* (whence springs the error). 'It was rough going, and more than once Philip blessed the broad pair of bucolic shoulders which were doing the most part of the work.' There are several

alternatives, all to be preferred: 'doing most of the work', '— the biggest share of the work', '—the larger part of the work'.

mostly is 'in the main', as in 'A man whose mind had been mostly fallow ground will not easily take to the mental plough and hoe'. Do not misuse it for *most,* as in 'The people mostly in need of assistance do not ask for it'. (*O.E.D.*)

motif is not a synonym of *motive.* It has four specific uses:—

i. In painting, sculpture, architecture, decoration, etc., it is a constituent feature of a composition or a distinct part of a design, hence a particular type of subject, hence the principal feature or the predominant idea of a work; as in 'That painter's favourite *motif* is cherubs'.

ii. Hence, in a novel, a biography, etc., a type of incident, a dominant idea, the predominant idea or theme.

iii. In dress-making, an ornament (e.g., of lace or braid) sewn on to a dress.

iv. In Music, be careful! (*Leitmotiv* or *subject* or *figure* is safer.)

Originally an adoption from French, it should now be written in roman characters. *Motiv,* a German term, has not been anglicized, except in *leitmotiv.* (*O.E.D.*)

motion pictures; moving pictures; the pictures; the movies. The fourth is slang, the third is a colloquialism. *Moving pictures* is more usual than *motion pictures,* although the latter is the more sensible term. The building in which a cinematographic programme is shown is in England a *cinema* [in the U.S.A. a (*motion picture*) theater].

moustache. See WHISKERS.

mouthfuls and mouths full. Cf. BASKET-FULS.

mowed and mown as past participles. Usage prefers 'He has mowed the grass', 'The grass was mowed yesterday', but 'Mown grass smells sweet', 'A mown field looks bare'.

Mrs, not *Mrs.,* is the form preferred in England. [In American usage, *Mr., Mrs.,* and similar spellings are considered abbreviations, not contractions; they are therefore followed by a period.]

much and many. Do not use the former where the latter is idiomatic, as in 'As much as twenty members have resigned'; *many* is the word for separables and units.

much and muchly. Avoid the archaic *muchly* unless you are sure that as a jocularity it is inoffensive.

much and very. With ordinary (i.e., non-participial) adjectives and with adverbs, use *very*: not 'much unkind' but 'very unkind'; not 'much soon' but 'very soon'. With participial adjectives, *much* is permissible, as in 'He was much pleased', though 'very pleased' is more usual; *much obliged* is a set phrase. Note, however, that one says 'much too soon', 'much sooner', 'much worse', 'much better', 'much the more praiseworthy', 'much the largest'.

much less (or still less) is sometimes illogically used through lack of clear thinking, by writers usually competent; e.g., 'The task of keeping the fire under, much less of putting it out, was beyond the resources of the fire-engines'. Obviously, if 'the task of keeping the fire under' was difficult, that of extinguishing it was *much more so*.

MUDDLING THROUGH, otherwise Hoping for the Best, is seen, in its results, in the article entitled WOOLLINESS.

mulct does not mean 'to *cheat* (a person)'. Correctly it = 'to punish (a person) by a fine', either as in 'The master was mulcted all his pay' or as in 'The new sect were . . . mulcted in heavy fines'.

multifarious; multiform; multiple. See MANIFOLD.

murder; manslaughter; homicide. These three terms are often confused. In the British Empire, *murder* is planned, intentional killing; *manslaughter* is unplanned, though possibly intentional killing; *homicide* is the generic term for all killing of one person by another. More precisely:—

Murder is 'the unlawful killing of a human being with malice aforethought; often more implicitly *wilful murder*'. In the U.S.A. there are two kinds of murder: *murder in the second degree*, where there are mitigating circumstances; *murder in the first degree*, where there are none.

Manslaughter (in Scotland: *culpable homicide*) is 'committed when one person causes the death of another either intentionally in the heat of passion under certain kinds of provocation, or unintentionally by culpable negligence or as a consequence of some unlawful act'. (*O.E.D.*)

Homicide, which includes both *murder* and *manslaughter*, occurs chiefly in

culpable homicide, which is *manslaughter*; excusable homicide, which is killing in self-defence or by accident or misadventure;

justifiable homicide, which is a killing in the performance of certain legal duties (e.g., the hangman's), by unavoidable necessity, or to prevent the commission of an atrocious crime. (*Webster's*.)

mutual = 'reciprocal', as in 'mutual fear', 'mutual friendship'—this being the safest sense in which to use it; and 'pertaining to both parties; common; in common', since ca. 1900 regarded as incorrect when applied to things, actions, sentiments, as in 'our mutual front door', (of a collaboration) 'their mutual work'; and in the same general sense, but applied to 'a personal designation expressive of a relation'—an application now regarded as incorrect except in *mutual friend(s)* and *mutual acquaintance(s)*, where the strictly correct *common* is ambiguous (still, one can always say *friends—or acquaintances—in common*). (*O.E.D.*)

myself, yourself, herself, himself, itself, ourselves, yourselves, themselves. There is a tendency to employ these pronouns where the simple *I* (or *me*), *you*, *she* (or *her*), *he* (or *him*), *it*, *we* (or *us*), *you*, *they* (or *them*) are sufficient. The *self* forms are either reflexives, as in 'I hurt *myself*', or emphatic additions, as in 'He *himself* did not know' (avoid the ambiguity of 'He did not know *himself*'). Here are three misuses:—

'You and myself will arrange this between us'
'Herself and himself will soon be getting married'
'He sent the enquiry to yourself'.

mystery is not used as an adjective by self-respecting writers. When Anthony Berkeley, in 1938, wrote that 'The local police were half disgruntled at being cheated of their mystery murder and half thrilled at being caught up into issues so far outside their own experience', he was poking fun at popular journalists. There is some—though inadequate—excuse for *mystery man* (short for *man of mystery* or *mysteries*).

N

naif, naïf; naive, naïve. *Naif* is inexcusable; *naïf* is unnecessary, being the masculine of Fr. *naïf*; *naive*, 'artless'. The *O.E.D.* recommends *naive*, written in roman and pronounced as a dissyllabic.

name (v.). See DENOMINATE.

name of, of (or by) the. See BY THE NAME OF.

name . . . who (or that). It is permissible to say, 'The editor telephoned to a big name from whom he wanted an article', although the present writer does not recommend such looseness. But the following use of *name* passes the bounds of decency: 'Picking up his telephone, he called for a certain number . . . Getting it, he asked for a certain name, who, in less than a minute, was upon the 'phone.'

nasty. Weseen is wrong in condemning this word as a colloquialism in the senses 'unpleasant, disagreeable' (as in 'a nasty day'), 'mean' ('a nasty trick'), and 'ill-natured, ill-tempered' ('to turn nasty'): they are faultless Standard English.

native(s). There is something not only inexact but offensive in the general use of this word for the dark-skinned inhabitants of Africa, India, etc., as though it applied exclusively to them and implied an inferiority of race. The inhabitants born in England or the United States are the 'natives' of that country.

natty. See TASTEFUL.

naught. See 'NOUGHT and NAUGHT'.

near and **near to.** *Near* and *near to* can be used of literal position, as in 'We lived quite near them', or, less usually, '. . . near to them'; *near to* is more general than *near* in transferred or derivative senses—sometimes, indeed, *near* would be wrong in such instances. As Dr Onions remarks, 'Notice that the different senses of *near* take different constructions, e.g., "The Prince of Wales stood *near* (or *near to*) [i.e., close *to*] the *throne*" and "The German Emperor [was] *near to the throne* of Great Britain" (i.e., in respect of succession). In the second sentence "near the throne" would be undesirable, as being ambiguous and suggesting the wrong meaning'; a neat exemplification of the difference.

near-by, as an adverb, is English dialectal and American; as a preposition, English dialectal; as an adjective, American.

Near East, the. See MIDDLE EAST.

necessaries and **necessities.** The former = 'essentials; requisites', as in 'Food, sleep and shelter are necessaries of life'. In this sense, *necessities* is obsolescent. The predominant current sense of *necessities* is 'pressing needs or wants; a situation of difficulty or of hardship', as in 'The necessities of every newly colonised country' and 'We must aim at a habit of gratitude, which has no relation to present necessities'.

The adjective *necessitous* = 'living or placed in poverty' or 'characterized by poverty'. (*O.E.D.*)

necessity is a misuse for (an) *essential*. 'Without the necessities of a good internal government, liberty is not likely to last long', meaning 'the needful elements' or 'essentials'.

neglect is *negligence* exemplified. When they are approximate equivalents ('Guilty of negligence', 'guilty of neglect'), *neglect* is the stronger word.

negligence should be used for *indifference* only in the senses 'careless indifference concerning one's appearance' and 'unaffected style'; not for *callousness*, as in 'Feigned negligence and real anxiety as it were cancelling each other out in his voice and rendering it quite toneless'.

negligent; negligible. Respectively 'careless' and 'not worth care (or attention)'.

Negro (capitalized). [In America *Negro* is not so acceptable as *colored* (*person*) to descendants of African races, except in formal statements. Of recent use is *race* (n. and adj.), e.g., 'race (phonograph) *recordings*' for recordings made by Negroes.]

negro; negrillo; negrito. For the first, at least, the capital letter would seem to be not merely more polite but grammatically more fitting. The plurals are *Negroes*, *negrillos, negritos*; and only *Negro* has a distinct feminine—*Negress*.

neighbourhood of, in the. 'The story . . . on the making of which Hollywood is said to have lavished in the neighbourhood of £300,000.' Here the expression is a bad and wholly unnecessary substitute for 'about' or 'nearly'. Cf. **region of, in the.**

neither followed by a plural verb. See EITHER.

neither should be restricted to two things, persons, actions, sets, groups, companies, etc. For three or more, *not any* or *none* is required. In 'Jack, Jill and Jim were present; neither had much to say', substitute *none* (*of them*) for *neither*.

neither . . . nor. The *number* of the verb has caused much trouble. The simplest general rule is that (*a*) if both of the subjects are in the singular, the verb is singular ('Neither Bill nor Jack is at fault'), and (*b*) if either of the subjects is in the plural, so is the verb ('Neither the men nor the woman are at fault'—'Neither he nor they are at fault'). Obviously if both of the subjects are in the plural, so is the verb.

Pronouns in different persons increase the difficulty. The rule that the nearer subject governs the verb in both person and number applies here as elsewhere. Thus:

'Neither he nor I *am* at fault'
'Neither he nor you *are* at fault'
'Neither you nor I *am* at fault'
'Neither you nor he *is* at fault'
'Neither I nor he *is* at fault'
'Neither I nor you *are* at fault'.

neither . . . nor, misplaced. 'Bertrand Russell has characterized pure mathematics as "that science in which we neither know what we are talking about, nor whether what we say is true" ' (Stuart Chase, *The Tyranny of Words*). Read '. . . we know neither what we are talking about nor whether what we say is true'.

neither . . . nor . . . nor. See NO . . . NOR.

neither of their (sakes). See GENITIVE, VAGARIES OF THE: penultimate paragraph.

neither . . . or is a rather childish mistake for *neither . . . nor*. A professional writer perpetrated this: 'Looking neither to the right or the left'.

NEOLOGISMS. 'A novel word or phrase which has not yet secured unquestioned admission into the standard [language] is called a *neologism*, which is simply a "new form of speech". There is no test but time. If a neologism seems to most speakers to supply a lack in the language, or to be peculiarly fit for the expression of some special idea, it is sure to maintain itself against the protests of the literary and scholastic guild.—On the other hand, nothing can force a new term into any language against the inclination of a large majority of those who speak it. The field of language is strewn with the dry bones of adventurous words which once started out with the paternal blessing to make their fortune, but which have met with an untimely end, and serve only, when collected, to fill the shelves of a lexicographical museum.' (The Fowler brothers.)

Neologisms, moreover, should be formed with some regard to etymological decency; the marriage of a so very English word as *swim* with a so very Greek vocable as *stad* strikes one as an unseemly misalliance. And what reason for *swimstad* when we have *swimming-bath*?

neophyte: 'a beginner, a novice, a tyro': is not to be overdone!

nett for *net*, as in *nett profit*, *nett result*, is without justification.

neurasthenic and **neurotic.** There is a scientific distinction between *neurasthenia*, 'a nervous weakness', and *neurosis*, 'a nervous disease' (*O.E.D.*), from which the adjectives are derived. Such terms should be left to the doctors.

never, as a mere equivalent of *not*, is a colloquialism and should, in serious writing, be used only after careful consideration. 'He never knew it was so chilly' for 'He did not know it was so chilly' is natural in dialogue, but incongruous in formal writing; cf. 'He spoke never a word' for 'He spoke *not* a word' (emphatic) or 'He did not speak a word' (neutral). In familiar speech 'He spoke never a word' is stronger than 'He did not speak a word'; in writing it is no stronger than 'He spoke not a word'.

never expected is loose for *expected never*, as in 'I never expected to see her there'.

never so is no longer good English for *ever so*, as in 'Beer is beer, be it never so weak'.

nevertheless. The combination *but nevertheless* is tautological for *nevertheless*.

new and **novel.** The former refers to time ('It is new to me') or to state or condition ('His suit was new'); the latter to kind ('It's a novel way or method'). *New* is opposed to *old*, *novel* to *common* or *well-known*.

New Year Day. Incorrect for *New Year's Day*.

New York City. The official name is *The City of New York*, rare except in official papers or formal statements. *New York City* (abbr. *N.Y.C.*) is common in both speech and writing, as is simple *New York* except where it leads to confusion between the city and the state. *New York, N.Y.* is a variant in writing and is sometimes preferred to *New York City*. Mail is addressed to *New York, N.Y.*, or *New York City*.

news. Anxiety to be correct causes people sometimes to put the verb in the plural, but the singular has been accepted as Good English, as in 'No news is good news'.

nice is a verbal counter; permissible in conversation, it is to be avoided in serious writing.

nicely for *satisfactorily* or *well*, or *very well*, is not a colloquialism; it is, however, far too common and should, as a general rule, be avoided. [According to *Webster's*, *nicely* (adj.) meaning *well*, *in good health*, is colloquial; *nicely* (adv.) is standard for *precisely*, *scrupulously*, *satisfactorily*.]

nigger belongs only, and then only in contempt or fun, to the dark-skinned African races and their descendants in

America and the West Indies. Its application to the native peoples of India is offensive.

nigh (adv.) for *near* is archaic in prose; current usage reserves it for poetry. Do not employ it as an adjective. *Well nigh* for *almost* or *very nearly* is a cliché.

no. See at NONE.

no + superlative + noun ('no slightest sign') = '*no* + that noun, *not even the slightest*'. Idiomatically, 'There was no slightest sign' = 'There was no sign at all, not even the slightest', and not, as one might think, 'There was no very slight sign, but there was a big sign'.

no admission is occasionally used ambiguously for *no admission-charge*, to which *admission (is) free* is preferable.

no more . . . than. A curious slip is made by that brilliant American writer, George Jean Nathan, in: 'Napoleon returned and had no more taken up his knife and fork than he was again called out of his tent . . .', where the meaning is '. . . had no more than taken up his knife and fork when he was called out . . .', or 'had no sooner taken up . . . than he was called out'.

no . . . nor for *no . . . and no* and *no . . . or*. This *no . . . nor* is permitted by *The O.E.D.* in its use as an equivalent of *no . . . and no*, as in 'We had no revolutions to fear, nor fatigues to endure'. This equivalence, however, is obsolescent. The man in the street tends now to say, 'We had no revolutions to fear and no fatigues to endure', and the modern stylist would write, 'We had no revolutions to fear; no fatigues to endure'. 'She took no interest nor part in outdoor sports' seems nowadays old-fashioned. Sometimes *or* would be preferred to *and no* as the modern equivalent of this *nor*, as in 'He had in him . . . no tincture of Scottish, Irish, Welsh, French, German, Italian, American nor Jewish [blood]', where a modern stylist would write 'He had . . . no tincture of Scottish, Irish, Welsh . . . American, or Jewish [blood]', with a comma after *American* to ensure dissociation. In the following sentence, 'They say that no novel in the first person can ever be true because no one can recall conversations as they actually occurred nor remember the physical details of past scenes',—I should have preferred '. . . no one can [either] recall conversations . . . or remember the physical details', which is neater than 'no one can recall conversations . . . and no one can remember

the physical details'. Here, as in all nuanced writing, discrimination is required; not the bull-at-a-gate courage of desperation.

no object. See OBJECT, NO.

no one; noone. The latter is incorrect.

no one (or **nobody**) **. . . they.** See ANYONE . . . THEY.

no one's (**nobody's**) **else** (else's). See ELSE'S.

no place is illiterate for *nowhere*, as in 'The jewel was no place to be found'.

no such. 'You can't have seen a letter from me, because no such exists' should be *no such letter* (or *thing*), for *such* ought not to be used as a pronoun except in the time-honoured formulas, 'such is life', 'such was the decision'.

no thing. See 'NOTHING and NO THING'.

no use is incorrect—or, at best, colloquial —for *of no use* or, more economically, *useless*, as in 'This pen is no use'.

nobody's else. See ELSE'S.

nom de plume is to be avoided: there is no such term in the best French, *nom de guerre* being usual. The correct English is *pen-name* or (literary) *pseudonym*, of which the former is a translation of the pseudo-French *nom de plume*; but in post-War French, *nom de plume* is very often employed: the popularity of *pen-name* + that of *nom de plume*, as used in England, has engendered a genuinely French *nom de plume* which is a writer's *nom de guerre*.

nomenclature means not, as in ' "Delpha" may be a popular nomenclature with the mystic sorority', but 'a system of names'—as in 'The Linnaean nomenclature'—or 'the terminology used in a science or in technics'.

nominal is incorrectly used in 'The figures are nominal'; he means *approximate*. *Nominal*: 'existing in name only, in distinction to real or actual' (*O.E.D.*). *Nominal*, in *at a nominal charge* or *cost*, *for a nominal fee*, is not 'low' but 'so low' as not fairly to be reckoned a charge, a cost, a fee. In short, *nominal* is not synonymous with *low*.

nominate. See DENOMINATE.

NOMINATIVE ABSOLUTE. There's nothing mysterious about this! 'She failing to keep the appointment, he went off and got drunk.'

none. (i) When *none = not one*, use the singular, as in 'None of the newspapers has appeared this week'.

(ii) When *none = no one, no person, nobody*, the singular is correct; but, as indeed for (i) also, the plural is not regarded as a solecism.

(iii) When *none* = *no persons*, the verb is plural, as in 'None have been so greedy of employments . . . as they who have least deserved their stations' (Dryden). The corresponding singular pronoun is *no one*. That is how I posed the problem in *Usage and Abusage*. But I was wrong —how very badly wrong, Mr R. B. Hamilton of Nottingham shows in a letter he has generously allowed me to quote.

'It is bad form nowadays to mention the Ten Commandments; so I will, with apologies, take you no further than the first, as it appears in the Prayer Book: "Thou shalt have none other gods but me". The turn of phrase is archaic; but if you had pondered it, you might have cleared up, instead of thickening, the fog of pretentious misunderstanding which surrounds the use of "none".

'May I submit for your consideration the following sentences:—

Q. Is there any sugar?
A. 1. No, there isn't any sugar. (collo-quial)
2. No, there isn't any. (colloquial and elliptical)
3. No, there is no sugar. (formal)
4. No, there is none. (formal and ellip-tical)

Q. Are there any plums?
A. 5. No, there aren't any plums. (collo-quial)
6. No, there aren't any. (colloquial and elliptical)
7. No, there are no plums. (formal)
8. No, there are none. (formal and elliptical)

'You will, I hope, agree that this arrangement has more than symmetry to recommend it. In the first place, all four replies in each case are exactly synony-mous; secondly, they are all logical; and, thirdly, they are all idiomatic—they all slip off the tongue of careful and careless speakers alike; you hear them all every day of your life.

'Are they all equally grammatical? It seems that they should be; for they are logical and idiomatic, and what is gram-mar but a mixture of logic and idiom? There is no dispute as to Nos. 1 to 7; but when you come to Number 8, you will find that there is a superstition that, in formal contexts, it should be re-written with the verb in the singular. The awk-wardness of this is apparent; for it seems to require the question to be either "Is there any plums?", which is bad gram-mar, or "Is there any plum?", which is not English at all. This awkwardness, however, recommends it to pompous or timid writers who, like fakirs, hope to gain merit by discomfort.

'The superstition was I think invented by some 18th-century sciolist, who, mis-led by appearances and regardless of his-tory and logic, decided that "none" was a contraction of "no one" and decreed that it should be followed by a singular verb. In point of fact, the truth is the opposite; for "no" itself is nothing but a shortened form of "none", standing in the same relation to it as "my" does to "mine"; so that "none other gods" is archaic only in retaining the longer form, before an initial vowel, in attributive use, and the phrase answers to the modern "no other gods" precisely as the Biblical "mine eyes" answers to the modern "my eyes". The phrase "no one" is therefore really a tautology (= not one one); and if Sentence No. 8 is wrong, No. 7 must be equally so.

'It is quite true that "none" contains the Anglo-Saxon *ān* (one), as also for that matter does "any". But Anglo-Saxon grammar is not English grammar; and both words have been indifferently singular and plural for six centuries.

'If you will now look back to the sen-tences, you will see that the facts are as follows:—(1) "No" is merely the attribu-tive form of "none"; (2) "None" and "no" do *not* (except by accident) mean "not one" or "no one" or "no persons"; they mean "not any", neither more nor less (it is impossible to construct any sen-tence which you cannot make into a ques-tion by substituting "any" for "none" and inverting the order of the words); and (3) "No", "none" and "any" are all singular or plural, according to the sense.

'Let me then urge you to throw in your lot with the "good-enoughists" (what is good enough for the Prayer Book should be good enough for you) and admit these simple facts. It is no disgrace to yield when etymology, logic, and idiom are all against you. To say (as you suggest we should) "None of the newspapers has appeared" is no better than to say "No newspapers has appeared". Indeed, it is worse; for vulgarity may be forgiven, but pretentiousness carries its own heavy punishment.'

none, misused with genitive. See GENI-TIVE, VAGARIES . . ., penultimate para-graph.

none such is very awkwardly, if not incorrectly, used in 'When he asked for the name, he was told that none such was in the register'.—Cf. NO SUCH.

nor for *or* and for *and no*. See 'NO . . . NOR for NO . . . AND NO'.

nor for *than*, as in Thackeray, 'You're no better nor a common tramper' (*O.E.D.*), is still frequent in low colloquial speech, but is a mark of illiteracy.

Occasionally, *nor . . . neither* is misused for *nor . . . either*, as in 'You've had a Boy Scout's training and they never have. Nor I neither.' One negatives not both members of *or . . . either* (that would produce a double negative) but the first only in this formula, which is quite different from '*neither* (you) *nor* I'; *nor I either* is merely an elaboration of *nor I*.

nor none is occasionally misused for *nor any*. ' "They have no Libel Law in France." "Nor none in Brazil", says Miles.'

normal, the. See:

normalcy, normalism, normality and normalness. The fourth is incorrect; the second, which is rare, has no special, no technical senses; the first is more American than British, but it is catching on in Great Britain; *normality* is the usual British form, although *the normal* is fast displacing it in the sense 'a normal variety of anything; an individual or specimen possessing normal characteristics or faculties'.

north. Inferior to *northward(s)* as adv.

northernly is inferior to *northerly* (adj.).

northward and **northwards.** The former is adj. and adv.; the latter, adv. only. Usage apparently prefers adverbial *northward* to the longer-established *northwards*.

nostalgia, nostalgic. *Nostalgia* 'means homesickness in acute form, verging on the psychopathic. Misconception of the meaning as any kind of intense yearning seems to be so widespread as to threaten that its true significance will soon be classed as archaic' (a correspondent, *The Times Literary Supplement*, Oct. 6, 1945). True; literally, the word means 'a painful desire to return home' and that, near enough, is the meaning in good English.

In the same way, *nostalgic*, instead of signifying 'from, in, of morbid homesickness', hence 'homesick', is frequently misused to signify nothing more than 'regretful' or 'yearning' or even 'reminiscent'.

not a one and **not one.** The former is incorrect: for 'Not a one of them did that' read 'Not one of them did that'.

not . . . any more is both wordy and colloquial for *no longer*, as in 'He was not hungry any more'.

not anything like. See NOTHING LIKE . . .

not hardly is incorrect for *hardly*. So too *not scarcely* for *scarcely*.

not . . . nor . . . nor is permissible when it is used instead of *neither . . . nor . . . nor*. Gladstone, 1870, writes 'Not a vessel, nor a gun, nor a man, were on the ground to prevent their landing', which, woolly though it is, is preferable to 'Neither a vessel, nor a gun, nor a man . . .'

not only . . . but (also), misplaced. 'This necessitated, not only the resignations of Essex and Manchester, against whom it was chiefly aimed, but also such valuable men as Lord Warwick, who as Lord High Admiral had successfully held the seas for Parliament during those anxious years' should read: 'This necessitated the resignations not only of Essex and Manchester, against whom it was chiefly aimed, but also of such valuable men as Lord Warwick, who . . .' Quoted by G. V. Carey, *Mind the Stop*, 1939; he adds: 'If you prefer to put "not only" after the first "of", you will not need a second "of" before "such".'

not . . . or for *not . . . nor*. 'Making certain there there was not, or was there likely to be, any alteration in the time of the boat's usual midday sailing . . . he disappeared.'

not scarcely. See NOT HARDLY.

notable and **noted.** The former emphasizes worth or worthiness; the latter, celebrity. The former is potential; the latter, actual. A notable man may not be noted; a noted man may not be notable.

notary; notary public. See LAWYER.—The plural of *notary public* is *notaries public*.

note and **notice** (vv.). *Note*, as merely 'to take notice of', is fortunately passing out of use. Usage now prefers *note* to = 'to *notice closely*'.

nothing and **no thing.** In the latter, the emphasis is on *thing*, as in 'No thing perturbs him'; many persons do'. 'Nothing perturbs him' connotes absence of, or freedom from perturbation. Whereas *nothing* is inclusive and general, *no thing* is exclusive and particular.

nothing but. In *nothing but* + a noun, it is *nothing* which determines the number of the verb; in other words, the verb after *nothing but . . .* should be in the singular. 'Nothing but dreary dykes occur to break the monotony of the landscape' should be 'Nothing but dreary dykes occurs . . .' (Onions, *An Advanced English Syntax*, 6th ed., 1932).

nothing like, adverbial ('Nothing like so fast'), is a colloquialism for *not nearly*.

notice. See 'NOTE and NOTICE'.

noticeable and **notable.** The former merely = 'worthy of notice', not—as *notable* does—'worthy of fame'; *noticeable* has the derivative sense, 'capable of being noticed; perceptible'.

notorious and **famous.** Both mean 'very well known (to the general public)'; but the former is unfavourable, the latter favourable; thus, 'a famous writer' but 'a notorious criminal'. *Notorious*, in short, is 'famous in a bad way—for crime or excessive vice'. The cliché *it is notorious that* properly means no more than 'it is common knowledge that . . .', but usage invests it with pejorative connotation.

n't for *not* is colloquial and familiar.

nought and **naught.** For the cypher or zero, use *nought*; for 'nothing' use *naught*,—that is, if you use it at all, for it is archaic except in poetry. [For the cypher or zero, *Webster's* prefers *naught*.]

NOUN ADJECTIVES. Frank Whitaker, having attacked the anti-possessive craze (*q.v.* at AMBIGUITY), continues thus:

'The noun-adjective mania is even more dangerous, in the sense that it is driving a wedge between written and spoken English. I read in a recent issue of the "Daily Sketch", picked up haphazard, these headlines: "Minister's Milk Bill Climb-down" (we must be grateful for the possessive there: "Minister Milk Bill" would have been a little difficult); "Navy bid to save stranded Britons" (no possessive there, you will notice), and "Brothers' big boxing bid". Now I know what is meant by the first two of those headlines—the third puzzles me—but heaven forbid that one man should ever go up to another in the street and say "Have you heard the latest about the Minister's Milk Bill Climb-down, or of the Navy bid to save stranded Britons?"

'I read in another paper, "Crime chief to retire", and I think I know what that means. But I am wrong. The man who is about to retire is not a gangster but a Scotland Yard superintendent. And what are we to make of the headline noted by William Empson in his book, "Seven types of Ambiguity", which reads, "Italian assassin bomb plot disaster"? We must be grateful again that the sub-editor did not follow the current fashion and write, "Italy assassin bomb plot disaster". But what did he mean? Was the assassin Italian? He was not. It was the disaster that was Italian. And what is an "assassin bomb plot"? I give it up.'

novel. See NEW.

noway; noways; nowise. All are correct; the third is the best; the second, the rarest.

noxious. See OBNOXIOUS.

number: whether it takes a singular or a plural verb. 'If a group of words, especially a partitive group, conveys the idea of plurality, a number of individuals, the verb is in the plural, even though the governing noun is singular, [but] the verb is singular if the group conveys the idea of oneness: "The greatest *part* of these years *was* spent in philosophic retirement", but "The greatest *part* of the Moguls and Tartars *were* as illiterate as their sovereigns". In "*a large number* of the garrison *were* prostrate with sickness" and "There *are a large number* of things that I desire to say" *number* is now felt not as a collective noun but as a component of a compound numeral, [and] the indefinite . . . *a large number* [as having] plural force, so that the verb is in the plural. . . . *Number* as a singular noun is still found occasionally where a writer follows the outward form rather than the inner meaning: "Chicago has as many more [models] and besides these there *is* probably *an equal number* of occasional sitters, transients" (Beecher Edwards, "Faces That Haunt You", in *Liberty*, May 22, 1926).' Such is the pronouncement of that great American grammarian, George O. Curme.

O

O and **Oh.** *O* and *Oh* were at one time used indifferently, but now the use of *O* is almost confined to poetry. *O* without punctuation is an invocation (vocative case) to some person or object named in the words that follow it, as in Milton:

O thou that with surpassing glory crowned,
Look'st from thy sole dominion, etc.,

or in the humbler verse, 'O lovely night! O! [or Oh!] lovely night!', which is two exclamations, the second explaining the cause of the first.

But *Oh, (a) lovely night, isn't it?* is not exclamatory; *Oh* in such cases implies a momentary pause for thought before speaking. Often it seems to call attention to a change of subject, a new idea: *Oh, have you heard, etc.?* Real hesitancy would be conveyed by *Oh—*. The mark of exclamation (*Oh!*) will always indicate some degree of feeling, surprise, pleasure or the reverse.

Dean Alford, complaining of the compositors' habit of inserting unnecessary and often misleading stops, says: 'If one has written the words *O sir* as they ought to be written in Genesis xliii, 20, viz., with the plain capital "O" and no stop, and then a comma after "sir", our friend the compositor is sure to write "Oh" with a shriek (!) and to put another shriek after "sir".'

object, no. E.g., 'distance no object' and 'price no object': catachrestic when 'no obstacle' or 'not an objection' is meant. The correct sense, 'not a thing aimed at or considered important' has been vitiated by confusion with *no objection*. Its absurdity is seen in the undertaker's advertisement: 'Distance no object'.

obligate (adj.), defined by *The O.E.D.* as 'that is of necessity such', is applied with scientific meaning by biologists, but is better avoided by all others.—As verb it is sometimes used for *oblige*, but means rather *to bind* (a person) *under an obligation.* An ugly and unnecessary word.

obliged. Correct uses:

(1) 'I am obliged by circumstances to do it.'

(2) 'I am much obliged to you for your kindness.'

(3) 'I shall be obliged if you stop making that noise.'

(4) 'I am'—or 'He or she is'—'your obliged servant', an old-fashioned letter-ending.

Of Nos. 2 and 3, *The O.E.D.* remarks, 'Now said only in reference to small services'. Except in dialogue, avoid the colloquialism exemplified in 'He obliged with a song'.

oblivion for *ignorance.* 'The necessity of keeping the common people in oblivion of the shortcomings of their material welfare.' (In reference to Germany and Italy.) **oblivious** for *unconscious* (*of*). *The O.E.D.* quotes Buckle, 'He was so little given to observation as to be frequently oblivious of what was passing around him'. Noun and adjective refer only to what has been known and is forgotten. Indeed, *oblivious* for *unconscious*, or for *impervious*, is a rather serious misuse. 'Fraim Falloway crouched morosely . . ., his face a puzzled mask' ['puzzled mask' is contradictory]; 'and when I offered him a cigarette he seemed utterly oblivious to my gesture'; moreover, one says *oblivious of*: cf. 'She continued brightly, oblivious to Martha's expression'. [*Oblivious* for *unobservant* is a colloquialism in American English.]

obnoxious, 'aggressively disagreeable', must not be confused with *noxious*, which means 'injurious', e.g., of poison-gas.

OBSCURITY. 'It may be better to be clear than clever, it is still better to be clear and correct.'

'Without distinction of speech there is never much distinction of idea', remarks Frank Binder. And without distinction of idea there cannot be distinction of speech —or style. 'Real and offensive obscurity comes merely of inadequate thought embodied in inadequate language', declared Swinburne in 1870. On the other hand, as a certain grammarian has said, 'In contemplating the way in which our sentences will be understood, we are allowed to remember, that we do not write for idiots'.

To begin with, two examples of that obscurity which arises from the desire to be brief ('I labour to be brief and become obscure', as Horace once remarked).

'I began to get excited over my new photographic outfit. It was natural, since it was new.'

'The bright naves of the wheels caught and played with the sun in their slow turning; and . . . at every fourth revolution, one of them creaked with a sort of musical complaint at a world which was perfect but for a drop of oil.' One is abruptly pulled up: *but for the lack of a drop of oil* would be better.

And then a number of miscellaneous examples which serve to show the dangers of obscurity.

'There are, of course, many uses of *colorful* which have no such [damning] implications—where, for example, that a thing should be full of colour is all we can ask where no ironical reserves and no disparagement can be intended.'

'There is no warrant for the placing on these inevitably rather light heads and hearts, on any company of you, assaulted, in our vast vague order, by many pressing wonderments, the *whole* of the burden of a care for tone' (Henry James). Cited by I. A. Richards (*op. cit.*) without comment. I pass it on—without comment.

'No, there was nothing left for him [David] in business . . . he was surfeited with success . . . David, too, though, had ideas. Vague, true, but ideas.' *Though* (= however) causes part of the trouble; *true* is so short for 'it is true' that ambiguity has arisen.

'He watched David talk, not too closely to make him self-conscious' (*ibid.*). The sentence would have been clear written thus: ' . . .; not too closely, lest he should make him self-conscious' or 'not so closely as to make . . .'

'Dales went first next day to the Registrar of Births and Marriages.' Dales was not the first to go there; probably not the first on even that day. The author meant, 'Next day, Dales went, first to the Registrar (and then elsewhere)'. Not content with that, the author continues, 'He found him a young man'.

'It was not Carol Berman alone to whom the jury's verdict came as a bewildering shock. Inspector Cambridge felt almost as dazed as she.' Obviously the passage should begin thus: 'It was not to Carol Berman alone that the jury's verdict came as a bewildering shock.'

observance and **observation**. The latter is no longer used for the former. *Observance* = 'the action or practice of keeping or paying attention (a law, custom, ceremony, etc.)'; also 'an act performed in accordance with prescribed usage; a practice customarily observed'. (*O.E.D.*)

observe is incorrect when used for 'to *preserve*' or 'keep' or 'retain'.—In the sense 'to make a remark', to 'remark' (v.t.), it is not incorrect but merely feeble.

obtain is incorrect when used for *to effect*. It seems to have arisen from a confusion of two senses, 'to gain or acquire'; and 'to reach'. See also 'PROCURE and SECURE'.

obverse. See CONVERSE.

occupy for *run to*, or *have*, or *comprise*, is loose. 'Such preparation may occupy six or seven stages.'

octopi, a mistaken plural of *octopus* by those who suppose it to be from Latin. The English termination should be used, *octopuses*; the pedantic prefer *octopodes*. [*Webster's* lists as plurals of *octopus* (New Latin): *octopuses, octopodes, octopi.*]

odd, 'strange', and **odd**, 'and a few more' (300 *odd*), must not be allowed to set up ambiguity, as in 'These 300 odd pages'. Write 'These 300-odd pages'.

odd number (or **odd-number**) is incorrect for *odd-numbered* in 'the odd-number tickets'.

odious and **odorous**. The former = 'hateful or detestable'; the latter = 'having a smell', i.e. *odoriferous*, which is generally used in the favourable sense, 'sweet-smelling, fragrant', the opposite being *malodorous* ('evil-smelling'). *Odorous* is never a pejorative.

of, carelessly omitted. This happens especially in *of which* clauses; e.g., 'The Colonel . . . departed to make arrangements, the exact nature of which Topper decided he would be more comfortable to remain in ignorance', where *the exact nature of which* should be *of the exact nature of which*.

of for *have* is a gross solecism, as in 'If I had of done it', where, moreover, *have* itself would be an illiterate intrusion.

of in *off of* is a Cockneyism and incorrect. *Off from* may in certain cases be allowed, but *away from*, *down from*, would always be better. [In American English *off of* is colloquial and vulgar.]

of, preposition. Incorrect uses of both *of* and *for* are exemplified in the following sentence, 'Even the very recent explanation of Mr Aldous Huxley for Swift's misanthropy is influenced by the theory of psycho-analysis'. Here 'of' should be 'by' and 'for' should be 'of'.

of all others. See OTHER, OF ALL.

of her—of hers; of his (+ noun)**—of his; of my—of mine; of your—of yours**. 'Note that "These are three friends *of mine*" and "These are three of *my friends*" have different implications; the second implies that I have more than three friends; the first does not' (Onions), though it does not exclude that possibility. There is, however, a further difference: 'A friend of the King' connotes dignity, whereas 'a friend of Bill Brown's' connotes familiarity in speech.

Certain writers have sought to confuse the issue by asking, 'What about *that long nose of his*?'; they point out that *his* cannot refer to more noses than one. Jespersen, *On Some Disputed Points in English Grammar*, deals fully with the entire *of my—of mine* question, and he shows that *that long nose of his* = *that long nose which is his*; he calls 'of his' (in *that long nose of his*) an appositional genitive.

George O. Curme, in *Syntax*, shrewdly remarks that 'There has become associated with the double genitive a marked liveliness of feeling, so that it now often implies praise or censure, pleasure or displeasure: "that dear little girl *of yours*", "that kind wife *of yours*", "this broad land *of ours*", "that ugly nose *of his*".' For the difficulties of this double genitive when a noun, not a pronoun is involved, see GENITIVE, VAGARIES OF THE, at the paragraph on the double genitive.

of old, as in 'A boy of twelve years old', is incorrect for *of age*. Or re-write thus, 'A boy twelve years old'.

of the name of. See BY THE NAME OF.

of whether. See WHETHER, OF.

of which. See WHOSE.

off of. See 'OF in *off of*'.

off-handed (adj.) is unnecessary for *off-hand*; *off-handedly* (adv.), for *off-hand*. These terms may be written as one word.

official = 'of, pertaining to, characteristic of office; authoritative; governmental'; whereas *officious* = 'meddlesome, interfering, obtrusive, pettily fussy'.

OFFICIALESE, JOURNALESE, COMMERCIALESE.

I. JOURNALESE. 'The style of language supposed to be characteristic of public journals; "newspaper" or "penny-a-liner's" English' (*O.E.D.*). *Webster's* defines it more fully thus: 'English of a style featured by use of colloquialisms, superficiality of thought or reasoning, clever or sensational presentation of material, and evidences of haste in composition, considered characteristic of newspaper writing.'

Journalese hardly needs exemplifying; but here is one example: 'Notwithstanding the genuine literary productions that have sprung out of the haunts of cotton-mills and weaving sheds, they have only here and there penetrated far beyond the immediate neighbourhood that called them into existence' (a Manchester journalist, 1850).

II. OFFICIALESE is that type of wordy English which has been—often justifiably—associated with Government offices.

In *The Times* of August 8, 1939, occurs this letter (which contains examples of both officialese and clegancies):

'*PLAIN ENGLISH*

'To the Editor of *The Times*.

'Sir,—May I contribute an example to Mr. Herbert's instances of deviations from "plain verbiage"? I had occasion some time since to ask a Government Department to supply me with a book for official use. I was informed in reply that, although the Department was not in a position to meet my request, I was "authorized to acquire the work in question by purchase through the ordinary trade channels". Or, as we should say, "buy it".

'It would be easy to add to Mr. Herbert's list of words which mark the tendency he deplores. "Assist" for "help", "endeavour" for "try", "proceed" for "go", "purchase" for "buy", "approximately" for "about", "sufficient" for "enough", "attired" for "dressed", "inquire" for "ask", are general in speech as well as print. I have noticed that whereas the waste in old lavatory-basins is marked "Shut", the up-to-date ones prefer the more refined "Closed". And, no doubt, some of these words and expressions are what Mr. Fowler, in his Modern English Usage, aptly termed "genteelisms". But others seem not to have even this justification.

'Mr. Herbert says with truth that even the Fighting Services have been corrupted. I have known one of them to be responsible for the use of "nomenclature" as a preferable equivalent for "name".

'August 3.   Your obedient servant,
CLAUD RUSSELL.'

In *The Listener* of April 10, 1947, the reviewer of the first edition of *Usage and Abusage* wrote thus:

'Mr. Partridge might have said more about Officialese. . . . This demon grows steadily more formidable as the Ministries multiply their number and their lists and schedules. They "initiate organisational preliminaries" instead of making preparations. They "integrate the hospitalisation services for the rehabilitation of mentally maladjusted persons". . . .

'One notes that the adjective "overall", which now appears in every paragraph of every Government report and is very dear to political journalists, had not cropped up in time for note. Apart from its sensible and proper application to certain garments, it can be rightly used of over-riding authorities. But the word has now become a vogue word, as Mr. Partridge would say, and is applied recklessly to figures and even situations. Inclusive figures are now always called "overall figures", which they are not. And how can a situation be overall? Another vogue word for him to watch is "bracket" to signify group. "The overall figures of the lower-income brackets" is typical economist's English today. "Economese" is a theme well worth his attention.'

But the most damning indictment of officialese—by far the most dangerous of these three menaces—is the one made in 1952 by 'Vigilans' in *Chamber of Horrors*, a glossary of British and American official jargon, with an introduction by E.P.

III. COMMERCIALESE OR BUSINESS ENGLISH (or, as Sir Alan Herbert calls it, *officese*).

A few examples of words and phrases used in commercial offices—and avoided by all self-respecting persons:—*advise* (inform), *as per*, *be in receipt of* ('We are in receipt of your letter'), *beg* ('We beg to bring to the notice of . . .'), *duly noted*, *esteemed favour* and *esteemed order*, (of) *even date*, *favour* (letter), *friends* (competitors: 'Our friends in the trade have been guilty of price-cutting'), *kindly* (for *please!*), *per*, *proximo*, *re* (of), *recent date*, *same* (for *it*: 'We have received same'), *service* (verb), *shop-lady*, *state* (for *say*), *a substantial percentage* (much; or merely some), *thanking you in advance*, *transportation* (a ticket), *ultimo*, *under one's signature*, *valuable asset*, *valued favour*, *your good self* (or *selves*).

Sir Alan Herbert, *What a Word!*, has a delightful section on commercialese. To those lively pages we send all those who wish a wittily scathing attack on the sort of English affected by business men (at least, in their offices). Sir Alan gives one example that simply cannot be omitted:—

'Madam,

We are in receipt of your favour of the 9th inst. with regard to the estimate required for the removal of your furniture and effects from the above address to Burbleton, and will arrange for a Representative to call to make an inspection on Tuesday next, the 14th inst., before 12 noon, which we trust will be convenient, after which our quotation will at once issue.'

Taking that letter as it stands, Sir Alan reduces it thus:—

'Madam,

We have your letter of May 9th requesting an estimate for the removal of your furniture and effects to Burbleton, and a man will call to see them next Tuesday afternoon if convenient, after which we will send the estimate without delay'; not counting 'Madam', we notice that the revised letter contains 42 words instead of 66. But Sir Alan goes further, by recasting, thus:

'Madam,

Thank you for your letter of May 9th. A man will call next Tuesday, forenoon, to see your furniture and effects, after which, without delay, we will send our estimate for their removal to Burbleton' (or 35 words against the original 66; or 157 letters against 294 letters).

Business English, in short, is extremely un-businesslike.

officious. See OFFICIAL.

offspring is properly used as a plural

('What offspring have you?'); as a singular it may have a curious ring, as in 'Here is my offspring, what do you think of him?'

oft is an archaism; *many times and oft*, a cliché.

often. According to *The Con. O.D.*, to pronounce the *t* is 'vulgar'. It is certainly unnecessary and is usually due to an affectation of refinement. [On the pronunciation in American English, see *Webster's*.]

To use *often* for *in many instances* sets up an ambiguity, as in 'A Danish house is often thatched with straw'.

oftener, oftenest are, in current usage, regarded as no less correct than *more often* and *most often*.

oftentimes and **ofttimes**. Both are obsolescent, though the latter still occurs in conventionally phrased poetry. Neither word means more than what is conveyed by *often*. [*Oftentimes* still occurs in American speech.]

old age, at an. Incorrect—or rather, unidiomatic—for *at an advanced age*.

older. See 'ELDER and OLDER'. Only *elder* is now used as a noun.

ology. See ISM.

omission. See OVERSIGHT.

omnibus. See BUS.

omnipotent; omniscient. The former = 'all-powerful'; the latter, 'all-knowing'.

on, used for *for*, is an error. 'To lay down the concept of free speech as practised in America *on* Asiatic peoples . . . is consistent if you like, but meaningless.'

on, misused for *on to*, e.g., 'I never notice what happens on the road, hanging on the back takes me all my time', a pillion passenger in a motoring case. The first 'on' is correctly used, the second incorrectly; to *hang on* anything is literally to be suspended, but to *hang on to* something is to cling or hold on with difficulty.

on and upon. See 'UPON and ON'.

on account of is unnecessary after *cause* or *reason*. For 'The reason is on account of (something or other)', read 'The reason is that . . .' or 'On account of something or other, something else happened'.

on behalf of. See BEHALF OF.

on time; in time. The former is colloquial, and American rather than English. *In time* = 'soon enough'; *on time* = 'punctually'.

on to. See ONTO.

one is often used unnecessarily or, at best, verbosely, as in 'If the opinion expressed is not one worthy of repetition, circulation should be restricted accordingly'.

one, use of plural in v. after. The rule is that the formula, *one of* + plural noun or pronoun, requires the ensuing verb to be in the plural. Thus 'He's one of those chaps who plays a lone hand' should be '. . . play a lone hand'. The use of the singular for the plural appears strangely inept when a subtle and notable writer employs it, as in 'We got out at one of those small country towns which is growing fast, but has not yet lost its character' (Joyce Cary). The rule becomes clear from an equation:

The cows
The red cows
The cows that *are* red in colour
One of the cows that *are* red in colour
It is one of the cows that are red in colour.

Therefore the *one* requires a singular verb:

One of the cows that *are* red in colour *is* for sale.

one and he. Nesfield condemns the use of *he* in: 'There are few demonstrations of affection; one is made to feel that he must trust himself'. It is strictly correct, but reads awkwardly; it would be better to say 'a man', 'each man' (is made to feel that he must trust himself). Correct, too, is the *one . . . one* mode; I confess that I prefer *one . . . one*, for it is less ambiguous than *one . . . he*.

Compare 'One readily admits that one may be wrong' (unambiguous) with 'One readily admits that he may be wrong'; in the latter it is not clear whether *he* refers to *one* or to a third person. Perhaps the simplest procedure is to determine whether the *one . . . one* or the *person . . . he* or the *you . . . you* mode is to prevail in the expression of your thought, and then to adhere to the mode chosen. Cf.: **ONE and YOU and WE modes.**

The *we* mode is—or should be—left to royalty, the Vatican, and editors of newspapers and other periodicals.

In friendly or familiar speech and in familiar writing, the *you* mode is permissible and often preferable: but care must be exercised against confusing the personal *you* ('When are you going to Town?') with the generic or impersonal *you* ('When you're dead, you're a long time dead').

In formal speeches and addresses, as in formal and literary writing, the *one* mode is preferable ('One does one's best to live the good life; but that best may fall so far short of merit as to seem, in the result, evil; nevertheless, it is one's effort which counts as virtue'). To employ the *one* mode in conversation, unless one does it with consummate skill, may produce a comic effect ('If one does one's best, one does all that one can be expected to do, doesn't one?').

one for *a* or *any*. 'Never has there been one complaint of any person having been robbed there.'

one another and **each other.** See 'EACH OTHER and ONE ANOTHER'.

one in (two . . . five, etc.) . . . takes a singular verb, and *two* (or *three* or *five*, etc.) *in* . . . takes a plural verb. The subjects respectively are simply *one* (amplified) and *two* (amplified), precisely as in *one horse in a million, one horse* is singular, and in *two horses in a thousand, two horses* is plural. In *John o' London's Weekly*, Jan. 6, 1939, 'Jackdaw' defends the advertisement-slogan 'Only one in five *clean* their [properly *his*] teeth . . .' on the unconvincingly ingenious ground that ' "one-in-five" contemplates not *one*, but as many *ones* as there are *fives*'. Am I, then, to presume that 'One horse in a million has a purple coat' should be '. . . have . . .' on the ground that there are as many *ones* as *millions*! Compare 'In every five [i.e., in every set of five persons], only one cleans his teeth' and 'Of every five, only one cleans his teeth'.

one or other is incorrect for *the one or the other* or *one or other of them*. 'Bennett . . . fought back (against Thoms), and only the interference of the Cut and Come Again staff prevented serious damage to one or other.'

ones for *those* is not wholly wrong, but it is loose and unidiomatic, as in 'Eminence is an accident in [the United States of] America, and it might befall anyone.—It does befall the most unlikely ones. . . . Ones who hoard fame and batten on it.'

one's for *his* or other pronoun. In 'Who would not wish to retrace the path of one's hero in the hope of becoming a hero on one's own?', A. R. Orage, *The Art of Reading*, *one's* is not incorrect; it is inelegant. In comparison with Orage's sentence, the revision 'Who would not wish to retrace the path of his hero in the hope of becoming a hero on one's own [account]' is preferable.

oneself and **one's self.** The difference between these two forms is precisely that between *myself* and *my self*, *yourself* and *your self*, *herself* and *her self*, *himself* and *his self*, *ourselves* and *our selves*, *yourselves* and *your selves*, *themselves* and *their selves*. The *oneself, yourself, themselves* form is that of the reflexive pronoun ('He hurt himself'), the appositive pronoun ('I myself did not understand what was happening'), and—in poetry—the emphatic pronoun ('Myself would work eye dim and finger lame', Tennyson —cited by Onions). In the *my self, their selves* form, *self* is synonymous with 'personality or personal entity'.

only, conjunction (approximately = *but*), should have a comma after it, for, otherwise, ambiguities are needlessly created, as in 'I do not know, only he does'. A semi-colon or a colon should precede *only*, as in 'I'd like to do it; only, I don't know how', for a comma looks odd and produces ambiguity, as in 'He came, only, he stopped for but a day'.

only, misplaced. Jespersen, *The Philosophy of Grammar*, 'The plural *feet* from *foot* was formerly only mentioned as one of a few exceptions to the rule that plurals . . . were formed in *-s*'. Not 'only mentioned' but 'mentioned only as one, etc.'—'We only heard it yesterday' should be 'We heard it only yesterday'. Coleridge, a careful writer, at least once committed a misplacement: 'The wise only possess ideas; the greater part of mankind are possessed by them': properly, 'only the wise'. Even G. K. Chesterton fell into the error of a misplaced *only*, as in 'His black coat looked as if it were only black by being too dense a purple. His black beard looked as if it were only black by being too deep a blue.' Nor are philosophers exempt: 'We can only substitute a clear symbolism for an unprecise one by inspecting the phenomena which we want to describe' (read '. . . one only by inspecting'), Ludwig Wittgenstein.
Merely is subject to the same vagaries.

only, tautological. See BUT.

only and **only not** for *except*(*ing*) or *but*. 'He never drinks, only when it's somebody's birthday', where *only* should be *except*.

only alternative. See ALTERNATIVE.

only too is defensible when it is used literally, as in 'One who has committed murder once is, as a rule, only too ready to commit it again'. But it should be avoided as a loose synonym of *very*: for instance, 'Only too pleased to help in a good cause' is absurd.

onomatopœia. See ECHOISM.

onset should not be used for (first) *sign* as it is in 'I'm getting stylised, and that's the onset of fossilisation via coagulation'.

onto is misused for *on to* in such a phrase

as 'to walk onto the next station'. (Cf. 'INTO for IN TO'.) Wherever *on to* is simply an adverb, *on to* is the correct form. But 'in the sense in which it corresponds to *into*, *onto* is a real compound', pronounced differently from *on to* (*on' to'*), for *onto* is a trochee (*on' to*), as *The O.E.D.* points out.

operative, adj. *Operative* has come to mean, all too often, 'most important, most significant' — especially in the phrase, *the operative word*, which was a vogue by 1938, when it occurred in, e.g., 'Nicholas Blake' (C. Day Lewis), *The Beast Must Die*. The late Charles Williams, symbolic poet, spiritual novelist, penetrating critic, wittily though punningly employed it in *The Figure of Beatrice*, 1943, 'The operative word of the last line is "move-moves" '. In this overworked phrase, *operative* has been made to bear not only the two senses noted above, but also those of 'notable', 'revelatory', 'solvent', 'sought-for', and 'key'; if *key* itself were not being overdone—'key man', 'key job', etc.—I should say that where 'key' or 'clue' is implied, 'the key word' is preferable to 'the operative word'.

operative and **operator**, nouns. *Operative* is now confined to workmen in mills or factories; it is common in American usage, whereas English usage prefers *millhand* and *workman* respectively. Not that *operative* is not used in Great Britain (and the Empire), but it is a technical word of industry, sociology and politics.
An *operator* may be a surgeon or a dentist, a telephone or telegraph operator, or, especially, one engaged in the buying and selling of stocks, shares, commodities, or in some speculative business. For a workman or mill-hand, it is to be avoided.

opinion, in my; I (myself) think, etc. Frequently, these phrases are unnecessary: usually, the context and the circumstances of one's statement make it clear that it is only an opinion; and if one wishes to stress *I*, it is enough to write (or say) '*I* think'.

opponent. See ANTAGONIST.

opportunity and **chance.** See CHANCE.

opposite (adj.) takes *to*, as in 'His house is opposite to mine'; the noun takes *of*, as in 'His is the opposite of that'. Incorrect are 'This is the opposite to that' and 'His house is opposite of mine'. ('His house is the opposite of mine' means something different and requires a particularization.)

opposite and **contrary.** See 'CONTRARY and OPPOSITE'.

optimistic, 'inclined to optimism, i.e., to take a favourable view of circumstances and therefore to hope for the best', should not be debased to equivalence with *hopeful* on the one hand nor with *cheerful* (or *sanguine*) on the other.

option, have no. This should be avoided, especially in 'I have (or, had) no option but to go'; 'I had to go' is infinitely better.

or and nor. Both *or* and *nor* are dissociative, not associative; these conjunctions 'do not link words so as to form a Compound Subject. The Verb is therefore not necessarily Plural.

Either he or she *is* in fault. . . .

Constructions like the following should be avoided: "Neither death nor fortune *were* sufficient to subdue the mind of Cargill" (Fox, *History of James II*).'

If either of the two subjects joined by *or* or by *nor* is plural, the ensuing verb must be plural; stylistically, it is advisable to set the plural subject nearer to the verb, as in 'Neither Britain nor the Dominions desire war'.

In sentences where the subjects are of different persons (*he* and *I*, *I* and *the dog*, *you* and *your brother*, *you* and *I*), the verb should agree with the subject nearer to it, as in

'Either my brother or I *am* going';
'Neither you nor he *is* in fault';
'Neither he nor we *have* any doubt of it'.

These examples have been taken from *An Advanced English Syntax*, by Dr C. T. Onions, who adds: 'In the majority of cases, however, this form of expression is awkward, and is especially so when the sentence is a question, *e.g.*, "Is he or we wrong?" Avoid the difficulty by saying:

Either my brother is going, or I am.
You are not in fault, nor is he.
He has no doubt of it, nor have we.
Is he wrong, or are we?'

A general caution: Where *nor* is preceded by *neither* (whether explicit, or, as in 'Friend nor foe can help me now', implicit), *nor* presents no difficulties; in all other instances, *nor* is—or should be—synonymous with *and not*; but if it isn't, then be careful!

or for and. 'As matters stood, no power the police had, or'—properly 'and'—'no action they could take, could prove Granadi to be lying.'

oral. See AURAL.

oral and verbal. In its general sense, *oral* is applied to that which is 'communicated in or by speech', i.e., 'spoken', as in 'Oral teaching is the best' and 'oral evidence'; it has two technical senses: (a) in Physiology and Medicine, 'of the mouth', 'pertaining to the mouth', the *oral cavity* being the cavity of the mouth; (b) in Theology, 'by or with the mouth', as in *oral communion*.

Verbal is applied to all words, not merely to spoken words, and it emphasizes the letter as opposed to the spirit, as in 'a verbal translation', 'verbal criticisms' (criticism rather of the words than of the ideas and sentiments), 'a difference that was verbal rather than real'; a *verbal agreement*, however, is simply an agreement in speech only. In Grammar, it is the adjective corresponding to the noun (and notion), *verb*.

ORDER OF SENTENCES AND CLAUSES. Sentences and clauses follow —or should follow—the natural flow of effective presentation: the minor is subordinated to the major: clarity is preserved, ambiguity avoided.

ORDER OF WORDS. 'In English', says Dr George O. Curme, 'there are three word-orders: the verb in the second, the third, or the first place.'

I. *Verb in Second or Third Place.*

'The most common order is: subject in the first place, verb in the second: "*The boy loves* his dog". This is called *normal order*.' Even when a sentence is inverted, it is usual to keep the verb in the second place; inversion, by the way, is now common only when it conveys interrogation or ensures emphasis. 'Bitterly did we repent our decision', 'Never had I dreamed of such a thing', 'Only two had merciful death released from their sufferings', 'When did you meet him?', 'Where did you say she put it?', 'Only when the artist understands these psychological principles can he work in harmony with them' (Spencer).

'When the principal proposition'—i.e., the principal clause—'is inserted in a direct quotation or follows it, the principal verb may sometimes still, in accordance with the old inverted order, . . . stand before the subject, but it is now more common [? usual] . . . to regulate the word-order by the modern group stress, so that the heavier word, be it subject or verb, stands last in the group.' Contrast: ' "Harry", *continued the old man*, "before you choose a wife, you must know my position" ' with: ' "George" *she exclaimed*, "this is the happiest moment of my life" '. Contrast also: ' "You have acted selfishly", *was her cold retort'* with: ' "You have acted selfishly", *she replied'*.

Compare too: 'The wind whistled and moaned as if, *thought Michael*, all the devils in hell were trying to break into the holy building' (Compton Mackenzie) and 'The wind whistled and moaned as if, *it sounded to him*, all the devils in hell . . .' To the latter arrangement, which Sir Compton Mackenzie would never have tolerated, it must, however, be objected that it is ambiguous.

Another type of inversion is that in which the subject comes at the end for emphasis. 'Now comes *my best trick'*, 'To the list may be added *the following names'*, and, from Galsworthy's *The Man of Property*, 'Fast into this perilous gulf of night walked *Bosinney* and fast after him walked *George'*, where there is a lesser stress on 'fast' (in both instances).

Inversions are the usual reason for a verb to go into the third place, as in 'Very grateful they *were* for my offer', 'Lucky it *is* that we know her name', 'This threat he *was* unable to carry out'. The verb goes into the third place also in exclamations. Thus, 'What cheek he *has*!', 'What good friends horses *have been* to us for thousands of years!' The old inverted order, however, is retained in 'How pleasant *is* this hill where the road widens!'

Dr Curme sums up in this way:—'The normal word-order [i.e., the subject before the verb, with the complement, adverb, or object after the verb] has become the form of expression suited to the mind in its normal condition of steady activity and easy movement, from which it only departs'—better, 'departs only'—'under the stress of emotion, or for logical reasons, or in conformity to fixed rules.'

II. *Verb in the First Place.*

In modern English the first place in the sentence—an emphatic position—is occupied by the verb 'in expressions of will containing an imperative and often in those containing a volitive subjunctive, also in questions that require *yes* or *no* for answer', as in:

'*Hand* me that book!'
'*Were* he only here!'
'*Come* what will.'
'*Did* he go?'

B. From these generalities, let us pass to the position of the adverb in the sentence or clause and to the order of adverbs or adverbial phrases when there are two or more.

For the splitting of the infinitive (*to earnestly pray*), see SPLIT INFINITIVE.

The fear of splitting the infinitive has been so insidious that it has become a fear of 'splitting' even a gerund, as in 'To reduce the infantry for the sake *unduly of increasing* the artillery', where the sensible (and correct) order is '. . . sake of unduly increasing'.

In a compound verb (*have seen*) with an adverb, that adverb comes between the auxiliary and the participle ('I have *never* seen her'); or, if there are two or more auxiliaries, immediately after the first auxiliary ('I have *always* been intending to go to Paris'); that order is changed only to obtain emphasis, as in 'I never have seen her' (with stress on 'have') or 'Never, never have I seen her'. Failure to ensure the necessary emphasis accounts for such an infelicity as '*No one has probably seen you*—so you can go home in peace' (a detective novel, 1937), instead of '*Probably no one has seen you . . .*' There is, however, a tendency to move an adverb from its rightful and natural position for inadequate reasons, as in 'Oxford must *heartily* be congratulated on their victory', where 'heartily' modifying 'must' instead of 'be congratulated' is as absurd as—if 'certainly' was substituted for 'heartily'—'certainly' would be if placed after 'be': logically, 'must *heartily* be congratulated' (instead of 'must be *heartily* congratulated') is no less absurd than 'must be *certainly* congratulated' (instead of 'must *certainly* be congratulated').

On the same footing are the errors in 'It would be a different thing if the scheme had been *found fundamentally to be faulty*, but that is not the case' (where '. . . *found to be fundamentally faulty . . .*' would be correct) and 'In these times it is rare that the First Lord of the Treasury *also is* Prime Minister' (where *is also* would be correct).

To separate a transitive verb from its object leads to awkwardness and generally discomfits the reader. 'I had to *second by all the means in my power diplomatic action*' should be 'I had, by all the means in my power, to second diplomatic action' or, less forcibly and less happily, 'I had to second diplomatic action by all the means in my power'. The rule holds good, however short the adverb. 'Have you *interpreted rightly the situation*?' should be 'Have you rightly interpreted the situation?' 'I should *advise, then, the boy to* take plenty of exercise' should be 'I should, then [better: therefore], advise the boy to take plenty of exercise'.

'There are', Fowler cautions us, 'conditions that justify the separation, the most obvious being when a lengthy object would keep an adverb that is not suitable for the early position too remote from the verb . . . But anyone who applies this principle must be careful not to reckon as part of the object words that either do not belong to it at all or are unessential to it.' In 'These men are *risking every day with intelligence and with shrewdness fortunes on what they believe*', *fortunes* is the object; not *fortunes on what they believe.* Put *fortunes* immediately after *risking.* But the sentence needs re-ordering: 'Every day, though with intelligence and shrewdness, these men are risking fortunes on what they believe'. In 'I can set most of the shocks that flesh is heir to at defiance' (Joan Jukes, 'On the Floor', in *New Stories*, 1934), *at defiance* should follow *set*, not only because it is too far separated from its verb but also because *set at defiance* is a verbal unit—*defy.* In 'Failure of the Powers to enforce their will as to the Albanian frontier would expose to the ridicule of all the restless elements in East Europe their authority, which, as it is, is not very imposing', *their authority, which, as it is, is not very imposing* should immediately follow *expose.* But had *to the ridicule . . . East Europe* been *to ridicule* (two words instead of eleven), then the sentence would properly have read 'Failure of the Powers to enforce their will as to the Albanian frontier would expose to ridicule their authority, which, as it is, is not very imposing', for to put the very long object in front of the short adverbial phrase would be to remove the adverb too far from the verb.

Many of the preceding examples seem to have sprung from wrong ideas of correctness. Probably, however, the most frequent cause of error is carelessness. 'The Freudian theories in the last few years have influenced the novelists greatly' should be 'In the last few years the Freudian theories have greatly influenced the novelists', for the original position of *in the last few years* makes it appear that the Freudian theories began to exercise an influence not until the middle-1930's; *greatly* was also out of position. 'It has been implied that Germany is a collectivist State, or, if not, that it has at least far advanced in Socialism' should be '. . . has at least advanced far in Socialism'.

These misplacings of the adverb (or the adverbial phrase) exemplify the need of caution. But all errors exemplify that need: and errors of word and errors of syntax are instructively frequent in the work of those popular authors who turn out three or four or five books a year—often under two (or even three or more) names.

But adverbs may depart from the positions recommended in the foregoing paragraphs—if there is a good reason. The best reason of all is clarity: but then, we hardly need give examples of this. The reason next in importance is that of emphasis. 'I met your father *yesterday*' is the normal order; 'I met *yesterday* your father', as we have already seen, is abnormal and unidiomatic in English (though correct in French); '*Yesterday* I met your father' stresses the day—the time—*yesterday*; 'I *yesterday* met your father' is now affected, although it was common enough in the 18th Century ('The jury now will examine the [article]', 1751).

The *yesterday* example comes from Geo. O. Curme's *Syntax*, where the author points out that sometimes the adverb or adverbial phrase modifies, not the verb alone but the sentence as a whole. 'In this case the adverbial element usually precedes the verb, verbal phrase, or predicate noun or adjective' (i.e., the object or the complement), as in 'He *evidently* thought so' or, more strongly, '*Evidently* he thought so'; 'He *absolutely* lives from hand to mouth', where 'lives *absolutely*' would, at best, change the sense or, at worst, create confusion; 'She *always* lets him have his own way' or, more emphatically, '*Always* she lets him have his own way'.

ordinance; ordnance; ordonnance. An *ordinance* is a regulation, by-law, rule, that is less permanent, less constitutional, less general than a law or a statute; especially a municipal or other local enactment; also it is a religious observance, and a decree, and a dispensation of Providence.

As a military term, *ordnance* = 'cannon' (mounted guns); but the chief sense of the term is, 'the public establishment concerned with the military stores and materials, the management of the artillery, etc.'

Ordonnance is a systematic arrangement of parts in a piece of architectural or artistic work, or of literary material; Sir Joshua Reynolds spoke of 'disproportionate ordonnance of parts' (*O.E.D.*).

orient (v.). See ORIENTATE.

Oriental and **Eastern.** *Eastern* refers to the East portion (or part or region or land) of any part of the world; *Oriental* only to the countries, regions, etc., lying to the east of the Mediterranean, and especially to Asia or rather to Asia-without-Siberia. *Eastern Europe, the Orient, Oriental lands, Oriental drugs,* and similar expressions require a capital letter, but one may with propriety drop the capital both in 'the eastern part of the island', 'the eastern extremity of Great Britain', and in *oriental* as an adjective in astrology or astronomy.

orientate and **orient** (v.). (Noun: *orientation.*) As an intransitive, 'to face in some specific direction, originally and especially to the east' (an ecclesiastical term), *orientate* is correct; in all other senses, *to orient* is preferable. One can *orient* one's behaviour, one's conscience, one's ambition, or another person, or one can, reflexively, *orient oneself,* i.e., guide or direct it, him, oneself, or to get one's bearings, put another on the right path or track.

ostensible and **ostensive.** The former = 'declared, avowed; pretended or merely professed', as in 'His ostensible reason was that . . .' *Ostensive* is to be avoided in this sense, both because it is obsolescent and because it may set up an ambiguity. In Philosophy, *ostensive* = 'declarative'; applied to a proof, it means 'specious'; in Logic it = 'directly demonstrative'. (*O.E.D.*)

other, omitted after *any.* See GENITIVE, VAGARIES OF THE, last paragraph.

other, used intrusively. *Other* is incorrectly and ambiguously introduced in the following: 'The Jingo element is strong in London, stronger than it is in the *other* provincial towns.'

other, the. Avoid clumsy use. 'While one man was baling out the water from his canoe, another tipped up the boat so that it shipped bucketsful. It was the fun-maker who suffered, for *the other* man got out and landed while *the other* sank with the canoe.'

other . . . except. *The News Chronicle,* March 4, 1938, speaks of 'every other country except ours'. Our country, to be excepted from, must first be one of those 'others', which is absurd. The sense is expressed by 'every country except (or, but) ours'.

other than is the correct form (as also the similar combinations, *different from, opposite to, contrasted with*). In *other than,* etc., writers occasionally forget that *other, different,* etc., are adjectives, not adverbs.

Thus *other than* should be *apart from* in 'Other than that'—a missed catch—'the batsmen were quite comfortable'.

other to. *Other to* is occasionally misused for *opposite to* or *across from,* as in 'On the other side to mine'.

others, of all, is a form of false comparison. The 'he' referred to in 'He was the best (cricketer) of all others' is not *one of the others,* but *best of all* (the cricketers), or *better than any of the others.* Nesfield (*Errors in English Composition*) puts it thus: 'The thing to which the Superlative refers must be *included* amongst things of its own class; otherwise no such comparison can be made'. E.g., 'The place which of all others in the wide world she had wished most to see'.

othertimes (at other times) is colloquial and *other time* (ditto) is incorrect; *otherwhen* and *otherwhere* are literary; *otherwhile(s)*, when not dialectal, is archaic.

otherwise for *other* is a misuse. 'What he expected from life, otherwise than a day-by-day relish of experience and some eventual recognition of his disinterestedness, could not be seen.'

ought (n.). See AUGHT.

ought is stronger than *should.* 'You ought to do it' is stronger than 'You should do it'.

ought, didn't—hadn't—shouldn't. ' "He shouldn't ought to behave like that. It's hardly decent" ', Ernest Raymond, *We, the Accused,* 1935 (in dialogue), for 'he ought not to behave like that'. *Ought* never requires the auxiliary, the use of which can lead to the most ridiculous grammatical confusion, as in: 'He didn't ought to have done it, had he?'

ourselves. See MYSELF.

out loud, colloquial, is stylistically inferior to *aloud,* as in 'She sobbed out loud'.

outdoor is the adjective, **outdoors** the adverb, as in 'She put on her outdoor clothes to go outdoors into the rain and wind'. Oddly enough, the corresponding noun is *outdoors,* as in 'The outdoors is stimulating' although *out-of-doors* is perhaps more usual ('He prefers the out-of-doors to the most comfortable house').

outline is a brief preliminary plan; **summary** an abridged restatement.

outside of is incorrect in 'Outside of the house, he could see quite well; inside of the house, he could hardly see'. Read 'Outside the house . . ., inside the house . . .', for the prepositions are *outside* and *inside.* [In American usage, *outside of* and *inside of* may occur in informal writing as well as in conversation.]

outward and **outwards.** The former is both adjective and adverb; the latter is only adverb. Of the two adverbs, *outward* is used of position or situation, to mean 'on the outside; without', as in 'Sheepskins, with the wool outward' (Defoe), although *outside* is now more usual; and 'from the soul or mind into external actions or conditions', as in 'His life radiated from within outward', but the adverb for the literal 'in an outward direction; towards that which is outside or without', is *outwards*, as in 'To cut a semicircular flap from within outwards'. (*O.E.D.*)

over for *about* or *concerning* is catachrestic or, at best, very colloquial, as in 'He was anxious over your misfortune'.

over should, to avoid ambiguity, be *for over* in the following: 'It was audacious, perhaps foolhardy. But not too daring for a determined man who at last had an opportunity to satisfy a grudge he had nursed over a decade.' *Over* in the time-sense is normally 'for the duration of', or 'spread over', not, as in the example, 'more than'.

overlay and **overlie.** The latter = 'to lie over or upon', lit. or fig.; hence, 'to smother by lying upon', more generally *overlay* ('She overlaid her child'). *Overlay* is much wider in its application: e.g., 'to cover *with*', 'to conceal or obscure as if by covering up'. Do not use *overlay* in the first sense of *overlie*. *Overlay—overlaid*; *overlie — overlay — overlain*.

overlook and **look over.** The latter = 'to look at, to inspect, to read through'; the former = 'to look over the top of', 'to look down upon', (of a place) 'to command a view of'; 'to disregard; to fail to see'.

oversight; omission; supervision. *Oversight* = 'supervision, superintendence; care or management', but is obsolescent in this sense. Its dominant current sense is 'failure or omission to see', hence 'inadvertence', hence 'a mistake of inadvertence', as in 'It may have been an oversight'. (*O.E.D.*)

overwhelming is misapplied when it is used as a mere synonym of *vast*, as in 'Though it can be said that, in the overwhelming majority of cases, secret messages can be deciphered and read by the trained expert, the fact remains that the time factor may make the decipherment valueless'. So, too, *an* (or *the*) *overwhelming proportion of* is infelicitous for *by far the larger part of* or *the vast majority of*.

overflowed; overflown. The preterite of *overflow* is *overflowed*; so too is the past participle. Reserve *overflown* for *overfly*, 'to fly over', hence 'to surpass in flight'.

owing to. See CONJUNCTIONS, DISGUISED.

ozone should be used neither as a synonym of *air* (especially, good or healthy air), as so many advertisers use it; nor of *oxygen*, for properly it = 'an altered condition of oxygen, existing in a state of condensation, with a particularly pungent and refreshing odour'.

P

pact is 'an agreement made between persons or parties, a compact' (*O.E.D.*): a dignified word, it should not be debased to trivial uses. Properly, it is applied to *formal* agreements; to solemn or weighty or important or significant agreements.

pailfuls and **pails full.** See BASKETFULS.

palate; palette; pallet; pallette. *Palate* is the roof of the mouth, hence one's sense of taste; *palette*, that tablet of wood (or occasionally porcelain) on which an artist lays and mixes his colours; *pallet* is a straw bed, hence a mean or humble bed or couch; and *pallette* (but more usually *pallet*) is a piece of armour for the head, hence in Scottish, the head or pate. (*O.E.D.*)

panacea should not be used for a cure for a particular ill, for *panacea* means 'a catholicon, a universal remedy'. Therefore to speak of 'a panacea for gout' is absurd.

panegyric is not merely *praise*, but either a public speech, or a public writing, in praise of a person, thing, achievement; a laudatory discourse; 'a formal or at least an elaborate eulogy', or, derivatively, 'laudation' or any 'elaborate praise'. (*O.E.D.*)

panic (v.i., v.t.) has present participle *panicking*, past participle (and tense) *panicked*.

paragon and **parergon.** A *paragon* is 'a model or pattern of excellence' ('a paragon of virtue'). A *parergon* is 'a literary by-work' (done in an idle period or off one's usual track) or 'employment supplementary or secondary to one's principal work'.

PARAGRAPHING. In the words of Alexander Bain, 'The division of discourse next above the Sentence is the Paragraph. It is a collection, or series, of sentences, with unity of purpose'—an orderly collection, a natural sequence.

'Between one paragraph and another there is a greater break in the subject than

F

between one sentence and another. The internal arrangement comes under laws that are essentially the same as in the sentence, but on a greater scale.

'The Paragraph laws are important, not only for their own sake, but also for their bearing on an entire composition. They are the general principles that must regulate the structure of sections, chapters, and books. The special laws applying to different kinds of prose composition—Description, Narrative, Exposition, and Persuasion—cannot supersede those general principles; they only deal with the matter in hand from a higher point of view. Apart from the application of those higher laws, we may adapt an old homely maxim, and say "Look to the Paragraphs, and the Discourse will take care of itself" ': each paragraph (or, on a larger scale, each section of a chapter) corresponds to a point to be made, described, narrated; to a head of discourse, a topic, an aspect. If you establish the ordonnance of your theme, you will find that there is one order superior to all others; in establishing the order in which you desire to make the points of your exposition or your argument, to set forth the incidents in your narrative, the aspects in your description, you simultaneously and inevitably establish the division into paragraphs and the order of those paragraphs. That is the nearest sensible thing to a general rule.

But here are several minor precautions.

I. If a paragraph shows signs of becoming tediously long, break it up into two or three or even four parts, linked one to another and casting back to the first head by such a conjunction or such a conjunctival phrase (e.g., 'in such circumstances as these, it was natural that . . .') as indicate the dependence of the second, third, fourth of the theme-involved paragraphs on the first and the relation of the second to the first, the third to the second, the fourth to the third.

II. Do not shred the story, the essay, the article, into a sequence of very short paragraphs. This is an irritating trick beloved of slick journalists.

III. But to interpose a one-sentence paragraph at intervals—at longish intervals—is prudent. Such a device helps the eye and enables the reader to regain his breath between one impressive or weighty or abstruse paragraph and the next.

IV. If the development of the theme is logical, natural, easy, one paragraph follows on its predecessor so inevitably that a conjunction may often be unnecessary. A long procession of *but, however, nevertheless, therefore, moreover* can become a weariness—and generally does.

V. Examine the paragraphing in the longer articles of this book. I do not pretend that it is perfect, but I believe that it is both simple and adequate. See my *You Have a Point There*, 1953.

parasol is a (carried) sunshade; an *umbrella* is a (carried or not carried) protection against rain or sun. One distinction between *parasol* and *sunshade* is that the former is small and umbrella-shaped; the latter may be anything designed to protect against the sun's rays, be it visor, large umbrella, lattice or awning. A more important distinction, as a friend has pointed out, is that 'the correct, educated word for the mushroom-like diverter of the sun's rays is *parasol*. To say "sunshade" is as damning as to say "greatcoat" for "overcoat" or "up to Town" for "up to London".'

parentheses. See BRACKET.

PARENTHESIS, USE AND DANGERS OF. The danger of losing the thread of grammatical sequences is illustrated by the following sentence: 'But the present Exhibition, arranged by him in connexion with the Jubilee of the British School of Athens (though the results of the discoveries at Knossos itself naturally still form the main theme on an amplified scale), the object has been to supply as far as possible the materials for a general survey of the Minoan culture in its widest range, etc.' Charles C. Boyd, in *Grammar for Great and Small*, hit the nail on the head when he remarked that 'The test of a parenthesis is whether the other words make sense without it'.

pardon me! See EXCUSE ME!

parergon. See PARAGON . . .

parson, technically, is 'a holder of a parochial benefice in full possession of its rights and dues; a rector'. Hence, colloquially, any beneficed clergyman—any clergyman, whether Anglican or Nonconformist: but in this colloquial sense, it is —except in rural use—depreciatory. In favourable or neutral contexts, therefore, *parson* is to be avoided, as of course it is also in formal speech or writing except in its technical sense. [In American usage, *parson* may have a familiar, affectionate connotation.]

part, misused for *some*, as in 'Part of the students fail their examinations'.

partake of is not simply 'to *take*': it means 'to take one's share of', 'to share in'.

'Being alone, I consoled myself by partaking of a glass of stout' is silly; 'Your papa invited Mr R. to partake of our lowly fare' (Dickens) is sensible.

partiality. See PREJUDICE.

partially, wrongly used for *partly.* Mr Harold Herd in *Watch Your English* gives an excellent example of the ambiguity caused by this misuse: 'The appeal was partially heard before the Lord Chief Justice . . . yesterday', where the proper meaning of 'partially' is *unfairly*, with a bias towards one side. However, the adj. *partial*, 'incomplete', as in *a partial success*, can hardly be avoided.

PARTICIPIAL PHRASES, DISCONNECTED. 'Upon landing at the quay the little town presented a strong contrast in styles.' 'After walking about two miles from Llangollen, a narrow valley opens on the right.'

See also CONFUSED PARTICIPLES.

PARTICIPLES, FUSED. See FUSED PARTICIPLES.

party should not, in formal English, be used for *person*: 'The old party looked ill' should be 'The old man'—or 'woman'— 'looked ill'.

pass, misused for *meet.* A train *passes* another if the latter is stationary; *passes* or *overtakes* another going in the same direction; *meets* one that is coming in the opposite direction.

passed and **past.** *Past* was formerly the common spelling of the past participle of *pass*, but this use is obsolete: *passed* is the past participle, and *past* is adj. or noun. We write 'the past month', 'in the past', but 'the month has passed quickly'.

PAST SUBJUNCTIVE FOR PRESENT (OR FUTURE) INDICATIVE or for **PRESENT SUBJUNCTIVE** 'softens the form of the expression', as in 'You *should*' for 'It is your duty to' (do something); '*Would* you help him?' for '*Will* you help him?'; '*Might* I say what I think?' for '*May* . . . ?'; '*Could* you come a little earlier than we arranged?' for '*Can* you . . . ?' The same applies to 'You *should* not speak so disrespectfully of your parents' for 'You *ought* not to speak . . .'

pastor should not be used as an exact synonym of *minister* or *clergyman*; it should be restricted to a 'minister in charge of a church or congregation, with particular reference to the spiritual care of his "flock" ' (*O.E.D.*). [When one American church member meets another, he may ask, 'Who is your . . . ?' (minister, pastor, priest, rector). Methodists and Baptists seem to prefer *pastor* or, old style, *preacher*; Presbyterians, *minister* or *pastor*; Congregationalists, *minister*; Episcopalians, *minister* or *rector* (High Churchmen, sometimes, *priest*); Roman Catholics, *priest*. *Preacher* and *parson* (Protestant) are now old-fashioned. *Clergyman* is usually Episcopalian though *clergy* is a common term. The Methodist pastor lives in a *parsonage*; the Presbyterian and the Congregationalist minister in a *manse*; the Episcopalian rector and the Catholic rector (priest in charge, sometimes *pastor*) in a *rectory*.]

pathos. See BATHOS.

'**patron** of the arts', but not of a greengrocer or a bookmaker. Tradesmen have *customers*, professional men have *clients* —though doctors have *patients*.

See also ' CLIENT and CUSTOMER '.

patronize for *trade with* (a grocer) or *at* (his shop) is commercial pretentiousness.

pattern. In *The Times Literary Supplement* of September 22, 1945, there was, from that formidably acute Classic, J. M. Edmonds, a letter editorially captioned 'The Over-Worked "Pattern" ': someone had recently condemned it as a 'vogueword'. *Pattern* has only since 1942 or 1943 become a fashionable term. It is ousting, for instance, 'design'; nowadays it occasionally means something perilously like 'mode' or 'manner'. I have heard 'a pattern for living', 'a pattern for a good life', and 'the pattern of wise thinking'. The word is losing its formality, but that is not necessarily a bad thing.

pavement is the usual English, *sidewalk* the usual American term for 'the paved footway at the side of a street, as distinct from the roadway' (*O.E.D.*). If at the side of a country road, it is a *footpath* in England, a *path* in America.

pay away; pay down; pay off; pay out; pay over; pay up. To *pay down* is to pay part of a due or a debt, also to pay on the spot or immediately; *pay off* is to pay a person in full and discharge him, whereas *pay up* is to pay in full for something or to discharge a debt in full; to *pay over* is to hand money (*to* a person) either in part or, less generally, in full; *pay away* is pay unexpectedly or reluctantly or with difficulty or (e.g., of a bill) to a third party; and *pay out* is to pay a sum from one's account or a fund, or to get rid of a person (e.g., an undesirable partner) by paying (e.g., his share of the capital).

peaceable and **peaceful.** The former is now restricted to persons, their character, their actions, their feelings, as in 'The inhabitants are shepherds, . . . simple, peaceable, and inoffensive'. *Peaceful*, 'full of or characterized by peace; undisturbed, untroubled, quiet', is applied to periods, occasions, countries, scenes, parties, states of mind, appearances, faces, as in 'The Thames Valley affords many peaceful scenes and vistas'. (*O.E.D.*)

peculiar(ly) is better avoided in the sense *particular(ly)* or *especial(ly)*; e.g., 'The Arabs regard the spot as peculiarly sacred'. (*O.E.D.*)

peer, misused for (a person) *superior*. 'He is the equal if not the peer of anyone in the club.' [The belief that *peer* means superior or at least connotes *superiority* is exceedingly common among Americans —so common and so strong that it actually has this meaning more often than not. And unfortunately, correction at school only drives the word from the vocabulary of expression (as opposed to the vocabulary understood).]

pence is the collective, PENNIES the distributive (or separative) plural of *penny*. Thus, 'The fare was fivepence'; 'I gave him three pennies', three coins, whereas 'I gave him threepence' refers to the sum, paid either in a threepenny piece or in three separate pennies; 'Pennies are brown, pence are money'. [In American English, *penny* colloquially = *cent*; pl. *pennies* (*pence* does not occur).]

pendant, -ent. See DEPENDANT.

penultimate is the last but one; **antepenultimate**, the last but two. Noun and adjective.

people, 'a nation, race, tribe, community', is singular, with plural *peoples*; *people*, 'persons', is plural. *The people*, 'the electorate', is singular, as is *the people*, 'the laity'; but *the people*, those who do not belong to the nobility or the ruling (or official) classes, is plural.

per is commercialese—and permissible in a Latin phrase, *per annum*. But it should not be allowed in good writing. 'Mr Chamberlain went to Munich per aeroplane.'

per cent. is occasionally misused for *percentage*; properly, *per cent.* is used after a numeral. [American usage prefers *per cent* or *percent* (without period).]

per day; per month; per week; per year. Inferior to *per diem*, *per mensem*, *per hebdomadem*, *per annum*; much inferior to 'a day' ('twelve shillings a day'), 'a year' ('£300 a year'), etc., or 'by the day or month or week or year'. Be either learned in Latin or easy in English; don't be mongrel. [For American usage this is a command not to use *per*. Certainly *per hebdomadem* would not be intelligible.]

percentage for *proportion*. 'In motor racing, the machine—not the man—does the larger percentage of the work.' Idiomatically, one would go a step further and write, 'In motor racing, the machine does most of the work'.

perceptible; perceptive; perceptual. In current usage, *perceptible* is 'able to be perceived by the senses or the mind; observable'; 'a perceptible difference' is a difference that can be seen, felt, or understood, but it is not synonymous with *considerable*, as certain careless writers have supposed.—*Perceptive* is 'capable of perceiving, belonging to or instrumental in perception', as in 'perceptive faculties'; hence, 'quick in perception, quick to notice; intelligent', as in 'Dickens was a most perceptive man'.—*Perceptual* is a learned term, meaning 'of or belonging to perception', as in 'perceptual images'. (*O.E.D.*)

perennially = 'permanently', 'constantly', 'perpetually', not 'year after year' as in 'Perennially subject to attacks of gout'. The same applies to the adjective, which does not = 'recurring year after year'.

perfect, more, most; less, least; all these are inadmissible. See COMPARATIVES, FALSE.—Used for *complete*, it is incorrect, as in 'The ship is a perfect loss'.

PERFECT INFINITIVE, wrongly used. The perfect infinitive seems to unpractised writers to accompany 'I (or you or he) should, or would, have liked', or 'He had intended', as in 'They would have liked to *have been* there, I'm sure', 'I should have liked to *have gone* to the cricket match', 'If he had intended to *have done* that, he might at least have told me': whereas the correct forms are 'They would have liked to *be* there', 'I should have liked to *go*', 'If he had intended to *do* that'. Compare 'If he had intended *doing* that'. The idea of the past is already in the finite verb ('would have liked', 'should have liked', 'had intended'): why repeat it? To good sense as to logic, the repetition is always irritating and occasionally confusing. (Based on Onions, *An Advanced English Syntax*.)

perfectly for *entirely* or *wholly*, as in 'A perfectly good motor-car', is a colloquialism that rings rather oddly in formal prose.

perform one's ablutions. See ABLUTIONS.

PERIODS, USELESS. See USELESS FULL-STOPS.

permit; allow. The former is active, the

latter neutral; the former connotes forbearance, sufferance, mere toleration, whereas the latter connotes approval and denotes sanction. One *allows* a thing by default or out of weariness; one *permits* it by express action—one states or even legalizes (certainly one formalizes) it. 'I allow him to come here; I permit him to stay past the agreed time.' 'That may be tacitly allowed which is not expressly permitted' (*Webster's*).

permit of. See ADMIT, ADMIT OF.

perpetually. In current usage, *perpetually* means 'incessantly; persistently; constantly recurrent; continually'.

perquisite, misused for *privilege*. (Concerning a fancy-dress ball) ' "I never dress up", said Maxim. "It's the one perquisite allowed to the host".'

persecute and **prosecute** are occasionally confused. The former is to 'pursue with malignancy or with enmity and injurious action'; to *prosecute* is 'to institute legal proceedings against' (a person).

persistently. See CONSISTENTLY.

personage, misused for *person*. 'She looked exactly the same cool, cynical personage as when she had spoken to him at the bank that morning'; 'That entirely mythical personage, "the man in the street".' A *personage* is someone important.

personal and **personally.** 'My personal opinion', 'I personally think', 'to pay a personal visit' are excessive—not to say absurd—for 'my opinion', 'I (*or I*) think', 'to pay a visit'. If you must have emphasis and wish to avoid italics, you can say 'my own opinion', 'I myself think'; and for 'to pay a personal visit' (as though one could visit otherwise than in person!) it is best to substitute some more sensible phrase. Instead of saying, 'Tom Mix paid a personal visit to London', say 'Tom Mix paid a visit to London' or, if you consider that event to be remarkable, 'Tom Mix actually paid a visit to London',—although 'visited' is more economical and telling than 'paid a visit to'.

personal is an adjective; **personnel** (stress on last syllable) is a noun, meaning 'the body of persons working in an establishment, especially of a public institution', and often opposed to *matériel*.

personality. In addition to retaining the basic sense, 'the fact (or the quality) of being a person, not, e.g., a thing', and the sense 'personal existence or personal identity', *personality* is now used chiefly in the sense 'distinctive personal or individual character, especially when *of a marked or notable kind*' (*O.E.D.*; italics mine); but that kind need not necessarily be *a pleasing* (attractive) *personality*; therefore a modifying word is advisable—e.g., *attractive, lovable, remarkable.*—See also:

personality and **personalty** are occasionally confused. *Personalty* is a legal term for 'personal estate'; or, as Henry Stephen defines it in his famous *New Commentaries*, 'Things personal (otherwise called personalty) consist of goods, money, and all other moveables, and of such rights and profits as relate to moveables'. *Personality* = 'personal existence, a distinctive personal character' (Harold Herd); do not loosely use it as a synonym of 'famous person'.

PERSONIFICATION. In personification, a quality or a thing is represented as a person: 'Confusion spoke', 'Vice is a monster', 'Poetry is a mellifluous rhetorician'.

Once so common, especially in poetry and perhaps above all in odes, personification is now suspect. When a writer personifies, he is looked at askance: 'He's ranting', say the critics; 'Getting a bit above himself', say his friends; and maybe he feels not too comfortable about it himself. But in impassioned verse and poetic prose, personification is permissible. It is, however, to be used sparingly and with the nicest discretion.

personnel is singular. Wrong in 'There are few more gloomy places in the early morning than a restaurant. Both the personnel—such as are about—as well as the furniture are in *déshabille*.' But do not use the word at all where *staff* will serve; *personnel* is a piece of official jargon.— Also see 'PERSONAL . . . PERSONNEL'.

persons is now less usual than *people* except after a numeral, as in 'eighty persons were present': 'Eighty *people* . . .' would be extremely colloquial. In short, *people* in the indefinite, *persons* the precise or definite plural.

perspective and **prospective.** *Prospective* means, on the one hand, 'regarding or concerned with or operative in the future', and on the other, 'future; expected or hoped for'. *Perspective* = 'of or belonging to perspective', i.e., to a particular 'art of delineating solid objects on a plane surface', hence 'the relation—especially the proportion—in which the parts of a subject are viewed by the mind; the aspect of an object of thought'.

perspicuity, 'clearness of statement' (*O.E.D.*), and *perspicacity*, 'clearness of understanding' (*ibid.*), are easily and often confused. Perspicacity is required to grasp the distinction, and perspicuity to explain it. The same applies to the adjectives, *perspicuous* and *perspicacious*.

perspiration and **perspire**. See SWEAT.

persuasion. Correctly used for 'religious (and less often political) beliefs or opinion', it is classified by *The O.E.D.* as 'slang or burlesque' when used for nationality, sex, kind, sort, description, as in 'She said she thought it was a gentleman in the haircutting persuasion'.

perturb and **disturb** alike mean 'to agitate'; in current usage, the former is reserved for mental and spiritual agitation, whereas the latter tends to be used of physical discomfort; and certainly *perturbation* is now applied only to the nonphysical, *disturbance* rarely to other than the physical. 'Disturbed at my studies, I fell into a vague perturbation of mind and of spirit.'

peruse is not synonymous with 'to *read*', for it means to read carefully from beginning to end. One *peruses* a contract, one *reads* an (ordinary) advertisement.

pessimistic is 'pertaining to or like or suitable to pessimism'; hence, 'disposed to take the gloomiest view of circumstances': but do not debase it to meaning nothing more than 'gloomy'.

phantasy. See FANTASY.

phenomenal should not be debased to equivalence with *unusual*; it may, however, be used as a synonym of *prodigious*, as in 'The success of Miss Kate Greenaway's "Birthday Book" was phenomenal'.

phenomenon; scientific plural, *phenomena*; ordinary plural, *phenomenons*; incorrect pural, *phenomenas* (cf. STRATAS and DATAS). Not to be used of anything unremarkable, nor to be confused with *feature* or *quality*.

phosphorous (adj.) is a frequent misspelling of *phosphorus* (n).

PHRASAL VERBS, CHANGEABLE POSITION OF ADVERBS IN. 'What rule governs "Take your hat off" and "Take off your hat"; "He laid his rifle down" and "He laid down his rifle", etc.?'

I should not care to say that there is a rule. But it would appear that where the emphasis lies on the object (*hat*, *rifle*), the order is 'Take off your hat' and 'He laid down his rifle'; where the emphasis lies on the adverb, the adverb comes last, as in 'Take your hat off' and 'He laid his rifle down'. This is a matter of idiom: and it is dangerous to be dogmatic about idioms.

picture is colloquial (and trivial) for 'a (very) beautiful or picturesque object', as in 'The room, when decorated, was a picture', 'The child was a picture'.

piece is now dialectal only, in the sense 'a portion of space' i.e., a short distance, a part of the way, or 'a portion of time', i.e., a while, especially a short while. As applied to a woman or a girl, it is, at best, trivial.

pinchers is dialectal for *pincers*. But whereas *pincers* has no singular, *pinchers* has a technical singular: '*Pincher* . . . a nipping tool fitting the inside and outside of a bottle, in order to shape the mouth'. (*O.E.D.*) [In American English *pinchers* is probably more common than *pincers*. However, small pinchers are nowadays called *pliers* and *nippers*.]

pipefuls and **pipes full.** Cf. BASKETFULS.

piteous; pitiable; pitiful. (And the corresponding adverbs in *-ly*.) *Piteous* is 'appealing for pity or exciting it; deserving it', hence 'lamentable' or 'mournful', as in 'a piteous groan'; but it is now less common than *pitiable*. *Pitiable* is used mostly in the sense 'deserving or needing pity, or exciting it; lamentable', as in 'The beggar was in a pitable condition'. *Pitiful* can be used in this sense, but one would do well to confine it to the sense 'full of pity, feeling pity, characterized by pity', hence 'compassionate' or 'merciful'; as a pejorative, it = 'miserably insignificant' ('A pitiful attempt to ape Royalty'), 'contemptible'.

placable, for *quiet*, *peaceable*, is misused; its true sense, *easily appeased*, *forgiving*, is distinct.

placable, placeable; placatory, placating. *Placeable* = 'capable of being placed'; *placable* = 'gentle, mild, forgiving; especially, easily pacifiable or appeasable', as in 'Though irritable, he was placable'. *Placatory* (rarely of persons) = 'conciliatory or propitiatory', as in 'a reply both dignified and placatory'. As an adjective, *placating* is a synonym of, and less formal than *placatory*; like *placatory*, it is not used of persons themselves.

The adverbs are *placably* (*placeably* doesn't exist), *placatorily*, *placatingly*.

The respective opposites are *implacable*, *unplaceable*, *unplacatory*, *unplacating*; the third and fourth are little used. (*O.E.D.*)

place is incorrect for *where* in *anywhere*, *everywhere*, *nowhere*, *somewhere*. More than that, it is illiterate.

plain, like *homely*, is to be avoided in descriptions of women, for, there, it is a euphemism for *ugly* or, at best, *unbeautiful*. *Homely*, however, is inoffensive in England, where it has the connotation of 'home-loving', 'unpretentiously housewifely'. [In American usage *homely* usually means plain and even unattractive when applied to persons and things. *Homelike* and *homey* (colloquial) preserve the connotation of affectionate welcome and comfortable ease.]

PLATITUDES are, to thinking, what clichés are to writing. 'The platitude is the prince of spiritual peace; his yoke is easy, his burden is light' (Frank Binder). **-ple**, as in the series *triple, quadruple, quintuple, sextuple, septuple, octuple*, etc., has a meaning easily deducible from the entry at 'TREBLE and TRIPLE', *q.v.* The *-ple* represents Latin suffix *-plex*, which corresponds exactly to the English suffix *-fold* (*q.v.*).

Duple is obsolete as a general term in the series, but it is retained in mathematics and music. For *multiple*, see MANIFOLD.

plead—preterite, *pleaded* (colloquial American, Scottish dialect: often *pled*)—past participle, *pleaded*.

PLEONASM. See VERBOSITY.

plethora is not mere *abundance*, but *superabundance*.

PLURALS, SNOB. Big-game hunters are in the habit of speaking of *a herd of antelope* or *giraffe* or *elephant*, *a troop of lion, a crash of rhinoceros, three tiger, five leopard*, etc. Perhaps on the analogy of *a herd of deer* or *three deer, a flock of sheep* or *five sheep.*

This sort of thing is all very well at 'The Travellers', on safari, and in the best lounge at Nairobi: after all, minorities have their rights. But when, at the zoo, you hear a man, who doesn't know the difference between a jaguar and a cougar, say to his son, aged seven, 'Just look at those two lion, Willie!', you feel that snobbery has become a symptom of 'the larger lunacy'.

For snobbish language in general, see 'The Speech-Habits of Snobs' in my *From Sanskrit to Brazil*, 1952.

PLURALS, UN-ENGLISH. Jespersen speaks of those 'abnormal plurals which break the beautiful regularity of nearly all English substantives—*phenomena, nuclei, larvae, chrysalides, indices*, etc. The occasional occurrence of such blundering plurals as *animalculae* and *ignorami* is an unconscious protest against the prevalent pedantry of schoolmasters in this respect.' But usage has consecrated *strata* as the plural of *stratum*.

The general rule is: Add *s* (or, to nouns ending in *s* or *x* in the singular, *es*). Therefore *nucleuses* and *chrysalises*. *Indices* differs from *indexes*—see the separate entry. For *phenomena*, see *phenomenon*. The plural of *formula* is *formulas* (not *-ae*, much less *æ*). The 'Greek' scientific singulars, *electron, ion, neutron*, and the rest take the normal English plural, as in R. A. Millikan's learned book, *Electrons, Protons, Photons, Neutrons, and Cosmic Rays*. This rule applies not only to Greek and Latin words (*octopus—octopuses; rhinoceros—rhinoceroses*), but to words from modern languages: thus, the plural of *stiletto* is *stilettos*; not, as in Italian, *stiletti*.

plurocentral for *pluricentral* ('having more than one centre) is typical of an error common among writers on science. The combining form of L. *plus*, 'more', is *pluri*.

p.m. See A.M.

poetize is gradually displacing *poeticize*.

point of view. See STANDPOINT.

policy and **polity.** The latter means 'civil organization; civil order', also 'civil government' or 'a particular form of government', 'a state'; *policy* is 'a *course* of action intended, or adopted and pursued by a ruler or a government'. Weseen gives a good example in 'The United Kingdom is democratic in polity, but each party has its own policy'.

politician and **statesman.** In the U.S.A., *politician* has a connotation of intrigue and jobbery; in Great Britain, where it is not so sinister a word, it means 'one skilled—or engaged—in politics', all M.P.s being politicians. A *statesman* is a Cabinet Minister—a good one—or, at the least, an M.P. that has much influence, wisely used.

populace is a noun, *populous* an adjective. *Populace* is now derogatory: instead of meaning 'the common people', as it used to do, it = 'the mob' or even 'the rabble'.

portend, misused for *signify*. 'The window had been open at the time . . ., though what it might portend Higgins was not prepared to say.'

portent is unfortunate when used for *significance*, as in: 'For signature there was the interlocking-squares symbol that had come to have such a sinister portent for us all', S. S. Van Dine.

portentious for *portentous* is seldom written but often uttered. Probably on the analogy of *pretentious*.

portion and **part.** *Portion* = 'share' (one's portion of food; of an estate); it is short for *marriage portion*; it is one's lot or fate ('Brief life is here our portion'); a (limited) quantity; not now used often for 'a part of *any* whole'. Roughly, a *portion* is an entity cut or taken from a mass or conglomerate, whereas a *part* is a fraction or a constituent: 'part of a house, a pen, a body, a country'. (*O.E.D.*)

POSITION OF WORDS. See ORDER.

positive for 'merely *sure*' or 'merely *certain*' is hyperbolical; the correct nuance is 'very sure' or 'dogmatically (or assertively) sure'. There is something odd about this sentence: 'The scientist finds his referents and makes positive that others can find them in the dark': despite the fact that *positive* is used as = 'very sure'. Idiom demands 'makes certain that . . .'

For 'complete', as in 'He's a positive fool', *positive* is a colloquialism.

possess is stronger than *have*. Where the two words are synonymous, euphony or dignity will decide which is the better. *Possess* is, for instance, never derogatory: one *has* faults, one does not possess them.

POSSESSIVE, DUPLICATED. 'Seyss-Inquart's sentimental contact with Austria has been very different from that of Hitler's' should be either '. . . different from that of Hitler' or '. . . different from Hitler's'. (G. V. Carey, *Mind the Stop*.)

POSSESSIVE ADJECTIVE, unnecessary. 'Mr Garston's, the pawnbroker's, voluntary contribution.'

POSSESSIVE CASE. See GENITIVE.

possibility is sometimes misused for *chance*. 'I had no possibility to eschew the confusion.' The author might, however, have written, 'There was no possibility of my eschewing the confusion'—but the sense would have been slightly changed. And sometimes for *potentiality*, as in 'The main theme . . . is . . . the vision which revealed men and women as they are in actuality and, simultaneously, . . . as they would be if all their stunted possibilities had attained maturity'.

possible for *necessary* or *unavoidable* would seem to be an improbable error. Nevertheless, it occurs — surprisingly often.

possibly for *perhaps*. In conversation it is both permissible and clear, but in writing it is sometimes ambiguous. Consider 'He cannot possibly do it' and 'He cannot, possibly, do it': the first is clear, the latter becomes ambiguous if a careless writer omits the commas.

post. In North America, one *mails* a letter; in England one *posts* it.

postscript and **p.s.** (or *P.S.*). Strictly, the latter is an abbreviation of the former; to say *p*—*s* is to speak colloquially. The plural of the word *p.s.* is *p.ss.*; but in a letter one's second *p.s.* is generally written *pp.s.*, one's third *pp.ss.* [American usage: *p.p.s.*]

potable and **drinkable.** See EATABLE.

potent and **potential.** *Potent* is 'powerful', whether of person or liquor; *potential* is 'possible as opposed to actual: latent'. A potential statesman is one who has the ability: all he needs is the opportunity.

practical, misused for *practicable*. 'She tried to open the window on the right, but it didn't seem practical.'

practical, when misused for *virtual*, leads to strange ambiguities; this misuse springs from that *practically* which means, not 'in a practical manner', but 'almost', 'virtually'.—'It provides proof positive that forgery by typewriter is a practical impossibility'—a very odd statement indeed. (Here, exaggeration or overstatement may have originated the error, '. . . is an impossibility' being all that was required.)

practically. In *What a Word!*, 1935, Sir Alan Herbert—that sturdy champion of the cause of good English—writes thus: 'As a rule, "practically" means "*Not* practically" or "Nearly". For example, we [foolishly] say of a reluctant engine that it "*practically* started" when it did not start but made a bronchial sound and is now silent.—Do not misunderstand me . . . Life would be impossible if we never said "practically". You may say that a family is "practically extinct" when the only survivor is a dying old man', although a stylist would much prefer '*virtually* extinct'. 'But', Sir Alan Herbert resumes, 'it would be silly to say that the horse placed second "practically" won the Derby. A boxer may be "practically" knocked out, though still on his feet: but you cannot "practically" hit the bull's-eye, unless you do hit it. It is not the word but the habit that is bad.' I should go further and say: Avoid the word when it synonymizes *almost* or *virtually*—as good as—to all intents—in effect—though *not formally* (or *explicitly*), and select whichever of those seven synonyms is the most suitable to the context.

practice (n.), **practise** (v.), are often confused in spelling. [*Webster's: practice* (n.); *practice* or *practise* (v.).]

precedence, precedent. *Precedence* means superiority, especially socially, as in 'An earl takes precedence of a baronet'; cf.

'The moral always takes precedence of the miraculous' (*O.E.D.*). A *precedent* is a previous example or case that establishes a moral, social, or legal ruling; a lawyer has virtually won his case when he has found a precedent. *Precedence* is wrongly used in this sentence, 'There is, he thinks, no precedence for the admission of such evidence'.

precession and **procession**. The former implies a *going before*, the latter a *going forward*, but is usually applied to a body of persons marching in ceremonial order. The man in the street knows *precession* only in *the precession of the equinoxes*.

PRECIOUSNESS (or Preciosity). The *O.E.D.*'s definition is 'affectation of refinement or distinction, especially in the use of language; fastidious refinement in literary style'. It is at times difficult to distinguish between art, artifice, and affectation: preciosity ensues when subtlety or delicacy or both subtlety and delicacy are employed in contexts that do not call for them.

Preciousness can be satisfactorily judged only in long passages; but long passages cannot be quoted here.

From Pater's essay, 'Aesthetic Poetry', comes this—'The choice life of the human spirit is always under mixed lights, and in mixed situations, when it is not too sure of itself, is still expectant, girt up to leap forward to the promise. Such a situation there was in that earliest return from the overwrought spiritualities of the Middle Age to the earlier, more ancient life of the senses; and for us the most attractive form of the classical story is the monk's conception of it, when he escapes from the sombre atmosphere of his cloister to natural light. Then the fruits of this mood, which, divining more than it understands, infuses into the scenery and figures of Christian history some subtle reminiscence of older gods, or into the story of Cupid and Psyche that passionate stress of spirit which the world owes to Christianity, constitute a peculiar vein of interest in the art of the fifteenth century.'

John Addington Symonds is often precious, as in the following reference to a passage in Lorenzo de' Medici's *Corinto*: —'Here we have the *Collige virgo rosas*, "Gather ye roses while ye may", translated from the autumn of antique to the April of modern poetry, and that note is echoed through all the love-literature of the Renaissance. Lorenzo, be it observed, has followed his model, not only in the close, but also in the opening of the

F*

passage. Side by side with this Florentine transcript from Ausonius I will now place Poliziano's looser, but more poetical handling of the same theme, subjoining my version of his ballata.'

precipitously is erroneously used for *precipitately* in 'She looked around her wildly, and precipitously left the room'; *precipitous* meaning 'very steep', and *precipitate* 'violently hurried'. One might leave a room 'precipitously' by jumping out of the window or falling downstairs.

precisian (not *precision*); **precisionist** (not *precisianist*). A *precisian* is a person rigidly precise; but one who makes a profession or practice of precision is a *precisionist*. Hence, *precisianism*, the abstract noun corresponding to *precisian*; *precisionism*, to *precisionist*.

PRÉCIS WRITING. The *O.E.D.* gives the word 'précis' as not yet naturalized: spells it not only with an accent (a procedure both justifiable and indeed necessary) but in italics, which, I propose, should be discarded. The plural is 'précis's'. [For American usage, *Webster's* gives the plural *précis*.] The verb 'précis', to make a précis of, has present participle 'précising' and past tense (and participle) 'précised'; I must say that I prefer 'précis'ing' and 'précis'd'.

By the same authority, the term 'précis' is defined as 'a concise or abridged statement; a summary; an abstract'. My impression is that *summary* is an exact synonym of *précis* and that *abstract* might be usefully restricted to a summary or epitome of scientific or technical information —above all, of figures (e.g., statistics). Admittedly, an *abridgement* is also either a compendium or an epitome: but the terms are not interchangeable at will, and it is better to maintain distinctions than to destroy them.—From *The O.E.D.*'s definition it would be dangerous to deduce that *abridgement* and *précis* are synonymous: one makes a précis of a paragraph, a passage, even a chapter, or of a letter, a report, a document; not of a book of any considerable size, the summary of a book being either (large scale) an abridgement or a compendium, or (small scale) a synopsis. An *abridgement*, as *The O.E.D.* says, is either 'a compendium of a larger work, with the details abridged, and less important things omitted, but retaining the sense and substance' or 'an epitome or compendium of any subject that might be treated much more fully'; it is also, *The O.E.D.* allows, a synopsis,—but that is a sense we should do well to ignore, at least to the extent of avoiding it. [In American usage the term *digest*, as synonymous with *abridgment* and *abridge*, has been popularized by *The Reader's Digest*. The term *digest* was borrowed from the law, where it means a compilation, systematically arranged, of legal rules, decisions, and statutes.]

There are four main ways in which a précis can be made:—

I. To summarize in one's own language and to cast the summary into Reported Speech (*oratio obliqua*)—or to retain reported speech if the original itself is oblique.

II. To summarize in one's own language and, unless the original is itself in Reported Speech, ignore the convention of reported speech—i.e., leave the summary in Direct Speech.

III. To retain, so far as possible, the language of the original and, unless the original is already oblique, to cast the summary into Indirect or Reported Speech.

IV. To retain, so far as possible, the language of the original, but to ignore the convention of Reported Speech, —unless the original is in Reported, in which case there is no sense in turning the Indirect into the Direct mode.

A certain Examining Board says, in its instructions concerning précis, that 'generally the recognized technique of "reported speech" should be expected, together with a formal title, and the date if relevant'; but it does not insist on Reported Speech. The custom of putting a précis into Reported Speech is an old one. That something is to be said for it—e.g., that the précis gains in impersonality (if that *is* a gain)—I admit. But much more can be said against it: one takes longer to cast a précis into Indirect Speech than into direct, unless the original is in Indirect Speech; a précis in Indirect is more difficult to make; therefore, the proportion of errors will be larger in an Indirect than a Direct précis; and the potentiality of ambiguity is much higher in Indirect than in Direct Speech. As a school exercise, Reported Speech has its intellectual value; but in the practical world, to turn Direct into Indirect Speech is a waste of time. Moreover, it is a relic of a rigid Classicism.

Examining Boards, in general, recommend Method I: a summary couched in one's own words and cast into Reported Speech. Failing that, they tolerate Methods II and III: III, a summary that, cast into Reported, retains much or even most of the wording of the original; II, a summary not in Reported, yet written in one's own words. But they frown on IV, which, abandoning the convention of Reported, yet sticks as close as possible to the wording of the original.

I have long urged the abolition of Reported Speech (unless the original is Indirect) from précis writing. Which, then, of Methods II and IV do I prefer?

As a training in composition, Method II (one's own language, in Direct Speech) is superior to Method IV; but as précis *qua* précis, IV (Direct Speech in words keeping as close as is idiomatically possible to those of the original) is superior, for this is the method that precludes error more than any other method does. In short, there is précis by recast and there is précis by reduction; the *literary* ideal is a recast of the reduction. If the reduction is carefully made, it will require only a slight recasting.

For easy reading, it is advisable to break a long, unparagraphed passage into paragraphs—not arbitrarily but according to the divisions of the subject. Do not tinker with an already satisfactory paragraphing. And do not alter the order of the narrative or the discourse unless the order is faulty: remember that you're not supposed to be presenting yourself; you are required to represent the author in brief. Don't show off by changing the ordonnance of a good writer: he knows better than you do how *he* wishes to set forth his subject.*

Here follow two passages set in a certain examination. They are preceded by these instructions:—'Write a Précis giving clearly the substance of the following passage and presenting *in a consecutive and readable shape*, briefly and distinctly expressed, the main points of the argument, so that anyone who has not time to read the actual passage may learn the substance of it from the Précis.'

The Capture and Defence of Arcot

Clive was now twenty-five years old. After hesitating for some time between a military and a commercial life, he had at length been placed in a post which partook of both characters, that of commissary to the troops, with the rank of Captain. The present emergency called

* See also my *Précis Writing* (Routledge, London).

forth all his powers. He represented to his superiors that, unless some vigorous efforts were made, Trichinopoly would fall, and the French would become the real masters of the whole peninsula of India. It was absolutely necessary to strike some daring blow. If an attack were made on Arcot, the capital of the Carnatic, and the favourite residence of the Nabobs, it was not impossible that the siege of Trichinopoly would be raised. The heads of the English settlement, now thoroughly alarmed by the success of Dupleix, and apprehensive that, in the event of a new war between France and Great Britain, Madras would be instantly taken and destroyed, approved of Clive's plan, and intrusted the execution of it to himself. The young captain was put at the head of two hundred English soldiers. and three hundred Sepoys armed and disciplined after the European fashion. Of the eight officers who commanded this little force under him, only two had ever been in action, and four of the eight were factors of the company, whom Clive's example had induced to offer their services. The weather was stormy; but Clive pushed on, through thunder, lightning, and rain, to the gates of Arcot. The garrison, in a panic, evacuated the fort, and the English entered it without a blow.

The intelligence of these events was soon carried to Chunda Sahib, who, with his French allies, was besieging Trichinopoly. He immediately detached an army of ten thousand men, under his son, Rajah Sahib, to invest the fort of Arcot, which seemed quite incapable of sustaining a siege. The walls were ruinous, the ditches dry, the ramparts too narrow to admit the guns, the battlements too low to protect the soldiers. The little garrison had been greatly reduced by casualties. It now consisted of a hundred and twenty Europeans and two hundred Sepoys. Only four officers were left; the stock of provisions was scanty.

During fifty days the siege went on. During fifty days the young captain maintained the defence, with a firmness, vigilance, and ability, which would have done honour to the oldest marshal in Europe. The breach, however, increased day by day. The garrison began to feel the pressure of hunger. Under such circumstances, any troops so scantily provided with officers might have been expected to show signs of insubordination. But the Sepoys came to Clive, not to complain of their scanty fare, but to propose that all the grain should be given to the Europeans, who required more nourishment than the natives of India. The thin gruel, they said, which was strained away from the rice, would suffice for themselves.

An attempt made by the government of Madras to relieve the place had failed, but Rajah Sahib learned that the Mahrattas were in motion; their chief, Morari Row, roused by the fame of the defence of Arcot declared that he had never before believed that Englishmen could fight, but that he would willingly help them since he saw that they had spirit to help themselves. It was necessary to be expeditious. Rajah Sahib offered large bribes to Clive; they were rejected with scorn, and he determined to storm the fort.

The enemy advanced, driving before them elephants whose foreheads were armed with iron plates. It was expected that the gates would yield to the shock of these living battering-rams. But the huge beasts no sooner felt the English musket-balls than they turned round and trampled on the multitude which had urged them forward. The rear ranks of the English kept the front ranks supplied with a constant succession of loaded muskets, and every shot told on the living mass below. After three desperate onsets, the besiegers retired.

The struggle lasted about an hour. Four hundred of the assailants fell. The garrison lost only five or six men. The besieged passed an anxious night, looking for a renewal of the attack. But when day broke, the enemy were no more to be seen. They had retired, leaving the English several guns and a large quantity of ammunition.

Lord Macaulay.

My version (by reduction and slight recasting) is this:—

The Capture and Defence of Arcot

Clive, promoted commissary captain at 25, represented that, unless vigorous efforts were made, Trichinopoly would fall: the French become masters of India. If an attack were made on Arcot, capital of the Carnatic and residence of the Nabobs, the siege might be raised. The heads of the English settlement approved of Clive's plan. He was put in command of 200 English soldiers and 300 Sepoys, with eight officers. Clive pushed on, through storms, to Arcot. The garrison, panicking, evacuated the fort; the English entered.

Intelligence was soon carried to

Chunda Sahib, who, with French allies, was besieging Trichinopoly. He immediately detached 10,000 men, under his son, Rajah Sahib, to invest Arcot fort, which seemed incapable of sustaining a siege. The garrison now consisted of 120 Europeans and 200 Sepoys with four officers and scanty provisions.

During fifty days Clive maintained the defence like a veteran. The breach, however, increased. The garrison began to feel hunger. But the Sepoys proposed that the grain should be given to the Europeans, who required more nourishment: the thin gruel strained from the rice would suffice for themselves.

An attempt by the Madras government to relieve Arcot had failed, but Rajah Sahib learned that the Mahrattas were moving; expedition was necessary. Rajah Sahib offered bribes to Clive; they were rejected; he determined to storm the fort.

The enemy drove before them elephants forehead-armed with iron plates: battering-rams. But the huge beasts, feeling the English bullets, trampled on the multitude behind; every shot told on the living mass below. After three desperate onsets, the besiegers retired.

There fell 400 assailants, only six defenders. The besieged passed an anxious night, but when day broke, the enemy had retired, leaving several guns and much ammunition.

Here is a passage to be précis'd in 260-300 words.

The Pitt-Newcastle Coalition.

The two most powerful men in the country were the Duke of Newcastle and Pitt. Alternate victories and defeats had made them sensible that neither of them could stand alone. The interest of the State, and the interest of their own ambition, impelled them to coalesce. By their coalition was formed the ministry which was in power when George the Third ascended the throne.

The more carefully the structure of this celebrated ministry is examined, the more shall we see reason to marvel at the skill or the luck which had combined in one harmonious whole such various and, as it seemed, incompatible elements of force. The influence which is derived from stainless integrity, the influence which is derived from the vilest arts of corruption, the strength of aristocratical connection, the strength of democratical enthusiasm, all these things were for the first time found together.

Newcastle brought to the coalition a vast mass of power, which had descended to him from Walpole and Pelham. The public offices, the church, the courts of law, the army, the navy, the diplomatic service, swarmed with his creatures. The great Whig families, which, during several generations, had been trained in the discipline of party warfare, and were accustomed to stand together in a firm phalanx, acknowledged him as their captain. Pitt, on the other hand, had what Newcastle wanted, an eloquence which stirred the passions and charmed the imagination, a high reputation for purity, and the confidence and ardent love of millions.

The partition which the two ministers made of the powers of government was singularly happy. Each occupied a province for which he was well qualified; and neither had any inclination to intrude himself into the province of the other. Newcastle took the treasury, the civil and ecclesiastical patronage, and the disposal of that part of the secret-service money which was then employed in bribing members of Parliament. Pitt was Secretary of State, with the direction of the war and of foreign affairs. Thus the filth of all the noisome and pestilential sewers of government was poured into one channel. Through the other passed only what was bright and stainless. Mean and selfish politicians, pining for commissionerships, gold sticks, and ribands, flocked to the great house at the corner of Lincoln's Inn Fields. There, at every levee, appeared eighteen or twenty pair of lawn sleeves; for there was not, it was said, a single Prelate who had not owed either his first elevation or some subsequent translation to Newcastle. There appeared those members of the House of Commons in whose silent votes the main strength of the Government lay. One wanted a place in the excise for his butler. Another came about a prebend for his son. A third whispered that he had always stood by his Grace and the Protestant succession; that his last election had been very expensive; that he had been forced to take up money on mortgage; and that he hardly knew where to turn for five hundred pounds. The Duke pressed all their hands, passed his arm round all their shoulders, patted all their backs, and sent away some with wages, and some with promises. From this traffic Pitt stood haughtily aloof. Not only was he himself incorruptible, but he shrank from the loathsome drudgery of corrupting others. He had not, however, been twenty years in Parliament, and ten years in office, without discovering how the Government was carried on. He was perfectly aware that bribery was practised on a large scale by his colleagues. Hating the practice, yet despairing of putting it down, and doubting whether, in those times, any ministry could stand without it, he determined to be blind to it. He would see nothing, know nothing, believe nothing.

It may be doubted whether he did not owe as much of his popularity to his ostentatious purity as to his eloquence, or to his talents for the administration of war. It was everywhere said with delight and admiration that the Great Commoner, without any advantages of birth or fortune, had, in spite of the dislike of the Court and of the aristocracy, made himself the first man in England, and made England the first country in the world; that his name was mentioned with awe in every palace from Lisbon to Moscow; that his trophies were in all the four quarters of the globe; yet that he was still plain William Pitt, without title or riband, without pension or sinecure place. Whenever he should retire, after saving the State, he must sell his coach horses and his silver candlesticks. Widely as the taint of corruption had spread, his hands were clean. They had never received, they had never given, the price of infamy. Thus the coalition gathered to itself support from all the high and all the low parts of human nature, and was strong with the whole united strength of virtue and of Mammon.

Lord Macaulay.*

The following is my suggestion:—

The Pitt-Newcastle Coalition.

The most powerful men were the Duke of Newcastle and Pitt. Alternative victories and defeats had made them sensible that neither could stand alone. The interest of the State, and their own ambition, impelled them to coalesce, in the ministry that was in power when George the Third became king.

The more carefully the structure of this celebrated ministry is examined, the more we marvel at the skill or the luck that had harmoniously combined such various and seemingly incompatible forces. The influences deriving from stainless integrity and from the vilest arts of corruption, the

* This passage, like the preceding one, is reprinted with the very kind permission of the Oxford & Cambridge Schools Examination Board.

strength of aristocratical connection, and democratical enthusiasm, all merged for the first time. Newcastle brought a vast mass of power; the public offices, the church, the courts of law, the army, the navy, the diplomatic service, swarmed with his creatures. The great Whig families, trained in party warfare, acknowledged him as their captain. Pitt had what Newcastle lacked, an imaginative and passionate eloquence, a high reputation for purity, and the confidence and ardent love of millions.

The partition of government was singularly happy. Each man occupied a province for which he was well qualified; and neither wished to intrude into the other's. Newcastle took the treasury, the civil and ecclesiastical patronage, and the bribing of members of Parliament. Pitt was Secretary of State, with the direction of the war and of foreign affairs. Thus all the filth was poured into one channel. Through the other passed only what was bright and stainless. Mean, selfish, self-seeking politicians flocked to Newcastle's great London house. There appeared ambitious Prelates and those M.P.s in whose silent votes the strength of the Government lay, —one wanting this; another, that. The Duke pressed all their hands, and sent away some with wages, some with promises. From this traffic Pitt stood haughtily aloof. Incorruptible, he shrank from the drudgery of corrupting others. He inevitably knew, however, how the Government was carried on; that bribery was practised on a large scale: but doubting whether any ministry could stand without it, he determined to be blind to it. He would know nothing.

Perhaps he owed as much of his popularity to his ostentatious purity as to his eloquence, or to his talents for the administration of war. It was everywhere said with delighted admiration that the Great Commoner had, in spite of the Court and the aristocracy, made himself the first man in England, England the first country in the world; that his name was mentioned with awe in every Palace of Europe; yet that he was still plain William Pitt, without title, pension, or sinecure. Whenever he should retire, after saving the State, he would be poor. Widely as corruption had spread, *his* hands were clean. Thus the coalition was strong with the united strength of virtue and of Mammon.

predicate is occasionally misused for *predict*; and vice versa. The former = to de-

clare, assert, affirm; the latter = to fore-
tell.

prefer ... than. See THAN.

preferable, more. See COMPARATIVES,
FALSE.

prejudice (n.) against, but *partiality for.*
The former word (except in legal terminology) is now unusually pejorative, the
latter usually favourable.

prelude. *Prelude* became, ca. 1930, almost
an inevitable for 'introduction', 'pro-
logue', 'pre-history', and what-have-you-
in-this-kind, and it is still being used far
too much, especially in titles of books.

premise, misused for *presumption, assumption.* 'Since then, nothing has been
seen or heard of him, and as that is the
case, the premise is that he's still there.'
The author misunderstands the meaning
of *premise*, a legal term for 'the previous
statement from which another is inferred'
(*The Con. O.D.*); the assertion that 'nothing has been seen or heard of him' is
the premise from which it is inferred that
'he's still there'.

prepared to admit, confess, state, etc., be.
'I am prepared to confess that I am the
culprit' is absurd; the verbosity is un-
dignified; one confesses, or one doesn't.

PREPOSITION AT END. Instances of
extreme awkwardness: 'The paper so
praised Boswell himself was the author
of' (J. Timbs, *The Romance of London*,
1865); 'When she prattles about herself
and her admirers, she makes the reader
blush for the shamefacedness she evidently does not even guess at the lack of'.
Yet too great a fear of putting the preposition at the end sometimes leads to
even worse errors. Thus, a certain author
has written, 'They who come here see it
as though it were a place of earth records,
in the form that in their own countries
such things are kept', meaning 'are kept
in', or better, 'the form in which such
things are kept'; here the writer shirks the
necessary repetition of *in*, and writes un-
grammatically. The same error, and for
the same reason, occurs in the inscription
on the monument to John, Duke of
Argyle, in Westminster Abbey: 'A General and Orator exceeded by none in the
Age he lived' [in].

Pearsall Smith called the preposition
at the end of a clause or a sentence an
anglicism; he added that it should not be
discouraged. The late H. W. Fowler
wrote thus:

'It is a cherished superstition that prepositions must, in spite of the ineradicable
English instinct for putting them late

("They are the fittest timber to make
great politics of" said Bacon; and "What
are you hitting me for?" says the modern
schoolboy), be kept true to their name
and placed before the word they govern.
. . . The fact is that the remarkable freedom enjoyed by English in putting its
prepositions late and omitting its relatives is an important element in the flexi-
bility of the language. The power of saying
*A state of dejection such as they are abso-
lute strangers to* (Cowper) instead of *A
state of dejection of an intensity to which
they are absolute strangers*, or *People
worth talking to* instead of *People with
whom it is worth while to talk*, is not one
to be lightly surrendered. . . . *That depends
on what they are cut with* is not improved
by conversion into *That depends on with
what they are cut*. . . . Those who lay down
the universal principle that final prepositions are "inelegant" are unconsciously
trying to deprive the English language of
a valuable idiomatic resource, which has
been freely used by all our greatest writers,
except those whose instinct for English
idiom has been overpowered by notions
of correctness derived from Latin standards. The legitimacy of the prepositional
ending in literary English must be uncom-
promisingly maintained; in respect of elegance or inelegance, every example must
be judged not by any arbitrary rule, but
on its own merits, according to the impression it makes on the feeling of educated English readers.'

**PREPOSITION REPEATED UN-
NECESSARILY.** 'An order, this, at
which the taximan would have jibbed at
violently . . . ', John G. Brandon; 'The
weak estate in which Queen Mary left the
realm in' (Milton: cited by Onions).

PREPOSITIONS, DISGUISED. See
DISGUISED PREPOSITIONS.

PREPOSITIONS WRONGLY USED.
The idea is owed to Charles Boyd's very
useful little book, *Grammar for Grown-
Ups*, which contains a tabulated list of
words. Here, the error precedes the correct use.

(of things) *accompanied by* for *accompanied with*; a person, however, is
accompanied *by* another
accounted for in consequence of for
accounted-for by
acquiescence to for *acquiescence in*
adherence of for *adherence to*; *an adherent to* for *an adherent of*; *adherent
(adj.) of* for *adherent to*
aim for for *to aim at*

assist (him) *to do* for *assist* (him) *in doing*
(of things) *attended by* for *attended with*
(one's) *belief of* (e.g., *revelation*) for *belief in*
careful with for *careful of* (e.g., one's money or reputation)
(one's) *character of honesty* for *character for honesty*
comment (n. and v.) *to* (a thing) for *comment on*
conducive of for *conducive to*
[*different to* is not a solecism, but the scholarly prefer *different from*; *different than*, however, is incorrect]
disgust at (or *of*) for *disgust with*
embarrassed at for *embarrassed by*
end by for *end with*, as in 'The service ended by a prayer'; or for *end in* (as in 'It all ended by his going off in a huff')
equal as (or *with*) for *equal to*
familiar to (the idea) for *familiar with*
favourable reception with (the public) for *favourable reception by*
ill of is now rare for *ill with*
in comparison of for *in comparison with*
in respect to for *in respect of*
in search for for *in search of*
inculcate (a person) *with* (something) for *inculcate* (something) *on* (a person)
inferior than for *inferior to*
instil (someone) *with* for *instil* (something) *into*
involved by for *involved in*
judged on (certain standards) for *judged by*
knowledge on for *knowledge of*
listen at for *listen to*
oblivious to for *oblivious of*
pregnant of for *pregnant with*
protest at for *protest against*
receptive to for *receptive of*
(one's) *relations towards* (another person) for *relations with*
sensible to for *sensible of*; contrast *sensitive of*, which is incorrect for *sensitive to*
solicitous to for *solicitous of*
sparing with for *sparing of*
suffer with for *suffer from*
superior than for *superior to*
tendency for for *tendency to*
tolerant to for *tolerant of*
with a view of for *with a view to*
write (*up*)*on impulse*, ambiguous for *write from impulse*.

prescience, misused for *presentiment*. 'The prescience [his own] of another European War harassed him', Gilbert Frankau, *Royal Regiment*, 1938.
present-day for *present* or *contemporary* is an unnecessary synonym; and why use two words for one? 'The present-day sys-tem in politics' drew my attention to this particular piece of ineptitude. ['Present-day English' is the awkward name of an American group devoted to the study of contemporary English.]
presentative and presentive. The former is the more usual; *presentive* is the opposite of *symbolic*; i.e., it = 'presenting an object or an idea direct to the mind'. In addition to its ecclesiastical sense, *presentative* is used in Psychology and Metaphysics in a sense wider than that of *representative*.
present writer, the, is inferior to *the author* in the sense 'I (or me), the writer'; and usually *I* is preferable to either.
president for *presidency* or *Presidency*. The American *run for president* (properly *President*) and *candidates for President* are colloquialisms for *run for the Presidency, candidates for the Presidency*.
presume. See ASSUME.
presumptious for *presumptuous* has become an illiteracy.
presumptive for *presumptuous*. 'If I am unhappy it is my own fault for being a presumptive fool'; in this sense never correct and now obsolete. *Presumptive* is defined as 'based on presumption or inference', and *presumption* as 'a belief deduced from facts or experience' (*O.E.D.*) or even from imagination. *Presumptuous* is 'unduly confident or bold'. The presumptuous man is too ready to act on a merely presumptive opinion.
pretend dominantly = 'to feign, represent falsely'; although the sense 'to profess' is admissible, it is better to use *profess*.
pretension, pretention. The latter, on which certain printers insist, has no justification; *The Con. O.D.* doesn't even mention it, nor does *Webster's*.
preventitive, preventative, preventive, are easily confused. The first is incorrect for either of the other two; *preventive* is the best form, whether for the noun or for the adjective.
previous is frequently used of a person acting too hastily, especially as in 'You have been much too previous'; this is slang. The meaning of *previous* is 'preceding' or 'former': 'The previous question', that came last before the one under discussion.
previous to for *before* or *until* is commercialese.
previously to this is catachrestic for *previous to this*, which is itself verbose for *before this* or *previously*. 'Previously to this we could toy with various ideas.'

priceless. See INVALUABLE.

primeval (preferable to *primaeval*) and primitive. Both words = belonging to or characteristic of the first age of the world or of anything ancient. But only *primitive* = rough, elementary; old-fashioned. *Primitive*, moreover, has learned senses (in, e.g., anthropology, medicine and philology) not possessed by *primeval*.

primordial; principal. See COMPARATIVES, FALSE.

principal, confused with *principle*. 'On the principal of taking the biggest first, I will begin with Eastbourne.'

priority has been foisted upon us by the Services, including the Civil Service, as a synonym for 'urgency', 'a matter of urgency', 'an essential', 'a prime necessity', as in 'The man-power of industry has become No. 1 priority'. Like *ceiling* it is to be treated with great disrespect.

probe, misused for *prod*. 'He probed about the hedge.' To *probe* is to *penetrate*.

procession. See CAVALCADE.

procure and secure. To *procure* is 'to gain or win; to obtain by care or effort'; to *secure* is 'to obtain for certain; to obtain for safe possession'. *Procure* and *secure* should not be so weakened that they become synonymous with the neutral *obtain*.

professor is illicitly used by pill-vendors, mountebanks, showmen of all sorts. To speak of a *professor of music* (or of *singing*) is permissible, if he be prominent or very capable in his profession. In general, it is best to reserve the term for university professors.

PROGRESSIVE INFINITIVE. See BE BEING . . .

PROGRESSIVE (or CONTINUOUS TENSES are often, by stylists, employed to avoid ambiguity: 'Fruit was eaten in large quantities' may refer either to habitual action or to a certain occasion; 'Fruit was being eaten in large quantities' is applicable only to continuous action on a certain occasion.

prohibit. See INHIBIT.

prohibit (a person) to (do something) is archaic. Either one *prohibits* a person *from* doing something, or one prohibits the thing in question: thus, 'The Prime Minister prohibits them from discussing the matter in public' or 'The Prime Minister prohibited public discussion of the matter'.

prolific is often misused for *profuse*. The former = 'fertile; abundant'.

PROLIXITY. See VERBOSITY.

promote should not be used with bad or evil things, for it means 'to further, to advance'. Do not say 'Drink promotes idleness' but 'Drink increases (or leads to) idleness'.

prone and supine. 'To lie *prone*' is to lie, face downwards, on one's belly, as in (normal) rifle-shooting; 'to lie *supine*' is to lie flat on one's back, face to the zenith. Both of these words may be applied to the person (or his body) or to the position.

PRONOUN, POSSESSIVE. 'The sound of martial music would be borne to eager . . . ears as regiment after regiment made their way.' The nominative 'regiment' is in the singular and the pronoun should be *its*.

'At a friend of my wife's there is a photograph . . .', omits a possessive; the sentence needs to be recast.

PRONOUNS JOINED by *and* or dissociated by *or* must not be in different cases, as they are in 'You and me will go now'; 'She didn't hit him or I'.

PROOF CORRECTING, HINTS ON. Not a subject to be treated in this book. But the inexperienced should consult G. V. Carey, *Mind the Stop*, last chapter.

propaganda is a singular (not, like *data* and *strata*, a plural); its plural is *propagandas*.

propellant and propellent; propulsion; propulsive. 'Wind is a propellant, that is to say, a propellent [= driving] force', Weseen; although *The O.E.D.* (which gives *propellent* for both noun and adjective) does not recognize *propellant*, *Webster's* has the *-ent* form as n. and adj. and *-ant* for a specific noun.

Propulsion is the action of driving or pushing forward or onward, or the being so driven, or the effort required therefor; *propulsive* is its adjective.

properly so called is needed in contradistinction to 'falsely (or improperly) so called', but generally it is a wordy synonym for *proper* (after, not before, the noun it qualifies). Thus 'The dialects properly so called' are merely 'The dialects proper'.

prophecy and prophesy. The latter is the verb, the former the noun.

proportion should not be used for *portion* (or *part*) or *number*, as in 'The greater proportion of journalists are men'.

proportions is commonly misused for *size* in such a sentence as 'the chair is not suited to a man of his proportions'; *proportions* being the relation of one part to another, whether large or small.

propose and purpose. To *purpose* is 'to set before *oneself* for accomplishment', as in

'My friend purposes to open an office';
His mother purposed that he should be a
preacher'; 'I purpose . . . keeping a sort
of journal'. In short, *propose* is encroach-
ing far too freely on the territory of *purpose*. (*O.E.D.*)

proposition, fast becoming a passe-partout, is in constant misuse. A *proposal* of
marriage is not a 'proposition', but the
word is properly applied to a draft of the
terms for a business agreement. *Proposition* is not synonymous with *affair*, *matter*, *task*, *undertaking*. For a slashing
attack on the word see Fowler's *English
Usage*; consult also Horwill's *American
Usage*.

prosaic and **prosy**. Both = 'commonplace, matter-of-fact', but *prosy* has the
connotation of tedious, so that its sense
is 'commonplace *and* tedious; dull and
wearisome'. Neither is now used for
'consisting of, or written in prose', *prose*
being the current adjective.

prosecute, confused with *persecute*. See
'PERSECUTE and PROSECUTE'.

prospective. See 'PERSPECTIVE and PRO-
SPECTIVE'.

prosy. See 'PROSAIC and PROSY'.

prostrate (adj.) and **supine** are sometimes
inexactly used. The former is lying face
downwards, the latter face upwards, on
the back. Two different states of mind
may be expressed in these attitudes.
[*Webster's* equates *prostrate* (adj.) with
prone or *supine*.] See also 'PRONE and
SUPINE'.

protagonist is occasionally confused with
antagonist, which is almost its opposite.
In literary terminology, *protagonist* means
'the chief character in a drama; hence in
a novel, a story, etc.'; derivatively, 'a person prominent in any contest or cause; a
champion of a cause'. *Protagonist* should
not be used loosely for any *supporter* (or
partisan) or *upholder*, for in its derivative
sense it means 'a *prominent* supporter or
champion of any cause'. (*O.E.D.*)

protest at. See PREPOSITIONS WRONGLY
USED.

prototype, misused for *predecessor* or
similar. 'The book . . . would have passed
into the limbo of the remainder lists with
thousands of its prototypes had not the
quality of one of the wilder anecdotes . . .
earned it a place in the news columns of a
Sunday paper.' There can be only one
prototype.

protrude, obtrude, intrude. 'I hope I don't
protrude', said the foreign gentleman, join-
ing the company uninvited. To *obtrude* (a
thing) is to force it on a person's attention.

prove, in 'the exception proves the rule',
is used in its primary sense, 'to test; to
make trial of', as in the Biblical 'Prove all
things and hold fast to that which is good'.

provide, misused for *form* or *constitute*,
as in 'Darts provides one of the most interesting games of skill and can be played
almost anywhere'.

provided and **providing** are less correct
(and often less clear) than *provided that*
and *providing that* in the sense 'it being
stipulated that', as in 'Provided that all is
safe, you may go' and 'I shall pay the
money, providing that you prove to me
the necessity'. It is, however, both permissible and indeed usual to omit *that*
when the sense is 'on condition that; in
case that, if only', as in 'Provided the
temperature remain the same, the volume
which a gas occupies is . . .'. (Based on
The O.E.D.)

psychological moment, at the, is now a
mere synonym for *in the nick of time*. In
the sense 'at the psychologically most
favourable moment', it is permissible,
though hackneyed.

psychology. Be sure to use this vague term
so precisely that its volatility is crystal-
lized, for it can be distressingly ambiguous. E.g., 'Shakespeare's psychology' has
at least four meanings, the two most
obvious being: 'Shakespeare's opinion of
or theories about the mind' and 'the way
in which Shakespeare's mind worked'.

psychosis. A recent vogue word.

publicity ; propaganda. The latter is 'any
association, systematic scheme, or con-
certed movement for the propagation of
a particular doctrine or practice' (*O.E.D.*),
whereas *publicity*, in its 20th-Century
sense, is 'the business [or the practice] of
advertising or making articles, schemes,
or persons publicly known' (*ibid.*).

punctilious and **punctual**. A punctilious
person—one who is scrupulously observant of fine points, or of details of action
or behaviour—is always *punctual*, scrupulously observant of an appointed time
(or, of trains, 'not late').

PUNCTUATION. Here is a newspaper
article that calls attention to its importance.

PUNCTUATION AND SPELLING

Dr Temple's Views

A Word to "Idle Examiners"

The Archbishop of York, Dr Temple,
thinks that correct punctuation is more
important—intellectually—than correct

spelling. He said so yesterday when he presented the school prizes at the Royal Infant Orphanage at Wanstead.

"In writing essays," said Dr Temple, "there are two things one has difficulty with—spelling and stops. Nearly everybody says it is the spelling that matters.

"Now spelling is one of the decencies of life, like the proper use of knives and forks. It looks slovenly and nasty if you spell wrongly, like trying to eat your soup with a fork.

'But, intellectually, spelling—English spelling—does not matter. Shakespeare spelt his own name at least four different ways, and it may have puzzled his cashiers at the bank.

"Intellectually, stops matter a great deal. If you are getting your commas, semi-colons, and full stops wrong, it means that you are not getting your thoughts right, and your mind is muddled." *The Observer*, Oct. 23, 1938.

Before making a few remarks on punctuation in general and giving some examples of mispunctuation, I shall refer the reader to certain authorities to be studied:—

F. Howard Collins, *Authors' and Printers' Dictionary*, 1905; 9th ed., 1946.
F. G. & H. W. Fowler, *The King's English*, 1906; 3rd ed., 1930 (excellent).
H. W. Fowler, *Modern English Usage*, 1926 (excellent).
W. Whitten & F. Whitaker, *Good and Bad English*, 1939 (short but valuable).
G. V. Carey, *Mind the Stop*, 1939 (the best short account).
R. Skelton, *Modern English Punctuation*, enlarged ed., 1949 (workmanlike).
G. H. Vallins, *Good English*, Library Ed., 1952: an attractive chapter.
E.P., *You Have a Point There*, 1953: a full-length study, with many examples. Contains an American chapter, by John W. Clark.

Before coming to intrinsic punctuation, let us for a moment consider extrinsic punctuation—punctuation in reference to quotation marks. There is a tendency among printers to put the period (full-stop) and comma inside the 'quotes', but the semi-colon and colon outside (though one often sees this sort of monstrosity: 'He was "hot-stuff;" he was "no fool:" he was formidable'), as in:—

'The word "breakfast," now always written as one word, was, before that, a hyphenated word, "break-fast." The natural course is for such words to begin as two vocables, "care free"; to become hyphenated words, "care-free": and to end up as single words, "carefree." '

But careful printers are beginning to follow the more logical rule of putting punctuation inside the 'quote' only when the punctuation mark is actually *part* of the quotation and also serves to round off the entire phrase or sentence that is concluded. A good writer will punctuate the above example thus:—

'The word "breakfast", now always written as one word, was, before that, a hyphenated word, "break-fast". The natural course is for such words to begin as two vocables, "care free"; to become hyphenated words, "care-free": and to end up as single words, "carefree".'

If one is quoting a person's actual words, the same rule should be observed as is observed in that example: with the caution that 'he said', 'as he said', etc., are to be treated as parenthetical; indeed, if you are in doubt, use parentheses.

In support of Dr Temple I quote from Mr Frank Whitaker's excellent address in *The J.I.J.*, January, 1939: 'Of punctuation I have time only to say this: that we ought to deplore the growing tendency to use only full stops and commas. Punctuation is an invaluable aid to clear writing, and I suggest that far too little importance is attached to it by many journalists.'

In very short sentences, the period (which marks the end of a statement) and the comma (which signifies apposition, as in 'Edward VII, King of England', or divides principal from subordinate clauses, as in 'When the girl arrived, the boy sat down') can—though not always happily —be made to suffice; but once you begin using long sentences, you need either the semi-colon, for a pause—a break—more important than that which is marked by a comma, as with the semi-colon in this sentence, or the colon, for a counterbalancing, a poising of the importance-stresses or significance-divisions: or for an addition that is too immediate to be marked by so definite and so final a stop as the period,—such an addition as you will have noticed in this rather long sentence, which exemplifies the ordinary dash and the strong or intensive comma-dash ('. . . the period,—such an addition as you will have noticed . . .').—And, of course, there is the period-dash, which marks a rather abrupt resumption or a dissociative break in the discourse. Such a break may conclude with '.—' as well as begin with one. The stop written ':—' is the colon-dash; it serves to introduce a list or anything else that has been formally announced; it might, in short, be defined as 'annunciatory'. Nowadays, however, the colon-dash often gives way to the simple period, especially when the list or more especially the illustrative sentence or passage begins on a new line.

But there are fine shades of distinction between the following:—

(a) 'The man rose to his feet, his opponent rushed at him, and both fell heavily to the ground.'

(b) 'The man rose to his feet; his opponent rushed at him; and both fell heavily to the ground.'

(c) 'The man rose to his feet: his opponent rushed at him: and both fell heavily to the ground.'

I think that, here, (c) is affected, for it is too literary for the context. In (a), the first comma is perhaps too weak to mark adequately the ensuing pause. Of these three, (b) is the best: but better still is the more varied 'The man rose to his feet; his opponent rushed at him, and both men fell heavily to the ground'.

At this point, I should like to draw attention to the recent revival, in literary prose, of the 18th-Century use of the semicolon: that use which produces the effect of a stressed pause or of a rhetorical break, as in the following example from Michael Harrison's novel, *When All the Trees Were Green*: 'And now we are coming to a clearing in the woods; a little glade, bright green with the soft moss-grass; in the centre of which glade a stream ran between deep banks . . .'.

There are, in fact, several ways of indicating a break or a pause.

(1) Parentheses, as in 'He was (God forgive him!) a scoundrel'.
It is worth one's while to remember that the contents of a parenthesis (the words between parentheses) must be such that their omission would neither alter the syntactic flow nor materially affect the pause.

(2) Dashes, as in 'He was—God forgive him!—a scoundrel'. This is stronger than (1).

(3) Commas, as in 'He was, God forgive him!, a scoundrel': but here the exclamation mark virtually precludes the use of commas.

(4) Semi-colons, as in 'He was; God forgive him!; a scoundrel!' though here, too, an exclamation mark looks odd in conjunction with a semi-colon.

But (3) and (4) are viable in: 'He was, as all men knew, a scoundrel' and 'He was; as all men knew; a scoundrel', the latter being very literary.

(5) Colons, as in 'He was: God forgive him!: a scoundrel', where, again, the exclamation mark induces a feeling of discomfort; a discomfort absent both from 'He was: as all men knew: a scoundrel' and from the preferable 'He was: all men knew: a scoundrel' —perhaps even more literary than (4).

The importance of punctuation—an importance that could hardly be over-emphasized—may be illustrated by the letter of invitation to Jameson at the time of his raid into the Transvaal. In telegraphic form, the text runs thus: 'It is under these circumstances that we feel constrained to call upon you to come to our aid should a disturbance arise here the circumstances are so extreme that we cannot but believe that you and the men under you will not fail to come to the rescue of people who are so situated.' If you put a full stop after 'aid', the message contains an unequivocal invitation ('Come at once!'). But if you put the full stop, not after 'aid' but after 'here', the message becomes merely a conditional invitation depending on a circumstance arising at some indefinite time in the future.

Now for some less momentous examples: In a publisher's list of books there appears:

'ANARCHY or HIERARCHY
by S. de Madariaga

Author of *Englishmen, Frenchmen, Spaniards, Disarmament, The Genius of Spain,* etc.'

Very confusing, that list of the author's works! Read, 'Author of *Englishmen, Frenchmen, Spaniards; Disarmament; The Genius of Spain;* etc.'

'The only student I have ever met who ever believed his ears was blind': the lack of punctuation is defensible on the score of fluency; but 'The only student I have met who ever believed his ears, was blind' does away with the ambiguity. The sentence, however, needs to be rewritten, perhaps in the form, 'Of all the students I have met, only one believed his ears: and he was blind' or '. . .; and he was blind'.

'Bush and Brown slept in cloak and

blanket on the bare soil, probably, Hornblower anticipated, most uncomfortably' (C. S. Forester, *Flying Colours*). The comma after 'soil' is too weak; I suggest, 'B. and B. slept ... on the bare soil; probably (Hornblower anticipated) most uncomfortably'.

In the British Museum copy of H. A. J. Munro's *Criticisms and Elucidations of Catullus*, 1878, someone has, against the sentence 'The latest editor of the text Baehrens believes it like me to be one poem', written the criticism, 'not grammatical'. Rewrite, 'The latest editor of the text, Baehrens, like me believes it to be one poem' or 'Like me, the latest editor of the text, Baehrens, believes it to be one poem'.

'There was no villa to be seen ... As they drew near it became evident that the narrow road ended by the villa itself' (Louis Bromfield, *The Strange Case of Miss Annie Spragg*). This passage obviously requires a comma after 'near'.

'For all the Loyalist Party know the girl may turn up at any second' (Laurence Meynell, *The House in the Hills*). Punctuate, 'For all the Loyalist Party know, the girl ...'

'The night it all began torrential rain fell' (Dale Collins, *Lost*): insert a comma after 'began'.

' "You don't really like it, you're only pretending to please me" ' (Muriel Hine, *Clear as the Sun*): a comma is required after 'pretending'; but that insertion weakens the comma after 'it'. Punctuate, 'You don't really like it; you're only pretending, to please me'.

'If there was any previous connection between Bennett and the Oultons that, and not Mrs O'Brien's name and address on their back, might account for Bennett's interest in Miss Molly's sketches' (E. R. Punshon, *The Dusky Hour*): put a comma after 'Oultons'.

'And once I had discovered that there was no longer any doubt as to whether a spark of life still lingered in him' (Stephen Maddock, *Doorway to Danger*). I had reached the end of the sentence before I realized that not the whole sentence but only 'once I had discovered that' is an adverbial clause; a comma is needed after 'that', which is pronoun, not conjunction.

In 'The opposite arrangement—that is to say, an abundance of short and unaccented syllables, and the more abrupt consonants alternated with the vowels, by making the pronunciation rapid, light and easy, corresponds to quickness of motion in the subject' (Alexander Bain, *English Composition and Rhetoric*, 1887–88, at II, 292) the punctuation is vague, probably incomplete, and certainly ambiguous.

In 'When the dreadful plague was mowing down the terrified people of London in great swathes, this brave man, instead of flying quietly, remained at his house' (Walter Thornbury), it is obviously the printer, not the author, who has erred by putting a comma after 'quietly' instead of before it.

And finally two examples from Stuart Chase's *The Tyranny of Words*, 1938:—
'What is the ultimate nature of matter? The question we know by now is meaningless.' Punctuate thus:—'. . . The question, we know by now, is meaningless.'
'A bank studied on the basis of what is going on inside without recourse to abstractions like "credit", "liquidity", "soundness", is a pretty whimsical thing.' A comma after 'inside' would remove an ambiguity.

[For American usage an important authority is the University of Chicago Press *A Manual of Style*.—Double marks of punctuation, such as :— and ,—, have almost disappeared from American printing.—Many American printers prefer a general practice of setting all periods and commas within the quotation marks, all semicolons and colons outside of the quotation marks. The small points dangling after the broad double quotes of American use are curious-looking. However, in typescripts, where every symbol takes an em space, double quotes after period or comma may jut out ridiculously, especially when only the last word is quoted.—Mr Partridge's account of punctuation shows by its wealth of possible effects that punctuation can be made a part of the art of writing—instead of the simple, almost mechanical routine that American schools recommend.*]

pupil and **student**. A *pupil* at a school, a *student* at a university. [In American usage we cater to the young people and speak of *high school students* as well as *college* and *university students*; and *grammar school pupils*. But a professor may talk of 'a former pupil of mine'. Musicians and painters have *pupils*, not *students*, though these are 'students of painting or of music' and some of them may study at 'the Art Students League'.]

* Part of Professor W. Cabell Greet's end-note to 'Punctuation' in *Usage and Abusage*.

puppet and **marionette**. A *puppet* is any figure representing a human being; usually it is small; generally it is a doll. Also it is 'a human figure, with jointed limbs, moved by means of a string or wires; especially one of the figures in a puppet-show; a marionette' (*O.E.D.*); but in this sense, *marionette* is more usual.

pure does = *mere*, but avoid it if, as in 'pure Nudism', it sets up an ambiguity.

PURE ENGLISH. See STANDARD ENGLISH.

Puritan and **puritan**. A *Puritan* is a member of that party of English Protestants who, in late 16th-mid 17th Century, desired a further purification of the Church and, especially, a simpler form of worship. A *puritan* is 'one who is, affects to be, or is accounted extremely strict, precise, or scrupulous in religion or morals'. (*O.E.D.*)

purport in the sense of 'purpose' is now so rare as to make its employment inadvisable: see the passage quoted at MALAPROPISMS. The general sense of the noun is 'meaning' or 'tenor'; and, properly used, the word is restricted to documents and speeches. As a verb, it is confined to documents and speeches and it signifies 'to have as its meaning' or 'to be intended to seem', 'to be made to appear', as in 'He received a letter purporting to be written by me and to contain my decision on an important matter'. (*Con. O.D.*)

PURPOSE. See FINAL CLAUSES.

purpose (v.). See 'PROPOSE and PURPOSE'.

purposely. See ADVISEDLY.

Q

quadra-; quadri-; quadru-. The first is always wrong; the second is the usual form, except in *quadrumanous* and in such other nouns as have a second element that begins with *p* (as in *quadruped*). The sense is 'having *or* consisting of *or* connected with four (things specified)'. (*O.E.D.*)

quaint is 'unusual, uncommon, or even odd', but at the same time either 'attractive' or 'agreeable' especially if it is either 'pretty or dainty in an old-fashioned way'. Do not use it to mean either 'merely odd' or 'amusing (or droll)': those are slangy or, at best, colloquial usages.

qualitive is incorrect for *qualitative* (referring to quality), which is often contrasted with *quantitative* (referring to quantity).

quality of is correct in 'a certain quality of paper' but wrong in 'To finish up in some club of the same quality of his own', where the first 'of' seems to have led the author astray.

quantative is incorrect for *quantitative*.

quantity and **number**. It is better not to speak of *a large* (or *a small*) *quantity* of things or persons when one means *a large* (or *small*) *number*; but in familiar (though not in literary) Standard English, *a quantity* may be used of an indefinite, i.e., of a fair or considerable number of persons or things, as in 'Four chairs and a quantity of pillows'. But avoid it if it leads to ambiguity; it is better to differentiate, as in 'He gave away a large quantity of canned goods but still has a number of cans'. (*O.E.D.*)

quarter after, a. See HALF AFTER, A.

query and **inquiry**; **quest**. A *query* is a specific question, a question of limited or particular or *singular* reference, whereas an *inquiry*, though it may simply mean 'a question', more usually means a set or a series of questions, an investigation, as in 'an official inquiry into the fate of *The Thetis*'. A *quest*, in current usage and apart from technicalities, is a search or pursuit, especially of something remote, or figuratively; e.g., 'the quest of the Holy Grail'.

question (v.) is used in a misleading manner in the following: 'Despite this popularity, Scott was questioned as to whether he was a suitable source for dramatists'. The meaning is not that someone asked Scott this question, but that *the question was raised*.

questionary is an adjective; 'having the form of, or consisting of, questions; conducted by means of questions', as in 'a questionary interview'; *questionnaire* is a list of questions; especially an ordered list —or a skilful set—of questions, designed to cover a certain field, or to fulfil an educational or official purpose. *Questionnaire* has displaced *questionary* in this sense.

quiescent; **quiet**. *Quiescent* means 'inactive, at rest, motionless', as in 'He lay quiescent', and, in Philology, (of a letter that is) 'not sounded'. (*O.E.D.*)

quit—quitted. The form *quit*, whether in the preterite or in the past participle, is English dialectal. [In American it is a standard variant of *quitted*.]

quite cannot properly qualify a noun. 'Quite the sensation of the day' and 'Not quite the thing' are colloquial phrases.

quite does not—in good English—mean 'rather', its two Standard senses being (i), 'completely, wholly, entirely, to the fullest extent', as in 'Haws . . . which often quite cover the hawthorn bushes' (Jefferies), 'Here have I sat . . . quite by myself', 'quite certain', 'a quite separate question' or 'quite another question (or, thing)'; and

(ii) 'actually; truly; positively', as in 'He died quite suddenly', 'She was so perturbed that she felt quite ill'. The exclamatory *quite* (or *quite so!*) ('I agree with you' or 'I heartily approve') is colloquial.

quite a for *a quite*. E.g., the colloquial 'He stayed there quite a long time' should be '. . . a quite long time'. But 'quite a while' is correct, because *a while* is indivisible.

quota, 'a predetermined share or proportion', is used unhappily in 'The Queen's Road was busy with its usual quota of life', Laurence Meynell, *The Dandy*, 1938.

QUOTATION MARKS, unnecessary use of; e.g., in 'It would seem that over all was hanging some menace which was real but intangible, something against which the sling-shots, the knives, the "silenced" automatics of gangdom, could not prevail'. The quotation marks would be appropriate only if the word *silenced* were a technical or slang term of which the reader was presumably ignorant.

QUOTATION MARKS IN GENERAL. See esp. my *You Have a Point There*, 1953.

quote. See CITE.

R

'rabbit, Welsh, generally supposed to be a corruption of *rarebit*, is actually a slang nickname for a local dish, similar to "Norfolk Capons" for red herrings, "Irish apricots" for potatoes, etc.', Ackermann. The form *rarebit* is incorrect.

racquet, a frequent spelling of (tennis-) *racket*, is quite incorrect; 'in some mysterious way', says Sir Gordon Lowe, 'it has got mixed up with the French spelling "raquette" '.

radical, Radical; radicle. A *Radical* is 'one who advocates sweeping changes'; *radical* means 'basic, fundamental'; *radicle*, is, in Botany, an embryonic primary root or, more generally, a rootlet; in Philology, however, a root is a *radical*.

radio (radiotelegraphy), for *wireless* (broadcasting), has been opposed by many Englishmen on the ground that it is an Americanism: regarded closely, it is seen to be at least as unobjectionable as *wireless* (whether noun, adjective, or verb). *Radio*, as verb, means either 'to send a message by radio' or 'to broadcast'; but in England, it has been, for the most part, restricted to the former sense;

radio, moreover, is also short for *radiogram*. Both 'to *radio*' and 'to *broadcast*' are preferable to either *radiocast* or *radiobroadcast*.

rail for *railroad, railway,* is a 'rubberstamp word' that should be eschewed by self-respecting writers. [In American usage the phrase *by rail* is probably standard.]

railroad is the usual term in the U.S.A., **railway** the usual term for the British Empire. But *railway* is much more widely used in the States than is generally believed in England, and in England *railroad* was, until ca. 1900, at least as common as *railway*. [*Webster's* states a distinction often made in American English: *railroad* for heavy steam transportation; *railway* for the lighter street-car (or tram) lines, for shops railways, crane railways, or any way for wheels.]

raise is transitive, *rise* is intransitive. The noun is *rise*, but *raise* is permissible (though less usual) in the sense 'an increase in amount (especially of money)' and correct in the sense 'a rising road or passage', though for 'a piece of rising ground; a hill', *rise* again is more usual. (*O.E.D.*)

raise and **rear.** One *rears* children; animals are either *reared* or *raised*. As applied to human beings, *raise* is depreciative, facetious. [Not so in American English. In the U.S.A. 'born and raised' is much more common than 'born and reared'.]

raison d'être is a wholly unnecessary Gallicism for *reason* or *explanation*.

ranch and **rancho; range; hacienda.** A *range* is 'the region in which cattle or sheep may pasture' (but chiefly the former), or, without *a* or *the*, 'grazing ground'. A *rancho* is 'a large grazing farm; a ranch;—distinguished from *hacienda*', a *hacienda* being a Spanish American term (*rancho* is Spanish American too, but also South-western U.S.) for 'a cultivated farm, with a good house, in distinction from a farming establishment with rude huts for herdsmen, etc.', i.e., a *rancho*. In Western U.S.A. and Canada a *ranch* is 'an establishment, with its estate, for the grazing and rearing of horses, cattle, or sheep', especially 'the buildings occupied by owner and employees, with the adjacent barns, corrals, etc.; also, the persons on the estate collectively'. Loosely and commonly, any farm in the West, esp. if large.

rang. See RING.

range (n.). See RANCH.

rapt. See at WRAPT.

rare and scarce. Weseen has neatly established the difference, thus:—'The adjective *rare* is often misused for *scarce*, as "Potatoes are rare this winter". *Rare* applies properly to things that are infrequent at all times and usually to things that have superior qualities, as "Great leaders are rare". *Scarce* applies to ordinary things that are temporarily not plentiful, as "Jobs are scarce this winter".'

rarely or ever. See 'SELDOM OR EVER'.

rather, had; rather, would. 'I had rather oppose prejudices than confute arguments'; but *would rather* when an hypothesis is expressed; e.g., 'Were a patriot reduced to the alternative of death or political slavery, I am confident he would rather die than live'.

rather a . . ., misused for *a rather* . . . 'He was rather a dandy' is correct, for 'a dandy' is, here, indivisible in the sense that one cannot say 'a rather dandy'; but 'He was rather a conceited dandy' is incorrect for '. . . a rather conceited'; cf. 'a very conceited dandy'.
A parallel is afforded by 'quite a dandy' and 'a quite recent dandy' (*not* 'quite a recent dandy').

rather than for *than*. 'All this was new to him, his experience having made him more knowing about bookies rather than books.' To correct this sentence, omit 'rather'.

rational ('endowed with reason'; hence, 'sane, sensible, reasonable') is now rare as a noun; *rationale*, 'a reasoned exposition of principles; hence, an explanation', also 'the logical or the rational basis (*of* anything)', is only noun. (*O.E.D.*)

re, from *in re* (Latin), 'in the matter of', which is supposed in commercial offices to be an abbreviation of 'referring to', can be properly used only in the driest of business communications.

re- and re (v.). If *re* = 'again', then hyphenate, as in *re-sound*; if it = 'back-(wards)', then write the verb as one word, as *resound*. Note especially *re-cover*, 'to cover again', and *recover*, 'to have good health again'.

reaction is often misused for *attitude* or *opinion*.—Cf. the next entry.

reaction is correctly used in *one's reaction to*, 'one's response (whether conscious or sub-conscious) to' or 'one's behaviour in relation to an influence (actual or presumed)', as in 'His reaction to the doctor's treatment was, all in all, satisfactory' or 'I fear that my reactions to his proposal were not quite what he expected'. But *reaction on* is incorrect, as in 'The reaction of the doctor's treatment on the patient was alarming'. One's reaction is one's action in reference *to* something, not one's influence *on* something.

real is often unnecessary. Particularly unnecessary in the phrase in which it so often occurs: *in real life*, as, e.g., in 'Very often in fiction, as in real life, one is appalled . . .', where *in life* (or *in reality*) would be much superior to *in real life*.
Always ask yourself whether *real* or *mere* or *actual* is necessary [not '*really* necessary']: if it is not, then omit the excrescential word. And cf. REALLY.

realize for 'to *obtain* or *gain*' is loose.

really, actually and definitely are usually unnecessary. The frequent use of 'really', 'definitely', 'actually', 'as a matter of fact', 'to tell you the truth', etc., shows the speaker's lack of confidence in his own credibility; he seems to need additional assurance that what he asserts is not a fabrication or a mere conjecture. He whose Yea is Yea and his Nay Nay has no need of these adverbial supports. Father Ronald Knox, in *Double Cross Purposes*, says that 'They found Victor Lethaby a tornado of well-bred apologies, all punctuated with an irritating repetition of the word "actually"—a habit of modern youth, particularly when he is lying'. It is a well known fact that *as a matter of fact* often prefaces a deliberate half-statement.

realm. See SPHERE.

realty is the legal term for 'real property', 'real estate': it can never be used as a synonym of *reality*.

reason. See CAUSE.

reason . . . because, or why . . . because, is often used redundantly for *reason . . . that*, as in 'The reason he does this (or, why he did this) is because he knows no better'.

receipt is now archaic for *recipe* (in cookery); a *receipt* is a written acknowledgement of money or goods received, or the receiving itself (as in 'On the receipt of the recipe, the cook immediately went to the kitchen and made the new dish'). [In American usage *receipt* is still current in cookery though less common than *recipe*.]

RECEIVED STANDARD. See STANDARD ENGLISH, II.

receptacle, of a thing; recipient, of a person. 'The recipient of the ornate receptacle was less pleased than its donors had hoped.'

recipe. See RECEIPT.

recollect and re-collect. Respectively 'to

recall to mind' and 'to collect again', as in 'I do not recollect re-collecting my MSS.'

recollect and remember. The former may be synonymous with the latter; but discriminating writers and speakers—discriminate. '*Recollect, when distinguished from *remember*, implies a conscious or express effort of memory to recall something [that] does not spontaneously rise in the mind' (*O.E.D.*), as in 'At last I recollected what, during my illness (lasting, you may recall, some nine weeks), I had failed to remember, important though it was'.

recompense is the v.; either *recompence* or, etymologically, *recompense* is the n.

recourse for *resource*. 'Most of us read detective stories and know all the tricks of the trade of the fiction-detective—but how many of us know how the *real* criminal investigators work, and what recourses they have at their command to help them in their fight against crime?'

recover and **re-cover.** Respectively, 'to get (a thing) back' and 'to cover again', as in 'I succeed in recovering that excellent chair which, sent to be re-covered, had gone astray'.

recreation and **re-creation** are to be kept distinct: the latter = 'creation anew', the former = 'refreshment, physical or mental or spiritual'. In 'This was a temperament singularly fitted for the recreation of life's little comedies and tragedies', *recreation* is the word required. The corresponding adjectives are *recreational* and *re-creative* (generally written *recreative*).

recrudescence has been so strongly and wittily condemned by Fowler that I, who have sinned but do now repent, need only point out that, etymologically, it = 'a breaking out again of a wound', 'a becoming raw of the flesh'; hence, it is used of a disease, a sore, an epidemic. Hence, figuratively, a renewal or a return of a quality, or a state of things, especially and *properly* if they are regarded as evil or objectionable, as in 'a recrudescence of calumny', 'the recrudescence of a metaphysical Paganism' (*O.E.D.*), and 'His headaches were less frequent and there had been no recrudescence of the [mental] blackouts'. Any extension of that 'figuratively' leads inevitably to absurdity.

rectify. See JUSTIFY.

recto. See VERSO.

rector and **vicar** puzzle all except the cleric and the knowledgeable. A *rector* is 'a parson [*q.v.*] or incumbent of a parish whose tithes are not impropriate' (i.e. held by the parson); a *vicar's* tithes, however, are impropriate (held by him). (*O.E.D.*) **rectoral** is applied only to God (as spiritual Ruler); *rectorial* to a rector. (The adjective corresponding to *vicar* is *vicarial*, which is not to be confused with *vicarious*.)

recumbent and **incumbent; superincumbent; decumbent.** *Recumbent* is 'lying down'; 'reclining' ('His recumbent form was scarcely visible'); so too is the now rare *decumbent* ('The advantages of a decumbent'—now preferably *recumbent* —'position'). In *incumbent*, the stress is on the weight of the 'lier'; cf. the figurative *incumbent on* ('obligatory upon'), as in 'It is incumbent on him to look after his aged mother'. In Geology, *incumbent* has, like *superincumbent*, the sense, 'overlying'; *superincumbent*, however, is not properly a geological term, though it is applied to overhanging rocks. (*O.E.D.*)

recurring for *frequent* is wholly unnecessary; and it is also catachrestic, for, as an adjective, it should be applied to that which recurs either at irregular intervals or, as in *recurring decimals*, to infinity, and for irregular recurrence the correct adjective is *recurrent*; 'It might well be that here the scientific criminologist will find one more means of dealing with a problem that is one of the most recurring in his work'.

REDUNDANCY. See VERBOSITY, last paragraph.

refer to. See ALLUDE.

reflection and **reflexion.** 'The etymological spelling with *x* is the [earlier], and is still common in scientific use, perhaps through its connexion with *reflex*; in the general [i.e., the non-scientific] senses the influence of the verb has made the form with *ct* the prevailing one.' (*O.E.D.*)

reform and **re-form.** To *reform* is 'to improve, to correct'; *re-form* is 'to form anew'. Thus, one re-forms clay models, but one reforms criminals (or tries to).

refute and **deny.** To *deny* an accusation is merely to assert that it is false; to *refute* an accusation is to prove that it is false. One can also *refute* (or *confute*) the accuser; and one may *confute* an accusation. Perhaps it would be wise to reserve *confute* for proving accusers and arguers to be wrong, and *refute* for proving accusations, arguments, theories to be wrong; certainly *refute* is much the more common in the latter application. A further distinction between *confute* and *refute* is that the former is the stronger word.

regal. See KINGLY.

regalia, 'insignia of royalty', is a plural.

regard. One says *in regard to* and *without regard to*, but *as regards*.

regarding, preposition = 'in respect of', can be ambiguous, as in 'He [an idiot] would have a child's mentality too, regarding likes and dislikes'.

regime is an English word. If it is italicized and so treated as a French word, it must bear an accent, thus: *régime*; cf. ROLE.

region is misused in the abominable verbosity *in the region of*, about: cf. *in the* NEIGHBOURHOOD *of*.

REGIONAL DIALECTS. See DIALECT and STANDARD ENGLISH, II.

regret (v.) is frequently ambiguous; as in 'For an instant Mr Pendlebury regretted the freshness of Berkshire. Then his natural buoyancy reasserted itself. After all, though it was hot here . . ., Central London must be an inferno.' The meaning is that Mr Pendlebury, who was not in Berkshire at the time, longed for—*not* 'was repentant (or apologetic) about'—the pleasant county of Berkshire.

reiterate and **repeat.** The latter is general; the former, particular, being applied only to words, statements, requests, expressions of feeling. *Iterate* (*q.v.*) is a literarism.

rejoinder is either 'the defendant's answer to the plaintiff's replication' (plaintiff's reply to defendant's plea) or, in general usage, 'an answer to a reply': it is a pity to weaken it to synonymity with '*any* reply'. (*O.E.D.*)

relation and **relative.** The writer is one of those who prefer *relative* to *relation* in the sense 'kinsman'.

relations towards. See PREPOSITIONS WRONGLY USED.

RELATIVE CLAUSES. For the use of *that*, *which*, *who* (the why and the when), see 'WHICH and THAT'.

'A moderate number of relative clauses may give charm and ease to the style, many consecutive ones are often felt as heavy and cumbersome', writes Jespersen in *Notes of Relative Clauses*. He gives an example from Medwin's *Life of Shelley*, 1847:—

'Lewis told that [i.e., the story] of Minna, *which* first appeared in *The Conversations of Lord Byron*; and one also sketched there, *which* is more stirring, of a haunted house, at Mannheim, *which* he had inhabited, *that* had belonged to a widow, *who* to prevent the marriage of her only son with a poor but honest maiden, had sent him to sea, *where* he perished in a wreck.'

The sentence might be rewritten thus:—

'Having told that story of Minna which first appeared in *The Conversations of Lord Byron*, Lewis went on to relate another and more stirring story, which had been briefly outlined there. It concerned a haunted house, which, inhabited later by Lewis, had belonged to a widow. This widow, to prevent her son's marriage with a poor but honest maiden, had sent him to sea—and to his death.'

RELATIVE CLAUSES, WRONG POSITION OF. See AGREEMENT, FALSE.

RELATIVE PRONOUN, omitted. In many instances, the omission of the relative pronoun leads to 'a form of expression which can hardly be matched for conciseness in English or any other language' (Onions). Thus 'The man I was talking about is a well known author', is preferred to 'The man about whom I was talking'. As Jespersen has remarked, this omission of the relative pronoun, so far from being a fault, 'is a genuine English idiom of long standing'.

relevant. See at REVELANT.

remain uncovered is often very ambiguous, for it means not only 'to stay uncovered after having one's (or its) cover (hat, etc.) removed' by oneself or another, or by an action or process, but also 'to stay without a cover that has never been put on'.

remediable; remedial. The former is passive, 'able to be remedied or redressed; curable', as in 'Where injustice, like disease, is remediable, there the remedy must be applied in word or deed' (Jowett); the latter is active, 'affording or constituting a remedy, tending to remedy, relieve, or redress; potentially curative, potentially effective in providing a remedy', as in 'The remedial part of a law' (Blackstone).

'Every good political institution must have a preventive operation as well as a remedial' (Burke). The adverbs are *remediably* and *remedially*; the opposites of the adjectives are *irremediable* (adverb in *-bly*) and—what? Perhaps *inefficacious* and *ineffectual*. There seems to be no such adjective as *irremedial*, though it is hard to see why there shouldn't be one! (Based on *The O.E.D.*)

remember. See RECOLLECT.

remembrance and **reminder.** *Reminder* is rare for 'memento'; *remembrance* is rare and obsolescent for *reminder*, 'something that reminds, or is intended to remind, a person; a mention designed to remind a person of something'; *remembrance* can-

not be interchanged with *reminder* in the latter's sense of 'a person that reminds'. In short, *remembrance* and *reminder* are, in current usage, never interchangeable.
reminiscent of for *indicative of* or *redolent of* is feeble: and incorrect.
remit and send. Remit = 'to *send*' only in the specific sense, 'to send or transmit (money or valuables) *to* a person or a place'. In any other sense of *send*, remit is incorrect.
Renaissance and **Renascence; renaissance** and **renascence.** As a synonym of 're-birth', only *renascence*; for a revival, e.g., in art or literature, either *renaissance* or *renascence*, though preferably the latter. For that great European revival of art and letters which began in the 14th Century and reached its English peak in the 16th Century, *Renaissance* is the more usual, the other being literary and perhaps a trifle affected: the adjectives are *Renaissance* or *Renascence*, preferably the former. The adjective corresponding to the 're-birth' sense of *renascence* is *renascent*.
rend, 'to tear, to tear apart'; preterite *rent*; past participle, *rent*.
render a decision, render decisions are inferior to *make a decision, make decisions*.
rendition, 'a performing or a performance'. is frowned upon in England, even in a musical connexion (*rendering* or *playing* is preferable); and as 'the amount produced or rendered; the yield (especially of silk)', it is American.
rent (v.). See HIRE . . . And cf. REND.
rent is misused when it is made synonymous with *let* or *lease*. The lessee, not the lessor, 'rents' a house, a room; the lessor 'leases' or 'lets' it. [In American English *rent* and *lease* are used of both the tenant and the landlord.]
reoccurrence is incorrect for *recurrence*.
repairable can be used for *reparable* only of material things (buildings, roads, boots); in the sense 'due to be repaired', either form is correct, but for material objects, *repairable* is preferred.
repast. See ELEGANCIES.
repeat. See 'REITERATE and REPEAT'.
repellent and repulsive. *Repellent* is confined to persons, their faces or expressions, their statements or demands; *repulsive* is synonymous with *repellent* in the sense 'repelling by coldness or excessive austerity or by some disagreeable feature; affecting one with distaste or aversion', though, here, *repulsive* is the stronger word; but *repulsive* also = 'repellent *to the mind*, i.e., disgusting', as in 'repulsive tropical plants, repulsive manners'.

repent for *regret* or *resent* is a misuse. 'She had treated them well and he no longer repented her coming to Graken-hill.'
repertoire and **repertory.** The latter is a storehouse (lit. or fig.) where something may be found, as in 'The established repertory of our statutes and usages' (Milman); it may be, but is better not, used as a synonym of *repertoire*, 'a stock of plays or musical pieces with which either a company or a player is accustomed—or prepared—to perform', hence one's stock of, e.g., stories; the adjective of *repertoire*, however, is *repertory*, as in *repertory company* and *repertory theatre*. (*O.E.D.*)
REPETITION, needless, has been described as 'a mark of illiteracy—or of a minor intelligence'. 'It looked bad, that it did! With all the . . . Very bad, it looked. Hersey wouldn't half be interested, he wouldn't!' Nor is repetition particularly effective in 'Denis had met the girl at Stern Bridge, and had gone there without going through Isle by going some round-about way'.
Words or phrases should be repeated only if the repetition is effective or if it is essential to clarity.
replace is frequently misused for *displace* (or *supplant*) or *put something* (or *someone*) *in the place of*. *The Observer*, Sept. 20, 1936, contained this: 'May I call attention to a regrettable misuse of English perpetrated—of all places!—at the Journalists' Congress? The point under discussion was the pressure alleged to be brought to bear on editors, with the result that "in more than one instance the correspondents have been replaced". To replace means, and can only mean, to put back in its place. Obviously the meaning was intended to be the opposite, to displace.—Stephen Tone, *Coventry*.' Dean Alford drew attention to this error as long ago as 1865, 'Lord Derby went out of office and was replaced by Lord Palmerston', pointing out that this literally means 'Lord D. went out and Lord P. *put him back again*'. The error seems, however, to be incurable; we find it again in *The Evening News*, March 7, 1938, 'But surely the time has come to replace complaints by action . . . to replace those deplorable examinations by a better and more practicable system'. [In American usage (as seemingly in British) *replace* means to *place again*, to *take the place of*, to *fill the place of*.]
replete is debased to mean *complete* or

furnished with, in the announcement, by a catering firm, of a branch café 'replete with every modern convenience'; *replete* means 'quite full', 'full to overflowing'.

replica should not be used as a synonym of *repetition*, as it is in 'His speech was an almost exact replica of one delivered by Disraeli'. Be careful with *replica*, which might well be restricted to its use as an art term; and as an art term, it is properly 'a copy, duplicate or reproduction . . . made by the original artist'. (*O.E.D.*)

reported. See 'REPUTED and REPORTED'.

REPORTED SPEECH. One excuse for reported speech is a desire to break up the monotony of verbatim dialogue by making it impersonal: but reported or in-direct speech (*oratio obliqua*) is, because of its artificiality, more apt than direct speech (*oratio recta*) to become mono-tonous. What, in 'They declare that they refuse to fight' or 'They declared that they refused to fight', is there that is prefer-able to ' "We refuse to fight", they declare' or 'They declare: "We refuse to fight" '?

The Classics started this cumbrous metamorphosis of the speaker's actual words, and despite the fact that the Romans often made a sad mess of it, we stick to an outmoded vehicle of thought. Newspaper reporters of Parliamentary (and other) speeches continue to use it; examiners of the young still set questions on it. The best justification is that it exer-cises the wits: but why exercise the wits in steering one's verbal craft between the Scylla of pedantry and the Charybdis of unwieldiness?

Nevertheless, for the sake of those who contrive to believe in the virtues of re-ported speech, perhaps I ought to say that an excellent exposition is made by Dr Onions in *An Advanced English Syn-tax*. Of the different kinds of reported speech, he gives an illuminating ex-ample.

He points out that the passage:— 'Croesus, king of the Lydians, said to Solon, the Athenian: "My Athenian guest, *your* great fame has reached even to *us*, as well of *your* wisdom as of *your* travels, how that as a philosopher *you have* travelled through various countries for the purpose of observation. *I am* therefore desirous of asking *you* a ques-tion. *Tell me*, who *is* the most happy man *you have* seen?" '—can be reported in three different ways, i.e., from the view-point of Croesus, from that of Solon, and from that of an outsider.

I. Croesus would say:—

'I said to Solon that *his* great fame *had* reached even to *us*, as well of *his* wisdom as of *his* travels, how that as a philosopher *he had* travelled through various countries for the purpose of observation. *I was* therefore desirous of asking *him* a ques-tion. *I asked him to tell me*'—or *would he tell me*—'who *was* the most happy man *he had* seen', the *would he tell me* repre-senting a possible 'Will you tell me?'

II. Solon would say:—

'Croesus told me that *my* great fame *had* reached even *to them*, as well of *my* wisdom as of *my* travels, how that as a philosopher I *had* travelled through various countries for the purpose of ob-servation. *He was* therefore desirous of asking *me* a question. *He asked me to tell him*'—or *would I tell him*—'who *was* the most happy man *I had* seen.'

III. An outsider's account (being in the 3rd Person throughout, this is the most usual form of reported speech) would run:—

'Croesus, king of the Lydians, said to Solon, the Athenian, that *his* (Solon's) great fame *had* reached even to *them* (the Lydians), as well of *his* wisdom as of *his* travels, how that as a philosopher *he had* travelled through various countries for the purpose of observation. That *he* (Croesus) *was* therefore desirous of ask-ing *him* (Solon) a question. *Would he tell* him, who *was* the most happy man *he had* seen?'

reprehend is 'to blame'; apprehend is 'to seize or grasp' (physically or mentally); comprehend is 'to understand'.

repulsive. See 'REPELLENT and REPULSIVE'.

reputed and reported. The former is occa-sionally misused for the latter (or for *said*), as in 'It is reputed that he tried to escape'.

requirement and requisite. A *requirement* is 'a want, a need; that which is needed', as in 'the requirements of a hospital', '£10,000 would meet the requirements of capitalization'; also 'a condition that must be fulfilled', as in 'The other profes-sors are under more stringent require-ments to teach'. A *requisite* is 'something indispensable, especially an indispensable quality or property', as in 'The form of febrifuge which combines . . . the two requisites of efficacy and economy'. A *prerequisite* is 'something required before-hand' (there being no such term as *pre-requirement*) or 'a condition previously necessary' (as in 'The . . . prerequisites of success are ability, courage, and luck'): there is, in the latter sense, very little difference between *requisite* and *prerequisite*; the latter does, however, emphasize the fact that before anything can be done at all, certain conditions must already have been complied with. (*O.E.D.*)

research (noun). There has, since about 1930, been a growing tendency to speak of research *on* a subject. But surely one does research—or one researches—*in* a subject and *into* a special aspect of a subject? Thus, 'His researches have been in history and in geography; especially into certain problems of historical geography'.

reserve and **preserve**. A *reserve* (in addition to non-competing senses) is 'something set apart for a specific purpose', including a district or a place; if for a native tribe, it is a *reservation*. A *preserve* is 'a piece of ground, set apart for the rearing (and protection) of game', also 'a pond for fish; a vivarium'; often figurative, as in *to poach on a person's preserves*.

reside and **live**; **residence** and **house**. To *reside* is to live permanently or at least for some considerable time *in* or *at* a particular place; to live officially (i.e., to *be in residence*) at a place. One's *residence* is one's settled abode, especially the house or mansion of a person of rank or distinction: you and I have a *house*, the President or the Prime Minister has a *residence*.

resolve (n.); **resoluteness; resolution**. As 'steadfastness of purpose', *resolve* is archaic, as in the set phrase, *of high resolve*; *resoluteness* is now the usual word in this sense. The dominant sense of *resolve* is 'a (specified) resolution or determination', as in 'She made up her mind never to marry again, and she kept her resolve'; as 'a formal resolution of a deliberative body', it may occur in American English, though *resolution* is the common term. As a scientific, medical, or musical term, *resolution* has no rivals. (*O.E.D.*)

resource is occasionally confused with and misused for *recourse*. You examine your *resources* (stock that can be drawn on to supply some need), and decide which of them *to have recourse to*, i.e., to adopt as means of help.—See also RE-COURSE.

respectable, 'worthy of respect'; **respectful**, 'showing respect'; **respective**, as in 'The practical sovereignty of all three brothers was admitted in their respective territories'.

respectively, misused for *both*. In 'He is a member of the hockey eleven and the "Rugger" fifteen respectively', omit *respectively*.

responsible should be restricted to human beings. [American usage permits such sentences as 'Great heat is responsible for many deaths', but here *responsible* is inferior to *the cause of*.]

restive and **restless**. Of horses, *restive* = 'refractory' or 'intractable'; the same applies to human beings. *Restless* = 'averse to being still, settled or quiet', or 'deprived of rest; hence, uneasy'. (*O.E.D.*)

restrain. See CONSTRAIN.

result for *fact* is feeble, as in 'The autopsy shows the curious result that Jensen was dead before the shot that was supposed to have killed him had been fired'.

results. See ACCIDENT.

resurrect is occasionally misused for 'to *find*', as in 'Where did you resurrect that hat?', when the hat is new; but if the speaker says 'When did you resurrect that hat?' and means 'When did you rescue it from the rubbish-heap?', he is simply using *resurrect* figuratively in the sense, 'restore to life, or to view, again'.

retiracy; retiral; retirement. *Retiracy*, an Americanism (nowadays rare), means either 'seclusion or privacy' (one of the two main senses of *retirement*) or 'a sufficient fortune to retire upon' (Bartlett); *retiral* is now rare in the sense 'an act of withdrawal or retreat' (the opposite of *advance*), and less common than *retirement* in the sense, 'the act—or the fact—of withdrawing from, or surrendering, an office, a position, a vocation' or from, say, street to house, drawing-room to w.c., or from noise to quiet, publicity to peace. In military terminology, *retirement* is now less common than *retreat*.

retort and **riposte** should not be used as colourless synonyms of *reply*; *retort* is to reply wittily; *riposte* (a term from fencing) is to reply sharply and wittily. ' "I love you", he said ardently.—"I love you too", she retorted [or riposted]' shows up the absurdity.

revelant, revelatory; relevant; also **revelative** and **revealing**. The first is a common solecism for the third (*relevant*, 'pertinent'); *revelatory* is the adjective corresponding to 'to *reveal*' and it = either 'serving or tending to reveal' or '(actually) yielding a revelation', as in 'a revelatory gesture', 'a most revelatory autobiography', 'a physic manifestation startlingly revelatory of the unseen'; *revelative* has the nuance, 'conveying a revelation', as in 'The Bible, to one who comes upon it for the first time, is a tremendously revelative book'. Ordinary people prefer *revealing*, as in 'A most revealing oath fell from his lips', 'a revealing book'. (*O.E.D.*)

revelation for *disclosure*—a strong word for a weak one—is not to be overworked. **Revelations** is incorrect for *Revelation* as the short title of *The Revelation of St. John the Divine*.

revenge and **avenge** (vv.); **revenge** and **vengeance** (nn.). See AVENGE.

reverent must not be confused with *reverend*; the former applies to the worshipper, the latter to the object of worship.

reversal; reversion. The former is the noun corresponding to *reverse* ('to reverse the order'). *Reversion* is a legal term, but it also = 'the right of succession to a thing or an office'; and it is the abstraction of *reversal*.

reverse (n.). See CONVERSE.

revolutionist (n.) is an unnecessary variant of *revolutionary*, which serves very well as both noun and adjective.

revue is confined to the theatrical entertainment. Do not italicize it: there's no other name for this diversion.

rewarding, adjective, barely antedates 1941 as a vogue word bearing the sense 'repaying' in the nuances 'profitable', 'satisfactory, agreeable or pleasant', 'gratifying'. It is one of those pseudo-psychological terms (cf. *inferiority complex*—see COMPLEX, above) which so easily attain popularity among the half-baked, the superficial, the cynical. 'It is so rewarding to be courteous to one's superior officers.' 'It is too, too rewarding, my pet, to be polite and charming to one's butcher, don't you know.' It is more justifiably employed, as one would expect of her, when in *The Observer* of October 21, 1945, Miss Claire Lejeune, concerning the film *The Man on America's Conscience* as seen by British soldiers in North Africa, writes that 'All found it intelligible; most found it unusual and rewarding'.

RHETORICAL, THE. Rhetoric, as Lord Baldwin of Bewdley once remarked, is the harlot of the arts.

There are two Rhetorics: the old and the new. Of the old, a typical expositor is Alexander Bain, who died early in the present century; of the new, the best expositor is Dr I. A. Richards, whose *The Philosophy of Rhetoric*, 1936, has done so much to rehabilitate both the art and the study thereof. But the subject would be out of place here. The curious may consult *Usage and Abusage*.

rhyme and **rime**. Although the former is

the usual spelling, the latter is not incorrect and has historical justification; it has of late years been to some extent revived to make clear its distinction from *rhythm*.

rid—preterite, *rid*—past participle, *rid*; *ridded* is permissible but not very common.

ride—preterite, *rode*—past participle, *ridden* (rarely *rid*).

riddle should not be used as a co-extensive synonym of *puzzle*. A *riddle* is an enigma or dark saying ('When is a door not a door?'), *puzzle* being no longer used in this sense; a mystery (*The Riddle of the Sands*), hence a mysterious person. On the other hand, *puzzle* may be applied to a person or a thing that puzzles us ('He's a bit of a puzzle'), though not with quite the sense of 'mystery'; and whereas a *puzzle* is used of any toy, device, or (non-verbal) problem designed to exercise the brain, *riddle* is applied only to a verbal problem.

right of ways is incorrect for *rights of way*.

right to, have a. See HAVE A RIGHT TO.

rigorous. See at VIGOUR.

rime. See RHYME.

ring (of bells)—preterite, *rang* (or *rung*: but avoid it)—past participle, *rung*. But 'to ring' a tree has both preterite and past participle *ringed*.

riposte. See RETORT.

rise. See RAISE.

Rockefeller is, except among Americans, often misspelt *Rockfeller*; and, except among Englishmen, *Rosebery* is often misspelt *Roseberry*.

role, without accent or italic, is correct; so is *rôle*, with accent and italic, but it is, in English, obsolescent; *role*, without accent but in italic, is incorrect; cf. REGIME.

Roman Catholic; Catholic; catholic. The first two are both noun and adjective; the third, adjective only. In the sense 'universal', *catholic* is obsolescent. The prevailing nuances of *catholic* are 'of universal human interest or use'; 'touching the needs, interests, or sympathies of all men', as in 'What was of catholic rather than national interest'; (of persons) 'having sympathies with all' ('He is catholic in his tastes'), (of things) 'embracing all' ('The sun poured its clear and catholic looks'). *Catholic Church* or *Church Catholic* formerly meant 'the Church universal, the entire body of Christians'; but since the Reformation it has also and more usually meant 'the Church of Rome', often designated *the Roman Catholic Church*; *Catholic* suffices in opposition to *Protestant* or to *Anglo-Catholic*; in short, it always suffices.

rooves as plural of *roof.* See SPOOF.

Rosebery. See ROCKEFELLER.

rotal; rotary; rotatable; rotating; rotational; rotative; rotatory.

Rotal: of a wheel; like or characteristic of a wheel ('vocal or rotal tumult').

Rotary (adjective): (of motion) circular; also, operating by means of rotation, especially in reference to that large class of machines in which the main action is dependent on the rotation of an importantly operative part; also as in 'Storms that are cyclonic; i.e., rotary and progressive'. In the U.S.A., *Rotary* = 'belonging to one of the Rotary Clubs'.

Rotatable: capable—or admitting—of a rotatory movement, as in 'a sounder, rotatable on a long shaft'.

Rotating (adjective): (*a*) turning round a centre (or an axis),—for which *rotary* is commoner; (*b*) causing rotation,—for which *rotatory* is more usual.

Rotational: acting in rotation, as in 'rotational members'.

Rotative: turning round like a wheel, a sense in which *rotary* and *rotatory* are more strongly established. Producing—or produced by—rotation, as in the astronomical 'rotative forces'; hence, connected with rotation: in these three nuances, *rotatory* is at least equally common; in the 'of the nature of rotation' sense of *rotative*, *rotatory* is more usual. A useful sense is 'recurrent', as in 'Cotton was cultivated in India as a rotative and not as a special crop'.

Rotatory: causing rotation (cf. *rotative*), especially in *rotatory apparatus.*— Working by means of rotation; and of things that *rotate* (v.i.): as in 'rotatory storms'.—Of the nature of, or connected with, rotation, as in (of a wheel) 'having a rotatory motion', 'a rotatory velocity'.

Rotation, basically, is either the action of moving or turning around a centre or axis (or on an axis), or the action of producing such a movement. (*O.E.D.*)

round for *on* or *about* is a characteristic of Cockney speech: e.g., 'Meet me round seven o'clock' and, from Edwin Pugh's *Harry the Cockney,* ' "If you don't gimme a bit . . . I shall punch you round the jaw".' [*Round* (*around*) for *about* is colloquial in American English.]

route is occasionally misused for *method* or *manner* or *procedure* or *process,* as in 'attaining fame by the political route'. [*Route* is generally pronounced *root,* but in the U.S.A. the pronunciation with the

diphthong of *out* survives in military use, railroad use, and often in business ('milk route', 'paper route'). (*Webster's.*)]

royal tennis. See TENNIS.

RUBBER-STAMP WORDS. See AMAZING.

rung. See RING.

rush (n. and v.) is being overworked by journalists. Nor is it an exact synonym of *haste.*

S

Sabbath, the, and **Sunday;** not forgetting **the Lord's Day** and **the Day of Rest.** But the best of these is *Sunday, the Sabbath* being slightly affected where it is not Scottish; in good, normal English, *sabbath* is short for *witches' sabbath* (a midnight meeting of demons, wizards, witches). The only serious objection to *the Lord's Day* is that it is so much longer than *Sunday,* than which it is also more formal; *the Day of Rest* is a rather trivial synonym.

sabotage, used for *to wreck,* is unhappy and introduces a mechanical note that is out of keeping. In *What a Word!,* Sir Alan Herbert quotes, as an example of its misuse, 'Sabotaged the Peace issue'.

sacrosanct and **sacred.** The former is, stylistically, an intensive of the latter; prudent writers, however, use it only in the specific sense (of persons; laws, customs, obligations; authority) 'secured by a religious sanction from violation, infringement, or encroachment', as in 'Truth, which alone of words is essentially divine and sacrosanct'. Based on *The O.E.D.*

sadism and **masochism.** In generalized and (at first) loose usage, the former is desire to hurt others and the ability to enjoy their pain; the latter is the desire to be hurt and especially the enjoyment derived from being hurt. But in medical and strictly correct usage, *sadism* is 'a form of sexual perversion marked by a love of cruelty' (*O.E.D.*), the name deriving from the Comte (*not* Marquis) de Sade (†1814); and *masochism,* from the Austrian novelist, Sacher-Masoch, is 'sexual perversion, in which a member of one sex takes delight in being dominated, even to the extent of violence or cruelty, by one of the other sex'.

said, the ('the said act'), is permissible for *this* in legal phraseology—and nowhere else. See also THE SAID.

sailer is either a *sailing ship,* or a ship with reference to her sailing powers ('A very strong tight ship, and a pretty good sailer', Defoe); a **sailor** is a seaman.

sake and sakes. 'When the preceding genitive is plural, the plural *sakes* is often used', as in 'For both our sakes, I would that word were true', 'Put yourself to no further trouble for our sakes'. (*O.E.D.*) True; but there are two points to be made: —(i) ' "For our sake" implies a common concern or purpose. "For our sakes" implies a difference of concern or purpose' (Weseen): a valid and valuable distinction. But (ii) except where metre needs *both our* (or *your* or *their*) *sakes*, a good writer would today write 'for the sake of both of us' (jointly) and 'for the sakes of both of us' (separately).

salary. See HONORARIUM (and also WAGE).

salon and saloon. *Saloon* is American for a bar-room, and general for a public room on a passenger-boat; American for a drawing-room (especially a large one); and general for a large apartment or hall in a hotel or restaurant. *Salon* is a reception-room of a Parisian lady of fashion, hence a recurrent gathering of notabilities at her house; hence, either the room or the gathering in other capitals. Also, a drawing-room on the Continent, especially in France.

same (adj.)—used tautologically. 'The comedian has repeated the same joke at least a thousand times.'

same (n.). 'We are in receipt of your favour of the 2nd inst., and thank you for same': *the same* would be correct, but it is stilted and too commercially conventional; *it* would be better.

same and similar. The former denotes identity; the latter implies mere likeness. 'He was positive it was the same man.'— 'It is a house of similar design to ours.' Harold Herd, *Watch Your English.*

same, the, is incorrectly followed by *which* in such a sentence as 'Is the agency referred to the same agency which the honourable gentleman repudiated the other day?' The correct form would be 'the same agency as that which' or 'as the one which'; but 'the same' is itself unnecessary, and the hon. member would have better expressed his meaning, 'Is the hon. gentleman referring to the agency which he repudiated the other day?' Cf. 'The post which the judge subsequently received is not the same that he was originally offered': where 'not the same that' should be 'not the same as that which' or 'not that which'.

same . . . of, incorrect for *same . . . as that of.* 'It was the same colour of'—properly *same colour as that of*—'the moundy platform where they stood.'

sample. See EXAMPLE.

sanatarium; sanatorium; sanitarium. The first is an occasional misspelling of the second; a misspelling probably caused by confusion with *sanitarium* (a variant—except for a school hospital or sick room—of *sanatorium*). The plurals are *sanatoria, sanitaria,* but soon the plurals in *-iums* will (as they should) oust the others.

sanatory and sanitary must be carefully distinguished, the former meaning 'conducive to healing', the latter 'intended or tending to promote health' or healthy conditions. [*Webster's:* Sanatory signifies *conducive to health; sanitary* has the more general meaning of *pertaining to health;* as, the camp is not *sanatory,* its *sanitary* conditions are bad'.]

sanction has, in the sense 'penalty', become a vogue word.

sang. See SING.

SARCASM. See IRONY, last paragraph.

sateen and satin. *Sateen* is a cotton (or woollen) fabric that has a glossy surface like that of satin; but sateen is to satin what *near silk* is to (*sheer*) *silk. Satin* is a silk fabric that has on one side a glossy surface produced by such a method of weaving as ensures that the warp threads are 'caught and looped by the weft only at certain intervals'. (*O.E.D.*)

save is obsolete for *unless,* 'elegant' for the preposition *except.* The conjunctival *save that* ('Then all was still, save that a vast gush of fire rose up for a moment') is archaic in prose, literary in verse. (*O.E.D.*)

saw—preterite, *sawed*—past participle, *sawed* or *sawn.* The past participle used predicatively is either *sawed* or *sawn,* but preferably *sawed* ('The wood to be sawed is in the yard, over there'); attributively in England always *sawn* ('Sawn wood is easier to handle'); [in the U.S.A. *sawed* or *sawn*].

scan is erroneously used for, and taken to mean, 'to glance through hurriedly and casually', but as will be found in the best dictionaries, it means *to examine closely or minutely, to scrutinize.* When one scans verse, one metrically analyses it.

scarcely. See HARDLY.

scarcely . . . than. See HARDLY . . . THAN.

scared of is incorrect for *afraid of* (or *frightened by*). [*Scared* has homely and forceful qualities in American English, and one may well hesitate to proscribe any of its idiomatic uses. *Scared to do it* is dialect or colloquial speech; *scared by dogs* is standard English; *scared of dogs*

is probably standard on a familiar level.]
scatheless and **unscathed.** *Scatheless* =
'without scathe', i.e., without harm, as
in 'It is a game from which you will come
out scatheless, but I have been scalded'
(Trollope). *Unscathed* = 'unharmed, un-
injured', as in 'Whatever his experiences
of this kind may have been, he passed
unscathed through them' (A. W. Ward).
(*O.E.D.*)
sceptic, sceptical; skeptic, skeptical. The
sk- forms are the usual ones in the
U.S.A.; *sceptical* is preferred to *sceptic*
for the adjective. (The *sc* is pronounced
as *sk*; there is an ancient pun about
sceptics that are *septic*.)
SCIENTIFIC ENGLISH. This important
and difficult subject has been very ably
treated in T. Savory's *The Language of
Science*, 1953.
Scot, Scotch, Scots, Scottish, adjectives;
Scotchmen, Scotsmen, Scots, the Scotch,
nouns.
    Of the nouns, the usual English name
is *Scotchmen*; the usual Scottish one,
Scotsmen. Of *Scot*, the noun, *The O.E.D.*
says that 'since the 17th Century till
recently chiefly Historical except in jocular and rhetorical use. In Scotland there
has latterly been a tendency (especially in
newspaper writing) to the more extended
use of the word'; *the Scotch* is unobjectionable but slightly obsolescent.
    Of the adjectives, *Scot* is a solecism;
the other three are admirably treated in
The O.E.D. at *Scotch* (adjective); their use
is 'somewhat unse tled'. Since about
1870, there has, in Scotland, been an increasing tendency to discard *Scotch* and
to use *Scottish* or, less frequently, *Scots*;
in England, *Scotch* is the usual adjective
in speech, but good writers prefer *Scottish*
in reference to the nation (*the Scottish
people*), the country at large (*Scottish
scenery, the Scottish border*), its institu-
tions, and characteristics (*a Scottish lawyer, the Scottish character, Scottish
poets*); nevertheless, it would be an affectation to speak of a *Scottish gardener* or
girl, usage prescribing *a Scotch gardener,
a Scotch girl*, and there simply isn't an
alternative for *Scotch whiskey* and *Scotch
tweeds.* Usage favours *Scots* in *Scots law*;
and *Scots* is obligatory in *a pound Scots, a
shilling Scots, a penny Scots*, and in such
variations from English weights and
measures as *Scots acre, Scots mile, Scots
pint, Scots stone*; moreover, in language
contexts, we say *a Scots dialect* or *phrase*,
although *a Scottish dialect* or *phrase*
would not be incorrect. *Scots* is invariable

in such regimental names as *Scots Guards*
and *Scots Greys.*
scrip and **script.** 'In loose or popular language', *scrip* is 'applied to share certifi-
cates in general'; properly, it is 'a provi-
sional document entitling the holder to a
share or shares in a joint-stock undertaking, and exchangeable for a more formal
certificate when the necessary payments
have been completed'; it is 'short for the
obsolete *subscription receipt*'. But *script* is
handwriting ('His is a beautiful script'),
hence a system of writing ('a cuneiform
script', 'the Babylonian script', 'the complicated Japanese scripts'); in Law, it is
the original document in opposition to a
counterpart (or *rescript*). (*O.E.D.*) [In
American usage *scrip* may also = a certificate of indebtedness used in place of
governmental currency. *Script* in theatre,
movie, and radio jargons = manuscript
or typescript—for theatre and radio, the
play; for motion pictures, the synopsis,
scenario, dialogue, etc.]
seamstress. See SEMPSTRESS.
seasonable is 'suitable to or to be expected
in the season referred to': 'It's seasonable
weather' is that infuriating remark for
which we must be prepared when, in winter, one experiences weather that might
be more aptly described as a blight.
Seasonal, however, means 'in season',
'characteristic of the seasons or, especially, of a particular season' ('seasonal
variations of weather'); hence (of trades)
'dependent on the season' or (of employees) 'engaged only in or for a particular season' ('Seaside-hotel waiters are
mostly seasonal'); applied to diseases, it
= 'recurrent' or 'periodical', as in 'Hay-
fever, fortunately, is a seasonal complaint'. *Seasoned* is 'matured' (worked on
by the season) or (of wood) 'dried—hence,
hardened—by keeping'; of persons or
animals it = 'acclimatized', 'fortified by
habit, especially familiarized with a certain occupation' ('4000 seasoned troops').
(*O.E.D.*)
secretarial is the adjective corresponding
to *secretary*; **secretariat** is the official,
especially governmental, establishment of
a secretary, hence the staff and the place
where a secretarial department works or
records are preserved. The position of a
non-official secretary is a *secretaryship.*
secretion for **concealment** is an error not
often met with, but Dean Alford quotes
The Times as referring to 'the secretion of
tobacco and written communications in
the food sent in (to prisoners)', and points
out that 'secretion' means 'that agency in

the animal economy that consists in separating the various fluids of the body'. **sector** is a technical term; **section** is (for the most part) a general one ('part, portion, division, subdivision, and slice'). The only sense in which they are confused the one for the other is the military one, 'a portion or section of a front, corresponding generally to a sector of a circle the centre of which is a head-quarters', the correct term being, not *section* but *sector*. A sector was that portion of the front which was, in practice during the War of 1914–18, occupied by a division. (*O.E.D.*; *Larousse du xxe siècle*.)

secundus and **junior.** *Junior* is 'the younger' and it is appended to a full name (*James Smith, Junior*) 'to denote the younger of the two bearing the same name in a family, especially a son of the same name as his father'; also after a simple surname (*Smith, Junior*), to denote the younger of two boys of the same surname at school. *Secundus* is 'the second'. Appended to a personal name, it means 'the second of the name' (*Dr Monro, secundus; James Thomson, secundus; Robert Chambers, secundus*), but it is not usually applied to a son in relation to his father. [In American English *second* is used instead of *secundus*.]

secure (v.). See 'PROCURE and SECURE'.— It is misused for *ensure* (or *effect*) in 'The police have got frightfully swollen heads; the conditions of the modern world all tend to secure that'.

see, do you. The frequent introduction, in conversational narrative and description, of *d'you see?, you see?*, or *see?*, is a bad habit with very many people and always a sign of unclear thinking. [*Listen!* as well as *See?* is a frequent interjection in low colloquial American.]

see where is incorrect for *see that* (and an astonishingly common error it is!), as in 'I see where they've had another storm at home', for 'I see that they've had another storm at home'.

seeing. See CONJUNCTIONS, DISGUISED.

seldom is not now to be used as an adjective, though it was formerly so employed by good writers.

seldom ever is pleonastic for *seldom* in such a sentence as 'I seldom ever go to town nowadays'. Cf. the following entry.

seldom or ever, like *rarely or ever*, is a not uncommon error for *seldom or never* (or for *seldom if ever* in the same sense). Nesfield finds this error committed by Sydney Smith:—'Those who walk in their sleep have seldom or ever the most dis-

G

tant recollection that they have been dreaming at all.'

selection and **composition.** *Selection* = an, or the, act of selecting or choosing, or a thing selected. Therefore, it should not be employed where there is no idea of selecting or choosing, as in 'What selection of Bach's do you like best?'

self is incorrect for *I* in, e.g., 'Self and family desire to extend to you our sympathy'. The plural is *selves* ('their dead selves'), not *selfs* as so often in A. S. M. Hutchinson's novel, *As Once You Were*.

semi. See DEMI.

semi-monthly; semi-weekly. See BI-MONTHLY.

semi-yearly is a hybrid for either *semiannual* or the more English *half-yearly*. (Adverbs: *semi-annually, half-yearly*.)

seminar and **seminary.** The former is a university technicality for 'a select group of advanced students associated for special study and original research under the guidance of a professor'; hence, 'a class that meets for systematic study under the direction of a teacher'.

A *seminary* is 'an institution for the training of those destined for some particular profession'—in the Catholic Church, a college for training young men to become priests.

The learner in either is a *seminarist* or a *seminarian*. (*O.E.D.*)

Semitic; Hebraic; Hebrew; Jewish. *Semitic* = 'belonging to or concerned with the Semitic group of languages' (Hebrew, Aramaean, Arabic, Ethiopic, Ancient Assyrian), as in 'a Semitic verb', 'a Semitic scholar', 'Semitic studies'; as a noun, *Semitic* is the Semitic family of languages; *Semitics* is the study thereof, or of the Semitic peoples.

Hebraic = 'of, concerning, or characteristic of the Hebrews or their language; having a Hebrew style or character', as in 'His features were Hebraic', 'His perception of nature . . . is mystical and Hebraic' (Emerson). A *Hebraist* is one versed in the Hebrew language, a Hebrew scholar.

Hebrew (n.) is an Israelite; historically, it is 'applied to the early Israelites'; 'in modern use', says The *O.E.D.*, 1901, 'it avoids the religious and other associations often attaching to *Jew*', but *Jew* is rapidly acquiring dignity and is now preferred to *Hebrew*; also the language spoken by the Hebrews. As an adjective, it = 'Israelitish, Jewish' and 'of, concerning, like or characteristic of the Hebrew language'. *Jewish* is now the predominant adjective in reference to the modern Jews (the nation, religion, literature, art, character, customs).

send a remittance is inferior to *make a remittance*.

SENSE-CONSTRUCTIONS. Sense-constructions are those in which grammar is set aside in the interest of ready understanding. Rarely are they justifiable: for, in almost every instance, the breaking of the rule tends to set up an ambiguity, or else it so shocks the cultured that the intended advantage is wholly lost.

For examples, see BETWEEN YOU AND I, EVERYONE . . . THEY, and FRIENDS WITH.

With the second, cf. ANYONE . . . THEY in the following extract from a letter that appeared in *The Observer* of March 12, 1939:—' "Anyone can call *their* house a hall" is a subtle recognition of the virtual plural in "anyone" ' (H. B. Bullen): but has not almost every noun or pronoun a virtual plural? Can that virtuality (so far taken for granted that one never thinks of it) be held to be a sufficient reason for dispensing with a simple and sensible rule?

Here is another example.

(Concerning a man that died with his hand outstretched to feed a beacon fire.) 'Death had taken him in the act of feeding his last desperate signal.' 'His act' for 'the act' would have been logical, but unidiomatic; but even 'his act' leaves us with an ambiguity—an ambiguity resolved by the fact that there is a unit: *him —in—the—|act —of—feeding—his—last —desperate—signal.* Where sense-construction is idiom, it is folly and presumption to meddle with it.

sensible and **sensitive.** The former is now obsolete for the latter in the nuances, 'having more or less acute power of sensation or feeling', 'apt to be quickly or acutely affected by some object of sensation', 'capable of delicate or tender feeling', and 'readily accessible to some specified emotional influence'. (*O.E.D.*) Those persons who have some French (but not enough) are misled by the French *sensible*, which = 'sensitive'. The English *sensible* is the French *sensé*; the English *sensitive* is the French *sensible*.

sensitiveness and **sensitivity.** The former is the general, the latter is the psychological term (as in 'sensitivity to stimuli', 'cutaneous sensitivity'). In short, *sensitivity* is merely the psychological version of *sensitiveness*, which is both 'the power or the capacity of sensation (feeling)' and especially 'a highly developed capacity or

power of sensation; keen or delicate susceptibility to outward impressions'; hence, '(excessive) touchiness', also 'the quality of being easily affected by or quickly indicating changes of condition'. (*O.E.D.*)

sensual, sensuous, sensory. *Sensory*, being the most technical, is much less likely to be confused with either of the other two than *sensual* is with *sensuous* or vice-versa. *Sensory* = 'of or relating to the sensorium' (physiology) or 'relating to sensation or sense-impressions' (psychology).

Sensual is predominantly 'lewd' or 'unchaste', and 'voluptuous' (as in *sensual pleasure*) or 'excessively inclined to the gratification of the senses' (especially in sexual activities).

Sensuous should be avoided in the now rare sense 'excessively addicted to the pleasures of the senses, especially to sexual pleasure'. Its nuances are these: 'Of or pertaining to the senses', 'derived from or perceived by or affecting the senses', 'concerned with sensation (feeling) or sense-perception'; (of pleasure) 'received through the senses' and 'sensitive, or keenly alive, to the pleasures of sensation'. Thus, a *sensuous* artist is not necessarily a *sensual* man; the pleasure derived from music is *sensuous*, not *sensual*. [Definitions: *O.E.D.*]

separate for *dissociate* is incorrect, as in 'It was intolerably easy to separate mentally the academic theories of war from the human side of it, even when one was engaged in it oneself'.

separate between. 'He had to separate between what was essential and what was accidental': where *distinguish between* or *separate . . . from* is meant.

SEQUENCE OF TENSES. See TENSE-SEQUENCE.

series, 'one set of . . .', is occasionally misconstrued as a plural. Thus, 'A series of cellars provide the various parts of our dressing-station'.

serried, 'closely ranked'; **serrated,** 'saw-toothed in shape'.

service (n.) is much overworked; *duty* is, in many contexts, preferable, and in others, *expert advice* or *expert assistance* or *expert attendance*.

session and **cession.** The former = a sitting, a séance; the latter, a surrendering, a surrender (of territory or rights).

set for 'to *sit*, be seated' is now a solecism when it's not dialectal. The same remark applies to figurative uses ('The matter sets heavily on her mind').

sets-off, sets-out, sets-to. Incorrect for *set-offs, -outs, -tos*; but these awkward combinations should be avoided.

several for *some* or *fairly numerous.* ' "Found these, sir", he said, producing several pieces of broken glass, some of which were evidently fragments of a spectacle-lens or lenses, and some of which had formed part of a tube with engraved markings on it.'

sew, sewed, sewed or, archaically, **sewn.** *Sewn* survives in *hand-sewn, machine-sewn.*

sewage ; sewerage. *Sewage* is refuse matter conveyed in sewers; *sewerage* is 'drainage or draining by means of sewers; a system, a method, of draining by sewers', hence 'sewers collectively; the system of sewers belonging to a particular locality'. Although *sewerage* can be used in the sense of *sewage* as here defined, careful writers do not so use it. (*O.E.D.*)

sewn. See SEW.

sex. See GENDER.

sez. See SAYS.

shake—shook—shaken. *Shook* as past participle is solecistic when not dialectal.

shall and **will.** 'The faultless idiomatic use of *shall* and *will* is one of the points which are regarded as infallible tests of the correct English speaker; it offers peculiar difficulties to Scots, Irishmen and Americans', says Dr C. T. Onions in *An Advanced English Syntax.*

The same rules affect all three kinds of future tense: the simple, 'I shall go'—the progressive, 'I shall be going'—and the perfect, 'I shall have gone'. Indeed they affect also the corresponding pasts, *would* of *will*, and *should* of *shall*; but *should* and *would* are here treated separately.

Mere futurity is expressed by *shall* in the first person ('I shall go', 'We shall go') and by *will* in the second and third persons ('You *or* he will go', 'They will go'): this may be regarded as the basic usage in modern Standard English, and it should be departed from only for a specific reason. In this usage *shall* and *will* are mere indications of time—auxiliaries of tense.

The chief modification of that general rule is a survival of the original senses of *shall* and *will.* Dr Onions summarizes thus: '*Shall* denoting obligation, necessity, or permission; *will* denoting resolve or willingness'. And the following are his examples:—*

---

* The parentheses *within* the example-sentences are Dr Onions's; the 'square' parentheses following the example-sentences are mine.

(1) 'I *will* (= am resolved to) live a bachelor.'

(2) '*Will* you (= do you intend or wish to) take it with you, or shall I (= am I to) send it?'

(3) 'We *will* send someone to fetch you.' [= 'We are resolved to send someone to fetch you'; mere futurity would require 'shall'.]

(4) 'He *will* (= is determined to) go, say what you may.' [But if *will* be employed, it must be stressed; otherwise 'is determined *or* resolved to go' is usual.]

(5) 'Thou *shalt* not steal'; 'You (he, they) *shall* go this instant'.

(6) 'Where the tree falls, there it *shall* lie.' [I.e., 'it must lie'.]

(7) 'He found the country in a state of unrest, for reasons which you *shall* hear.' [I.e., 'for reasons which you will be permitted to hear'. This usage is now a literary, not a spoken one.]

(8) 'You *shall* repay me at your convenience.' [This stresses the obligation or the permission, according as the speaker intends his statement to be understood.]

(9) '*Wilt* thou have this woman to be thy wedded wife?' Answer: 'I *will*.' I.e., 'Do you wish to have . . . ?' Answer: 'Yes, I do wish to . . .'

Dr Onions modifies his general modification, thus:—'*Shall* is sometimes stronger than *will*; e.g., "You will not go away?"—"I *shall*". *Will* is occasionally used to express command; e.g., "You *will* not go out to-day; you *will* stay in and work".' Closely connected with this use of *will* is that use whereby *will* serves to soften a request, as in 'You *will* have breakfast ready by eight o'clock' (of which a still milder alternative is 'You *might* have my breakfast ready by eight o'clock'), and also in the interrogative '*Will* you tell me the time, please', which is rendered still more polite by substituting *would* for *will.*

Dr Onions notes that the future tense is 'not uncommonly employed to express an inferential fact of the present:

'This *will* no doubt be the book he referred to.' But such an inferential fact is equally well expressed by '*This*, doubtless, is the book he referred to'.

Contrast the usage in Sheridan's 'Courage *will* come and go', where *will* connotes (rather than expresses) tendency or present habitual action; an even better example is 'These things *will* happen'.

Dr Onions notes that in independent questions the rule for *shall* and *will* is the same as in independent statements; 'but in the 2nd Person that auxiliary is used which is expected in the answer: ' "*Shall* you go to London to-morrow?" (The expected answer is "I *shall*".) The substitution of *will* would convert the sentence into a kind of request.' But not if the progressive tense be used, for '*Will* you be going to London to-morrow?' asks what the addressed person intends to do on the morrow, and 'Are you going to London to-morrow' stresses futurity.

Literary uses of *shall* for all three persons are these:—

(*a*) In those clauses in which the action is mentioned or implied as being under consideration or in prospect:—'Permission to use the reading-room will be withdrawn from any person who *shall* write on any part of a printed book.' (Good sense and idiomatic usage would seem to prefer 'Permission . . . will be withdrawn from any person who writes on any part of a printed book'.) 'There will I hide thee, till life *shall* end.' (I.e., 'There am I resolved to hide thee . . .'. The corresponding past is 'There did I'—or 'was I resolved to'—'hide thee, till life should end'.)

(*b*) In implied commands, e.g., 'My aunt intends that you *shall* accompany us'. Current idiom, however, prefers 'My aunt intends you to accompany us'.

In colloquial and indeed all spoken English, however, *will* is fast displacing *shall* in all cases in which *shall* was formerly used and in which we are recommended to use it. That there should be this tendency is a pity, for once *shall* has disappeared, we shall have lost many useful distinctions.

shape of, in the, is incorrect for *in the form of* in such sentences as these cited by Weseen: 'He gets his pay in the shape of commissions'; 'He gets his exercise in the shape of golf'. But even *in the form of commissions* (or *golf*) is verbose for *by commissions, at golf* or *by golfing*.

shape—shaped—shaped. The past participle *shapen* survives in the obsolescent *well shapen* and, though somewhat archaic, in poetry.

share and part. Do not misuse *share*, 'an allotted portion', for *part*, as in 'A large share of the meadow'.

sheared. See SHORE (v.).

shelffuls; shelves full. Cf. BASKETFULS.

shew; show. The latter is now the usual spelling. (But *shew-bread* has survived.)

shine (v.i.); preterite *shone*; past participle, *shone*. But the v.t. has preterite and past participle *shined*. 'The sun shone yesterday', 'The sun has not shone the last few days'; 'He shined *or* has shined my boots': these are correct.

shipment. See CARGO.

shook. See SHAKE.

shore of an ocean, a sea, a lake, or even of a great river; *bank* of all other rivers.

shore is archaic for *sheared* as the preterite of 'to *shear*'; the past participle is either *sheared* or *shorn*, the former only as a verb, the latter as both verb and adjective ('the shorn lamb').

short. See BRIEF.

shortly is to be avoided as a synonym of *briefly* in such a sentence as 'She spoke shortly', which conveys the idea of curtness or abruptness. Still more ambiguous is 'She will speak shortly', which conveys that 'she will speak before long'.

should and **would.** See 'WOULD and SHOULD'.

show. See SHEW.

show—showed—showed or, preferably, **shown.** In the passive, *shown* is obligatory ('He was shown to be a thief'); in the active, *showed* is less common than *shown*.

shut. See CLOSE.

sick. See 'ILL and SICK'.

sick and sickly. The former refers to temporary, the latter to habitual, illness.

sidewalk. See PAVEMENT.

sideward is adverb and adjective; **sidewards**, adverb only.

sideways; sidewise.

Sideways is current, in good use, only as an adverb, 'with the side foremost; facing the side' ('Two people could not pass in the passage without turning sideways'); 'in a lateral direction; obliquely' ('The lark came down sideways'); 'inclining to one side' ('with head bent sideways').

Sidewise is occasionally used as an adjective = 'sideward' ('Each man gave a sidewise bow'). As an adverb, it = 'sidewards', 'to one side', 'laterally', as in 'He glanced sidewise at me'; it is less common than *sideways* both in 'a house standing sidewise to the street' and in 'to hold the head sidewise'. (*O.E.D.*)

signature. See SUPERSCRIPTION.

significant. *Significant* has, in the world of art and, imitatively, of music and literature, much the same position as that occupied by *implement* in the academic world, and, though a whit studio-soiled it retains most of its vogue. It now does duty for 'outstanding', 'most important or notable', 'most interesting', 'most valuable', and so forth. It has, however, been used effectively, fundamentally, 'significantly' in the following sentence from Stapledon's *Beyond the Isms*: 'The whole language of religion, formerly significant, has degenerated into a mere jargon'.

sillily may be difficult to pronounce, but it is easy to write, and much more economical than *in a silly manner*.

similar, exactly, is a misuse for either *same* or *very closely resembling*; 'similar' is too vague to be made 'exact'. The *Daily Express* often uses it: and on Nov. 27, 1937, it defended the phrase, 'This thing is exactly similar to that'.

similar and **analogous.** *Similar* is 'having a marked resemblance or likeness; of a like nature or kind' ('We are on our guard against similar conclusions', Burke); constructed with *to* ('This is similar to that'). *Analogous* is 'similar in certain attributes, circumstances, relations or uses; having something parallel'; it is constructed with *to*; 'Disorders analogous to those of Syracuse' (Grote). In the sense 'expressing an analogy', it is inferior to *analogical*.

similar and **same.** See 'SAME and SIMILAR'.

similar for *corresponding*; **similarly** for *correspondingly*. 'In accepting a definition wider than political for Left and Right, we must similarly accept a definition of Socialism wider than that of a particular political programme.' Misuse.

similar as for *similar to* or *same as* is probably caused by a confusion between those two phrases. It is an odd mistake to find in so distinguished a writer as 'Nicholas Blake', yet in *There's Trouble Brewing* we come on: 'The remains appear to be of similar height and physique as Bunnett'.

similar to, misused for *the same as*. J. H. Vaux, the convict, writing from Newcastle (N.S.W.) and speaking of robbery with violence, says, in 1812, 'This audacious game is called by *prigs* [i.e., thieves] *the ramp*, and is nearly similar to *the rush*'.

SIMILES, BATTERED. Here is a short list of similes that are working overtime. Think twice before you use any of the following.

as similes: see the key-words
aspen leaf, shake (or *tremble*) *like an*

bad shilling (or *penny*), *turn up* (or *come back*) *like a*
bear with a sore head, like a

behave: see *bull*
black as coal—or *pitch*—or *the Pit, as*
blush like a schoolgirl, to
bold (or *brave*) *as a lion, as*
bold as brass, as
bright as a new pin, as [obsolescent]
brown as a berry, as
bull in a china shop, (*behave*) *like a*

cat on hot bricks, like a; e.g., *jump about*
caught like a rat in a trap
cheap as dirt, as
Cheshire cat, grin like a
clean as a whistle, as
clear as crystal (or *the day* or *the sun*), *as*; jocularly, *as clear as mud*
clever as a cart- (or *waggon-*) *load of monkeys, as*
cold as charity, as
collapse like a pack of cards
cool as a cucumber, as
crawl like a snail
cross as a bear with a sore head (or *as two sticks*), *as*

dark as night, as
dead as a door-nail, as
deaf as a post (or *as an adder*), *as*
different as chalk from cheese, as
drink like a fish, to
drop like a cart-load of bricks, to
drowned like a rat
drunk as a lord, as
dry as a bone (or *as dust*), *as*
dull as ditch-water, as
Dutch uncle, talk (to someone) *like a*
dying duck: see *look like . . .*
dying like flies

easy as kiss (or *as kissing*) *your hand, as*; also *as easy as falling off a log*

fight like Kilkenny cats
fighting cocks: see *live . . .*
fit as a fiddle, as
flash, like a
flat as a pancake, as
free as a bird, as; *as free as the air*
fresh as a daisy (or *as paint*), *as*

good as a play, as; i.e., *very amusing*
good as gold, as; i.e., very well behaved
good in parts, like the curate's egg
green as grass, as
grin: see *Cheshire cat*

hang on like grim death
happy (or *jolly*) *as a sandboy* (or *as the day is long*), *as*
hard as a brick (or *as iron* or, fig., *as nails*), *as*
hate like poison, to
have nine lives like a cat, to
heavy as lead, as

honest as the day, as
hot as hell, as
hungry as a hunter, as

innocent as a babe unborn (or *as a new-born babe*), *as*

jolly: see *happy*

keen as mustard, as
Kilkenny cats: see *fight*

lamb to the slaughter, like a
large as life (jocularly: *large as life and twice as natural*), *as*
light as a feather (or *as air*), *as*
like similes: see the key-words
like as two peas, as
like water off a duck's back
live like fighting cocks
look like a dying duck in a thunder-storm
look like grim death
lost soul, like a

mad as a March hare (or *as a hatter*), *as*
meek as a lamb, as
memory like a sieve, a
merry as a grig, as [obsolescent]
mill pond, the sea [is] *like a*

nervous as a cat, as

obstinate as a mule, as
old as Methuselah (or *as the hills*), *as*
plain as a pikestaff (or *the nose on your face*), *as*
pleased as a dog with two tails (or *as Punch*), *as*
poor as a church mouse, as
pretty as a picture, as
pure as driven snow, as

quick as a flash (or *as lightning*), *as*
quiet as a mouse (or *mice*), *as*

read (a person) *like a book, to* (*be able to*)
red as a rose (or *as a turkey-cock*), *as*
rich as Croesus, as
right as a trivet (or *as rain*), *as*
roar like a bull
run like a hare

safe as houses (or *as the Bank of England*), *as*
shake: see *aspen leaf*: also *shake like a jelly*
sharp as a razor (or *as a needle*), *as*
sigh like a furnace, to
silent as the grave, as
sleep like a top, to
slippery as an eel, as
slow as a snail (or *as a wet week*), *as*
sob as though one's heart would break, to
sober as a judge, as
soft as butter, as
sound as a bell, as

speak like a book, to
spring up like mushrooms overnight
steady as a rock, as
stiff as a poker (or *as a ramrod*), *as*
straight as a die, as
strong as a horse, as
swear like a trooper
sweet as a nut (or *as sugar*), *as*

take to [something] *like* (or *as*) *a duck to water*
talk like a book; and see *Dutch uncle*
thick as leaves in Vallombrosa, as
thick as thieves, as [conspiracy]
thin as a lath (or *as a rake*), *as*
ton of bricks, (e.g., *come down* or *fall*) *like a*
tough as leather, as
true as steel, as
turn up: see *bad shilling*
two-year-old, like a

ugly as sin, as

warm as toast, as
weak as water, as
white as a sheet (or *as snow*), *as*
wise as Solomon, as
work like a nigger (or *a horse* or a *Trojan*)

simpleness is being superseded by *simplicity*, except in the sense. 'foolishness; lack of intelligence; lack of shrewdness'.
SIMPLICITY. Simplicity of language or style is 'absence or lack of elegance or polish' or, in the modern acceptation, 'freedom from ornateness or over-elaboration; plainness or directness of an attractive kind'. (*O.E.D.*)

Simplicity is an admirable ideal; it can, however, be pushed to that extreme wherein the style becomes inadequate.
simply should, in many contexts, be avoided in the sense of *merely* (as in 'He is simply careless'), for it often sets up an ambiguity. Note, too, that 'He spoke simply' = 'in a simple, unaffected, sincere manner', whereas 'He simply spoke' = 'He only spoke; he spoke but did not act, sing, etc.' As an intensive, *simply* is familiar English; 'simply too lovely for words' may be amusing, but it is trivial.
simulate and **dissimulate.** The difference is important. To *dissimulate* is to hide or disguise one's real thought or feeling, to pretend not to have or feel; to *simulate* is to pretend to be, have or feel that which one is not, has not, or does not feel.
simultaneous. See COMPARATIVES, FALSE.
since (conj.) leads to errors in the use of tense. It is obviously incorrect to write 'He is a notability since he has written that book'; less obviously incorrect is

'He has been a notability since he has . . .', the logical (and correct) form being 'He has been a notability since he wrote . . .'.

'You had a row with him and are not' —it should be *have not been*—' on speaking terms since.' Advertisement: 'What a difference since I have used —— soap!' should read 'since I used, or began to use'; here the verb must be in the preterite.

sing—preterite *sang*—past participle *sung*. *Sung* is the only form for the participle, but the preterite has the alternative *sung*.

sink—**sank**—**sunk** are the usual forms in current speech and in prose. The preterite *sunk* is becoming rare. The alternative past participle *sunken* is attributive, as in 'a sunken road', 'sunken cheeks', 'sunken rocks': yet *sunk* is preferred where (deliberate) human agency is implied: 'a sunk ditch', 'sunk carving', 'sunk cistern'. (*O.E.D.*)

situate; situated. In general, *situated* is to be preferred; in legal phraseology, *situate* is sanctified by custom, but elsewhere it is an absurd affectation.

size; sized. *Every-size, fair-size, medium-size, middle-size, small-size, large-size*, etc., as adjectives are incorrect for *fair-sized, medium-sized, middle-sized, small-sized, large-sized*; *every-sized* seems illogical, and *of every size* (after the noun) is preferred. So too *larger-sized, smaller-sized* are unnecessary for *larger* and *smaller*.

skilful; skilled. Possessing skill; showing skill. Usage, however, restricts *skilled* to labour—to craftsmen or technicians—and to their work. E.g., 'a skilled woolsorter' but 'a skilful batsman'. (Harold Herd.)

sky-light (or **sky light**) and **skylight.** *Sky light* is precisely what one would expect it to be: light from the sky. *Skylight* is that small opening which admits daylight.

slander. See LIBEL.

slang is incorrect for *slung* (preterite of *sling*); the past participle is *slung*.

SLANG.

I. DEFINITIONS; EXAMPLES.

The *O.E.D.* defines the almost indefinable *slang* as 'language of a highly colloquial type, considered as below the level of standard educated speech, and consisting either of new words or of current words employed in some special sense'; *Webster's* as 'Language comprising certain widely current but usually ephemeral terms having a forced, fantastic, or gro-tesque meaning, or exhibiting eccentric or extravagant humor or fancy'.

It stands below colloquialisms, but above cant. If a cant word gains wider currency, it is by its admission to the vocabulary of slang; if a slang word is promoted, it is to the ranks of colloquialism. (See the articles CANT and COLLOQUIAL.)

Here are a few examples exhibiting the difference between slang and colloquialism and Standard English (or Standard American). Standard *man* is colloquial *chap* and slang *bloke* or *cove* or *cully* or *guy* or *stiff* or *bozo*, of which slang terms the first three were originally cant; and *old man* is colloquial *old* (or *ancient*) *chap* (or *fellow*) and slang *old buffer* or *old geezer*; *money* is colloquial *wherewithal* or *shekels* and slang *spondulicks* (originally American) or *tin*; *doctor* becomes the colloquial *doc* and the slang *vet*, *croaker*, *pill-shooter*; *lawyers' clerk* becomes colloquial *limb of the law*; *lawyer*, colloquially *pettifogger*, becomes in slang, *landshark* (English), *mouthpiece* (English and American), *fixer* (American); a clergyman is colloquially *parson* and slangily *amen wallah, fire escape, holy Joe, sky pilot*.

II. ORIGIN; REASONS FOR USE.

* Slang, being the quintessence of colloquial speech, is determined by convenience and fancy rather than by scientific laws, philosophical ideals and absolutes, and grammatical rules. As it originates, so it flourishes best, in colloquial speech. 'Among the impulses which lead to the invention of slang,' Henry Bradley once remarked, 'the two most important seem to be the desire to secure increased vivacity and the desire to secure increased sense of intimacy in the use of language.' The most favourable conditions of growth are those of 'crowding and excitement, and artificial life.'

But why is slang used at all?

Slang, I believe, is employed for one, or several, of the following sixteen reasons —and there are doubtless others.

(1) In sheer *joie de vivre*, by the young in spirit as well as by the young in years; 'just for the hell of it'.
(2) As an exercise either in humour or in wit and ingenuity.
(3) To be different from others.
(4) To be picturesque.

* The ensuing paragraphs represent a condensation of chapters II–III of my *Slang To-day and Yesterday.*

(5) To be arresting, striking, or even startling. (*Épater les bourgeois.*)

(6) To avoid clichés.

(7) To be brief and concise.

(8) To enrich the language. This purposiveness and deliberateness is rare except among the well-educated, Cockneys forming the most important exception.

(9) To impose an air of solidity and concreteness on the abstract; of earthiness on the idealistic; of immediacy and appositeness on the remote.

(10) To lessen the sting of, or on the other hand to give additional point to, a refusal, a rejection, a recantation; to reduce, perhaps also to disperse, the solemnity, pomposity, or excessive seriousness of a conversation—or on rare occasions, of a piece of writing; to soften the starkness, to lighten or to 'prettify' the inevitability of death, the hammerblow of madness, or to mark the ugliness or the pitiableness of profound turpitude; and thus to enable the speaker or his auditor to endure.

(11) To talk, or to write, down to an inferior, or to amuse a superior, public; or merely to be on the same speechlevel with one's audience or one's subject-matter.

(12) For ease of social intercourse.

(13) To induce friendliness or intimacy.

(14) To show that one belongs to a certain school, trade or profession, artistic or intellectual set, a social class; in brief, to establish contact or to be 'in the swim'.

(15) To show or prove that someone else is not 'in the swim'.

(16) To be secret—not understood by those around one.

III. ATTITUDES TO SLANG.

Slang now excites much less disapprobation than was its lot before the present century; disapproval, indeed, had coloured the views of some notable 19th Century philologists and grammarians. In 1825, J. P. Thomas, in *My Thought Book*, bluntly declared that 'the language of slang is the conversation of fools'; O. W. Holmes was scathing at its expense. Greenough & Kittredge condemn it on the ground that, being evanescent, vague and ill-defined, slang has a deleterious effect on those who use it often, for it tends to destroy all those delicate shades of meaning which are at the root of a good style; they hold that it is the speech of lazy persons; and assert that when a slang word becomes definite in meaning it has almost ceased to be slang, —which is manifestly false, for most slang words are unconventional synonyms of conventional words. A fairer view is that expressed by Professor H. C. K. Wyld: 'While slang is essentially part of familiar and colloquial speech, it is not necessarily either incorrect or vulgar in its proper place', which, the Fowler brothers assert in *The King's English*, 'is in real life'— that is, in conversation.

With regard to the use of slang, the Fowlers raise an important point when they say that 'The effect of using quotation marks with slang is merely to convert a mental into a moral weakness'. But there I must join issue with the authors of *The King's English*. They say that if a man uses slang at all in writing, let him do so in a courageous, not a cowardly manner: let him use it frankly, without quotation marks. So far as it goes, that is admirable; it does not go far enough. A good writer wishes to indicate that the word or phrase he puts into inverted commas is *not* Standard English, is not pure English, is not to be aped by the young nor unreflectingly copied by a foreigner; its status, he implies, is suspect, but he is using it because it is necessary to the atmosphere or to the characterization he wishes to make. True; he will use slang sparingly; he will use it only when it is necessary to the effect he is desirous of creating: but, precisely because he employs words scrupulously, and precisely because he is anxious to avoid being taken as an examplar of slang, a supporter of this particular word or phrase, he fences it off with quotation marks.

IV. THE ROLE OF SLANG.

'An analysis of modern slang', wrote Brander Matthews in 1893, 'reveals the fact that it is possible to divide [it] . . . into four broad classes, of quite different origin and very varying value. Two unworthy, two worthy. Of the two unworthy classes, the first is that which includes the survivals of "thieves' Latin". . . . Much of the distaste for slang felt by people of delicate taste is, however, due to the second class, which includes the ephemeral phrases fortuitously popular for a season [e.g., *Where did you get that hat?*]. . . . The other two classes of slang stand on a different footing . . . They serve a purpose. Indeed, their utility is indisputable, and it was never greater

[—the remark is still valid—] than it is today. One of these consists of old and forgotten phrases and words, which, having long lain dormant, are now struggling again to the surface. The other consists of new words and phrases, often vigorous and expressive, but . . . still on probation': these two classes help to feed and refresh the vocabulary. 'It is the duty of slang to provide substitutes for the good words . . . which are worn out by hard service.' Of the fourth class— vigorous new slang—he goes on to say that it is 'what idiom was before language stiffened into literature': compare Lounsbury's description of slang as 'the source from which the decaying energies of speech are constantly refreshed'.

V. THE ESSENCE OF SLANG.

Slang tends to be 'Saxon' rather than 'Latin-Greek'—native rather than learned in its elements; except among the very cultured and the innately supple and subtle, it is simple and direct rather than complex and concealed or insinuatory; it reduces the peculiar and the particular (in which, nevertheless, it rejoices and is, on occasion, 'at home') to the level of general comprehension; it abridges rather than develops or elaborates; so far from padding, it omits the incidental and the contingent; rather than divest them of colour, it renders them pictorial and metaphorical; except in humour and wit, it eschews sentimental hyperbole and philosophical high-falutin'; it takes nothing too seriously, yet (very faintly) it implies a moral or an intellectual standard, usually at the level of good sense or, at the lowest, of common sense; it universalizes words and phrases rather than exclusively or snobbishly confines them to one social class; it refers itself to human nature rather than to Nature; it dispels hypocrisy and humbug; in short, it is catholic, tolerant, human and, though often tartly, humane.

Inherent in human nature as a psychological tendency and potentiality, slang is indicative not only of man's earthiness but of his indomitable spirit: it sets him in his proper place: relates a man to his fellows, to his world and the world, and to the universe.

See esp. E. P., *A Dictionary of Slang and Unconventional English* (5th ed., 1954) for the British Empire and, for the U.S.A., L. V. Berrey and M. Van den Bark's *The American Thesaurus of Slang*, several editions.

G*

slank is incorrect for *slunk*, the preterite of *slink*; *slunk* is also the past participle.
slant (n.). See STANDPOINT.
slattern. See SLOVEN.
slayed is incorrect for *slew*, the preterite of *slay*; the correct past participle is *slain*.
sled, sledge, sleigh, as vehicles. As 'a vehicle running on ice or snow', the three terms are synonymous, *sledge* being in the U.S.A. the least used, *sled* the most; in the British Empire, *sledge* is the most used, *sled* the least. (*O.E.D.*) [In the memory of many Americans, a *sleigh* was a more comfortable and stylish vehicle than a *sled*. The two compared much as a car and a truck today. A *sledge*, sometimes called a *sled*, is a low vehicle on runners used for very heavy work in summer or winter. Every child in the snow country has a small *sled* (or *handsled*) for his pleasure and, formerly, his chores.]
sleuth for *detective* should be employed only in a facetious way.
sloven and **slattern.** The former is common to the two sexes; the latter is used only of the female—'a woman or girl untidy and careless in clothes and cleanliness (and other habits) and in housework'. A *sloven* is any untidy or dirty person; hence also a careless, slipshod workman, craftsman, or writer. *Slut* is stronger than *slattern*: a *slut* is a foul *slattern*; hence, a low or loose woman or girl, or a forward, impudent one (especially of a girl); yet, unlike *slattern*, it may be used playfully: 'Ah! you're a wheedling slut!' (*O.E.D.*)
slow; slower or **more slow,** adverbially *more slowly*; **slowest** (rarely *most slow*), adverbially *slowest* (occasionally *most slowly*). 'He walks slowly' and 'go slowly' (literal) or 'go slow!' (figurative). The forms *more slow(ly), most slow(ly)* are literary or poetical. [*Go slow* is literal as well as figurative in American usage. *Slow* adv. is occasionally interchangeable with *slowly* adv. Sometimes it is more forceful; sometimes it better suits the rhythm.]
slut. See SLOVEN.
small fry is occasionally misused as a singular. 'Garston takes your overcoat on Monday and lets you have it back again on Saturday night—for a consideration. Or will buy it for that matter. Small fry.' It is also misused in: 'It resulted in murder [the murder of a prominent lawyer politician]—and not just the usual shooting of some small fry.' *Fry* is 'a collective term for young or insignificant beings'

(especially newly-hatched fish), as *The O.E.D.* reminds us.

smell—smelled, smelt—smelled, smelt; but in both preterite and past participle, *smelt* is now the usual form. 'I smelt something' but 'something smells unpleasantly' and 'something smells of (e.g.) oil'.

SNOB PLURALS. See PLURALS, SNOB.

so (adv.), emphasizing the adj. following, as in *I was so pleased*, is a weak and slovenly form of expression. *Much* or *very* is preferable.

so, ambiguous. 'A prosperous, carefree foreigner, probably visiting Monte Carlo for the first time in his life, and so eager for adventure': should not *so* be *therefore*? *So* for *therefore* or *accordingly* is much overworked.

so for *so that* or *in order that* is always colloquial and sometimes ambiguous, as in 'I do not ask you to believe these things, but I will give you proof, so you can judge them for yourself'.

so, pronoun, is frequently misused: sometimes because it is asked to do too much. There is a considerable strain on *so* in 'King Carol today . . . proclaimed to his people: "Rumania must be saved, and I have decided to do so" ' (*The Star*, Feb. 11, 1938); and here is a parallel misuse in *The Daily Herald* of the same date, 'Mr B. said later: "Much as we hate doing so, we are reconciled to the fact" '.

so, superfluous. As, e.g., in 'Both Karl and his mother discussed the crisis with Sir Oscar Bloom, but separately so, and from different viewpoints'.

so as for *so that*, in the sense *in order that*, is catachrestic, for *so as*—if used at all—should be confined to consequence. And in any event, it should be followed by *to* + the infinitive. Therefore 'He did this so as he might win the prize' is doubly unfortunate. 'He did this vigorously—so as to fall down exhausted' (result) is not incorrect; but it is clumsy for 'He did this so vigorously as to fall down exhausted'.

so . . . as, omitted. Do not omit this preparatory formula: to omit so necessary and basic a piece of sentence-material is to incur the certainty of ambiguity and abruptness. 'It may turn out that nature can be so embraced,'—i.e., embraced in any one formula,—'but thinking must be organized not to demand it as a necessity' should read '. . . but thinking must be so organized as not to demand it . . .'.

so far as. See AS FAR AS.

so that = *with the result that* (generally)

and *in order that*. Keep it for the former.

sociable and **social**. *Sociable* is 'naturally inclined to be in company with others', hence 'inclined to seek their company and to enjoy it', 'affable'; hence of occasions, 'of or characterized by companionship, especially friendly or at least pleasant companionship' (*sociable habits* or *manners, sociable life, sociable talk*). *Social* = 'consisting of persons associated in friendly intercourse or pleasant companionship' (*in every social circle*); 'living—or desiring to live—in communities' ('Man is a social being'); 'of or like, connected with or due to society as an ordinary condition of human life' (*social usefulness, the social order* or *state*); 'concerned with or interested in the constitution of society and its problems' (*a social reformer*). (*O.E.D.*)

society and **Society**. The former = 'companionship, fellowship; the state or condition of living in association with others of the same species; and especially the aggregate of persons living together in a more or less ordered community'. The latter = 'the aggregate of leisured, cultured, or fashionable persons regarded as forming a distinct class or body in a community'. (*O.E.D.*) The capital *S* serves to indicate the distinction in a way so convenient that it is not to be lightly disregarded.

SOCRATIC IRONY. See IRONY, third paragraph.

solar topi is incorrect for *sola topi* (or *topee*). The pith helmet used in India is so called from the sola, a swamp plant producing the pith, and is misspelt *solar* from the mistaken idea that the adjective refers to the *solar rays*.

sole. The two commonest senses in nontechnical English are 'one and one only', as in 'the sole support of his mother', 'the sole manager of these estates'; and (of properties, rights, privileges, duties, obligations) 'exclusive', as in 'A theory of which he claims the sole invention', 'This is a task in which he has the sole obligation'. (*O.E.D.*)

SOLECISM AND SOLECISMS. *Solecism*, the Greek *soloikismos*, derives from the offensive and illiterate corruption of the Attic dialect as spoken by those Athenian colonists who settled at *Soloi* (Soli), in Cilicia, a province of Asia Minor.

The O.E.D. defines it, in the linguistic sense, as 'an impropriety or irregularity in speech or diction'—a gross mispronunciation, a stress wrongly placed (especially in a well-known word); 'a violation of the rules of [accidence] or syntax'.

It is approximately synonymous with *illiteracy*, which, however, includes also misspellings. "E ain't a-comin' 'ere' contains three solecisms (*'e, comin', 'ere*) and five illiteracies (*'e, ain't, a-, comin', 'ere*).

solicitor. See LAWYER.

solidity should not be made synonymous with *solidarity* ('community or perfect coincidence *of* (or *between*) interests'), nor with *stolidity*, which is 'dull impassiveness' or 'a natural incapacity for feeling', the former sense being favourable, the latter unfavourable. (*O.E.D.*)

some for *part* is misused, as in 'I shall spend some of the day in Town'.

some for *somewhat* (or *rather*) is a solecism ('He is some better to-day'); for *very* (or *much*), *very pleasant, large*, it is slang ('He speeded some'; 'We had some holiday').

some few. See 'FEW and A FEW'.

some place, some place else: solecisms for *somewhere, somewhere else*: as in 'The enemy was some place near', 'The jar is obviously some place else'.

some reason or another. See SOME WAY OR ANOTHER . . .

some thing and **something; some time** and **sometime.** Written as separate words, these two expressions are dissociative ('I'll see you at some time before midnight'; 'Some thing, not some person, was revealed'). When units are required, *something* and *sometime* are required. In current usage, *sometime* has two main senses, 'at some future time' ('Will you tell me?'—'Yes, sometime') and 'at some indefinite or indeterminate point of time; at some time or other' ('The prisoner escaped, sometime after nightfall'); in the sense 'now and then; occasionally', *sometimes* is right. (*O.E.D.*)

some way or another; some reason or another. These are wrong for *some way or other, some reason or other*, e.g., 'In some way or other they escaped', 'For some reason or other, he left home'.

somebody (or **someone**) . . . **they.** See ANYONE . . . THEY.

somebody's (or **someone's**) **else** or **else's.** See ELSE'S.

somerset; somersault. The former is either dialectal or obsolescent for the latter.

something of that extent is misused for *something of that kind* or *sort*.

somewhat the same. Eric Partridge in *The French Romantics' Knowledge of English Literature*, 1924, speaks of 'a group of critics . . . possessing similar literary opinions as well as ability of somewhat the same high standard', but his subsequent study of English leads him to condemn the use of *somewhat* in the sense of *approximately* or *nearly* or *almost*.

somewhere near is infelicitous and slovenly for *somewhere about*, 'at (or in) approximately' (a specified period or date), as in 'I woke up somewhere about five o'clock', and also for *approximately*, as in 'He was ill somewhere about a month'. Note, too, that *somewhere about*, in these two nuances, is clumsy for *about*. (*O.E.D.*)

son-in-laws is incorrect for *sons-in-law*.

sooner is familiar but good English for *rather* in 'He'd sooner play than work'; not a colloquialism.

sophisticate (adj.) is obsolete for *sophisticated*. But *sophisticate* (n.) is both convenient and justifiable for *sophisticated person*.

sort of for *rather, somewhat*, is colloquial. At the end of a sentence and usually following an adjective, it is a slovenly form of modification. 'He is queer, sort of': 'He is rather queer' or 'He is, in a way, queer' is much to be preferred. Cf. KIND . . . OF.

sort of, these or **those.** In 'these sort of things are done by conjurers' there is a confusion between 'this sort of thing is done . . .' and 'these sorts of things are done . . .'. Cf. KIND . . . OF, ALL.

sound (v.). One may say that 'A thing sounds all right' (which is rather colloquial, of course), but *sound* is misused in 'In a moment or two blows would be exchanged and after that anything might happen, but most likely a miniature razor battle, particularly as the voices of both parties sounded to be of foreign origin': where 'seemed to be' would be better, as also would 'the voices . . . sounded like those of foreigners'.

sound out is tautological—and it rings oddly—for *sound*, 'to test'. Perhaps on the analogy of *try out*. 'President is sounding out sentiment by undercover [= secret] observers in European capitals', cited by Stuart Chase in *The Tyranny of Words*.

source and **cause.** *Source* cannot be used indiscriminately for *cause*, as in 'The source of his injury was a motor collision', but it is permissible in 'The source of many failures is neglect of duty'. The *O.E.D.* makes it clear that a *source* is 'the chief or prime cause *of* something of a non-material or abstract character', as in 'The free election of our representatives . . . is the source and security of every right and privilege' (Junius); generally, however, there is a reference (actual or implied) to the quarter whence something non-material or abstract arises, as in 'Evil-smelling gases are a source of annoyance to all those who live within a mile of the factory' and 'One source of danger is the carelessness of the garrison'.

sourkrout is incorrect for *sauerkraut*.

southernly is obsolete for *southerly*; and *southerly* is obsolescent for 'situated in— or towards—the south', for which *southern* is the correct term. *Southerly* is reserved for '(wind) blowing from the south', as in 'In the greater part of Europe the southerly and westerly winds bring rain' (T. H. Huxley) and for 'facing southwards or tending southwards', as in *A southerly aspect, a southerly direction*. (*O.E.D.*)

southward; southwards. The latter is adverb only; the former is both adjective and adverb, and even as adverb, now more usual than *southwards*.

sow—sowed—sowed (or, in poetry and as adj. before a noun, **sown**). The verbal noun is *sown*; 'The desert and the sown'.

spake is archaic for *spoke*.

span is archaic for *spun* (preterite).

sparing with. See PREPOSITIONS WRONGLY USED.

special. See ESPECIAL.

speciality and **specialty.** *Specialty* is now preferred to *speciality* in the following senses:—A special line of work (including study and research); a manufacture or product characteristic of a certain locality, firm, factory, etc.; 'an article specially dealt in or stocked' by, e.g., a shopkeeper: thus, 'His specialty was inlaid-work' (Leland), 'The brass work of Birmingham has long been one of its specialties'. In the abstract, 'the quality of being special, limited, or restricted in some respect', *speciality* is the right word ('Some . . . are general and vague directions, . . . others . . . the extreme of speciality', Grote). (*O.E.D.*)

specie and **species.** *Specie* is coined money; *in specie* = in actual coin; *specie* has no plural. *Species* is both singular and plural, and it = 'a class composed of individuals having some common qualities or characteristics, frequently as a subdivision of a larger class or genus'. (*O.E.D.*)

spectators. See AUDIENCE.

speed—sped—sped. But *speed*, 'to drive a motor-car very fast', and *speed up*, 'to hasten the acceleration or tempo of' (e.g., a business, a dance), more often than not have preterite and past participle *speeded*.

spell—spelled or **spelt—spelled** or **spelt.** Purists prefer *spelled* for the preterite, *spelt* for the past participle; usage accepts either form in the preterite but prefers the shorter form in the participle.

SPELLING lies beyond the scope of this work. See esp. G. H. Vallins, *Spelling*, with a chapter, by John W. Clark, on American practice.

Spencer, philosopher (adj. *Spencerian*); **spencer,** a wig, a garment, a lifebelt; **Spenser,** poet (adj., *Spenserian*).

sphere (or **realm,** or **world**) **of** (e.g., **sport**) for *sport*. 'In the sphere (or realm or world) of sport, one should play for the side, not for oneself' would not be weakened by reducing it to 'In sport, one should . . .'.

spill—spilled or **spilt—spilled** or **spilt.** Those who like to differentiate, reserve *spilled* for the preterite, *spilt* for the participle; but usage scarcely supports them, except that it prefers *spilt* as a participial adjective, as in 'His words are like spilt water' (Carlyle) and *to cry over spilt milk*.

spit, 'to expectorate'—preterite, *spat* in U.S.A., *spit*)—past participle, *spit*; but *spit*, 'to transfix'—*spitted*—*spitted*.

spite of. See DESPITE.

SPLIT INFINITIVE, THE. In *An Advanced English Syntax*, Dr C. T. Onions writes: 'The construction known by this name consists of the separation of *to* from the Infinitive by means of an adverb, e.g. "He used *to continually refer* to the subject", instead of "He used *continually to refer*", or "He used *to refer continually*". The construction is becoming more and more frequent, especially in newspapers, but it is generally admitted that a constant and unguarded use of it is not to be encouraged; some, indeed, would refuse altogether to recognize it, as being inelegant and un-English. (Instances like "For a time, the Merovings continued to *nominally rule*" are particularly ugly.) On the other hand, it may be said that its occasional use is of advantage in cases where it is desired to avoid ambiguity by indicating in this manner the close connexion of the adverb with the infinitive, and thus prevent its being taken in conjunction with some other word': e.g., 'Our object is to further cement trade relations' is obviously preferable to 'Our object is to cement further trade relations' (which yields a sense different from the one intended), and is no less surely preferable to 'Our object is further to cement trade relations', which leaves it 'doubtful whether an additional object or additional cement is the point' (Fowler). H. W. Fowler writes thus:—'We maintain that a real split infinitive, though not desirable in itself, is preferable to either of two things, to real ambiguity, and to patent artificiality'. As an example of patent artificiality he cites 'In not combining to forbid flatly hostilities', instead of the natural and sensible 'In not combining to flatly forbid hostilities'; 'In not combining flatly to forbid hostilities' would obviously have been ambiguous.

Fowler, we see, speaks of 'a real split infinitive'. Is there, then 'an unreal split infinitive'? Of course; there is one in the following sentence: 'The sentence ought *to be differently constructed*', which is as blameless as '*to be mortally wounded*' or '*to have just heard*'. There is a 'split' only when an adverb comes between *to* and an infinitive '*to clearly see*'.

Avoid the split infinitive wherever possible; but if it is the clearest or the most natural construction, use it boldly.

spoil—**spoiled**, **spoilt**—**spoiled**, **spoilt**. *Spoiled* is the correct form in both preterite and participle, but *spoilt* is permissible in the senses 'so damaged as to be rendered unfit or useless' ('Supper had been waiting until it was quite spoilt'); 'to affect detrimentally or injuriously (an immaterial object)', as in 'His day will be spoilt by rain'; 'to injure (a person's character) by excessive leniency'—as in 'She spoilt her only son'; and intransitively, 'to deteriorate; to decay', as in 'The fruit soon spoilt in the very hot weather'. (*O.E.D.*) As adjective, *spoilt* is usual: 'A spoilt child is an unhappy child'.

spoof and its plural. A correspondent wrote as follows to *The Radio Times* of Jan. 15, 1938: 'In a recent *Radio Times* the plural of the word hoof is spelled hooves in two instances. One would not spell the plural of roof rooves, and how supremely ridiculous the plural of spoof would appear if it were spelled spooves!' *Hooves* is allowed by *The O.E.D.*, though it is less commonly used than *hoofs*; but good authors have preferred it. *Rooves* also was common in our early literature, and is (like *loaf*, *loaves*) consistent with the genius of our language. But *spoof* is quoted as analogous. Has *spoof* a plural? Originally a game, it was no more capable of taking a plural form than *cricket* or *golf*. *Spoof* is the abstract quality of jocular deception inspiring some trick or practical joke; it is in fact an adjective derived from the game. If it is to be used in such a sense that a plural is required, there will be nothing in *spooves* more 'ridiculous' than in *spoofs*.

spoonfuls and **spoons full**: cf. BASKETFULS.

SPORTING PLURALS. Sportsmen tend to use the singular for the plural—*trout* for *trouts*, *lion* for *lions*, etc.—and to look with scorn upon those who speak of *trouts* and *lions*. The ordinary person, unacquainted with the jargon of these specialists, should not allow himself to be intimidated by the snobs of sport. If you wish to shoot three *lions* or to hunt *tigers*, do so.

SPORTS (field-sport) **TECHNICALITIES.** There are, in field sports, numerous terms that baffle or are unknown to the ordinary man and woman. The best book on the subject is Major C. E. Hare's *The Language of Sport*.

sprain and **strain** (v.). The former is 'so to twist or wrench (a part of the body) as to cause pain or difficulty in moving', now mostly confined to wrenching one's ankle. To *strain oneself* is so to exert oneself physically as to be in danger of injury.

spring—**sprang** or **sprung**—**sprung**.

squirt. Blood *spirts*, not *squirts*, from a wound; here is an idiom that careless writers tend to ignore.

St, not **St.**, and **Ste**, not **Ste.**, are the best forms. Reserve *St.* for *Street*.

staff of persons, pl. *staffs*; *staff*, a stick, rod, pole, pl. *staffs*, although the earlier plural, *staves*, is still preferred in the senses 'a stick carried in the hand as an aid in walking', 'a rod used as an instrument of divination or magic', 'a stick or pole used as a weapon', 'a spear- (or lance-) shaft'. In music, *staff* has plural *staffs*; obviously the variant *stave* has plural *staves*. (*O.E.D.*)

staid and **stayed.** Reserve the former for the adjective ('of grave or dignified or sedate deportment, demeanour, conduct'), the latter for the verb. 'The staid girl has stayed—a girl.'

stair; stairs. A *stair* is one of a succession of steps leading from one floor to another; *stairs* means either the steps of staircases or a series or 'flight' of such steps; *staircase* is usually one flight of steps, occasionally a series of flights. *Stairs*, as the plural of *stair*, hence as '(two or more) steps', is now avoided, *steps* being used instead.

stalactite; stalagmite. The former deposit of calcium carbonate is one that descends from the roof of cave or cavern; the latter, one that rises from the floor.

stanch; staunch. For the adjective, much the commoner form is *staunch*; for the verb, *stanch* is preferable. [For both, *Webster's* gives *stanch, staunch*.]

stand for *withstand* is unhappy. Whereas *stand* for 'tolerate, endure, bear' is a colloquialism to be avoided in good writing, *stand* for 'withstand' or 'resist' is the product of a meagre vocabulary; and it may be a rank mistake, leading to ambiguity, as in 'The avaricious man could not stand the solicitations of easy money'.

STANDARD ENGLISH and STANDARD AMERICAN. If we accept the definition, 'Standard English and Standard American are the speech of the educated classes in the British Empire and the United States' (when, that is, they are not speaking slangily), we may yet desire to know where, and how, Standard English arose. That rise provides material for an interesting story.

I. HISTORY.

Old English had a standard, but that standard disappeared with the Norman Conquest. In the victorious reigns of Edward I (1272-1307) and Edward III (1327-77), there was a strong growth of national feeling; national consciousness was certainly accompanied by an increasing hostility to the use of French in England and consequently an increasingly favourable attitude towards the use of English. 'In the second half of the Fourteenth Century', says McKnight, 'the English language came once more to its own, into use not only in Parliament and the law courts and in schools, but in the literary productions composed for English cultured society.'

In this revival of English as a literary language, after it had so long been a merely spoken language, the particular kind of English adopted was the East Midland dialect. The reasons for this adoption, says McKnight, are these:— 'The dialect of the East Midland district lay between Northern and Southern dialects and, as the Northern differed considerably from the Southern, the Midland served as a midway compromise understandable by all; it formed the speech of Oxford and Cambridge, the two great centres of higher education and of a culture more profound and mellow than that of London; it formed also the dialect of London itself, the centre of the political, official and commercial life of the country. And thus it was the speech of Chaucer, who, the greatest English writer until the 16th Century and, during the 11th–14th Centuries, the only great writer to employ English at all, passed most of his life in London; as the dialect spoken at Oxford, it was used by Wycliffe, who discarded his native Yorkshire for this smoother speech; as the dialect of London and hence of the Court, it was used by Gower, who might have been expected to employ the Kentish dialect.' Chaucer's and Gower's best work appeared in the last twenty years of the 14th Century; in the 15th, their disciples—and others—followed their lead and wrote in the East Midland dialect. The supremacy of the East Midland dialect was unquestioned by the dramatists and the poets of the Elizabethan age.

The language of the 16th and early 17th Century, however, was far from being so fixed and regularized as that of the 19th and, though less, the 20th Century. Spelling was idiosyncratic, syntax experimental, and vocabulary a glorious uncertainty; these features and tendencies were counterbalanced by 'the freedom enjoyed by the writers of that period in the adoption of new words and the combination of existing words in word-compound and in phrase'. Regularity in spelling and vocabulary, along with order in accidence and syntax, came in the approximate period, 1660–1800.

For more than 300 years the East Midland dialect, 'at first, no doubt, merely held to be the fashionable mode of speech, has gained in prestige, until, at the present day, it is spreading all over [Great Britain], and among all classes' (Wyld, *The Growth of English*). This dialect has become Standard English: the criteria of that standard are the choice of words and phrases, the syntax, the pronunciation. Of Standard English as we know it in the 20th Century, we may say that it 'is a kind of English which is tinged neither with the Northern, nor Midland, nor Southern peculiarities of speech [and] which gives no indication . . . of where the speaker comes from. . . . It is the ambition of all educated persons in [Great Britain and Northern Ireland] to acquire this manner of speaking, and this is the form of our language which foreigners wish to learn' (*ibid.*).

II. STANDARD ENGLISH: DEGREES AND KINDS.

There are, however, different kinds of Standard English. The best of these is Received Standard,* for it fulfils all the requirements of good speech; Modified Standard is Standard English that differs from Received mainly in pronunciation; and Literary Standard lies beyond any matter of pronunciation and is confined to written English.

Of Literary English—Literary Standard—it is necessary only to say that it is the more conventional, stylized, and dignified, more accurate and logical, sometimes the more beautiful form that Received Standard assumes, like evening dress, for important occasions; it is also more rhythmical and musical.

What then of Received Standard and Modified Standard? 'It is proposed', says Wyld in his *Short History of English*, 'to use the term *Received Standard* for that form which all would probably agree in considering the best, that form which has the widest currency and is heard with practically no variation among speakers of the better class all over the country. This type might be called Public School English.' (The stress here, you see, is on pronunciation and enunciation.) 'It is proposed to call the vulgar English of the Towns, and the English of the Villager who has abandoned his native Regional Dialect'—dialect in the ordinary sense of the term—'*Modified Standard*. That is, it is Standard English, modified, altered, differentiated, by various influences, regional and social. Modified Standard differs from class to class, and from locality to locality; it has no uniformity, and no single form of it is heard outside a particular class or a particular area.'

III. THE LIMITS OF PURE (or, RECEIVED STANDARD) ENGLISH.†

There is a perhaps startling difference between pure English and the English spoken by the uncultured. In the American 'Them guys ain't got no pep' and the English 'Them blokes ain't got no go', not even a single word satisfies the standard exacted by pure English, whether American English or British English. In both versions, the first word (*them*) is ungrammatical (for 'these' or 'those'); the second

is slang (for 'men'); the third (*ain't*) is illiterate; the fourth (*got*) is unnecessary —and colloquial; the fifth (*no*) is illogical, the sense demanding *any*; and the sixth (*pep*: *go*) is slang. Both versions are not merely uncultured but illiterate.

There are, however, inestimable advantages to be obtained from uniformity of vocabulary and from regularity of syntax: that uniformity and that regularity do at least make understanding much easier: and communicability is the primary requisite of both speech and writing.

Since the 17th Century, English has gained tremendously in precision. Language has not been evolved to be the sport of the illiterate, any more than to be the plaything of the highbrow or the chopping-block of the journalist. Language is the chief means of communication. 'It is important that the language medium should offer as little as possible resistance to the thought current, and this end is attained only when the symbols of language are ones that convey precisely the same meaning to all who use the language.'

But we may raise a question concerning the degree to which a language can be healthily standardized. A language cannot be at the same time entirely standardized and truly vital: a rigorously regimented language would die from stiffness of the joints and atrophy of the spirit. 'Ideas inherited from the past . . . may find adequate expression in the idiom of the past. . . . The shifting, developing forms assumed by living thought, however, demand the plastic medium of a living language.' It is only natural that new systems of thought and new modes of living should, by the very strength of their processes and by their widespread currency, generate new words, new compounds, new phrases and even new modes of expression: in linguistics, as in politics, the will of the nation is all-powerful.

On this question of the limits of pure English (Received Standard), Logan Pearsall Smith has written: 'Since our language seems to be growing year by year more foreign, abstract and colourless in character, it stands in greater need than ever of this vigorous and native reinforce-' ment' which we could obtain from dialect in particular and popular speech in general. This reinforcement could be enlisted and fruitfully employed by all of us, 'were we not paralysed by that superstitious feeling of awe and respect for standard English [i.e., Received Stan-

---

* 'Received Standard' and 'Modified Standard' are Professor Wyld's designations, whereas 'Literary Standard' is mine.

† In this section I draw heavily on G. H. McKnight's *English Words and Their Background*.

dard] which is now [1925] spread by the diffusion of education'. We are enslaved by the tyrant Correctitude.

But why should Standard English have to resort to dialectal and popular speech for vitality and picturesqueness instead of drawing on its own resources? 'It is inevitable', Pearsall Smith continues, 'that when any form of speech becomes a standard and written language, it should as a consequence lose much of its linguistic freedom. All forms of speech have of course their rules and usages, but in a written language these rules and usages become much more settled and stereotyped': so that, finally, words and phrases are adjudged to be good or bad, not by their strength, clarity and aptness of expression, but by the external criterion of correctness. 'Such an attitude . . . tends . . . to fix grammar and pronunciation, to discourage assimilation [of picturesque or vigorous outsiders], and to cripple the free and spontaneous powers of word-creation.' Then, too, 'a standard language, in modern conditions, tends to be rather a written than a spoken language. The printed word becomes more and more the reality, the spoken word an echo or [a] faint copy of it. This inversion of the normal relation between speech and writing, this predominance of the eye over the ear, of the written symbol over its audible equivalent, tends to deprive the language of that vigour and reality which comes, and can only come, from its intimate association with the acts and passions of men, as they vividly describe and express them in their speech.'

The foregoing, however, is not to be taken as a depreciation of the *virtues and advantages* of Standard English, for this, the accepted form of English, with its national scope and its national use, with its rich and varied vocabulary, with its often subtle and, for the most part, flexible syntax, with all the historical associations inevitably and naturally garnered in the course of centuries, and these and other associations enriched by successive generations, is the inestimably precious inheritance of the English people, as any such language is of any ancient people. The position of good English is, in essentials, impregnable: for as it arises from, so does it serve, a social need. The danger lies, not in its being set aside (with the result of linguistic chaos, and hence of a lack of national unity), but in its being so unreflectingly and blindly respected that we may forget the very

existence of popular speech and widespread colloquialism, of slang and dialect, and thus forget both their intrinsic value and their value as readily available sources of freshness and invigoration.

'Human speech', as Pearsall Smith has remarked, 'is after all a democratic product, the creation, not of scholars and grammarians, but of . . . unlettered people. Scholars and men of education may cultivate and enrich it, and make it flower into all the beauty of a literary language', but they should not, in their efforts to keep the language pure, forget that it should also be kept vigorous.

IV. STANDARD ENGLISH IN THE DOMINIONS AND COLONIES.

Except among Public School men and women resident there, the Dominions and Colonies have not a Received Standard pronunciation, although the vocabulary is, among the cultured and the well educated, that of Received Standard. They may be said to speak Modified Standard. One may hope that, in the Dominions, the clarity and subtlety of the best Standard English will always exercise a beneficent influence. Certainly it would be idle to fear that these Dominion writers might be unduly cramped thereby.

Colonial scorn of Public School English, like English scorn of Colonial accents, should be allowed to die. There is a reason for Colonial accents; much virtue in Public School English.

V. STANDARD AMERICAN SPEECH AND WRITING.*

The United States presents a knottier problem, for, there, a much larger population is concerned than that of the English-speakers in the Dominions.

In writing, there is an American Literary Standard, which so closely resembles English Literary Standard as to establish no basic, no important difference. But is there, in American speech, a Received Standard? Or is there nothing but a number of Modified Standards? One might, on first thought, say that there are only Modified Standards, although one might add that some of these modifications are more pleasing to the British ear or more widely used than others. But the fact remains that, although there is, in the United States, no speech that can be classified as Received Standard with the

* See esp. E.P. & John W. Clark, *A History of British and American English since 1900*.

same feeling of certainty as Public School speech can be said to be Received Standard in England, yet the speech of the cultured elements of American society is as close to being a Received Standard as can be expected in so vast and many-peopled a land as the United States. That the criterion is neither so severe nor so rigid as that of English Received Standard does not make it any the less a genuine criterion.* But in America even more than in Great Britain, the speakers of Modified Standard are more numerous than the speakers of Received Standard.

It must, however, be remembered that the differentiation between Standard and popular speech, between Standard and slang, between slang and cant, is, on the whole, less marked in the United States than in the British Empire.

standpoint, point of view, viewpoint; angle and **slant**. The first is a blameless variant of the second, whether literal or figurative. *Viewpoint*, however, though admitted by *The O.E.D.*, has been deprecated by purists; not being a purist, I occasionally use it, although I perceive that it is unnecessary.

Angle, modern and permissible, is not to be used to the exclusion of *standpoint*. Americans tend to overdo *slant* in the figurative sense ('mental point of view').

stanza. See VERSE.

starlight and **starlit**. The former is a noun, and attributively an adjective ('a starlight night); *starlit* is only an adjective ('a starlit night'). But *starlit* is the commoner adjective predicatively: 'The night was starlit' is—quite apart from euphony—preferable to 'The night was starlight'. *Starlit* = 'lit up, or lighted, by the stars' ('The whole of the star-lit sky') and so does *starlight* ('A starlight evening, and a morning fair'): in this sense, *starlit* is to be preferred. But in the transferred sense, 'bright as the stars', only *starlight* is used, as in 'starlight eyes'. (Based on *The O.E.D.*)

start for *begin* is familiar—not literary—English, whether it is used transitively or intransitively; but for inanimate objects, *begin* is better, 'That story begins on page 79' being superior to '. . . starts on page 79', 'He began to work when he was only twelve' to 'He started . . .'.

state, 'alarm, anxiety', is a colloquialism.

state and **say**. *State*, being much stronger

* [The best account of American pronunciation is Professor Kenyon's admirable 'Guide to Pronunciation', *Webster's New International Dictionary*.]

than *say*, should be reserved for formal or impressive contexts. 'I wish to state that I like fish' is an absurd overstatement. **stately** is now rare as an adverb; so is *statelily*. *In a stately manner* is the locution sanctified by usage.

States, the. See AMERICA.

statesman. See POLITICIAN.

stationary is the adjective ('static; not moving'); *stationery*, the n. ('writing materials').

staunch. See STANCH.

staves. See STAFF.

stay, in law = 'to delay', 'to arrest (an action) for the time being'—not 'to put an end to'.

stayed. See 'STAID and STAYED'.

steal, 'a theft', 'something stolen', 'a corrupt transaction or a fraudulent one', is an American and Canadian colloquialism.

sticker and **stickler**. A *sticker* is a person constant to a cause or persevering in a task, whereas a *stickler* (for something) is a pertinacious contender for, or supporter or advocate of, a cause or a principle, a person or a party, also one who insists on the letter as opposed to the spirit of, e.g., a form or ceremony.

still more yet is redundant for *still more* or *yet more*, as in 'Still more yet is to be said for a strong defensive force'. *Still* (or *yet*) *more* is an intensive of *more* and should not be used unless an intensive is required.

stimulant and **stimulus.** *Stimulant*, in medicine and physiology, is 'something that temporarily quickens some vital process, or the function of some organ'; hence, in general use, 'an alcoholic drink'. *Stimulus* is a medical synonym of the medical sense of *stimulant*, and also, in medicine, it = 'the resulting stimulation'; in general use it is 'an agency or influence that stimulates to action or that quickens an activity or process'; hence, a 'quickening impulse or influence' (as in 'Difficulty is a stimulus'). Plural, *stimuli*. (*O.E.D.*)

sting—**stung** (archaic: **stang**)—**stung**.

stingy and **economical.** An *economical* person is careful of his money, but when occasion calls for liberality he may be generous; a *stingy* person is one who, too careful of his money, is always niggardly.

stolidity. See SOLIDITY.

stomach. See BELLY.

stop in the sense of *stay, remain, sojourn* (at a place or with a friend), though general, is strictly a misuse of the word; *The O.E.D.* allows it, cautiously saying that *stay* 'is more correct'. To *stop off at*, e.g., a hotel, is an American colloquialism.

STOPS. See PUNCTUATION.

storey and story. In the British Empire it is possible and useful to reserve *story* for 'a narrative', *storey* for 'a set of rooms on (or, one large room constituting) one floor or level': this is merely a matter of convenience, for etymologically *storey* is a variant of *story*. *Storey* is to be recommended on the score of clarity: 'the story of a story' is readily distinguishable from 'the story of a storey'; consider, too, 'the storey in this story is the fifth'.—See also 'FLOOR and STOREY'. [In American English the spelling *storey* is exceedingly rare.]

strait, 'narrow, constricted', is occasionally confused with *straight*, 'direct'.

strata is a plural ('layers') and should not be used as a singular, the correct singular being *stratum*. 'Woman, from her childhood, except perhaps in that strata of society which has divorced itself from the common cause of mankind, is ever the mother.' *Data* (singular *datum*) is occasionally misused in the same way. [*Webster's* notes that *data* is 'not infrequently used as a singular'; it brings no such comfort, however, to the users of *strata* as a singular, and for good reason. It is important to distinguish one stratum from another; but *data* is usually collective.]

stratosphere. See TROPOSPHERE.

stress. See VOGUE WORDS.

strike—struck—struck (archaic, stricken). But *stricken* as a participial adjective is actively extant in *a stricken deer* (wounded in the chase); in the science of percussion, it = 'struck with a blow'; in music, *a stricken note* is one produced by striking a blow; *fever-stricken*, *poverty-stricken*, *sorrow-stricken*; in the sense of '(mind, heart) afflicted with frenzy or madness'; jocularly *love-stricken* (*maiden* or *swain*); *stricken measure* (a measure 'having its contents levelled with the brim'); and *stricken field*, 'a pitched battle' (*not* a ravaged field).

string—strung (dialectal, strang)—strung (except as in next entry).

stringed, not *strung*, is the participial adjective to be used

(*a*) of musical instruments ('wind and stringed orchestras'); hence it = 'produced by strings or stringed instruments' (stringed music);

(*b*) in heraldry;

(*c*) and of a running-track divided into 'lanes'.

strive—strove—striven (solecistic: strove).

student. See PUPIL.

studio and study. A *study* is a room in which a student or a scholar studies or works, or a room in which a writer writes, whereas a *studio* is the work-room of a painter or a sculptor—or of a photographer; hence, in cinematography, a room in which cinema-plays are staged; in wireless, a room in which items to be broadcasted are produced; and a room in which gramophone records are made.

stupid person. See MORON.

STYLE. An aesthetic discussion of style would be out of place in this book. Moreover, many of the practical questions of style are dealt with elsewhere: especially, on the positive side, at SUITABILITY and, on the negative side, at WOOLLINESS. Particular aspects are treated here; for instance, the use of the SUBJUNCTIVE, FALSE AGREEMENT, ARCHAISMS, AMBIGUITY, COLLOQUIALISMS and DIALECT and SLANG, CLICHÉ, CONFUSED PARTICIPLES and FUSED PARTICIPLES, ELEGANCIES, GRAMMAR in general, JARGON, LITERARISMS, METAPHOR, OBSCURITY, ORDER, PRECIOUSNESS, PUNCTUATION, SIMPLICITY, kinds of CLAUSE, STANDARD ENGLISH AND AMERICAN, SIMILES (battered), SYNONYMS, TAUTOLOGY, TENSE-SEQUENCE.

But it may be well to recall to the aspirant writer's as to the student's and even the critic's mind, the too often forgotten fact that style is not something that one assumes on special occasions (like dress clothes), but that which one *is* when one writes; so far from being compelled to seek it, one cannot avoid it.

In writing, hence in style, the primary consideration is comprehensibility—therefore clarity; one's first duty is to make oneself understood.

The second is to be adequate to one's theme: the style should be thoroughly suitable to the subject.

The third, which is partly implied in the second, is to write well: forcibly when force is required; beautifully when loveliness is to be described or conveyed; concisely when concision is advisable.

'Without distinction of speech', says Frank Binder, 'there is never much distinction of idea, and therefore it need hardly be said that in no age have men so striven [as in the 20th Century] to be different and yet so frantically failed to be anything but the same. That the style is the man, we know, but this is one of those unfortunate truths which have the licence of all lips and the hospitality of few hearts, and whilst everyone is sighing for personality in others, he shuns the labour of attaining it for himself. He is

pleased with such facility as he has, the facility that comes not of power but of habit, the averaging habit of familiar fluency and of the practised drumming of ordinary ideas. And the thinner the fluid the faster the flow.'
Here is a very brief list of *some* of the more important books on style.

Walter Pater: *Appreciations* (with an essay on style), 1889.

John Addington Symonds: 'Notes on Style' in *Essays, Speculative and Suggestive*, 1890.

Herbert Spencer: *The Philosophy of Style*, edited by Fred Newton Scott, 1895.

Walter Raleigh: *Style*, 1897; very strongly recommended.

Remy de Gourmont: *Le Problème littéraire*, 1902.

Robert Louis Stevenson: *Essays on the Art of Writing*, 1905.

Sir A. Quiller-Couch: *On the Art of Writing*, 1916.

Fred Newton Scott: *Contributions to Rhetorical Theory*, 1918 and after.

J. Middleton Murry: *The Problem of Style*, 1922.

Vernon Lee: *The Handling of Words*, 1923.

Joseph Warren Beach: *The Outlook for American Prose*, 1926.

Herbert Read: *English Prose Style*, 1928.

John Brophy: *English Prose*, 1932.

F. Duchiez & P. C. Jagot: *L'Education du style*, 1934.

Bonamy Dobrée: *Modern Prose Style*, 1934.

S. P. B. Mais: *The Fun of Writing*,* 1937.

E. P.: *English: A Course for Human Beings*, Book III; 1949.

G. H. Vallins: *Good English*, Library Edition, 1952, and *Better English*, Library Edition, 1954.

subconscious. See UNCONSCIOUS.

subject (n.). In 'Roberts shared in all the contraband—many and various in subject—that Smith managed to get hold of', *subject* is misused for *kind, sort*.

subject (v.) is occasionally used catachrestically for *subordinate*, as in '[Newspaper] editors must subject their personal interests to the interests of the community'.

SUBJUNCTIVE. The vexed question of the subjunctive mood has been admirably treated by Dr C. T. Onions in *An*

* A book for young people.

Advanced English Syntax. On his exposition rests the whole of the following article.

'The Subjunctive is a Mood of *Will*; in its simplest uses it expresses *desire*, and all its uses can be traced to this primary meaning.'

In modern English the subjunctive is much less used than formerly—much less, too, than in many of the other European languages. In short, the English subjunctive is, and has long been, in a state of decay:† partly because the English people has become increasingly careless of distinctions of thought; partly because, in subordinate clauses, *may, might, shall, should* have been increasingly substituted for the true or simple subjunctive. For example, *lest he die* has, for the most part, been supplanted by *lest he may die* or *lest he should die*.

But, although it is freely admitted that the use of the subjunctive has been restricted and even, in its survivals, modified, it is foolish 'to say (as is sometimes said) that the Subjunctive, except in the case of *be* and *were*, is an extinct Mood. . . . A careful examination of both the [spoken] and the literary language shows that the Subjunctive is really a living Mood, and that it can never become extinct without an entire reconstruction of certain classes of sentences, e.g., the Conditional sentences [of Group II]. In these sentences we have the Past Subjunctive referring not to Past time but to Present or to Future time, which a Past Indicative could not do', as in '*Were* my brave son at home, he *would* not suffer this' (Present) and in 'If he *were* to do this (or, If he *did* this), he *would* sin' (Future).

Except in certain forms (e.g., *be* and *were*), the subjunctive has been *disguised*: that which, by itself, appears to be an Indicative, may, from the context, emerge clearly as a subjunctive: to the test of form and inflexion must be added the test of *meaning*.

Here is a test of Mood:—In 'It is necessary that I remain here', *remain* is subjunctive because we can also say 'It is

† In *We Who Speak English* Prof. C. A. Lloyd discusses 'the living subjunctive' and the contemporary use of the present subjunctive in substantive clauses after *beg, command, arrange, ask, warn, insist, suggest*, etc. This usage is not noticed by Jespersen or Fowler, and it seems to be predominantly American, although, as Professor Lloyd carefully reports, Fowler himself uses it in the article on *foam, froth* (*Modern English Usage*, p. 184): 'One demands of foam that it *be* white'. So should I.

necessary that he *remain* here'. In 'I wish I had a violin', *had* is subjunctive because we could change the sentence to 'I wish it *were* possible for me to have a violin'.

The most important point, for practical purposes, is the uses of the subjunctive; the most difficult point is the correct tense to employ.

Let us examine the uses of the subjunctive, *A*, in simple sentences and the principal clauses of complex sentences, and *B*, in subordinate clauses.

A. In Simple Sentences and Principal Clauses the subjunctive is used to express 'a wish or request that something may be', as in 'God *bless* you' and 'So *be* it'; or a concession, as in '*Be* that as it may . . .' These subjunctival wishes and concessions are confined to the present tense.

Also 'in the principal clause of conditional sentences implying a negative', as in 'I *would* not say, even if I knew' and 'Had we done it, we *should* have let you know'. It is worth remembering that the only verbs so used are *could*, *would*, *should*, *might* and *must*, although in poetry and poetic prose two others are permitted—*were* (= would be) and *had* (=would have), as in 'If thou hadst been here, my brother *had* not died' (the Bible).

So, too, where the *if*-clause has been omitted, as in 'I *should* like to go' (i.e., if I could), 'How *would* you express it?' (i.e., if you were asked), and 'Anyone *might* see that he is not well' (i.e., if he looked).

B. In Subordinate Clauses the uses of the subjunctive are more numerous—as might be expected.

i. In conditional sentences of Group II (see CONDITIONAL SENTENCES) the tense is either the past or the pluperfect.

ii. In clauses introduced by *if* or *though* subordinated to *as* or then representing a comparative clause, as in 'I feel as if I *were* going to fall'. See COMPARATIVE CLAUSES.

iii. In conditional sentences of Group III, 'where the Subjunctive implies *reserve*, or is *restrictive*', as in 'If it *be* so. . .' . See CONDITIONAL CLAUSES.

iv. In noun clauses depending on a verb of *will* or *request*. This is usual in statutes and notices. 'It is requested that letters to the Editor *be* written on one side of the paper only': 'The regulation is that no candidate *take* a book into the examination room'. Also 'It was requested . . .

should be written . . .'; 'The regulation was that . . . should take . . .', though even here the present subjunctive is more common, this present-for-past-subjunctive being a hall-mark of officialese.

In noun clauses dependent on *it is* (*not*) *right*, *it is wrong*, *it is necessary*, *it is not possible*, and *is it possible?*, as in 'It is right (or, not right; or, is it right?) that you *be* dismissed', 'It is necessary that he *go*'. Note, however, that the simple subjunctive is less usual than a subjunctive-equivalent, as in 'It is right (etc.) that he *should be* dismissed' and 'Is it necessary that he *should go?*' After *is it possible?* and *it is impossible* the subjunctive-equivalent, as in 'Is it possible that he *should be* such a fool?', is almost obligatory, for 'Is it possible that he *be* such a fool?' and 'It is impossible that he *be* such a fool', are archaic. Where 'is it possible?' is merely exclamatory, the indicative is obligatory, as in 'Is it possible that he *has* left England?'

In noun clauses dependent on *wish* and the archaic *would*, to indicate the object of the wish, as in 'I wish I *were* there' or 'had been there' or 'could have been there'; and in '*Would* that he *had* lived', where *would* = *I would*.

In noun clauses dependent on a verb of emotion, 'where the speaker contemplates the *thought* of something happening rather than its actually happening'; not the simple subjunctive but the *should*-equivalent is used here. 'I grieved that you *should* be so angry'; 'That he has acted thus is a misfortune, but that he *should* have acted thus is not surprising'.

v. In temporal clauses of a certain type; i.e., when the temporal clause refers to the future, whether from a present or from a past viewpoint. The simple subjunctive is now confined to poetry and poetic or, at the least, lofty prose, as in 'This night, before the cock *crow*, thou shalt deny me thrice' and 'The sun a backward course shall take ere aught thy manly courage *shake*'. But the *shall* and *should* equivalents—in which, by the way, it is *shall* or *should* in all persons and both numbers—are common in ordinary good prose as well as in lofty prose, as in 'When his eyesight *shall fail*, he will apply for a pension' and 'He decided to wait until the car *should pass* him'; here too, however, the indicative is fast becoming more usual, as in 'He decided to wait until the car passed him'. I ought to have written 'apparent indicative', for *passed* is a virtual subjunctive in this sentence, whereas it is indubitably indicative in 'He decided to wait—until the car passed him. The car's passing made him immediately change his mind.' It is obvious that the discarding of the subjunctive in such temporal clauses as these would lead to ambiguity.

vi. In final clauses (clauses of purpose) introduced by *less*:

Lord God of Hosts, be with us yet,
Lest we *forget*, lest we *forget* (Kipling).

vii. In concessive clauses:

'Though he *do* his best, his best is bad';
'Try as he *might*, he failed'.

viii. In general relative clauses, especially in the past—

Calm, but not overcast, he stood
Resigned to the decree, whatever it *were*
(Byron),

where it would now be avoided even in poetry; Bacon's 'However it *be* between nations, certainly it is so between man and man' is archaic, though not ludicrously so, but if we change his sentence, to 'However it *may be* . . . , certainly . . .' we get an effect of good prose; the substitution of the subjunctive-equivalent for the simple subjunctive has made all the difference, as indeed it would in a general relative clause in the past tense: change Byron's two verses to prose and you get 'He stood calm, but not overcast: resigned to the verdict, whatever it *might be*', which is ordinary good prose.

ix. In dependent questions:

'All men mused [= wondered] whether he *were* Christ' (the Bible); 'Even those who had often seen him were at first in doubt whether he *were* the brilliant and graceful Monmouth' (Macaulay).

TENSES OF THE SUBJUNCTIVE. In the subjunctive, as in the indicative, the tenses are those which conform to that general and invaluable principle which is known as the sequence of tenses. See TENSE-SEQUENCE.

'I have told you that you *may* know';
'The headmaster said that we *might* have a holiday';
'He took care that his form master *should* not see him';
'If you *did* it [either now or in the future], you *would* repent it' (either now or in the future);
'She looked as though she *were* fainting'.

sublimate is occasionally misused for 'to *subordinate*'.

sublimation. A recent vogue word.
sublime, sublimated; subliminal. Of these three terms, the first is the only one now in general as distinguished from psychological use. *Sublime* = 'elevated, lofty, exalted', literally and figuratively; hence, 'supreme', 'perfect'; in literature and aesthetics, it = 'apt or designed to inspire awe, deep reverence, lofty emotion, by beauty or grandeur'. *Sublimated* in the sense 'lofty, sublime', is obsolescent: better discard it! In chemistry, it = 'produced by the process of sublimation'; in psychology, it = (of a primitive impulse) 'modified and adapted, especially to the needs of civilization', as in *sublimated sex, sublimated savagery*. *Subliminal* is also a psychological term; it = 'below the threshold of sensation or consciousness, pertaining to the subliminal self', as in *subliminal consciousness*.—The corresponding nouns are *sublimity* or *the sublime*; *sublimation*; *a* or *the subliminal*.

submit for *subject* is not wrong, but it is virtually obsolete, as one realizes on encountering such a sentence as: 'He submitted the carpet . . . to the same microscopic scrutiny'.
submittance is obsolete for *submission*.
subnormal. See ABNORMAL.
subscription. See SUPERSCRIPTION.
subsequent. See CONSEQUENT.
subsist. See EXIST.
substantial and **substantive.** Apart from technical senses, these terms are synonymous except in the following senses of *substantial*:—real or true in the main ('On the whole, substantial justice had been done'); of real worth, repute, reliability ('The substantial intellect of the country'); (of persons) wealthy, weighty, influential ('A substantial Scottish grazier'); (of structures) made of solid material, of good workmanship ('a substantial house'); (of food) very nutritious, (of a meal) solid. And except in these senses of *substantive*:—(Of persons, nations, groups or associations of persons) independent ('substantive inventors'); not transitory ('Let us call the resting-places the "substantive parts", and the places of flight the "transitive parts", of the stream of thought', Wm James). The chief senses in which *substantial* and *substantive* are synonymous are:—Material or essential; not imaginary, not illusory; i.e., real; having a firm basis, solidly established; of considerable amount or quantity, valuable or effective because of large numbers. (*O.E.D.*)

substitute, misused. 'He must substitute sugar by saccharin' should be 'He must substitute saccharin for sugar'.

substract is a surprisingly common error for *subtract.*—*Subtract* and *detract* are occasionally confused. Both mean to deduct, but *detract* is applied only to virtue, reputation, status (see DE-TRACT . . .); *subtract* is rare in a figurative sense, George Eliot's 'The transient pink flush . . . subtracted nothing from her majesty' now seeming obsolescent; *subtract* is, in current usage, virtually confined to mathematics.

subtile is archaic for *subtle* in every sense except the medical one: (of feeling or sense) 'acute, keen'. In Dorland's *Medical Dictionary* it is defined as 'keen and acute, as, a subtile pain'.

succeed and **follow** are not synonymous; the latter having usually 'a literal and physical sense' and being applicable 'to many persons or things at the same time' ('A thousand sheep followed the bell-wether'); *succeed* 'usually means to come next after and take the place of. It implies only two individuals' or two groups or bodies viewed as units, as in 'Haig succeeded French', 'Winter succeeds autumn', 'A National government succeeds a Labour one'.

successively and **successfully** are sometimes confused. The latter = 'with success', the former = 'in succession', 'consecutively'.

such for *any* or *any such* or *this* or *that* (or *these* or *those*). 'For the sake of verisimilitude the scenes of this story have been laid in real places. All the characters introduced, however, are wholly imaginary, and if the name of any living person has been used, this has been done inadvertently and no reference to such person is intended'; 'Of the Roman's earthworks, if such were made, no traces remain'.

such for *of them*. This odd misusage occurs in ' "Will you suggest some names as possibilities?"—"No, there are too many such." '

such for *similar*: to be used cautiously.

such for *so* (pronoun). 'With this being such he will always be an ever-awake and useful member of society.'

such for *some one*. ' "Can you suggest . . . anyone who wished his death?"— "Mercy, no!"—"Yet there must have been such. Somebody killed him." '

such for *such a thing*. 'No unauthorised objects or materials could . . . have been included. He wished to take strong excep-tion to the suggestion that such might have occurred.'

such for *such part* or *such portion*. 'His eyes ran quickly over such of the interior . . . as they could reach', John G. Brandon.

such for *such things*. '. . . Cabalistic figures . . . French kept all such, though he doubted they would be helpful'; 'They [500 petrol-electric sets] were to be larger than such are usually made'; 'We had seen enough of the folly of complete strangers maiming and slaughtering each other under conditions of extreme discomfort and degradation for the sake of national honour and glory. Like Old Caspar, we had come to recognise from bitter experience, that no good ever came of such.'

such, none. See NONE SUCH.

such a (or **an**) + adjective + noun for *so* + adjective + *a(n)* + noun or for noun + *so* (or *thus*) + adjective, is to be avoided. In the sentence:

'The critics attacked McCabe, the author, for having invented such an un-believable character [the detective, Smith], instead of attacking Smith, the [actual] man, for being what he was': write, 'for having invented so un-believable a character' or, better here, 'a character so [or, thus] unbelievable', for any of these three changes (especially the third) would dispel the ambiguity; 'such an' leads some readers to suppose that the sentence will continue in some such way as this—'[The critics attacked McCabe . . . for having invented such an unbelievable character] as he, the author, makes him out to be'.

such a much 'That is why . . . Rugby is such a much better game than Associa-tion' is ugly and incorrect; for it should be 'Rugby is so much better a game . . .'; 'She was going to copy her stepfather, who was such a much smarter proposi-tion than her own father': 'So very much smarter a proposition' would be pre-ferable.

such another, a transposition of the correct *another such*. Edwin Pugh, ' "Ah, that was a funeral!" "I'm sure Marsh Street ain't likely to see sech another for many . . ." '

such as for *as, for example* or *for instance*. 'When the resistance to the complex is weakened, such as in sleep, the com-plexes may reappear'; 'The same lan-guage may predominate over a very large area, such as the English language pre-dominates in England.'

such as for *what* or *so much as*. 'Then he mooched to another window and surveyed such as was to be seen of the rear of the place from that point.'

such . . . that for *such . . . as*. 'He was even allowed to dust such objects of the precious collection that were not kept under glass.'

such . . . which (or who) is incorrect for *such as*. '[She had] a real compassion for such cases of hardship which were clamped down under her eyes'; 'Such of my acquaintances who care to submit themselves . . .'; 'The very fact that they lived in an enclosed intimacy not to be found in an ordinary road is sufficient to exaggerate such small annoyances and dissensions which from time to time arise'. The mistake probably arises from a confusion with *those . . . which.*—Cf. SUCH . . . THAT.

suffer with for *suffer from* a disease or disability is bad English; the 'suffering' is caused by and derived *from* the disease.

sufferance; suffering. The former is archaic as a synonym of the latter noun. Except for a legal sense, *sufferance* is extant only as = 'acquiescence, consent, sanction, permission, toleration', and mostly in the phrase *on sufferance*; 'He is on sufferance', 'a Cabinet on sufferance'. (*O.E.D.*)

sufficient and enough. The main difference between them as adjectives is that, before a noun, *enough* takes no article; *sufficient* does take one, or omits it, according to the context ('a sufficient income' but 'sufficient money'). The adverbs are *sufficiently* and *enough*. The nouns are *sufficient* and *enough*; despite Weseen, *sufficient*, which never takes an article, is faultless English in 'Sufficient has been done for pride; now let us think of comfort'; 'We saw sufficient to account for the noise'. *Sufficience* is archaic; *sufficiency*, which generally takes an article (except in the sense 'adequate provision of food; adequate bodily comfort'), has three main senses:—A competence ('to retire on a sufficiency'), though this is obsolescent; adequacy ('to report on the sufficiency of an examination candidate's work'); enough ('a sufficiency of wood for fuel'). (*O.E.D.*)

suffragette; suffragist. The former is—or rather, was—a rabid female supporter of female suffrage; the latter is merely any supporter (not necessarily violent nor militant) of female suffrage.

SUITABILITY AND ADEQUACY. *Ingenium par materiae* (ability equal to one's theme).

Broadly, adequacy* is such treatment of a theme as is felt to be not only and merely in keeping but also fully worthy of it, no matter how profound, moving, subtle or lovely the theme. To be adequate, therefore, is more than to be suitable; one may have—or adopt—a style suitable to a subject and yet prove unequal to that subject. One's conception may be excellent, but one's execution faulty: the road to style is paved with good intentions. Style must be clear, effective, aesthetically and emotionally adequate.

Here, more than anywhere else, practice is better than precept. And so I adduce a certain number of passages in which the manner suits the matter and the style is adequate to the theme. (The ensuing examples have been taken from Sir Arthur Quiller-Couch's *The Oxford Book of English Prose*.)

'Let us now praise famous men, and our fathers that begat us. The Lord hath wrought great glory by them, through his great power from the beginning. Such as did bear rule in their kingdoms, men renowned for their power, giving counsel by their understanding, and declaring prophecies: leaders of the people by their counsels, and by their knowledge of learning meet for the people, wise and eloquent in their instructions. Such as found out musical tunes, and recited verses in writing. Rich men furnished with ability, living peaceably in their habitations. All these were honoured in their generations, and were the glory of their times. There be of them, that have left a name behind them, that their praises might be reported. And some there be, which have no memorial, who are perished as though they had never been, and are become as though they had never been born, and their children after them. But these were merciful men, whose righteousness hath not been forgotten. With their seed shall remain a good inheritance, and their children are within the covenant. Their seed stands fast and their children for their sakes. Their seed shall remain for ever, and their glory shall not be blotted out. Their bodies are buried in peace, but their name liveth for evermore.'
Ecclesiasticus (Authorized Version, 1611).

That is a rhetorical style, drawing much

---

* I use the word, not as = bare adequacy (cf. the common phrase, 'barely adequate'), but as = complete adequacy.

of its beauty and effectiveness from rhythm, sense-repetition, word-repetition. Contrast it with:—

'All the powder of the *Revenge* to the last barrel was now spent, all her pikes broken, forty of her best men slain, and the most part of the rest hurt. In the beginning of the fight she had but one hundred free from sickness, and fourscore and ten sick, laid in hold upon the ballast. A small troop to man such a ship, and a weak garrison to resist so mighty an army. By those hundred all was sustained, the volleys, boardings, and enterings of fifteen ships of war, besides those which beat her at large. On the contrary, the Spanish were always supplied with soldiers brought from every squadron: all manner of arms and powder at will. Unto ours there remained no comfort at all, no hope, no supply either of ships, men or weapons; the masts all beaten overboard, all her tackle cut asunder, her upper work altogether razed, and in effect evened she was with the water, but the very foundation or bottom of a ship, nothing being left overhead either for flight or defence. Sir Richard, finding himself in this distress, and unable any longer to make resistance . . .; and that himself and the ship must needs be possessed by the enemy . . .: commanded the master gunner, whom he knew to be a most resolute man, to split and sink the ship; that thereby nothing might remain of glory or victory to the Spaniards . . .'

Sir Walter Raleigh, The Last Fight of the Revenge, from a Report, published in 1591.

With this plain prose compare the following passage on death from Raleigh's *A History of the World*, 1614, concerning 'the kings and princes of the world':—

'They neglect the advice of God while they enjoy life, or hope it; but they follow the counsel of Death upon his first approach. It is he that puts into man all the wisdom of the world without speaking a word. . . . He tells the proud and insolent that they are but abjects, and humbles them at the instant; makes them cry, complain, and repent, yea, even to hate their forepassed happiness. He takes the account of the rich and proves him a beggar. . . . He holds a glass before the eyes of the most beautiful, and makes them see therein their deformity and rottenness; and they acknowledge it.— O eloquent, just and mighty Death!

whom none could advise, thou hast persuaded; what none hath dared thou hast done; and whom all the world hath flattered, thou only hast cast out of the world and despised: thou hast drawn together all the far-stretched greatness, all the pride, cruelty, and ambition of man, and covered it all over with these two narrow words, *Hic jacet*.'

With Raleigh on death, compare Bacon:—

'Men fear Death as children fear to go in the dark; and as that natural fear in children is increased with tales, so is the other. Certainly, the contemplation of Death, as the wages of sin and passage to another world, is holy and religious; but the fear of it, as a tribute due unto Nature, is weak. . . . It is as natural to die as to be born; and to a little infant perhaps the one is as painful as the other. He that dies in an earnest pursuit is like one that is wounded in hot blood, who, for the time, scarce feels the hurt; and therefore a mind fixed and bent upon somewhat that is good doth avert the dolours of Death: but, above all, believe it, the sweetest canticle is *Nunc dimittis*, when a man hath obtained worthy ends and expectations. Death hath this also, that it openeth the gate to good fame, and extinguisheth envy.'

I have spoken elsewhere of poetic prose, but there I gave no example. Here is one, chosen from Thomas Traherne's *Centuries of Meditations* rather than from Sir Thomas Browne's more famous works.

'You never enjoy the world aright, till the Sea itself floweth in your veins, till you are clothed with the heavens, and crowned with the stars: and perceive yourself to be the sole heir of the whole world, and more than so, because men are in it who are every one sole heirs as well as you. Till you can sing and rejoice and delight in God, as misers do in gold, and Kings in sceptres you never enjoy the world.—Till your spirit filleth the whole world, and the stars are your jewels; till you are as familiar with the ways of God in all Ages as with your walk and table: till you are intimately acquainted with that shady nothing out of which the world was made: till you love men so as to desire their happiness, with a thirst equal to the zeal of your own: till you delight in God for being good to all: you never enjoy the world.'

In *Some Fruits of Solitude* (1693), William Penn, on 'The Comfort of

Friends', wrote thus:—'They that love beyond the world cannot be separated by it.

Death cannot kill what never dies.

Nor can spirits ever be divided, that love and live in the same divine principle, the root and record of their friendship.

If absence be not death, neither is theirs.

Death is but crossing the world, as friends do the seas; they live in one another still.

For they must needs be present, that love and live in that which is omnipresent.

In this divine glass they see face to face; and their converse is free, as well as pure.

This is the comfort of friends, that though they may be said to die, yet their friendship and society are, in the best sense, ever preserved, because immortal.'

Let us turn to Addison and take a short passage from his paper on the Royal Exchange (*The Spectator*, 1711–14):—'Our ships are laden with the harvest of every climate: our tables are stored with spices, and oils, and wines: our rooms are filled with pyramids of China, and adorned with the workmanship of Japan: our morning's draught comes to us from the remotest corners of the earth: we repair our bodies by the drugs of America, and repose ourselves under Indian canopies. . . . For these reasons there are not more useful members in a commonwealth than merchants. They knit mankind together in a mutual intercourse of good offices, distribute the gifts of Nature, find work for the poor, add wealth to the rich, and magnificence to the great. Our English merchant converts the tin of his own country into gold, and exchanges his wool for rubies. The Mahometans are clothed in our British manufacture, and the inhabitants of the frozen zone warmed with the fleeces of our sheep.'

From Gibbon comes this:

'It is a very honourable circumstance for the morals of the primitive Christians, that even their faults, or rather errors, were derived from an excess of virtue. The bishops and doctors of the church, whose evidence attests, and whose authority might influence, the professions, the principles, and even the practice, of their contemporaries, had studied the scriptures with less skill than devotion, and they often received, in the most literal sense, those rigid precepts of Christ and the apostles to which the prudence of succeeding commentators has applied a looser and more figurative mode of interpretation. Ambitious to exalt the perfection of the gospel above the wisdom of philosophy, the zealous fathers have carried the duties of self-mortification, of purity, and of patience, to a height which it is scarcely possible to attain, and much less to preserve, in our present state of weakness and corruption. A doctrine so extraordinary and so sublime must inevitably command the veneration of the people; but it was ill calculated to obtain the suffrage of those worldly philosophers who, in the conduct of this transitory life, consult only the feelings of nature and the interest of society. . . . It was not in *this* world that the primitive Christians were desirous of making themselves either agreeable or useful' (*The Decline and Fall of the Roman Empire*, 1776–1781).

With that, the grand style, contrast this simpler style of Robert Southey in *The Life of Nelson*, 1813:—'Early on the following morning he reached Portsmouth; and having dispatched his business on shore, endeavoured to elude the populace by taking a by-way to the beach; but a crowd collected in his train, pressing forward, to obtain a sight of his face: many were in tears, and many knelt down before him, and blessed him as he passed. England has had many heroes; but never one who so entirely possessed the love of his fellow-countrymen as Nelson. All men knew that his heart was as humane as it was fearless; that there was not in his nature the slightest alloy of selfishness or cupidity; but that, with perfect and entire devotion, he served his country with all his heart, and with all his soul, and with all his strength; and, therefore, they loved him as truly as and as fervently as he loved England. They pressed upon the parapet, to gaze after him when his barge pushed off, and he was returning their cheers by waving his hat. The sentinels, who endeavoured to prevent them from trespassing upon his ground, were wedged among the crowd; and an officer, who, not very prudently upon such an occasion, ordered them to drive the people down with their bayonets, was compelled speedily to retreat; for the people would not be debarred from gazing, till the last moment, upon the hero—the darling hero of England.'

And now, one of the great masters of

prose—Walter Savage Landor ('Aesop and Rhodope', *Imaginary Conversations*):

Rhodope. . . . Let me pause and consider a little, if you please. I begin to suspect that, as gods formerly did, you have been turning men into beasts, and beasts into men. But, Aesop, you should never say the thing that is untrue.

Aesop. We say and do and look no other all our lives.

Rhodope. Do we never know better?

Aesop. Yes; when we cease to please, and to wish it; when death is settling the features, and the cerements are ready to render them unchangeable.

Rhodope. Alas! Alas!

Aesop. Breathe, Rhodope! breathe again those painless sighs: they belong to the vernal season. May thy summer of life be calm, thy autumn calmer, and thy winter never come!

Rhodope. I must die then earlier.

Aesop. Laodameia died; Helen died; Leda, the beloved of Jupiter, went before. It is better to repose in the earth betimes than to sit up late; better, than to cling pertinaciously to what we feel crumbling under us, and to protract an inevitable fall. We may enjoy the present, while we are insensible to infirmity and decay; but the present, like a note in music, is nothing but as it appertains to what is past and what is to come. There are no fields of amaranth on this side of the grave; there are no voices, O Rhodope, that are not soon mute, however tuneful; there is no name, with whatever emphasis of passionate love repeated, of which the echo is not faint at last.

Rhodope. O Aesop! Let me rest my head on yours: it throbs and pains me.

Aesop. What are these ideas to thee?

Rhodope. Sad, sorrowful.

Aesop. Harrows that break the soil, preparing it for wisdom. Many flowers must perish ere a grain of corn be ripened. And now remove thy head: the cheek is cool enough after its little shower of tears.

Again in contrast, an extract from that admirably lucid and effective writer, Macaulay (from his essay on Clive):—
'The river was passed; and, at the close of a toilsome day's march, the army, long after sunset, took up its quarters in a grove of mango-trees near Plassey, within a mile of the enemy. Clive was unable to sleep; he heard, through the whole night, the sound of drums and cymbals from the vast camp of the Nabob. It is not strange that even his stout heart should now and then have sunk, when he reflected against what odds, and for what a prize, he was in a few hours to contend. . . . The day broke, the day which was to decide the fate of India. At sunrise the army of the Nabob, pouring through many openings from the camp, began to move towards the grove where the English lay. Forty thousand infantry, armed with firelocks, pikes, swords, bows and arrows, covered the plain. They were accompanied by fifty pieces of ordnance. . . . The cavalry were fifteen thousand. . . . The force which [Clive] had to oppose to this great multitude consisted of only three thousand men. But of these nearly a thousand were English; and all were led by English officers, and trained in the English discipline. . . . The battle commenced with a cannonade in which the artillery of the Nabob did scarcely any execution, while the few field-pieces of the English produced great effect. Several of the most distinguished officers in Surajah Dowlah's service fell. Disorder began to spread through his ranks. His own terror increased every moment. . . . He ordered his army to fall back, and this order decided his fate. Clive snatched the moment, and ordered his troops to advance. The confused and dispirited multitude gave way before the onset of disciplined valour. No mob attacked by regular soldiers was ever more completely routed. The little band of Frenchmen, who alone ventured to confront the English, were swept down the stream of fugitives. In an hour the forces of Surajah Dowlah were dispersed, never to reassemble.'

Before passing to an example of contemporary prose, I should like to quote John Henry Newman's definition of a gentleman (*The Idea of a University*, 1852):—'It is almost a definition of a gentleman to say he is one who never inflicts pain. . . . He is mainly occupied in merely removing the obstacles which hinder the free and unembarrassed action of those about him; and he concurs with their movements rather than takes the initiative himself. . . . The true gentleman . . . carefully avoids what may cause a jar or a jolt in the minds of those with whom he is cast;—all clashing of opinion or collision of feeling, all restraint, or suspicion, or gloom, or resentment. . . . He has his eyes on all his company; he is tender towards the bashful, gentle towards the distant, and merciful towards the absurd; he can recollect to whom he is speaking; he guards against unseasonable allusions, or topics which may irritate; he is seldom prominent in conversation and never wearisome. He makes light of favours while he does them, and seems to be receiving when he is conferring. He never speaks of himself except when compelled, never defends himself by a mere retort. He has no ears for slander or gossip, is scrupulous in imputing motives to those who interfere with him, and interprets everything for the best. He is never mean or little in his disputes. . . . He has too much good sense to be affronted at insults, he is too well employed to remember injuries, and too indolent to bear malice. He is patient, forbearing, and resigned, on philosophical principles; he submits to pain, because it is inevitable, to bereavement, because it is irreparable, and to death, because it is his destiny. If he engages in controversy of any kind, his disciplined intellect preserves him from the blundering discourtesy of better, though less educated minds. . . . He may be right or wrong in his opinion, but he is too clear-headed to be unjust; he is as simple as he is forcible, and as brief as he is decisive.'

In conclusion, an extract from Frank Binder, *Dialectic*, 1932.

'Life has its alternative, the ironic one of being angled at the bank or netted at the weir. We may escape the philosophy of form with its interplay of fate and personality, of the world without and the will within, and flee to the philosophy of measures with its processes of evidence, fact and proof. Here at least we are safe, or think we are, from the flats and shifting sands of superstition, and may sail on our daylight ways, scientific, assured, and open-eyed, along the charted paths of the seas. The port is fixed, the track defined, the times determined, yet even these our modern ways, like all the wisdom of the world, are writ on water. For just as religion is fallibly poised on the floating mote of faith, so science is no less parlously embarked on the dubious bubble of a measure, on something that has no absolute standing, a something that, in want of niches in space and time, cannot be measured itself nor be assessed in ultimate units. Indeed, were the world in flux, pulsating to all sizes yet keeping the ratio in every part, or speeding and staying the flight of time with proportional pace and delay in ourselves, we should not know it, and still should deem our measures, which swelled and lapsed in concert, as fixed and final for the universe itself. And to this myth of immutable measures comes the illusion of simultaneity, since for all experiments, comparisons, and proofs, whereby a synchronism is assumed, there is a passage through space and time, the measure being brought to the object measured, the proof following by an interval of thought. Yet we are asked to believe that in transpositions from spot to spot, and in references from a moment to a moment succeeding, there is a constancy in the object thought of, that it keeps a congruence in all its motions, and ceteris paribus always is what it was before. But how are we to prove this when no two points in space or time may be placed together for comparison? and since by the latest theory matter determines the space whereby it is contained, so with equal truth may space determine matter. With an equal truth we may assume that change is a change in the medium which surrounds us, that we fall like a fluid into the mould of the world, into the play of its principles and lineament of its seasons, and take on by adaptation the idiosyncrasies of time. And though we scout the thought as dialectic, how without a synchronism is this to be proved?'

A careful study of the preceding examples will show what is meant by *adequacy*, for these examples are in styles that are more than merely *suitable*.

summary; précis; abstract; abridgement. See PRÉCIS, par. 2.

Sunday. See SABBATH.

sung. See SING.

sunk. See SINK.

sunlight and **sunlit**, adjectives. Cf. the entry at 'STARLIGHT and STARLIT'.

sunlight; sunshine. The former is simply the light of the sun, whereas the latter is the shining of the sun, but also 'direct sunlight uninterrupted by cloud'. (*O.E.D.*) 'Sunshine peeping through some little window' (Dickens), 'There was a long fight between mist and sunshine' (Tyndall), 'He sat in the sunshine'; 'Sunlight is dispensed mainly from carbon'. (*O.E.D.*)

sunshade. See PARASOL.

super, in the senses 'very good', 'very efficient (or, effectual)', is becoming so general that even educated persons are beginning to forget that it is slang.
superincumbent. See RECUMBENT.
superior than. See INFERIOR THAN.
superlative. See COMPARATIVES, FALSE.
SUPERLATIVE DEGREE. The general rule is that the superlative is to be used only when there are three or more persons or things, as in 'He is the better runner of the two', 'She was the prettiest of them all'. But the pair *the former . . . the latter* ('There were two battles, A. and B.: the former was at X., the latter at Y.') is beginning to break down—to yield to *the first . . . the second*: a tendency to be resisted. Where only one of the two is mentioned, *former* and *latter* retain their potency: we say 'There were two battles . . .; only the former was important' or '. . . only the latter can be described here'.
superscription; subscription; signature. The first does not, the second does (though now rarely), mean a signature. *Subscription* is an act, or the action, of affixing a signature or of signing one's name; *superscription*, a heading, a piece of writing at the beginning of a document, is archaic in the sense 'address (on an envelope containing a letter)'.*(O.E.D.)* The same remarks apply to *subscribe*, *superscribe*.
supersede (to take the place of) is occasionally misused for *surpass*. 'Women supersede men in scholarship.'
supine. See PRONE.
supple is sometimes confused with *subtle*. If, greatly daring, one speaks of 'a supple mind', one means, not a subtle but an agile mind or a mind readily adapting itself.
supplement and **complement**. Whereas a *complement* is an integral second part or portion, a *supplement* is additional to something that was at first thought to be complete. To *supplement* is to augment or to add something to (to supplement something *with* something else; to supplement an income); to *complement* is to complete by adding an essential part, to supply what is (conspicuously) wanting. The adjectives are *complementary* and *supplementary*.
suppose. See SUSPECT.
supposedly, misused for *presumably*. 'X. is supposedly the guilty party' should be 'X. is presumably the guilty party'.
suppositious and **supposititious; suppositional**. For 'supposed; based on—or at

the least, involving—supposition', *suppositional* is now more common than *suppositious*. *Supposititious* (child) is one 'set up to displace the real heir or successor'; as applied to a writing, or a passage or even a word therein, it = spurious, counterfeit, false, forged. *(O.E.D.)*
supra-normal. See ABNORMAL.
surmise. See SUSPECT.
surprise. See ASTONISH.
surprised; astonished, amazed, astounded. As adjectives expressive of the feeling of wonder, these four are in ascending order of intensity. Originally, *surprised* meant 'suddenly attacked, assailed without warning', then 'taken unawares', hence 'detected, suddenly discovered', of which the first survives only as a military term.
suspect; surmise; suppose. 'To *suspect*' may be employed as a synonym of 'to *surmise*', but it is better to reserve it for pejorative uses. To *surmise* is 'to form a notion that the thing in question may be so, on slight grounds or without proof; to infer conjecturally', as in 'Whatever you may surmise about a future life, it is your duty to do your best by this one'. To *suppose* is 'to posit, for argument's sake'; especially, 'to incline to think; to entertain as an idea', as in 'Do you suppose that she wished to remain unmarried?' and 'The roads were no better than the old Squire had supposed'. *(O.E.D.)*
SUSPENDED PARTICIPLE, THE. Also known as the Misrelated Participle, this is treated fully at CONFUSED PARTICIPLES.
'Informing a maidservant that I desired private speech with her master, she explained that Mr Mannering was still at breakfast', Eden Phillpotts. 'Having said so much, you will expect me, I suppose, to begin talking about . . .', Hilaire Belloc.
suspicion for 'to *suspect*' is to be avoided.
sustain, in *to sustain a fracture*, is a bad, unnecessary word, and appears to be suggested only by an excessive sense of the gravity of the occasion or by a wish to imitate (bad) medical jargon. 'He fell from a ladder and broke his leg' says all that can be conveyed by 'sustained a fracture', and the use of *sustain* in this sense robs it of its true meaning, *to support, to uphold*. *Sustain injuries* is, by many newspaper editors in their style sheets, condemned as incorrect for *receive injuries*.
swang. See SWING.

sweat (n. and v.) is a better word than *perspiration* and *perspire*. Obviously if you do not wish to offend a lady, you do not tell her that she seems to be sweating freely, but the euphemistic, mealy-mouthed days of 'Horses sweat, men perspire, and women glow' have gone; certainly, men at least prefer to sweat. *Sweat—sweated* (less usual, *sweat*) *—sweated* (rarely *sweat*); participial adjective, *sweated*.

swell—swelled—swollen, less commonly **swelled**. The participial adjective is *swollen*.

swim—swam—swum.

swing—swung (rarely **swang**)—**swung**.

Sybil (or s-), **sybyllic** (= the next), **sybylline**, **sybyllism**, **sybyllist**, **sybyllistic**; inferior to the spellings in *si-* (*Sibyl*, etc.): for the old French is *Sibile* or *Sibylle*; Med. Latin, *Sibilla*, *Sibylla*, *Sibulla*; Greek *Sibulla*.

syllabification (a dividing into syllables) is preferable to *syllabication*.

synonym of and **synonym for**; **synonymous with** (not *of*, nor *for*). The correct use may be exemplified in three short sentences, thus:—'A synonym of *quick* is *fast*'; 'Synonyms for *rapid* are hard to find'; '*Mankind* is not synonymous with generic *man*'.

SYNONYMS: AND THE HERESY OF VARIETY, especially in dialogue.

There are extremely few exact synonyms; but here, as usually, *The O.E.D.* puts the case so well that to attempt to vie with its definition is not merely ineptitude and self-conceit but a form of madness.

'Strictly, a word having the same sense as another (in the same language); but more usually, either or any of two or more words having the same general sense, but each of them possessing meanings which are not shared by the other or others, or having different shades of meaning or implications appropriate to different contexts: e.g., *serpent, snake*; *ship, vessel*; *compassion, fellow-feeling, sympathy*; *enormous, excessive, immense*; *glad, happy, joyful, joyous*; *to kill, slay, slaughter*; *to grieve, mourn, lament, sorrow*.'

The educated person does not need to be told that, in the desire for variety, to consult a dictionary of synonyms (so called) and take haphazard an apparent synonym is to expose himself to the risk —almost to the certainty—of making himself ridiculous. But, as a stylistic device (for the sake of emphasis or

euphony), synonyms are frequently used. Some are imbedded in idiom (*to have and to hold*) and cliché (*free, gratis and for nothing*); others are stylistic (*the inaudible and noiseless foot of time*; *a figure, type, symbol, or prefiguration*); and both sorts are tautological.

If you are in doubt as to which of two synonyms to use, consult a good dictionary that cites abundant examples.

It is dangerous to achieve variety at the expense of the meaning. Do not hesitate to use the same word or even the same phrase twice in the one sentence, if the repetition prevents an ambiguity. Such variety as is seen in 'The person did not know what to do. This individual asked someone what he should do. Indeed, the man asked several by-standers what they advised' is absurd.

A very useful book is *The Choice of Words*, by V. H. Collins.

systematic and **systemic**. The general word is *systematic*; *systemic* being confined to physiology, in which it now = 'belonging to, supplying, or affecting the system or body as a whole', as in 'The . . . systemic sensation of hunger', 'systemic effects'; and to pathology, in which it now = 'belonging to or affecting the nervous system or special parts of it', as in 'systemic sclerosis of a small but defined tract of the spinal cord'. (*O.E.D.*)

systematize is superior to **systemize**.

T

TAGS. See CLICHÉ.

take leave, as in 'I take leave to argue the point', is inferior to *take the liberty* (of arguing the point).

take on, in the sense of *get excited, be 'upset'* about anything, is a harmless vulgarism: 'There's Missis walking about the drawing-room, taking on awful'.

talent. See GENIUS.

talisman has plural *talismans*—not *talismen*. Do not confuse *talisman*, amulet or charm, with *talesman* (pl. *talesmen*), one of the *tales* or persons added to a jury to make up a deficiency in number.

talk is infelicitous—too informal—for *speech* or *address* or *lecture* in such examples as the following:—'A talk on disarmament', 'Twelve talks on French Romantic Literature'.

talkies, the. See MOTION PICTURES.

tall is opposed to *short*, as *high* is to *low*. 'A tall hill, a tall house' should ordinarily be 'a high hill', 'a high house'; *tall timber* (woods with high trees) is an Americanism. But ships and trees are *tall* when they are high in proportion to their width, especially in such collocations as *a tall chimney* or *house, a tall mast* or *ship, a tall column* or *spire*, Also, *tall* is applied to things that are 'of more than average length measured from bottom to top'— e.g., *a tall hat, a tall copy* of a book.

tankard for *mug*. 'What pseudo-ancient inns miscall a tankard—but Mr Freeman and I still call a mug—of draught ale', R. H. Mottram, in Preface to H. W. Freeman's *Joseph and His Brethren*, 1928. A *tankard* is a drinking-mug made of metal, usually pewter; an earthenware *mug* would certainly be 'miscalled' a tankard.

tantamount. See PARAMOUNT.

Tartar, tartar; Tatar. The correct spelling of the native of Tartary is *Tatar*; the *r* crept in as a result of the influence of *Tartarian*, an inhabitant of *Tartaros*. From the ruthless *Tatars* and hell's *Tartarians*, comes *tartar*, a savage or unmanageable person—now mostly in *catch a tartar*.

tasteful(ly); tasty, tastily. The former pair (= in good taste) is admissible, the latter (in the same sense) is as vulgar as *natty* (e.g., *natty gent's suiting*) or *nattily*. Even *tasty* in the literal sense, 'pleasant to the taste', is a colloquialism.

TAUTOLOGY. *Tautology*, as defined by *The O.E.D.*, is 'a repetition of the same statement' or 'the repetition (especially in the immediate context) of the same word or phrase, or the same idea or statement in other words: usually as a fault of style'.

adequate enough
and etc.
appear on the scene
ascend up
at about (e.g., 3 p.m.)
attach together
attached hereto
both alike (see 'BOTH for *alike*')
burn down and *burn up* (see separate entry)
classified into classes
collaborate together
connect together and *connect up*
consolidate together
continue on and *continue yet*
co-operate together
couple together
debate about (v.)
descend down
discuss about

divide off and *divide up*
drink up and *drink down*
early beginnings
eat up
enclosed herewith (or *herein*)
end up
endorse . . . .: see *indorse . . .*
equally as
file away (commercially)
final completion
final upshot
finish up (v.t. and v.i.)
first begin
flood over
follow after
forbear from
forbid from
free, gratis, and for nothing
fresh beginner
from hence
from thence
from whence
funeral obsequies
gather together
have got (for 'have' or 'possess': see separate entry)
good benefit
hoist up
hurry up
important essentials
in between
indorse on the back
inside of
join together
joint co-operation
just exactly
just merely
just recently
lend out
link together
little birdling
meet together
mention about
merge together
mingle together
mix together
more inferior
more superior
more preferable
mutual co-operation
necessary requisite
new beginner
new creation
new departure and *entirely new departure*
new innovation
not a one
(it) *now remains*
open up (v.t.)
original source
outside of
over again

over with (done, ended, finished)
pair of twins
past history
peculiar freak
penetrate into
plan on (v.)
polish up
practical practice
(one's) presence on the scene
proceed on(ward)
protrude out
raze to the ground
really realize
recall back
reduce down
relax back
remember of
renew again
repay back
repeat again
repeat the same (e.g., story)
(to) rest up
retire back
return back
revert back
revive again
rise up
seldom ever
(to) separate apart
settle up
shrink down and shrink up
sink down
steady on!
still continue
still more yet
still remain
study up
sufficient enough
swallow down
taste of (for taste, v.)
termed as
than what
this next week
twice over
two halves (except when from different wholes)
two twins (of one pair)
uncommonly strange
unite together
used to (do something) before
we all and you all
where at
where to
whether or not
widow woman
young infant

Now, certain examples.
'That should leave me with twenty houses left' (Frank Tilsley, I'd Hate to Be Dead).

'Count A. was made the recipient of a national presentation' (The Times Literary Supplement: cited by Sir Alan Herbert).

'She set herself a standard of endurance and privation approximately as nearly as possible to that which she understood prevailed on the Western Front' (Ian Hay, The Willing Horse).

'The first layer of cloth was plain. The second had a lovely border on.'

'It sounded quite natural enough' (Henry Holt, Wanted for Murder). Omit either 'quite' or 'enough'.

'Treadgold gave orders that Ragusi was to be watched carefully. . . . For some half hour afterwards he sat at his desk with his head in his hands' (Anthony Weymouth, Tempt Me Not). 'Afterwards' is unnecessary.

'Occasionally she made a sale, but very seldom' (E. R. Punshon, The Dusky Hour) = 'She rarely made a sale'.

' "A canting hypocrite named Arpendrake," he began again, "has just absconded from England with the funds from an institution which really was supposed to be in the light of a great philanthropic affair" ' (John G. Brandon).

'It was a piece of ruled note-paper. . . . The quality was of a very cheap, coarse nature, such as comes in thick tablets which can be bought for a trifle at any stationer's' (S. S. Van Dine, The Kidnap Murder Case). Read '. . . It was of a very cheap, coarse quality, such as comes . . .'.

'He idled along from one street to another. . . . But never once, so far as we could ascertain, did he appear to glance back' (Stephen Maddock, Doorway to Danger): 'appear to' is unnecessary, and 'never' is enough.

'He could form no estimate at all of with how much favour he was regarded at the Admiralty' (C. S. Forester, A Ship of the Line, 1938). This sentence would be improved if 'of', which rings oddly, were omitted; after 'no', 'at all' is superfluous. Rewrite thus, 'He could not estimate with what favour he was regarded at the Admiralty'—or, better still, 'He could not estimate (or judge) how he stood with the Admiralty'. This example merits careful consideration, for it has been taken from one of the most economical (and best) of English post-1920 novelists.

'Further whimsicalities consist in . . . demanding . . . that all the books he finds in any guest-room be forthwith removed as insults to his intelligence and that the hostess see to it at once that the complete works of Maxwell Bodenheim be substituted in their stead' (G. J. Nathan, *Intimate Notebooks of George Jean Nathan*).

teach. See at LEARN.

technic, technics; technique; technology. *Technic* is a collective term for 'technical methods and details', especially 'the formal or mechanical part and aspect of an art or science', as in 'In the technic of this art, perfection can be reached only by long training' (Lowell), but *technique* is now more general. *Technics* (construed either as plural or as singular) may be used in the same sense: but here again, *technique* is more common. *Technics* in the sense 'the science or study of art or arts, especially of the mechanical or industrial arts' is inferior to the more usual *technology*. *Technique* also means skill or ability in the formal, practical, mechanical details of one's art, especially in one of the fine arts, and above all 'in reference to painting or musical performance'. Likewise, *technology* has the further meaning, 'practical arts collectively' and 'technical terminology or nomenclature'. (*O.E.D.*)

TECHNICALITIES. See JARGON.

teeming with is incorrect for *rich in*. 'Salamanca . . . a glorious old city, teeming with history.'

tempestive and **tempestuous.** The latter means 'stormy'; the former, 'seasonable'.

temporal and **temporary** are sometimes confused; the former is 'of or belonging to this life', as opposed to *spiritual*, 'belonging to the eternal'; the latter, 'not meant to last long', 'not permanent'.

temporize and **extemporize.** In good use, *temporize* is always intransitive; as = 'to improvise or extemporize', it is incorrect. To *temporize* is to adapt oneself, to conform to time and circumstance; *temporize with* is so to parley as to gain time. To *extemporize* (v.i.) is 'to speak extempore; in music, to improvise'; v.t., it is 'to compose off-hand; to compose and utter off-hand; hence, to produce on the spur of the moment, to invent for the occasion'. (*O.E.D.*)

tend and **trend.** In the sense, 'to have a general tendency, to have a disposition to', *trend* is obsolescent; *tend* is the right word. *Trend*, however, is correct for 'to turn off in a specified direction; to tend to take a direction expressed by or implied in the context', and, of rivers, currents, coastlines, mountain ranges, strata, territories or regions, 'to run, stretch, incline, bend in some direction', as in 'The coast trends to the northward', 'In its course to the north, the Gulf Stream trends more and more to the eastward'. (*The O.E.D.*)

tend for for *tend to cause.* 'Dainty underwear was certainly intriguing, but tended for delay,' Cecil Freeman Gregg.

tend to has become incorrect for *attend to*, in, e.g., 'I must *tend to* my business'. *Tend* is now used in *tending herds* or *flocks*.

tendencious is inferior to *tendentious*, which, by the way, means, not 'prejudiced' nor 'quarrelsome', but 'having a purposed tendency'.

tennis for *lawn tennis* is a colloquial convenience. *Tennis* properly so called is that royal game which arose in the Middle Ages and from which, in the 1870's, sprang the game of lawn tennis.

TENSE-SEQUENCE. In 'Devas had struck from an angle he had not considered, though it may well have been expected', *may* should be *might.*—'The threat of danger gave me a fierce, triumphant determination that, come what may, one little estate would stand inviolate' should read '. . . come what might'; and a careful writer would prefer *should* to *would*.

Those examples serve to indicate how necessary it is to ensure a right tense-sequence; to depart from that sequence is to produce always an effect of inelegance and often an actual ambiguity.

'The *Sequence of Tenses*', writes Dr Onions, 'is the principle in accordance with which the Tense in a subordinate clause "follows" or is adjusted to that of the principal clause'; thus, in general, when the governing clause has a Present [e.g., 'he says'], a Present Perfect [as in 'he *has said*'], or a Future [as in 'he *will say*'], the subordinate clause has a Present (*Primary Sequence*); when the governing clause has a Past [whether progressive, as in 'he *was saying*', or preterite, as in 'he said'] or a Pluperfect [as in 'he *had* said'], the subordinate clause has a Past (*Secondary Sequence*). The Sequence of Tenses applies chiefly to Final and Noun Clauses.

'I tell ⎫
have told ⎬ you that you *may* know.'
shall tell ⎭

'I told ⎫
was telling ⎬ you that you *might* know.'
had told ⎭

'The master *says* we *may* have a holiday', but in the past it is 'The master *said* we *might* have a holiday', the master's actual words being, 'You *may* have a holiday'.

'I *took* care that he *should* not hear me.'

'If it is desired to mark something as true universally or at the time of speaking', the tense is not adjusted:

'Columbus proved that the world *is* round.'

'I *asked* the guard what time the train usually *starts*.'

terminal and **terminus**. In Britain, they are distinct, but in the U.S. they tend to overlap.

terminate for *end, close, finish*. 'The proceedings terminated with a vote of thanks to the Chairman.' Why not 'The meeting ended'? Sometimes *expire* would be preferable, as in 'His subscription terminated last month'. *Terminated* = ended, for good and all.

TERMS OF ADDRESS. See TITLES.

testament, for *testimony*, is an occasional error; the former is a *will*, the latter 'an attestation in support of a fact or statement'. (*O.E.D.*)

testimonial on is incorrect for *testimonial to*, as in 'I dislike testimonials, but . . . here is a testimonial on mathematics'.

testimony. See EVIDENCE.

tetralogy. See TRIUMVIRATE.

than, misused for *other than*. 'He disliked the clash of personality, regarding any personality than his own as an intolerable intrusion'.—*But* or *differing from* might also be substituted here for *than*.—Cf. 'He had scarcely won . . . the place . . . than his health was found shattered' (Froude), where 'when' should be substituted for 'than'.

than, misused for *than that*. 'We have borne so much for the peace we pray for, that I think that I would rather see all humanity lying dead like this German boy, than it should blunder blindly into a war more terrible than this has been', Warwick Deeping, *No Hero—This*. To omit the second 'that' would not be a grave error, but a *that* is necessary after the first 'than'.

than, misused for *to*. 'Modern dictionaries are pusillanimous works, preferring feebly to record what has been done than to say'—read, *to saying*—'what ought to be done.'

than, misused for *when*. See BARELY THAN.

than, different . . . 'Here was quite a different kettle of fish than the one they had served up in the past', Samuel Putnam. The impeccably correct construction is *different* . . . *from*, although

H

different to (cf. French *différent à*) is permissible; if one says that 'one thing differs *from*' (never *to*) 'another', why does one not, with equal naturalness, say 'is different from'? [*Different* . . . *than* seems to occur more and more frequently in the New York daily and weekly press. Evidently the comparative sense of the word rather than the fact of its positive form may govern the syntax.]

than, else, is incorrect. See ELSE THAN.

than, inferior. See INFERIOR THAN.

than me or **than I** may occur in a sentence such as 'You are a much greater loser than *me* or *I*' (here Swift wrote *I* and was, I think, incorrect). The arguments are (1) that *than* is here a preposition and governs an object; and (2) that *than* is a conjunction introducing a clause, only the subject of which is expressed, the remainder being an ellipsis. I much prefer the use of the objective case (in this example, *me*); and all authorities agree that *than whom* (not *than who*) is correct in 'He is a king than whom there has never been a greater'. [American grammarians, even the liberals Krapp and Perrin, insist upon the second argument —which seems a pity, especially because school teachers have so much trouble trying to overcome the student's disinclination to use the nominative case in the final position.]

than what. 'His productions certainly do not belong to Mr Prentis's £5 class (than what is more wretched?), nor to his £25,000 class (than what is more vulgar?), but are adequate, etc.' There is no grammatical sense in 'than what'; the writer means 'than which, what is more wretched/vulgar?', though the juxtaposition of *which, what* is clumsy, and might be avoided by saying 'and what more wretched than that?' Often *than what* is merely tautological for *than*, as in 'It was easier than what he thought'.

Thanksgiving Day is preferable to *Thanksgiving day*; *Thanksgiving* is not bad English, but it is too familiar for formal occasions.

that (conj.) misplaced. 'There is just a chance where there is any ornamentation that a stain might creep under it', for 'There is just a chance that, where . . ., a stain might . . .'.

that (conj.) omitted. The omission of the conjunctive *that* sometimes causes a momentary confusion. In Milton Propper's *The Great Insurance Murders*, we find: 'There were no marks or scratches that indicated the lock had been forced' and 'Rankin ushered her to a chair and learned her name was Mrs Emily Reilly'. 'Indicated the lock' and 'learned her name' might possibly have been independent, self-contained statements: but with something of a jar, one finds that the sentences continue.—This defect is much commoner in American than in English writers.

that (conj.), redundant. This occurs in such a sentence as 'The sooner that this is altered, the better', where *that* is entirely uncalled for; and in 'He said that, as the mistake was irreparable, that it was useless to discuss the subject again'.

that, misused for *so far as* or *for all that.* 'He found that it was unlocked; indeed, that he could see. [it] seemed to have no means of locking.'

that, misused for *thus* or esp. *to that degree* or, loosely, *so very.* 'Oh, it's not that urgent', said the doctor on the telephone—and, in so doing, he used a colloquialism; his remark would have sounded better if he had said 'It's not so urgent as all that'. But because, when it = 'so . . . as all that', it has the merit of forceful brevity, the adverbial *that* is fast gaining ground. "You *are* wonderful, aren't you?"—"Not *that* wonderful!" may shock the purists; I don't use it either, but I respect it.

that, at. *At that,* a colloquialism, should be eschewed in formal, official, and other serious writing. Its most frequent senses are 'moreover', 'even so', and 'in any case'.

that and **which; that** and **who.** See 'WHICH and THAT; WHO and THAT'.

that same day (month, etc.) is not so much incorrect as unnecessarily emphatic for *that day* or the stronger *the same day*; e.g., 'On that same night, he went to London'.

that . . . that is clumsy or, at best, cacophonous for *that . . . which* or *that . . . who(m)*, as in 'That man that you saw yesterday is a swindler' and 'That box that the porter took was valuable'.

the for *this* or *that*, especially preceding a relative clause beginning with *who* (or *which*), is not so much wrong as inadequate, as in 'The man who says such things is obviously unfit to occupy so important a position', where *that man* would be an improvement; '*the* man *that*', however, is both admissible and usual.

the and **The** in titles. See TITLES OF BOOKS.

the author is to be used for *I* (or *me*) on formal occasions only.

the said. Inadmissible except in legal documents. 'The said playboy was a millionaire's son' is absurd. (Harold Herd.)

the which is obsolete and now incorrect for *which*, as in 'The which barn is for sale'.

their, them, they for singular *his* or *her*, etc. 'It was rather like a jig-saw puzzle to which everyone contributed their own little bit of knowledge.' An error commonly found in both speech and writing, and arising from our lack of a relative pronoun meaning *his-or-her.*

'I wore the fillet of the Golden Cobra, which could only be worn by one who had overthrown the cobra of the seventh ordeal, and in so doing had added strength to their will.' In such contexts the right pronoun is 'his', unless a woman is clearly referred to.

their's is incorrect for *theirs*—and astonishingly common.

them is constantly used for *they* (as *me* is for 'I'), after *as* and after *is, are, were*; 'It was not them' is incorrect, but, 'It was not them we wanted' has some justification since *them* represents *they whom.*

themselves. See MYSELF.

then, adj. See ALMOST.

then for *than* is an error much commoner than highbrows seem to think: it is not merely the illiterate who fall into it. The reason is not that, several centuries ago, *than* and *then* were spellings and pronunciations frequently interchanged, but that, where *than* bears no stress and is spoken very rapidly and lightly, it tends to approximate to *then.*

thenceforth. See THEREAFTER and THENCEFORTH'.

theory is occasionally used loosely for *idea* (or *notion*), *view* or *opinion* or *expectation*, as in 'My theory of the war is that the mechanically stronger side will win', where *expectation* or *opinion* would be preferable.

there, introductory, is apt to cause the verb to fail to agree with the subject in number, as in: 'There was at this time, within the horrid confines of that prison, several fellows who were very much respected by the others'; 'There was my wife and daughter to consider, and my whole career'; 'There still remains a few wilderness areas on the continent'. It is difficult to avoid the impression that the authors subconsciously regarded *there* as a noun (therefore singular), hence as the subject of the sentence. Cf. following entry.

there is many is incorrect for *there are many*, the subject being *many*; contrast French *il y a*. 'There is many a . . .' is correct.

thereabout and thereabouts. The latter is the more usual form.

thereafter and thenceforth. The former = 'after that date or time or place in a sequence'; *thenceforth* = 'continually or continuously from that time; indefinitely from that time; from that time *onward*'. *Both are formal words*, not to be used indiscriminately. (*O.E.D.*)

thereby making. See THUS MAKING.

therefore and therefor. 'The reason *therefor* (i.e., *for it* or *for this*) is *therefore* (i.e., *for that reason*) unsatisfactory' exemplifies the difference between the two words.

theretofore. See ARCHAISMS.

these kind or **sort of.** George Parker, 1781, 'Queer as this *rig*' or underworld dodge 'may appear, there is a larger shop in London where these kind of rings are sold, for the purpose of going on the *Fawney*', the trick of ring-dropping.

they, their, misused for *he, his* as in 'Anyone thinks twice, when their life is at stake': read 'his life'.

think as a noun is colloquial when it is not dialectal, whether for 'an act of thinking; meditation' ('An act of thinking does one much good') or for 'an opinion' ('My think is that he's a fool'). (*O.E.D.*)

thoroughbred and **pure-bred.** *Thoroughbred* is preferred to *pure-bred* for horses, dogs, bulls, rams, but the terms are synonymous. *Thoroughbred* may be applied to persons, and it is also a noun.

those that is inferior to **those who.**

though and **although.** *Although* is the more formal; *though* is usual in speech and in writings couched in familiar English.

though (or **although**) is sometimes used to introduce a subordinate clause in a highly irrelevant way; Dean Alford quotes 'He, though a gentleman of property, was unhappily paralysed in his lower limbs'.

though and **however.** The former should no more be used for the latter than the latter for the former! *Though*, like *although*, comes at the beginning of a clause—not, as in 'I did not like him though', at the end; nor in the middle, as in 'I must, though, discuss the doctrine'.

thrash; thresh. The latter is retained in reference to corn; in all other references, *thrash* is preferred, and is obligatory in figurative senses.

through for *by means of* or *by*, is allowed

by *The O.E.D.*; nevertheless, the best writers avoid it. E.g., 'Through an addition to his salary, he was enabled to purchase the house he wanted' is unsatisfactory.

thus for *therefore* is an error. 'Freedom to individuals means that they can do as they like; thus we should see what they like to do before we congratulate them.'

thus (or **thereby**) **making** is often very loosely used, as in 'The conversation and food were good, thus making the dinner very pleasant'. Turn thus: 'The conversation and food were good; consequently the dinner was very pleasant'.

tidy. Such expressions as *a tidy step, a tidy few*, are colloquialisms, whereas *pretty good* and *pretty well* are standard speech.

till is inferior to *until* in formal prose.

time for *by the time that* is illiterate. 'It'll be openin'-time, time I get down there.'

timid and **timorous; apprehensive.** *Apprehensive* is 'anticipative of something unfavourable', as in *apprehensive of danger* and *apprehensive for one's life. Timid* is 'easily frightened or over-awed', as in 'Poor is the triumph o'er the timid hare'. *Timorous* is synonymous with *timid*, but with emphasis on 'shrinking (with fear, or from doing something that requires courage)'; but one tends also to use *timid* of temporary fear, and *timorous* of a person habitually lacking in courage. (*Webster's*.)

titanic. See GIGANTIC.

TITLES OF BOOKS AND PERIODICALS. I have already discussed this question at the entry *the* in my *A Dictionary of Slang*.

Had I chosen the title *Dictionary of Slang*, it would have been incorrect to refer to it either as *A Dictionary of Slang* or as *The Dictionary of Slang* (very pretentious this, for there are other dictionaries of slang); had the title been *The Dictionary of Slang*, it would have been incorrect to refer to it as either *A Dictionary of Slang* or *Dictionary of Slang*; but as it is *A Dictionary*, why impute telegraphese by calling it *Dictionary*, or conceit by changing it to *The Dictionary*? Hence I write 'My *A Dictionary of Slang*'. If the title had been *The Dictionary . . .*, I should have referred to the book as 'my *The Dictionary of Slang*'.

And let us italicize the initial 'A' and 'The' or, if the inverted-commas mode is preferred, have inverted commas before them. 'A correspondent on the *Times*' or

'A correspondent on the "Times" ' is a feeble substitute for 'a correspondent on *The Times*' or 'a correspondent on "The Times" '.

Admittedly, the general practice is against 'my *A Dictionary of Slang*': but should not exactitude overrule a practice that can hardly be classified as idiom? In familiar speech, 'my *Dictionary of Slang*' is permissible: it is a colloquialism. But I do recommend that scholars and reputable writers and cataloguers should retain the *A* and *The* that form the first word in a title. Is it not better to speak of J. M. Barrie's delightful book as 'Barrie's *A Window in Thrums*' than to refer to it as 'Barrie's *Window in Thrums*'? Is not the latter both ambiguous and impertinent? After all, we do not speak of 'Michael Sadleir's *Foolish Things*', but of 'Michael Sadleir's *These Foolish Things*'; we speak, not of 'Michael Arlen's *Charming People*' but of 'Michael Arlen's *These Charming People*'. *A* and *The* have their rights no less than *These* and *Those*.

In the titles of periodicals, however, there is an exception, consecrated by usage and justified by convenience: when the title becomes an adjective, *The* is omitted. 'A *Times* correspondent' is more convenient than, and is idiomatic for, 'A correspondent on *The Times*'. I do not suggest that we should either say or write 'a *The Times* correspondent' or 'the *The Times* correspondent'. But there is no excuse for 'The editor of the New York Times snorts balefully on discovering this sorry stratagem': either 'The editor of *The New York Times*' or 'The editor of "The New York Times" ' is required.

There is no doubt concerning what is to be done with 'a' and 'the' *within* titles. They are always written *a* and *the*, as in '*The Lady in the Case*' is a good book'; but where a book-title or a periodical-title is involved, the above-enunciated rule is to be observed, as in '*The Ghost at The Times*' is an excellent book' or, for the sake of clarity, '*The Ghost at "The Times"*' is an excellent book'.

Not only *a* (or *an*) and *the* require small initial letters ('lower case', as printers say). So do prepositions—*at* and *from* and *in* and *of* and the rest of them.

There is no generally accepted rule concerning the other parts of speech. My own practice is to 'capital' every word that is neither an article (*a* or *the*) nor a preposition. I see little reason for writing 'be', 'is', 'are', 'was', 'were', 'will', 'shall', 'would', 'should', 'must',

'ought' in lower case when all other verbs are written in upper case: why *The Lady is Dead* but *The Lady Fell Dead*? Why not *The Lady Is Dead*?

In this matter of titles, I advise authors not to submit to 'the rules of the house'—those rules which printers have formulated in self-protection—when they are *sure* of the rightness of their own titling.

[For the citing of titles the most generally available American authority is probably the University of Chicago Press *A Manual of Style*.—As first words the articles *a* and *the* are part of the titles of books and one would expect them to be so treated—i.e., capitalized and set within the quotation marks or in the italic type that distinguishes the title. However, titles that make for awkwardness or misunderstanding—as in 'his *A Dictionary of Slang*' and 'Dr Vizetelly's *The Standard Dictionary*'—will inevitably be shortened, now and again, when they interfere with the English language. The American rule for capitalization of titles is that the first word and all important words are capitalized. Often, however, on a title page the title is set entirely in caps as is the case with Mr Partridge's dictionary. American librarians have solved the problem in this fashion: Partridge, Eric. Dictionary of slang . . ., a. They capitalize the first word and no other, and treat an initial article as an addendum. Editors, less bold than librarians, muddle along according to publishing house precedents or their own taste. In fact, no one style solves all problems. Authors can help by quoting rather than italicizing special words in titles.

There is no easy way of finding the correct and complete titles—if they exist—of the thousands of American newspapers. The two complete lists are arranged by states, towns, and short titles, as Texas, El Paso, Herald, Post, Times. (Moreover the banner heading on the front page of a paper may not be exactly the same as the masthead above the first column of editorials.) If an editor wishes uniform citations of newspapers, his most practicable course is to italicize or quote only the short title, as in the El Paso *Times*, the New York *Times*, the *Times*. The alternative is to give the masthead titles of newspapers he is acquainted with and to set the others by an arbitrary rule. The *Literary Digest* used to have three ways of citing newspapers (as I remember): one in the text, another in the credit line following a quotation, and still another in the credit line below a cartoon. Magazines are fonder of their articles than are newspapers. *The Atlantic Monthly* and *The Saturday Review of Literature* wish *The* (and so, by the way, does The Johns Hopkins University—known locally as The Hopkins). It may be difficult to remember whether the *American Mercury* or *The American Mercury* would be most flattering. *The* or *A Life, Time, Fortune* would be ruinous. Should it be *The Reader's Digest*? Some quite literate editors follow what our friend Mr Partridge would call the illiterate practice of ignoring the article in common citations of the periodical press. If we were presenting a Pulitzer prize or a sheepskin suitably inscribed, then we should ask the editor what he liked best. If the reader thinks the problem simple, let him consider —— magazine: it is **Harpers** MAGAZINE on the cover, *Harper's Magazine* on the contents page, **Harpers** *Magazine* on the masthead above the first article, and HARPER'S MONTHLY MAGAZINE on the running heads. What should an editor do? Call it *Harpers* for short and *Harpers Magazine* for long, and quote it often—that is good practice.]

to, omitted. 'For years it was disputed as to whom the word referred.' *Whom* is correct, but the *to* of *refer to* has been omitted owing to the influence of *as to*. The sentence should read 'For years it was disputed as to whom the word referred to'.

to for *to* + infinitive is colloquial, not Standard English; it is avoided in good writing. 'I shall go; he doesn't want *to*'.

to, in *other to* and *different to*. See OTHER.

to, misused for *as to* (or *in respect of*), is exemplified in 'Since the two of them had been at a loss to what else to do, they had made the journey to St. Johns'. In this example, *to* could have been omitted.

to-morrow and **tomorrow.** The O.E.D. prefers *to-morrow, to-day*, to the variants; *Webster's, tomorrow* and *today*—so do I.

tomorrow is and **tomorrow will be.** The latter is more logical, except when, in a vivid and graphic context, the morrow is pulled back into the present, as in the catch-phrase, 'tomorrow is another day'.

too for *very* is a trivial colloquialism, as in 'Isn't it just too sweet!'

too is occasionally misused for *either* in negative sentences and phrases. 'I don't mean that we should shut our eyes to it; but it shouldn't make us shut our eyes to

other things too.' A sense construction? Perhaps; but it jars.

toper and **drunkard; drinker.** *Toper* (mainly literary) is synonymous with *drunkard*, 'a hard drinker'; for *drunkard*, see also DRUNK. *Drinker* requires a qualifying word or phrase, as in 'a hard drinker', 'a moderate drinker', 'a drinker of nothing but water'.—For *dipsomaniac*, see DRUNK.

topic and **subject.** *Topic* is virtually confined to a subject that is *topical*, 'of or pertaining to the topics of the day—the subjects of the day's discussions, subjects that are, at best, a nine days' wonder'. (*O.E.D.*)

topography, geography, chorography. Whereas *geography* relates to the entire earth, or a considerable part of it, and treats the subject in general terms, *topography* is the detailed description of, say, a town or a district; *chorography* stands midway between the two—it deals with districts and regions but not with towns, villages, hamlets, valleys, etc.

tornado. See CYCLONE.

tortuous is sometimes misused for *torturous* and for *tortious* (a legal term).

totally destroyed appears, as a tautology, on the style sheets of many newspaper editors. 'A house is destroyed' is usually sufficient. But suppose that one is describing a row of houses subjected to fire: one house is *half destroyed*, i.e., destroyed as to one-half; the next, however, is wholly destroyed—*totally destroyed*.

trade-union and **trades-union.** The plurals are *trade-unions* and *trades-unions*. In England, the preferred form of the singular is *trades-union*; in the U.S.A., *trade-union*.

tragedy. See DISASTER.

tragic; tragical. *Tragic* is correct in the sense 'of, pertaining to, belonging to, proper to tragedy (a branch of the drama)'; but 'resembling tragedy in respect of its matter; relating to or expressing fatal or dreadful events, hence sad, gloomy' requires *tragical*, as does the sense 'excited with, (of a mood) coloured with, tragic feeling' ('This tragical mood', Miss Braddon); *tragic* is the right term for 'fatal, disastrous, calamitous; terrible' ('His short life had a tragic close'). (*O.E.D.*)

transfer is occasionally misused for *change* and *transpose*. The former error occurs in '. . . Some pencilled figures. Ten thousand dollars. Rebecca found him a pen and watched him transfer dollars into pounds.'

transitory and transient. Both are correct for 'temporary; fleeting; momentary'.

transpire is loose for *happen* or *occur*.

treachery and treason. The former has the wider meaning, being both general (when it is synonymous with *treason*) and particular (= 'an act of treason or perfidy'). In the general sense, 'deceit, cheating, perfidy; violation of faith, betrayal of trust', *treachery* is preferred to *treason*, but in the special application, 'deception or desertion of one's sovereign' or of the government of the state to which one owes allegiance, *treason* is preferred, with the variant *high treason*; and *treason* is, in all references and contexts, the legal term. *Treacherousness* is only an abstract, 'the quality of being treacherous'. (*O.E.D.*)

treasonable and treasonous. In the extended sense, 'perfidious', only the former is used. In the nuances, 'involving treason, characterized by, hence characteristic of, treason', the terms are synonymous: both 'a treasonable conspiracy' and 'a treasonous conspiracy' are correct; 'a treasonous libel', 'a treasonable letter' might also be 'a treasonable libel', 'a treasonous letter': but *treasonable* is gradually superseding *treasonous*. (*O.E.D.*)

treat; treat of; treat on. *Treat on* is incorrect for *treat of*. To *treat of* is 'to deal with (some matter, whether in speech or in writing); to discourse on', as in 'His book treats of a most abstruse subject'. To *treat* a subject is to discuss it (in speech or writing), now generally 'to deal with [it] in the way of literary art', the former nuance occurring in 'What subjects did he treat?', the latter in 'I wonder how he will treat the subject'. (*O.E.D.*)

treble and triple. In the sense 'three times as much or many; multiplied by three; of three times the measure or amount', *triple* is preferable to *treble*; thus, 'a triple scale' (*not* in music), 'The quantity should not be less than triple the weight of the solids consumed'. In the sense 'consisting of three things (or sets of things) or members; threefold', *treble* and *triple* are synonymous; thus, 'a treble enclosure', 'A kind of shirt of double or treble elk-hide', and 'A triple bank of oars'; but *triple* is now the commoner. In the sense 'having three applications or relations; of three kinds', *treble* is preferred, as in 'Every part and episode has its double and treble meaning'. In music: *triple* does not occur—except in *triple*

counterpoint, triple fugue, triple rhythm, triple time. (*O.E.D.*)

trek is 'a journey performed in an ox-waggon', 'an organized migration or expedition by ox-waggon'; hence, 'any migration or collective journeying'—but not properly of a holiday movement to the sea-side (etc.). It has, among journalists, become a 'rubber-stamp word' (see AMAZING). [Among American journalists the once-popular *trek* has been replaced by *hegira*; thus is misuse compounded.]

trend. See TEND.

triad. See TRIUMVIRATE.

trial for *attempt* is incorrect, as in 'Like a fussy old man who is afraid of losing his dignity, and in the very trial at keeping it, is seen without it'.

trilogy, trio. See TRIUMVIRATE.

tri-monthly, 'occurring once every three months' or 'lasting for three months'. In the former sense, *quarterly* is preferable; in the latter, *of three months*. Yet the sense in which a term is especially needed is 'occurring three times a month': therefore, why not adopt *tri-monthly* in that sense?

trip is a short voyage, a short journey. *Journey* refers to the land, *voyage* to the sea; a *trip* may be made on either.

triple. See TREBLE.

triumvirate is never, *trio* rarely, applied to things. To write of 'a triumvirate of test matches' (for three such matches), is faintly ridiculous. A series of three novels or (long) poems or plays is a *trilogy*; of four, a *tetralogy*. *Triad* may be used of three heroes, three matricides, three film stars, and so on; and is obligatory in certain learned or technical connexions.

troop; troops; trooper; troupe; trouper. A *troop* is that sub-division of cavalry which corresponds to a company of infantry and a battery of artillery; *troops* is 'armed forces collectively' without *the*, as in 'to raise troops'; *the troops* is a colloquialism for 'soldiers' or 'the soldiers', as in 'The spirit of the troops is excellent'; there is no singular to either *troops* or *the troops*. A *trooper* is a cavalryman, hence a cavalry horse. A *troupe* is a company of actors, dancers, or performing animals; a member of a troupe is a *trouper*.

troposphere, stratosphere, atmosphere. The third is the gaseous envelope that surrounds the earth; the first, that layer of atmospheric air which extends upwards, for some seven miles, from the surface of the earth and in which the temperature falls, as one moves higher; and *stratosphere* is that layer of air which lies beyond the troposphere and in which the temperature is constant. In short, the *atmosphere* consists of the *stratosphere* and the *troposphere*.

troubled; troublesome; troublous. *Troubled* is applied to a sea or other water, or a sky, that is stormy; to wine or water that is turbid (coloured with sediment; made muddy or thick); also to moods, thoughts, attitudes, minds, hearts, sleep, periods of time that are disturbed, disordered, disquieted, agitated, afflicted ('a troubled ghost'; 'these troubled times', 'troubled reign'; 'goaded by this troubled thought . . .'). *Troublesome* means 'giving trouble; causing annoyance; vexatious or distressing', as in 'a troublesome cough', 'troublesome neighbours': *troublous* is also used thus, but is now less usual. *Troublous* is a literary synonym of *troubled* as applied to a stormy sea; hence it is applied to a violent wind—another literary application; to periods, reigns, lives, state (of an institution); but in its own right, and without the competition of either *troubled* or *troublesome*, it further means '(of persons or their attributes) turbulent, disorderly; restless, unquiet', as in 'Troublous and adventurous spirits', (Motley), but even here it is rather literary than general for 'turbulent; restless, unquiet'. (*O.E.D.*)

trout; plural *trouts*, except in sporting use: 'He may guddle trouts in a stream', 'Pike and trout are to be had in the lochs'. When various species are concerned, the plural should be *trouts*, as in 'There is a good book on the trouts of the Catskills'.

truculent does not mean 'surly'. It = fierce, cruel, barbarous; (of things, writing, etc.) harsh, violent, scathing.

trustworthy; trusty. The former = 'worthy of trust or confidence; reliable'; so does *trusty*, but *trusty* is slightly archaic in this sense, except in the phrase *our trusty and well-beloved* (in letters from sovereign to subject).

truth. See VERACITY.

try and do (something) is incorrect for *try to do* (something). [This usage is approved by some grammarians as a comfortable English idiom; it is labelled *colloquial* by *Webster's*.]

tubercular; tuberculous. The latter is now reserved for pathological and medical contexts ('tuberculous tissue', 'tuberculous meningitis', 'tuberculous pork', 'hospitals for the tuberculous sick'),

whereas *tubercular* is, in discriminating usage, reserved for natural-history contexts, where it = (*a*) 'of a tubercle, consisting of a tubercle, of the form and nature of a tubercle' (a small tuber), or (*b*), 'tuberculate', i.e., having tubercles. (*O.E.D.*) [In popular American usage, *tubercular* is often used for *tuberculous*.]

tubfuls; tubsfull. See BASKETFULS.

two first. See at FIRST, TWO.

two halves, cut into, is verbose, redundant, absurd for *to cut into halves*. But *two halves make a whole* is, of course, correct.

two twins is tautological for *twins* when only one pair is understood; properly used, however, *two twins* = four persons.

tycoon is being overdone in the U.S.A., for 'big shot' in business, politics, etc. The Tycoon is 'the title by which the Shogun of Japan was described to foreigners'. (*O.E.D.*)

type (of), like *case (of)*, is often used unnecessarily or infelicitously; as in 'He's not that type of person'; 'Events of that type generally arouse suspicion'; 'The rose is not that type of flower'. Keep *type* in its right place.

typhoid (fever) and **typhus.** The former, once supposed to be a mere variety of the latter, is now usually called *enteric (fever)*. *Typhus* is a very acute, infectious fever.

typhoon. See CYCLONE.

typical should be modified only after due consideration. Such a sentence as the following strikes one as odd: 'Now there I had Smith's début—a rather typical performance which gave me quite a good idea of his methods'; why *rather*?

typist is the person operating a *typewriter* (the machine); 'to *typewrite*' is obsolescent for 'to *type*'.

typographic is perhaps obsolescent; **typographical,** current.

U

uglily sounds ugly in many contexts; not all, for in the following two quotations from *The O.E.D.* it is not cacophonous— 'In those representations man indeed was not more uglily than fearfully made' (Sayce); 'The town is . . . uglily picturesque'. It is much more economical than *in an ugly manner*.

ultra (adj.) is both ugly and odd for *excessive* or *immoderate*, as in 'ultra reverence'.

umbrella. See PARASOL.

unable. See INCAPABLE.

un- and **in-** in adjectives. See IN-. Here, however, is appended a short list of *im-* or *in-* and *un-* terms.

impecunious
impenetrable
impertinent
imperious
implacable
inadmissible
incapable
incomparable
inconsequent
inconsolable
incredible
incredulous
indecisive
indelible
indirect
inexact
infamous
infelicitous
inhuman
intransigent
unable (but *incapable*)
unbalanced
unbelievable (but *incredible*)
unblessed
unbounded
uncomparable
unconsoled (but *inconsolable*)
uncrowned
undecided (but *indecisive*)
unequal
unfaithful
unfavourable
ungrateful
unhappy (but *infelicitous*)
unhorsed
unimaginative
unimportant
unpenetrated (but *impenetrable*)
unpleasant
unpretentious
untenable
untruthful

unambiguous should not be used as an exact synonym of *perfectly clear*. Thus L. Susan Stebbing, in *Logical Positivism and Analysis*, writes: 'An *unambiguous* expression is not equivalent to a *perfectly clear* expression*, since we may understand more or less clearly. It is important not to confuse *ambiguity, vagueness, unclearness*; these three are quite different, and mutually independent.' This footnote is increased in significance when we see that the passage it glosses is: 'Moore holds that to *understand an expression* is not equivalent to being able *to give a correct analysis* of its meaning. He has pointed out that the failure to see that these are *not* equivalent has been responsible for a good many mistakes with

regard to the nature of philosophical problems.'
unanimous. See COMPARATIVES, FALSE.
unapt. See INAPT.
UNATTACHED PARTICIPLES. See CONFUSED PARTICIPLES.
unavoidable, misused for *unchangeable* or *unchanging*. 'As was his unavoidable custom, he observed the faces of the crowd around him' (Carolyn Wells).
unaware, adjective; **unawares**, adverb.
unbeknown is not dialectal. As a variant of *unknown*, it is perhaps unusual, but certainly not rare, as in 'the land of the unbeknown'; its commonest role, however, is that which it plays in the phrase *unbeknown to* (= *unknown to*), 'without the knowledge of', as in 'The bottle had been opened, unbeknown to the purchaser'. The elliptical *unbeknown*, 'without anybody's knowledge; unnoticed, undetected', is now rare: 'My love rose up so early And stole out unbeknown', Housman. (*O.E.D.*)
unbelievable and **believable**, for *incredible* and *credible*, are somewhat unusual and almost catachrestic; certainly they are to be avoided in connexion with persons. Obviously 'It is unbelievable' is permissible and even idiomatic when it applies to a fact or a rumour. But *unbelievable* rings oddly in 'The first readers of Mr McCabe's book . . . rightly refused to believe that there could possibly be a detective as unconventional and unscrupulous as Smith. The critics, therefore, attacked McCabe, the author, for having invented such an unbelievable character.'
unbeliever. See DISBELIEVER.
uncomfortable and **discomfortable.** The latter is the stronger, for it connotes discomfort, whereas the former connotes mere absence of comfort.
uncomparable is not the same as *incomparable*; it is a hybrid word, necessary to distinguish its meaning 'that cannot be compared' from that of *incomparable*, 'above or beyond comparison'.
unconscious and **subconscious.** *Subconscious* = 'partially or imperfectly conscious; belonging to a class of phenomena resembling those of consciousness but not clearly perceived or recognized'; hence, 'belonging to that portion of the mental field the processes of which are outside the range of attention'.
Unconscious, in psychology, means 'performed, employed, etc., without conscious action', as in *unconscious cerebration*. In ordinary language, it = 'unaware, unregarding or regardless' (as

in 'He was unconscious of the danger'), 'not characterized by—not endowed with—the faculty or presence of consciousness'; 'temporarily without consciousness' (*knocked unconscious*); 'not known to or thought of as possessed by or existing in oneself' ('The boxer had an unconscious grace').
With thanks to *The O.E.D.*

uncourteous. See DISCOURTEOUS.

uncreditable. See CREDIBLE.

unctious is a frequent misspelling and mispronunciation of *unctuous*.

undeceived, as a participial adjective, can be ambiguous, for there is a verb *undeceive*, to tell the truth to, to inform a person of a mistake, with a past participle *undeceived* employable as an adjective. 'But she shook her head, undeceived', Agatha Christie, *Dumb Witness*, where the meaning is 'not deceived', but where one is delayed by the possibility of the meaning 'informed' (of something).

under. See 'ABOVE and OVER'.

underlay and **underlie.** Apart from the former as a printing technicality and the latter as a geological as well as a mining one, the essential difference is this:— *Underlay* is 'to support (something) by placing something else underneath it; to furnish *with* something laid below', as in 'You ought not to stitch any wounded finger, . . . but underlay it with little splinters' and 'Their project of underlaying the sea with electric wires'.

To *underlie* is 'to form a basis to; to exist beneath the surface-aspect of', as in 'That germ of truth which underlies all falsity and every falsehood'.

undersigned, I (or **we**) **the.** Permissible in law; affected or tediously jocular elsewhere. In 1868 Dickens could write, 'The undersigned is in his usual brilliant condition'; that was a long time ago.

understandable. See COMPREHENSIBLE.

UNDERSTATEMENT or *Meiosis*; and *Litotes*. *Understatement* is the everyday synonym of the learned *meiosis*; understatement itself is the supreme virtue of the middle-class and upper-class Englishman. If an Englishman says, 'I dislike that woman', that woman should remove herself as expeditiously as possible; if he says that some contretemps is 'rather a nuisance', he means that it is utterly damnable or extremely unfortunate.

Litotes is that 'figure of speech, in which an affirmative is expressed by the negative of the contrary; an instance of this' (*O.E.D.*), as in 'a citizen of *no mean city*', 'He is no coward'.

H*

under the circumstances. *The O.E.D.*, defining *circumstances* as 'the external conditions prevailing at the time', says: 'Mere situation is expressed by "in the circumstances", action affected is performed "under the circumstances" '; thus, e.g., '. . . who found himself in circumstances to which he was unequal' (Froude); 'The desire to obtain the money will, under certain circumstances, stimulate industry' (Ruskin). When in doubt use *in*, which is always correct.

undiscriminating and **indiscriminate.** Usage tends to confine the former to persons, the latter to aim, purpose, motive, impulse, selection, plan, method, treatment, behaviour; a tendency that, if given effect, makes for clarity and for that distinctiveness which characterizes all sensitive or subtle writing. The senses of *indiscriminate* are: 'not marked by discrimination or discernment; done without making distinctions', hence 'confused or promiscuous'.

unduly is often used unnecessarily and hardly less often misused for 'too' or 'very'. The same stricture applies to *undue*, beloved of bureaucrats. Be on guard against these insidious words.

undying. See DEATHLESS.

unelastic and **inelastic.** Either is permissible, though the latter is preferable. Figuratively, *inelastic* is much the commoner.

unendurable. See COMPARATIVES, FALSE.

UN-ENGLISH PLURALS. See PLURALS, UN-ENGLISH.

unfertilized is correct; but rather *infertile* than *unfertile*, *infertility* than *unfertility*.

unfrequent is inferior to *nfrequent*, but *unfrequented* is correct, *infrequented* incorrect; *unfrequency* is rare for *infrequency*.

unharmonious is inferior to *inharmonious*.

unheard of = 'not before heard of, hitherto unknown', hence 'new, strange', hence 'unprecedented'. To be used with care.

unhospitable is inferior to *inhospitable*.

unhuman is much weaker than—not an error for—*inhuman. Unhuman* should be reserved for the sense 'not pertaining to mankind'; for the sake of clarity, use it neither for *inhuman* nor for *superhuman*.

unique, most or **rather** or **very.** An object that is 'unique' is the only one of its kind in existence; there can be no qualification of the absolute without a contradiction of the quality which it asserts. The use of *unique(ly)* to express excellence is incorrect.

unity for *entity* is a quaint mistake.

universal. See COMPARATIVES, FALSE.

universal(ly) for *general(ly)* is not only loose, but also the cause of deterioration in the former word; as in 'Mr George Bernard Shaw's theories may be more universally accepted by future generations than they are to-day'.

unless, misused for *except*. 'Unless when carried out on a set purpose, it [i.e., alliteration] offends the ear.'

unloosen is obsolescent for '*to unloose*'. It is not synonymous with *loosen*.

unmeasurable is preferable in the two literal senses 'incapable of being measured, on account of great size, extent, or amount, in reference to material things, to dimensions, to time', as in 'The tower . . . was of an unmeasurable height', and 'insusceptible of measurement; immeasurable', as in 'The Church is unmeasurable by foot-rule'. (*O.E.D.*) But in transferred applications, in figurative uses, *immeasurable* is preferable, as in 'immeasurable ambition', 'the immeasurable grace of God'.

unmoral, amoral, non-moral, immoral. The last—opposed to *moral*—is positive ('evil; corrupt, depraved'); the others are negative, and synonymous one with another. Purists prefer *non-moral* to *unmoral*. *Amoral* is the best word for the sense 'not to be judged by a moral criterion; not connected with moral considerations'.

unpayable is incorrect for *non-paying* and *improfitable*. 'That would be a most unpayable business.'

unpracticable is obsolete for *impracticable*; **unpractical** is obsolescent as a synonym of *impractical*. Good writers distinguish *unpractical* (merely not practical) from *impractical* (decidedly the opposite of *practical*).

unqualified is not, as some persons assume, synonymous with *unrestricted* or *entire*. This erroneous assumption vitiates the homely force of 'To have unqualified charge of a garden makes a vital difference in a person's outlook on gardening'.

unreadable is subjective ('too dull or obscure to be read with patience'); *illegible* is objective ('indecipherable').' Thus, 'Many of the manuscripts of unreadable novels are illegible'.

unreligious is neutral, 'not religious', or pejorative, 'ungodly'; *irreligious* is pejorative, 'ungodly, impious'.

unresenting of is incorrect for *unresentful of* (or *not resenting*), as in 'Unresenting of his old friend's raillery'.

unresponsible = 'not in a position of responsibility; not yet at the age at which responsibility sets in'; *irresponsible* may be used in the same sense ('You shouldn't have handed the question-paper to an irresponsible person'), but generally, in current usage, it = 'feckless, undependable'.

unretentive. See IRRETENTIVE.

unsanitary should be reserved for 'not possessing sanitation'; *insanitary* = 'injurious to health; unhealthy'. 'An uninhabited desert is merely unsanitary; a camp of nomads may be offensively insanitary.'

unscathed. See SCATHELESS.

unsuccess means, negatively, 'lack of success'; positively, 'failure'.

unsufferable is less usual than *insufferable*.

until. See at TILL.

untouchable. See COMPARATIVES, FALSE.

uphold. See HOLD UP.

upon and **on.** Of these synonyms, *upon* is stronger and more formal and impressive than *on*; but it is slowly falling into disuse in speech; in writing, *upon* is often preferred to *on* on the score of euphony.— To convey both elevation and contact, *up on* is required.

upstair, whether as adverb or adjective, is obsolescent for *upstairs*; as a noun, only *upstairs* is permissible.

upward and **upwards.** *Upward* only is adjective, both *upward* and *upwards* are adverbs, but *upward* is the more usual. *Upwards* is idiomatic form in the sense 'to a higher aggregate, figure, price, height, length, etc.', as in 'Accommodation for three guineas upwards'. (*O.E.D.*) **upwards of** is incorrect for *rather less than* or *nearly* or *not quite*, as in 'upwards of a hundred' (some number in the 90's).

urban is 'of or belonging to or characteristic of or resembling a city', whereas *urbane* is 'having the manners or culture regarded as characteristic of a city', hence 'civil, courteous', hence 'blandly polite', indeed 'suave', and is used in transferred senses ('urbane manners', 'urbane mind').

urge, noun, has gone some way towards superseding '(strong) desire', 'eagerness', 'appetition', '(powerful) ambition'. It has, in the form 'body-urge', been burlesqued in that shrewd satirical novel, *Cold Comfort Farm*, and it is disliked by many—not all of them purists. Yet it is used by numerous thinkers, scholars, writers; for instance, Sir Arthur Thomson, Professor A. N. Whitehead, Olaf Stapledon, A. B. Cox. Its least objectionable use appears to be 'the creative urge' (or 'the urge to create').

USAGE. See IDIOM.

us both and **us each.** See WE BOTH . . .

use (v.). See CONSUME.

USELESS FULL-STOPS (PERIODS). *Dr, Ld, Mr, Mrs, St,* and *Mlle, Mme,* are correct; *Dr., Ld., Mr.,* etc., are incorrect—and silly.

USELESS LATIN ADJECTIVES. There are numerous Latin- and Greek-derived adjectives that are unnecessary, for they duplicate a satisfactory 'Saxon' adjective (or noun used adjectivally). To speak of the *hodiernal post* (or *mail*) for *to-day's post, avuncular* for *uncle's,* is intolerable; but then, very few of us would.

usual to is infelicitous for *usual for.* 'Ward Syme at six-thirty in the evening was in the state of cheerful confusion usual to that time of day.' It would have been still better to write 'usual at that time of day'.

utmost, utter, uttermost. See COMPARATIVES, FALSE.

Etymologically, *utter* is the comparative, and *utmost* the (double) superlative of Old English *ut,* 'out' ('external'); *uttermost* = *utter* + *most,* an etymological absurdity.

Utter now = 'extreme, absolute, complete, entire', as in 'utter darkness'; (of denials, refusals, recantations, etc.) 'unmodified' or 'decisive'; (of persons) 'complete', as in 'an utter fool'.

Uttermost is obsolescent in the senses 'outermost' ('He flew to the uttermost island of the Hebridean group'), and 'extreme' or 'utmost', as in Ruskin's 'To speak with the uttermost truth of expression'; its only active sense is the very restricted one, 'last in a series', as in 'I shall pay to the uttermost farthing'. *Uttermost,* in short, is disappearing from general use.

Utmost physically = 'outmost' (most remote; most external), as in 'Knights of utmost North and West' (Tennyson); hence, it = 'furthest extended', as in 'With my utmost sight I could only just discern it'—a sense now rare. The predominant sense is 'of the greatest or highest degree, number, amount; extreme', as in 'The utmost profit of a cow', 'With the utmost cheerfulness'.

V

vagaries is an ill-chosen word in this sentence, 'Primitive man realized that he must have some protection from the vagaries of Nature—from the biting wind, the cold wet rain, and even the blazing sun'. Here the writer might better have used 'the vicissitudes (of Nature)'. *Vagary,* 'an aimless wandering', implies something indefinite, whereas these natural phenomena, though often unforeseen, are definite.

VAGUENESS. See WOOLLINESS.

valuable is that which has intrinsic value; **valued** is (that which is) regarded as having value. A *valuable* thing is perhaps not properly *valued*; a *valued* one is not necessarily *valuable.*

valueless. See INVALUABLE.

vantage. See ADVANTAGE.

vapid (pronounced *vappid*) and **insipid.** *Vapid* (L. *vapidus,* savourless) is (of liquors, beverages) 'flat', (of food) 'flavourless'; hence, fig., 'devoid of animation, zest, or interest' (esp., 'vapid talk', 'vapid amusements'). *Insipid* (L. *insipidus,* tasteless) is, lit., 'without taste, or with very little taste'; hence, fig., 'lifeless; dull or unexciting', as in 'insipid compliments'. The nouns are *vapidity* and *insipidity; vapidness* and *insipidness* are inferior forms. (*O.E.D.*)

vari-coloured and **variegated** are, the former obligatorily, the latter preferably, to be used of or in reference to colour. *Varied,* already falling into disuse, can safely be discarded by those who fear to confound it with *various,* for every sense of *varied* is shared by *various.* As for *various*: the discriminating writer refrains from using it in the weakened senses 'more than one; several; many'. 'We met various times' is, at best, infuriatingly vague: say *several* or *many* as the context demands.

varied. See VARI-COLOURED.

VARIETY. See SYNONYMS, last paragraph.

various, misused for *certain,* as in 'There are various things that no decent man will do'. See at VARI-COLOURED.

venal and **venial,** often confused, have opposite meanings; the former being 'purchasable', 'subject to mercenary or corrupt influences', the latter 'pardonable, excusable'. (*O.E.D.*)

vengeance and **revenge** (nn.). See AVENGE.

venom and **poison.** The former is the poison secreted by snakes and certain animals; also it is used figuratively for 'virulence; bitter spite or malice'.

venture. See ADVENTURE.

veracity and **truth.** *Veracity* = 'truthfulness; accuracy', or even 'a truth' but not 'truth' itself.

VERB + (PRO)NOUN + GOVERNED VERB ('I *saw it gain* on him'); and **VERB + (PRO)NOUN + ing FORM OF VERB** ('I *saw it gaining* on him'). In the former, the second or governed verb expresses a single, definite, time-precise, completed action, whereas in the latter the *-ing* form ('gaining') expresses a continuous, incomplete action. In the former, the sense is 'I saw that it gained on him', but in the latter the sense is 'I saw that it was gaining on him, but I did not see what eventually happened'.—Cf. 'I shall see it gain on him' and 'I shall see it gaining on him', likewise 'I see [the true, not the historic present] it gain on him' and 'I see it gaining on him': the same nuances hold good in those two tenses, except that the limiting of the action in 'I see it gain on him' is less clear-cut than it is in 'I saw it gain on him'.

VERB UNCOMPLETED. 'Political upheavals in Europe influence the Londoner's daily life in strange ways, and they always have.' Such ungrammatical short cuts are bad English; the change of tense necessitates a correct completion of the verb; 'and have always done so' would be correct and would avoid the jolt caused by leaving the auxiliary in suspense.

verbiage and **verbosity** are occasionally confused. Roughly, *verbosity* results in *verbiage*; nowadays, *verbosity* is applied mostly to speaking, *verbiage* mostly to writing; *verbosity* is both tendency and result, whereas *verbiage* is only result.

VERBOSITY.
'A plethora of words becomes the apoplexy of reason.' C. A. Ward, *Oracles of Nostradamus,* 1891.
The *O.E.D.* defines verbosity as 'superfluity of words', with the alternatives 'wordiness; prolixity'.

A few brief examples of a fault exemplified best by long passages:—
'Such are the vicissitudes of this our sublunary existence': for 'Such is life'.

'Lassitude seems to be a word unknown to the vocabulary of the swallows' (Morris, *British Birds*): an amusing instance of ponderous circumlocution, all the heavier because it was intended to lighten the dullness of direct statement.

'Modern Stockholmers, *irrespective of class*, are accustomed to fairly substantial midday meals in restaurants, and typists must have shared the indignation of their managing directors at *being forced this week within the confines of a packet of sandwiches*' (*The Daily Telegraph*); the italics are mine.

'Are we quite sure that newly emancipated woman has yet acquired a sound biological status, or secured for herself a harmonious psycho-physiological equilibrium?' (cited by Sir Alan Herbert).

'Your eyes will scarcely believe that cameras could record its roaring climax of catastrophe and desolation' (advertisement of a film).

* * * * * * * *

Verbosity, therefore, is almost the same thing as *pleonasm*, which is 'the use of more words in a sentence than are necessary to express the meaning; redundancy of expression'—except that *verbosity* has certain connotations absent from the most extended signification of *pleonasm*.

Vergil is inferior to *Virgil*, the Latin being *Virgilius*. Hence *Vergilian* is also to be avoided. [*Vergil, Vergilian* are the spellings preferred by *Webster's* and by *Harpers' Latin Dictionary*.]

vernacular is often used loosely for *low language* and *jargon* (technicalities). Properly, the noun and adjective = '(the language) naturally spoken by the people of a particular country or district', i.e., 'native or indigenous (language)'; hence, 'written, spoken or translated into the native language'; 'belonging to or characteristic of the native language'. In the 16th–17th Centuries, English was the vernacular, Latin the learned language, and French the language of diplomacy.

verse and **stanza.** For the sake of the valuable distinction, reserve *verse* for 'one line of verse or poetry' and use *stanza* for 'a small number of metrical lines forming a unit in a longer composition'.

verso and **recto.** The *recto* is the front, the *verso* the back of a manuscript or printed leaf or sheet. As The *O.E.D.* remarks, 'The left-hand page of a book is the verso of that leaf, and faces the recto of the next'.

vertebra has plural *vertebrae*.

very modifies adjective (*very angry*) or adverb (*very foolishly*), but not a past participle (*It is very improved* being wrong, *much improved* being right).

Vèry or **Vèrey; Verey; Verry:** misspellings of *Very*, the name of the flare, light, pistol.

very interesting but **much interested** or, less commonly, **very much interested.** Purists object to *very interested, very*

pleased, very disappointed, very annoyed,
etc. They prefer *much interested, much*
(or *very much*) *pleased, much dis-*
appointed; for the last, however, both
idiom and precision demand *acutely*
disappointed.
Clearly, idiom forbids *much interest-*
ing, much pleasing, much disappointing.
vest and **waistcoat.** A *waistcoat* is that
part of a man's suit of clothes which he
wears under his coat and which is of the
same material as the coat and trousers,
unless it is an *odd* waistcoat or a fancy
one—usually called a *vest* in the U.S.A.
In English usage, *vest* is the more
common non-commercial name for a
man's undershirt. In both English and
American usage, *vest* is, with reference to
women's apparel, (*a*) an undershirt, (*b*)
'part of a woman's dress bodice'.
Singlet is 'an unlined woollen garment
. . . worn as a man's undershirt'.
vestigial, misused for *rudimentary* or
rough-and-ready. This error occurs
several times in John Gunther's *Inside*
Asia.
via, 'by way of', refers to the direction of
a journey, not to the means of travelling;
therefore the following is wrong: 'Out
at the end of the wharf a man sold
tickets to'—'for' would be better—
' "excursion" trips via a speed boat',
Erle Stanley Gardner, *The Case of the*
Dangerous Dowager.
vicar. See 'RECTOR and VICAR'.
vicarial. See RECTORAL.
vicinage and **vicinity; neighbourhood.**
Vicinage is less usual than *neighbourhood*
in the collective sense, 'a number of
places lying near, one to another'; in this
sense it is preceded by *a* or *the, this* or
that, and it possesses a plural; 'The
agricultural and mineral treasures of its
vicinage'; frequent in the phrase, *in the*
(or *this* or *our* or . . .) *vicinage. In the*
vicinage of, like *in the neighbourhood of,*
= 'near to, contiguous to'. Moreover,
both *vicinage* and *neighbourhood* bear
the transferred sense, 'the people living
in a certain district or locality; the
people living near to a certain place or
within a certain range', as in 'The
vicinage applied . . . to the bishop for
leave to dig up the body and burn it' and
'The neighbourhood had scandalized
her'. Both *vicinage* and *vicinity* mean
'nearness, propinquity, proximity', as in
'The common white pottery . . . will not
bear vicinage to a brisk kitchen fire for
half-an-hour' and 'Under these conditions all vicinity of watercourses, unless

bridged, should be avoided'. Also *in the*
vicinity = *in the vicinage, in the neigh-*
bourhood; and *in the vicinity of* = *in the*
vicinage (or *neighbourhood*) *of* = 'near
or close (to)', as in 'The . . . ship
"Marseilles" capsized in the vicinity of
Portpatrick'. In a transferred sense, *in the*
vicinity of, like *in the neighbourhood of,* =
'something near to (a specified amount)',
as in 'In the vicinity of a hundred dollars',
'in the neighbourhood of sixteen pence'.
(*O.E.D.*) [*Vicinage* is not current in
American speech.]
victuals is not a mere synonym of *food,* as
the elegancy-lovers render it, for it
means 'articles of food; supplies, or
various kinds, of provisions; in later use,
especially articles of ordinary diet
prepared for use' (*O.E.D.*). [In American
usage, *victuals* is limited to dialect and
comic stories.]
vide = 'see!, consult!'; **viz.** = 'that is to
say: namely'. 'This strange event (*vide*
Motley) has never been satisfactorily
explained'; 'Three of Plumer's men . . .,
viz. Troopers Abrahamson, White and
Parkin'. Both *vide* and *viz.* (short for
videlicet) should be written in italics.
view (v.), misused for *look.* ' "If 'e can git
aht o' 'ere", 'Big Bill' said, viewing
round the place in the light of a candle
he had lit, " 'e's a dam' sight cleverer'n
what 'e looks" ' (John G. Brandon).
viewpoint. See STANDPOINT.
vigil, properly a prolonged night-watch,
is often misused to mean any wait, even if
trivial and extremely brief. 'Selecting the
most comfortable seat, and placing his
beer on the floor beside him, Dick
settled down to wait. It was not a long
vigil; for in less than a couple of minutes
Mr Potter made his appearance.'
vigour for *rigour.* Frank Shaw, *Atlantic*
Murder, 'Even the crew-quarters under-
went a microscopic examination. . . .
[The new hands,] naturally, were the
ones to be watched with extra vigour.'
vintage should be used only in reference
to wine: to speak, as the jocularly careless occasionally speak, of 'a (motor) car
of ancient vintage', has ceased to be
amusing.
violin. See at FIDDLE.
violincella is an incorrect spelling and
pronunciation of *violoncello.*
virility should not be used of sexual
power in women.
visa has been adopted at the expense of
visé. Visa, therefore, should not be
italicized.
vivarium and **vivary.** *Webster's* gives the

latter as a mere variant of the former;
The O.E.D. regards *vivarium* as the
superior form. The learned plural is
vivaria, the general plural is *vivariums*
(cf. *aquariums*). A *vivarium* is 'a place
where living animals [L. *vivus*, alive],
especially fish, are maintained or preserved for food'; also, 'a stretch of water,
specially adapted or prepared for the
keeping of living animals under their
normal conditions'. It is best to distinguish it from *aquarium* (used in
reference to fish and aquatic plants).
(*O.E.D.*)

viz. See VIDE.

vocation. See AVOCATION.

VOGUE WORDS. Many words (and a
few phrases) have acquired a power and an
influence beyond those which they originally possessed; certain pedants say, Beyond
what these terms have any right to mean
or to imply. But, like persons, words cannot always be taken for granted. It just
cannot be assumed that they will for ever
trudge along in the prescribed rut and for
ever do the expected thing! Journalists,
authors, and the public whim—sometimes,
also, the force of great events, the compulsion of irresistible movements—have
raised lowly words to high estate or invested humdrum terms with a picturesque
and individual life or brought to the most
depressing jargon a not unattractive general currency. Such words gain a momentum
of their own, whatever the primary impulse may have been.

Examples: *blueprint, complex* (n.),
*fantastic, glamour, integrate, operative,
pattern, reaction, rewarding, sublimation,
urge* (n.).

voluptious is a misspelling and a mispronunciation of *voluptuous*; cf. PRESUMP-
TIOUS for *presumptuous*.

voyage. See TRIP.

**VULGARISMS AND LOW LAN-
GUAGE.** *Vulgarisms* and *low language*
(*vulgar language*) are often taken to be
exactly synonymous. But it is well to
differentiate. *Low* (or *vulgar*) *language* is
of two kinds: (1) words foisted on one
social class by a lower class; words
brought from trade into drawing-room.
And (2)—closely connected and often
merging with (1)—those which have been
originated in and are used mostly by the
proletariat (a word employed here as a
necessary classification).

With (1) we need not concern ourselves
further: (2), however, is important. Examples of (2) are *dotty* and *dippy* for
'mad', *lolly* (a sweet), *codger* and *geezer*,

old woman (wife), *to cop, to bash, to do* or
diddle (the latter being no longer adjudged low). Of these, some are slangy,
others merely lowly and familiar. The
connexion between the slangy and the
lowly words is so intimate that, the
moment they cease to be slangy or
lowly, they tend to become admitted to
the class of ordinary colloquialism. Yet
the distinction between such lownesses
and slang is as desirable as it is legitimate.
Low words are those which, used by the
poorest and meanest of the poorer
classes, are yet neither cant nor 'good'
colloquialisms (admitted into decent
society): some are slang, some are
idiom. Excellent examples are found in
'deep' Cockney, where we see that much
low language is an almost inextricable
tangle of slang and idiom; some of it so
racy and picturesque and expressive that
it may put much Standard English into
the shade. Take such a passage as this
from *Arthur's*, by Neil Lyons:—

' "So it's corfee fur everybody", Jerry
the Twister had explained upon his
arrival at Arthur's stall. "Give me a quid,
'e did, as a start-off an' then blighted well
fought me fur it, the blighter. Where am
I? ses 'e. Kennington Road, ses I. Lead
me to the Strand, ses 'e. It was a lead, I
give you *my* word. 'E was a 'ot un.
Climb down nigh every airey we passed,
stole the milkcans, an' tied 'em up to the
knockers. Pinched a rozzer in the leg,
give 'im a visitin' card, an' stole his
whistle. Put 'is dooks up to a fireman,
tossed 'im fur 'is chopper, an' kissed 'is
wife. Run fur 'is very life into Covent
Garden Market (me after 'im), bought a
cabbidge, took it into a resterong where
all the nobs was dinin'. sends fur the boss
an' ses: Cully, cook this for my dinner." '

In such language as that, there are
many faults: but it is ruddy with good
health, and bursting with life. As G. K.
Chesterton said in 'A Defence of Slang'
(*The Defendant*, 1901), 'The lower classes
live in a state of war, a war of words.
Their readiness is the product of the
same fiery individualism as the readiness
of the old fighting oligarchs. Any cabman
has to be ready with his tongue, as any
gentleman [had once] to be ready with
his sword.'

Now we come to *vulgarisms* in the
sense in which I have for some years
tried to fix it, to stabilize it, to get it
accepted by the pundits and the philologists.

Vulgarisms are words that belong to

idiomatic English or denote such objects
or processes or functions or tendencies or
acts as are not usually mentioned by the
polite in company and are never, under
those names, mentioned in respectable
circles. Doctors may speak of them by
their medical names, and anyone may
refer to them—though not usually before
members of the opposite sex—by their
technical and generally Latinized or
Grecized designations, and persons
secretly libidinous or coprological delight
to drag such words into their talk in
terms of Freud and his followers. *Arse*,
an excellent Old English word, is no
longer obscene; it occurred in Frederic
Manning's great war novel, *The Middle
Parts of Fortune*, in 1930, and has since
appeared in print with increasing frequency. Ca. 1850–1920, the usual 'Saxon'
word was *backside*, but since the early
1920's—thanks largely to such 'choice
spirits' as Sir Alan Herbert—*behind* has
taken its place.* *Bum*, now decidedly
vulgar, has become mainly a schoolboys'
word; as used by Shakespeare, Dekker,
Jonson, it was much more dignified.
Bottom, in very general use since ca. 1830,
has always been considered more genteel
than *backside*, which is mainly a man's
word, whereas *bottom* is a woman's
word; since *behind* acceded to the throne,
bottom has taken to itself a moral recti-
tude even greater than *behind's* and an air
of primness happily absent from *behind*.
Posterior is politer still, but if we use the
plural we connote *buttocks*, which, so
much more precise and 'Saxon', is not
quite so acceptable to the prudish.
Euphemism, here as in all such words, is
often employed, sometimes in some
childish form as *sit-me-down*. *Chest* need
not be a euphemism: as a synonym for
the breast, it is merely—a synonym. But
as equivalent to the female breasts, it is a
silly, inexact euphemism. The 'Saxon'
words for the sexual parts are excellently
idiomatic and belong to the aristocracy
of the language, but, because they denote
these intimates, they are regarded as
vulgar and, though they are certainly not
slang, even as slangy. (A useful collective
noun is *genitals*, usable of either sex.)
The 'Saxon' words for 'to urinate' and 'to

defecate' are idiomatic and perfect English,
but association and prudery have put them
into quarantine; for the latter function,
however, there exists the estimable *stool*.
  These are vulgarisms. The *slangy* synonyms, which are numerous, belong to
low language.

W

wage; wages. *Wages*, construed as a
singular ('The wages of sin is death'), is
an archaism. In ordinary English, *wages*
(construed as plural) = 'the amount paid
periodically, especially by the day or
week or month, for the labour or service
of a workman or servant' (as opposed to
a *salary*, which is paid for non-manual or
non-mechanical work); but the singular,
wage, 'has sometimes a special convenience with reference to a particular
instance or amount', as in '[Masters]
commonly enter into a private bond or
agreement, not to give more than a
certain wage' and 'a day's wage for a
day's work'. Note *wage-labour* and, in
Political Economy, *wage-fund* (or *wages-
fund*).
wait is the intransitive ('Will you wait, or
not?'); **await** (or **wait for**) is the transitive
form ('Will you wait for me?'; 'He awaits
our arrival'). There is now an awkwardness in 'Wait what she's going to say';
but this transitive use of *wait* is still
acceptable in some locutions, such as,
e.g., 'Keeping her thoughts from the
ordeal that waited her' (Alec Waugh,
Going Their Own Ways). See also AWAIT.
waive, 'to relinquish, refrain, forbear', is
occasionally confused with *wave*, to make
a certain motion with the hands.
wake; waken. See AWAKE.
want (wish, desire). *Want* (v.i.) is 'to be
lacking'; archaic except as *to be wanting*
(to be lacking). *To want for nothing* is 'not
to lack the necessaries or comforts of
life'. As v.t., *want* = to *desire*, to *wish for*
(something); also with infinitive as in
'He wants to do it' (he desires or wishes
to do it); also 'to *want* a person to do
something'; also it = 'to wish to see, or
to speak to, a person', as in 'You're
wanted at the door', which is familiar,
not literary English.
-ward is a suffix both adjectival and adverbial, whereas **-wards** is adverbial only.
warn, 'to give timely notice of impending
danger or misfortune' (*O.E.D.*), with
other slightly varying senses all implying
danger or penalties, is often misused for
to give preliminary notice or information

* [In American usage *behind* has for a long time
been the usual nursery and homely word, much
commoner than *backside* and somewhat effeminate
as contrasted with the masculine *arse* (always pronounced, and popularly spelled, *ass*). But the present slang is *fanny*, which has had a spectacular
career in smart publications and stage-shows; and
in the home and nursery, whence it may have come
(cf. *doll*), challenges *behind* itself.]

without the implication of unpleasant consequences if the *warning* be neglected; 'I wonder if it is at all possible to be warned if there is likely to be a return of the aurora borealis at any time?'

warn of is incorrect for *warn against*, in 'Against unwarranted identification Korzybski delivers his major attack. He constantly warns of the *subject-predicate* form.'

warrant, warranty; guarantee, guaranty. For the last two, see GUARANTEE. *Warranty* is noun only; *warrant*, both noun and verb. *Warranty*, in Law, is 'an act of warranting'; in literary use, it = 'substantiating evidence (or witness)', as in 'By what warranty A deed so hateful say you I have wrought?' (Whitelaw's *Sophocles*), and also 'a justifying reason or ground' (*for* an action or a belief), as in 'The Pope was claiming powers ... for which there was no warranty in the history of the Church'; for the second literary sense, *warrant* is a synonym ('Have we any warrant for a belief in immortality?'). *Warrant* bears the senses, 'authorization; an act of authorization; evidence of authorization', as in 'An assembly that is without warrant from the sovereign is unlawful'; concretely, *warrant* is 'a document conveying authority or security' (*search warrant*), 'a writ or order issued by some executive body'. The verb *warrant* = 'to guarantee as true, to make oneself answerable for (a statement), especially in *I warrant*; 'to attest the truth or authenticity of; to authenticate', as in 'That [his confession] was genuine could not be doubted: for it was warranted by the signatures of some of the most distinguished military men living' (Macaulay); 'to authorize (a person to do something), as in 'Who has warranted this step?'; hence (of things), 'to furnish adequate grounds for (a course of action), to justify', as in 'It is impossible to say whether this accusation was warranted by facts'; to 'guarantee (goods, articles) to be of the quality, quantity, make, etc., specified', as in *warranted free from adulteration*. (*O.E.D.*)

was or **were** in conditionals. If there is no doubt, use *was*, as in 'He was instructed to determine whether this *was*'—not *were*—'practicable'. When there is doubt, use *were*, as in 'If it *were*'—not *was*—'justifiable, the head-master would take the necessary steps'. See also SUBJUNCTIVE.

washwoman is American (but not the best American) for *washerwoman*, as *washman* is similar American for *washerman*; *washerlady*, *washlady* are absurdities, illustrative of euphemism - cum - genteelism.

watch out for *watch* is not only colloquial but unnecessary, as in 'I knew that something was going to happen. . . . So I watched out, thinking that perhaps I might be able to prevent the worst.'

'way (adv.) is short for (*far*) *away* in such phrases as 'sold, way below cost', 'way down South', 'to go way off' (afar), 'way down East', 'from way back' (from a rural, or a remote, district): all are Americanisms (dialectal and colloquial). **'way** for *entirely* is colloquial, as in 'He wrote and wrote, 'way through the night'.

way of being, by. 'I am by way of being an artist' is permissible, except in literary English, when the speaker wishes to make his statement appear more modest; but 'He is by way of being an artist' is a senseless circumlocution when nothing more is meant than 'He is an artist'.

ways, in *come* (or *go*) *one's ways*, is now either dialectal or solecistic. So, too, for *a little ways* and *a good* (or *great* or *long*) *ways*—a short or a long distance.

we aren't and **we're not.** (Reversed: only *aren't we* is possible as a shortening of *are not we?*) Let us take *we're not ready* and *we aren't ready*. If the emphasis is on *ready*, at least as many people would say, 'We aren't *ready*, you know', as would say 'We're not *ready*, you know'; if on *not*, 'We're *not* ready' is preferable; if on *we*, '*We* aren't ready' is probably as common as '*We're* not ready'.

we'll is allowed by *Webster's* to represent either *we shall* or *we will*.

wed for *marry* is overdone by journalists, especially in headlines, where the short word is *so* convenient. Mr Frank Whitaker has stigmatized it as a 'rubber-stamp word' (see AMAZING).—*Wed* is, in ordinary English, inflected thus: *wed*— *wedded*—*wedded* (*wed* being dialectal or poetical).

wedding for *marriage* is to be used with care. Properly employed, *wedding* = 'the performance of the wedding-rite' or 'the ceremony of a marriage, with its attendant festivities', as in 'weddings, christenings, burials', 'Are you to be at the Milton wedding next week?'

week-end. A *week-end* (or *short week-end*) is from Saturday afternoon until Monday morning; a *long week-end* is from Friday evening until Monday morning.

weigh is incorrect for *way* in *under weigh*, 'in preparation'. 'Getting under weigh', W. H. G. Kingston, *Lusitanian Sketches*, 1845; Louis Bromfield, *It Had to Happen*, 1936, 'Now that he had a project under weigh his spirits rose'. (The metaphor is nautical.)

well nigh. See NIGH.

Welsh Rabbit. See RABBIT, WELSH.

we're not. See WE AREN'T . . .

were to + infinitive + preposition. See 'IS TO + infinitive + preposition'.

westerly and **western.** Cf. the remarks at 'EASTERLY and EASTERN'.

Westralians is not a blend that the inhabitants of *Western* (not *West*) *Australia* like. But *West Australians* is permissible.

westward; westwards. As adjective, only *westward* ('a westward view', 'a westward journey'). As adverb, either is correct, but *westward*, besides being much the older, is preferred by current usage.

wet—wet or **wetted**—wet or **wetted.** With *have*, *wet* is the commoner participle; with *be*, *wetted* is as common as and less ambiguous than *wet*.

wharfs; wharves. Both are correct; *wharves* is the more euphonious, and the usual American form; in Great Britain, *wharfs* has become commoner.(*Webster's*.)

what, as subject, takes the singular verb, whether the complementary noun be singular or plural: thus, 'What I like is sprouts', not 'What I like are sprouts'; 'What the public wants are crime stories' should be 'what the public wants is crime stories'.

what and **which**, as interrogative adjectives. See 'WHICH and WHAT . . .'

what for *those which* is incorrect. ' "The bullets . . . known to have been fired by young Mr Moffatt . . . are the same as what killed this Bennett bloke".'

what for *which*. Until the present century, only purists objected to *what* in, e.g., 'He told the truth and, *what* is more, people recognized his statement to be true'. Nowadays, it is pretty generally conceded that the sentence should read, 'He told the truth and—which is more—' [or commas] 'people recognized his statement to be true'. *What*, here, could be only a compound relative = *that which*, but 'He told the truth and, that which is more, people recognized his statement to be true' can be defended only with difficulty and dialectic. The correct form is, 'He told the truth and, which'—i.e., which fact—'is more', i.e., more important, 'people recognized his statement to be true'.

A good example of the correct use occurs in Cameron McCabe's *The Face on the Cutting-Room Floor:* 'Yet, these very few blunders excepted, McCabe understood his opponents amazingly well, and—which is more important—made no attempt to deceive himself about their superiority in many stages of the "fight".'

what, as. 'But that I did see, sir, as plain as what I see you now', E. C. Bentley and H. Warner Allen in *Trent's Own Case*, 1936. The speech of an uneducated person, who should have said '*as plainly as I see you now*'.

what . . . for?, as an inverted form of *for what*, is sometimes ambiguous, as in the question (overheard), of mother to child: 'What did he change his bright new penny for?', which might mean '*Why* did he change it?'

what . . . is when. A not unusual form of grammatical clumsiness, as in 'What is really shocking is when an artist comes to a serious subject such as this'. This sentence might be better expressed in other ways, e.g., 'It is really shocking to see an artist come, etc.', or 'What is shocking is to find that an artist can come, etc.'

what use is incorrect in 'What use is it to learn Greek?' 'Of what use is it . . .?' would be correct.

when can be used for *in which*, after, e.g., *year*, as in 'The year when it happened'— 'The year in which it happened'.

when, misused for *whereas*. 'When the old Rhetoric treated ambiguity as a fault in language . . ., the new Rhetoric sees it as an inevitable consequence of the powers of language', I. A. Richards. Was this particular error the result of a conscientious desire to avoid *while* = *whereas*, and of a too hasty solution of that stylistic crux?

when . . . ever is often misused for *whenever*. ' "And the next time, Mac, don't tell me that if I'd just buckle down to the job a little sooner I could finish it with time to spare." "When did I ever say that?" I demanded with some heat.'

whence, from. Though found in the work of good writers, the 'from' is redundant. Swinburne, *Studies in Prose and Poetry*, 'The quarter from whence the following lucubration is addressed': this would be more correctly written 'The quarter whence . . .' or 'The quarter from which'.

Whence is clumsily used in 'Here Machiavelli's earth returned to whence it rose' (Byron), where *to whence* =|*to*|*that place whence*.

where for *that* is incorrect, as in 'I see where they had a heat wave'—i.e., 'I saw, in the newspaper, that they had a heat wave'.

where for *whither* is now usual, as in 'Where are you going?' ('Where are you going *to*?' is redundant.)

where; wherein; at (or **in**) **which:** omitted. Although syntactically and structurally on a par with the omission of the relative pronouns, *that, which, who*, the omission of *where(in)* and *at* (or *in) which* is not the same analytically or verbally, for *where* = *at* (or *in) which*, and *wherein* = *in which*; *where* and *wherein* = combinations of preposition + pronoun, whereas *that, which, who* are simples or singles (pronoun only). The result of omitting *where, wherein, at* (or *in) which*, is subjectively one of momentary ambiguity, objectively one of abruptness, as in 'Neil was for storming Erchany like young Lochinvar and carrying her to some place they could be married in secret'.

where from and **from where.** *Where* can = *to where* (or *where to*), as in 'Where are you going?' and thus take the place of *whither*; but *where* does not take the place of *whence*, for which either *where from* or *from where* must be used. 'I took that passage from Thucydides.' 'From *where*?' 'Where did that man come from' is more idiomatic than 'From where did that man come?'

whether, of. 'The whole question of whether we like it is ignored' is redundant for 'the . . . question whether' or 'the question of our liking it'.

whether or no; whether or not. *Whether or no*, as in 'Whether or no it is possible, I cannot say', is obsolescent for '*Whether or not* it is possible, I cannot say'. But *whether or not* is tautological for *whether*, except where the doubt is to be emphasized.

which and **that; who** and **that.** Of these relative pronouns, *which* refers to things only; *that* to things and persons; *who* to persons only. But *that* is not a syntactical synonym of either *which* or *who*.

With the caution that 'the tendency to appropriate *who* and *which* to persons and things respectively often outweighs other considerations; thus, "People *who* live in glass houses" is preferred to "people *that*"; this is particularly the case with *those, they*, and other pronouns of common gender. "Those *who* are in favour of this motion", is more usual than

"those *that*".' It is to be noted that relative clauses are used for two purposes:—

(1) The more sharply to define or to limit the antecedent, which without the ensuing relative clause would either make no sense or convey a sense different from the intended one. 'This is the book that G. K. Chesterton wrote'; 'Uneasy lies the head that wears a crown'. Here, the relative cause is ushered-in by *that*, except after a preposition ('He is a man for whom'—not 'for that'—'I have the deepest regard') or where *whose* is inevitable ('He is a man whose opinion means much to me'). No stop is to be used to separate this relative clause from its antecedent, a rule applying also when *who* and *which* are used with a preposition or when *whose* is obligatory, as in 'The man whose son is alive is not heirless'. (In 'His recovery was hastened by . . . games on the enchanted heath, near which he lived', the comma after 'heath' is necessary, for there was only one enchanted heath, whereas 'His recovery was hastened by games on an enchanted heath near which he lived' would restrict the connotation of 'heath' and imply that there was more than one such heath.) The comma-less form is restrictive; the comma'd form is non-restrictive; i.e., it falls into the next class. —The relative may be omitted, as in 'This is the book G. K. Chesterton wrote'. The *that* relative occurs especially where the antecedent is shown to belong to a class, a group, a kind, a species, as in 'All that live must die' and 'The greatest dramatist (that) we've ever had'.

(2) The more fully to give information about something (the antecedent) that is already defined sufficiently to make sense; this class of relative has various names, such as 'non-restrictive', 'parenthetical', 'explicative'. Compare 'His brother is very rich' with 'His brother, who owns a brewery, is very rich'; 'This book is excellent' with 'This book, which was written by Chesterton, is excellent'. Here, the relative clause must be ushered-in by *who* (*whom*) or *which*; a comma should separate the relative clause from the antecedent; and the relative pronoun cannot be omitted. Here, too, the relative clause may be supplanted by a conjunction + a noun or a pronoun (and, of course, the rest of a sentence), thus: 'This book is excellent, and Chesterton wrote it'.

A useful rule is this: the restrictive or

defining or limitative or necessary relative clause (relatives of Class 1) forms an integral, irremovable part of the sentence and cannot be put within parentheses, whereas the non-restrictive relatives (Class 2) can always be put within parentheses and their omission would not render the sentence senseless.

In speech, the use of *which* for *that* is less reprehensible, for intonation will convey the sense. 'But in the written language the need of discrimination between the two classes described is often felt, and the non-observance of the distinction is liable to lead to misunderstanding. Example: "All the members of the Council, who were also members of the Education Board, were to assemble in the Board-room". This would naturally imply that all members of the Council were members of the Education Board. "That", instead of "who", would clearly express the meaning intended, which is that "those who are members of the Education Board as well as of the Council were to assemble". . . . Observe the significance of the distinction in the following: "In two of the instances, *which* have come under my notice, the system has worked well"; "In two of the instances *that* have come under my notice, the system has worked well". The first means: "Two of the instances have come under my notice; in [all of] these instances the system has worked well". The second means: "Instances have come under my notice; in two of them the system has worked well".' (Quoted from Onions, *An Advanced English Syntax*: on which the preceding part of the article has, in the main, been based.)

which and **what**, as interrogative adjectives. As, to a stranger, one says, 'What do you want?' and, to a friend that has indicated the range of his desire, 'Which do you need?' so, if one knows the genus, one says 'Which sort of book?', or, knowing the species, 'Which kind of novel—adventure, love, detection?', or, knowing the sub-species, 'Which author?' or, knowing the author, 'Which book of his?' Likewise, with a number of books available one asks not 'What book do you want? but 'Which book do you want?': yet one often hears people ask, 'What book do you want?'—'What book do you choose?'—and so forth. Compare the following questions (where the suitable interrogative is employed): 'What sort of cooking do you get here?' —'Good, very good!'—'And which sort

of food—English, American, or Continental?'—'English?'—'And what drinks are there?'—'No beers, no ales, no spirits; only wines.'—'Which wines—the expensive? French or Italian? Or both French and Italian?'—'The prices range from the absurdly low to the million-airish-high, and as for the country and the growth, why! you choose which(ever) wine you fancy.'

In short, *what* is vague and implies ignorance in the speaker, *which* is precise and therefore implies some specific knowledge.

which and **who** lead frequently to lapses from good grammar and good sense.

Gilbert White commits the error of writing *and which*, where either 'and' or 'which' is unnecessary: 'This is their due, and which ought to be rendered to them'.

A more illiterate error is *which he*, as in Dorothy Sayers, *Unnatural Death*, 1927: 'Ironsides . . . a clerk on the Southern, which he always used to say joking like, "Slow but safe, like the Southern—that's me" '; and "I believe the gentleman acted with the best intentions, 'avin' now seen 'im, which at first I thought he was a wrong 'un'.

which for *which fact* is clumsy and sometimes ambiguous, as in 'That rifle cost me fifteen pounds, which has left me short of cash'.

which, like. See LIKE WHICH.

which . . . were for *which . . . was* may, to the sceptical, appear to be an error unlikely to be committed by the educated person. It is an error more frequent than the sceptical realize. For instance, in so good a writer as Wilfranc Hubbard, there occurs this sentence, 'You ask me which of the two lives were least'— better, 'the less'—'worthy of record' (*Orvieto Dust*).

while and **whilst.** See 'AMONG and AMONGST'.

while, whilst for *whereas* or *and* (or even *but*). Sir Alan Herbert gives a comic example of this: 'The Curate read the First Lesson while the Rector read the Second'.

while for *although* is a perverted use of the correct sense of *while*, 'at the same time as', 'during the same time that . . .'.

whiskers and **moustache.** *The O.E.D.* settles the frequent confusion, thus:— '[whiskers.] The hair that grows on an adult man's face; formerly commonly applied to that on the upper lip, now called *moustache*, and sometimes to (or including) that on the chin (*beard*); now restricted to that on the cheeks or sides of the face.'

who and that (relative pronouns). See 'WHICH and THAT'.

who and whom. Such phrases as 'the man who I saw there' are very common in speech, for people appear to think that *whom* sounds pedantic. *Whom* for *who*, however, is the more frequent error in literary use. Thus Sir Wm Gell refers to a character 'whom it is possible may be at some future time introduced to my reader'; and Mrs Beatrice Kean Seymour has ' "We've met several people here, who remember him." She had not said whom they were.' Such a sentence as 'Men say who I am' becomes, as an interrogative, 'Who do men say that I am?', not as in the Authorized Version of the Bible, 'Whom do men say that I am?' (cited by Onions).

who else's. See WHOSE ELSE'S.

whoever for *who . . . ever*; and vice versa. In 'Whoever saw him do such a thing? I've known him for twenty years and have never known him to do it', *whoever* should be 'Who ever (saw . . .)'. But 'Who ever says such a thing is a liar' is incorrect for 'Whoever says such a thing is a liar'.

whole, the. 'The whole three of them' is incorrect for 'all three' or 'all the three'. 'The whole lot', however, is correct, whereas the common 'all the lot' is illiterate, for *lot* is singular, though meaning a group or number of things. Nesfield quotes *The Daily Telegraph*, February, 1900, 'This was the cost for removing snow from the whole of the thoroughfares of the metropolis' ('all the streets of London').

whom. See 'WHO and WHOM'.

whomever, whomsoever; whosever, whosesoever. These are the correct accusatives and genitives respectively of *whoever* and *whosoever*. But *whosever* is rare and *whosesoever* is archaic; for either of these genitives, modern usage prefers *whatever person's*. *Whomever* and *whomsoever* are subject to the same confusion with *whoever* and *whosoever* as *whom* is with *who*; e.g., 'They shall not be impeded by whomsoever it may be' (Ruskin).

whose for *which*. Strictly, *whose* refers to persons only. But *whose* for *of which* is permissible when employed to avoid the awkwardness of *the* [noun] *of which*, as in 'A large number of brass discs, *whose* workmanship [= the workmanship of which] shows that they belong to the later

period of Celtic art, have been found in Ireland'. (Onions).

whose, and, misused for *whose*. 'She who swore away the life of Kidden the porter and whose (Kidden's) blood still cries aloud for vengeance'.

whose else's. ' "You are sure it was Mr Inglethorpe's voice you heard?" "Oh, yes, sir, whose else's could it be?" ' The correct form for familiar Standard English is *who else's*; less common but permissible when the noun does not follow is *whose else*. See ELSE'S.

why for. See FOR WHY.

wide and broad. (See BREADTH . . .) In 'Cliff nodded and clenched and unclenched his wide mobile hands', we feel that *broad* would have been better. Whereas *broad* connotes amplitude (*broad shoulders*), *wide* emphasizes the distance between the limits—underlines the separation (*at wide intervals*). Wherever generosity or freedom from narrowness or pettiness is involved, *broad* is used (*broad-minded, in broad outline*). Then take 'a *wide*—a *broad*—range of subjects': in the former, number is chiefly important; in the latter, weight or generosity.

wiggle and wriggle. To *wiggle* is now colloquial when it is not dialectal, whether it is v.i. (to waggle; to wriggle) or v.t. (to wriggle something about, to cause something to wriggle).

will and shall. See 'SHALL and WILL'.

will be to + infinitive + preposition. See IS TO + infinitive + preposition.

windward and windwards. The latter is obsolescent; it occurs only in *to windwards*, for which *to windward* is much commoner. As an adjective, *windward* = 'moving against the wind', as in 'Windward Great Circle Sailing' (J. Greenwood, *The Sailor's Sea Book*); 'weatherly', as in 'An excellent windward boat'; and 'facing the wind', as in *the Windward Islands* (opposed to *the Leeward Islands*). As an adverb, *windward* = 'to windward, facing the wind', as in 'Tacking about, and so getting to Windward of them, they . . . gain'd a great advantage' (James Tyrrell, 1700). (*O.E.D.*)

wish-fulfilment and **wishful thinking.** Vogue words.

with. Except where ambiguity would result, I urge that *with* should be used of the instrument and *by* restricted to the agent. 'He was killed with [not by] a spanner.'

with + plural verb. 'Michael, accompanied by his wife, is at the door' is clearly correct; so is 'Michael, with his wife, is at the door' where the stress is on Michael, but if Michael and his wife are equally important (or unimportant), then 'Michael, with his wife, are at the door' (in which case, it is better to omit the comma after 'Michael'). See Onions, *An Advanced English Syntax.*

withal is an archaism.

within. See 'IN for *within*'. N.B.: this is not an error but an infelicity. When it is so easy to avoid confusion, why not avoid it? A good example occurs in the legend to be seen on the vans of a certain London firm: 'Goods delivered in 36 hours'.

without for *unless* is now illiterate, as in 'Without something unexpected happens, the murderer will be hanged to-morrow'.

without doubt should be used as an adjective only with sedulous care. In e.g., 'It is not only McCabe's objectivity—though that is without doubt—but also a natural equality between the two opponents', where 'indubitable' or, better, 'indisputable' would have been preferable.

witness, debased to = 'to *see*'. To *witness* is not merely to *see*, but to *testify.*

womanish; womanly; womanlike; female; feminine. *Womanish* is now mainly pejorative; *womanly,* mainly favourable. *Womanish* = 'resembling a woman in her weakness' (physical disabilities, mental disabilities), as in 'Her spitefulness is, in short, womanish'; but if applied to a (young or youngish) girl, it = 'like a grown woman (in figure or in her ways)'. *Womanish* is often (contrast *mannish*) applied to effeminate men, as in 'that womanish exquisite!' *Womanly* = 'of, belonging to, characteristic of a woman' (neutrally or favourably), whether of women or their qualities or their actions, as in 'Her womanly kindness and gentleness redeemed her from insipidity'; also 'having the character of—befitting—a woman as opposed to a girl', as in 'A womanly sort of bonnet'. *Womanlike* is the feminine of *manlike. Female* is merely the adjective corresponding to *male; feminine* corresponds to *masculine.* (*O.E.D.*)

wonder for *wonderful* ('a wonder child') is an example of journalistic 'rubber-stamp words' (*q.v.* at AMAZING).

wonderful—more wonderful—most wonderful. The forms *wonderfuller* and *wonderfullest* are not recommended.

wondrous (adj.) is literary; as adv., it is archaic for *wondrously* (itself literary).

wooded, wooden, woody. *Wooded* = 'covered with growing trees; abounding in woods and forests', usually with adverb, as in 'The neighbourhood was richly wooded'. *Wooden* = 'made of wood; consisting of wood' ('A waggon with wooden wheels'); hence, 'produced by means of wood; relating to wood; hard or stiff like wood', as in 'a wooden (now also *wood*) fire', 'The fingers have . . . become . . . pale and wooden'; figuratively, 'spiritless, dull and inert, unintelligent, insensitive', as in 'A dryasdust, wooden antiquary', 'He has a wooden head', 'a wooden notion'. *Woody* is a synonym of *wooded* (but without adverb), as in 'The rose-hung lanes of woody Kent' (Morris). Its other senses are 'of a wood, situated in a wood' ('a woody nook', 'They left the woody path for a field'); 'of the nature of, or consisting of, wood; ligneous' (as in 'the woody knobs of rose-bush roots', 'Fibrous and woody elements . . . exist . . . in all vegetable foods'); (of plants) 'having stem and branches of wood'; 'resembling wood; having the consistence or texture of wood' ('a large, woody apple'); 'characteristic of wood; having some quality of wood', as in 'clean woody odours'; 'having a dull sound, like that of wood when struck', as in 'A little cottage piano, woody and dull of tone'. (*O.E.D.*)

WOOLLINESS.

Woolly. Lacking in definiteness or incisiveness; 'muzzy'; (of the mind [style], etc.) confused and hazy. (*O.E.D.*)

Woolliness is that fault of style which consists in writing around a subject instead of on it; of making approximations serve as exactitudes; of resting content with intention as opposed to performance; of forgetting that whereas a haziness may mean something to the perpetrator, it usually means nothing (or an ambiguity) to the reader or the listener. The ideal at which a writer should aim—admittedly it is impossible of attainment—is that he write so clearly and precisely that his words can bear only one meaning to all averagely intelligent readers that possess an average knowledge of the language used.

But to generalize further on woolliness would serve no useful purpose. I shall particularize by giving, first, a number of brief examples and commenting on them, and, secondly, some longer passages and leaving them to the reader's angry bewilderment.

'Not a ship, nor a gun, nor a man, were on the ground to prevent their landing' (Gladstone, *Gleanings*, 1870). Why *ground*? (If Gladstone means 'at this part of the coast', why does he not write 'at this place'?) Does *gun* mean literally 'a cannon', or does it mean *gun-crew* or, rather, a *gun and its crew*?

'After dinner, they drove on to London, and found Mr Pegley's address was on the top floor of a new and very smart block of flats' (E. R. Punshon, *The Dusky Hour*). Better, '. . . found that Mr Pegley lived on the top floor . . .'

'As essayists, the writings of Addison and of Steele are familiar to all readers of eighteenth-century literature' (John Dennis, *The Age of Pope*, 1894). And all he needed to say was 'As essayists, Addison and Steele are familiar . . .'; the intrusive 'the writings of . . . of' has produced a ludicrous example of false agreement and put the reader out of his stride.

'It will be for him to decide if we proceed further' (Vernon Loder, *The Button in the Plate*, 1938). The author—as the context shows—intends 'whether'; 'if' yields a very different sense.

'His point is, I think, evidently mistaken' (I. A. Richards, *The Philosophy of Rhetoric*, 1936). Read, either 'His point is, I think, mistaken' or 'His point is evidently mistaken'. If the error is *evident*, why 'I think'? And if it isn't, why 'evidently'?

'In most prose, and more than we ordinarily suppose, the opening words have to wait for those that follow to settle what they shall mean' (*ibid.*). It is not the opening words which have to wait, but we who read them: *we* must wait for the ensuing words before *we* can settle what the opening words mean in the sentence.

'Put very simply, a causal law may be taken as saying that, under certain conditions, of two events if one happens the other does' (I. A. Richards, *ibid.*). Should this not read, 'Put very simply, a causal law may be taken as saying that if, under certain conditions, one of two events happens, the other happens also'?

' "Billy the Dip's" job was, as usual, outside man; which most important duty he would perform in the company of another ferrety-eyed person not present, who owned to the name of Abe Snitzler, and in whom was combined the cunning of the rat with the swiftness of the eel. These two would station themselves, the first on the corner of Regent and Maddox Street, the second in the alley at the rear

of the premises by which route the loot and getaway would have to be made' (John G. Brandon, *The Regent Street Raid*). Concerning this paragraph, a much longer paragraph might be written.

'They say you can't kill a newspaper man or even one who wants to become one' (Russell Birdwell, *I Ring Doorbells*, 1939). The first 'one' is the impersonal 'one' (a person); the second = 'a newspaper man'. Hence, confusion.

'Money won at billiards cannot be recovered' (Hay & Son Ltd's *Diary*, 1939). Not *won* but *lost* is the right word.

'It was more as if he lived in the shadow of something that no man could remain quite sane while contemplating' (Michael Innes, *Lament for a Maker*, 1938). The sentence has not been worked out; or rather, the thought has not been worked out. Perhaps '. . . something that, if he contemplated it, left no man quite sane while he contemplated it'. The original sentence is too condensed and too pregnant with meaning to be either clear or comfortable.

'He doesn't go out much, but he gives a man's dinner now and then, which are the best in London' (John Buchan, *The Power-House*). Read, '. . . now and then, and these are the best dinners in London'.

'The handwriting was like a sick man of ninety' (John Buchan, *The Moon Endureth*); better, 'like a sick man of ninety's' or 'like that of a sick man of ninety'.

'But probably he did, as we still may, find much to interest us in the work of the Lancashire poets' (Eric Partridge, *A Critical Medley*, 1926). For 'us', read 'him'.

'Not only are the frontiers of science traced out, its specialist lines of development where they are most significant, but its social and philosophic meaning are set out in direct form' (a publisher's booklist). Either 'meaning is' or 'meanings are'; the latter is preferable.

'Another mode of spending the leisure time is that of books' (Cobbett: cited by Nesfield).

'The fifteenth century has been termed "the golden age" of the English labourer, and up to the middle of the nineteenth century this may have been so' (W. O. Massingberd, in vol. II of *The Victoria County History* of Lincolnshire).

'A third public school man writes: "If one thinks a little, retailing is a very real, alive and gripping 'profession', and well it may be termed, perhaps never before a profession, it is highly specialised where one brings into play every faculty one has been given. To those men who have been fortunate to have a good education, there is nothing else I know where every subject he has been coached in has been brought into use at one time or another. With this being such he will always be an ever-awake and useful member of the community" ' (*The New Statesman*, quoting advertisements by members of the staff of a great London shop). That, I think, is the best example I have had the good fortune to find: it is perfect.

Now for a few examples from Mr Ramsay MacDonald, the Rt Hon. David Lloyd George, Mr Elihu Root, and Herr Adolf Hitler. They will evoke irreverent chortles from all who prefer clear to blurred, and definite to hazy writing.

'Relativity was written plainly across the pages of history long before Einstein applied it to the universe. Relatively, Capitalism has justified itself in relation to the absolute criterion of Capitalist aims; but in relation to the absolute criterion'—as though there were one!—'of social wealth, harmony and happiness, and individual welfare, Capitalism has not justified itself and has to be transformed into something that is higher' (James Ramsay MacDonald, 'Socialism for Business Men').

'No employer can appeal straight to the hearts of his people [his employees] to sacrifice themselves in the national interests, because the moment he does that he raises in their minds the problem of the relationship between employer and employed.—He raises in their minds that unfortunate conflict of the economic, industrial and social interests of the two sides to this economic problem. Until we can abolish the two sides, and unite them in a new form of social service, we shall not be able to appeal to the communal sense of both, in order to do sacrificial work for the benefit of the whole community. There lies the philosophical basis of the class conflict, and you cannot remove it except by re-organisation' (*ibid.*).

'Socialism is an idea. The growth of Socialism is shown by the continued application of sound ideas, modifying the form and structure of the society in which we live, and moulding it so that as time goes on the form becomes more and more like the absolute idea itself.—It is the same in architectural conception and the religious conception. It is the same as

the ideas in a man's mind when he starts out to build up a business' (*ibid.*).

'Mr Chairman, I am one of those people who never hide the fact that I am a patriot. You get sometimes queer definitions of patriotism, and in accordance with those definitions I am ruled out. But I am one of those people indifferent to what "they say" ' (Ramsay Macdonald, 'Patriotism True and False').

'I daresay I have not many years now here and certainly I am in the position of a man who feels that the remaining sands in the upper part of the sandglass become more and more golden in their preciousness, and therefore I am not anxious to waste them. I am not interested, therefore, so much in looking back and trying to devise agreements such as might apply under circumstances which I believe, if you and I make up our minds, are now dead' (Ramsay MacDonald, 'Among Old Friends'). The first sentence is a bewildering abomination, and the second sentence lacks a tail.

'We have been working as well as preaching in Europe and I think we have been working with a considerable amount of success. We have been seeing to this—and this is of fundamental importance—that public opinion is demanding that those responsible for governments should not only take the risk of war, which they take when they begin to build competitively their armaments, but they should take the risk of peace' (Ramsay MacDonald, 'The Risks of Peace').

On Oct. 21, 1929, to the assembled staff and students of McGill University, on the occasion of a Doctorate of Laws conferred on him by that university, Ramsay MacDonald spoke thus: 'As Prime Minister of Great Britain, I take this as an evidence on your part of the abiding and enduring loyalty to the common Empire to which we both belong. As one who has come over in order to try and bring a little closer not in the form of an alliance, but in the form of a closer and more affectionate unity of spirit and understanding these two great nations I take it in conferring this degree you have also had in mind.'

But let us pass to that more celebrated orator, David Lloyd George. His was a different sort of woolliness—the woolliness that results from an excess of metaphor and from a surfeit of words; a woolliness much less woolly than Ramsay MacDonald's, for the general (as opposed to the particular) meaning is nearly always clear, as in 'The Curse of Feudalism'—a speech that begins thus: 'The progressive forces in this country [Great Britain] are bending their energies to the task of uprooting the mischievous power of feudalism. The reactionary elements in the country, on the other hand, are, with the same [i.e., an equal; or, a similar] energy, with the same zeal, but, perhaps, with different weapons, undertaking the task of nourishing and feeding these roots [*which* roots?], and deepening their hold on the soil, and by tariffs and by something they call reform of the House of Lords, real progress in this country is barred in every direction by the feudal power.' Here the luxuriant verbiage rather induces a sense of woolliness than produces sheer woolliness: the passage, indeed, is far from being sheerly woolly: and as it fell, unhalting, from the orator's silver tongue, it was, one cannot doubt, eloquent and perhaps even impressive.

'Belgium, once comfortably well-to-do, is now waste and weeping, and her children are living on the bread of charity sent them by neighbours far and near. And France! The German army, like a wild beast, has fastened its claws deep into her soil, and every effort to drag them out rends and tears the living flesh of that beautiful land. The beast of prey has not leapt to our shores—not a hair of Britain's head has been touched by him' ('A Holy War', Feb. 28, 1915). The accumulation of imperfect metaphor produces a sense of discomfort; the effect is—woolliness. Cf.:

'This desolating war has been forced upon us by an arrogant military caste that sought to enslave Europe, who thought they had perfected a machine that would tear through her vitals and leave her crushed and bleeding at their feet. The Prussian means to dominate the world. That is a mania which has possessed the military castes in every century. Once or twice it has succeeded, and that has upset the balance of many who thought they could follow. But although they will not succeed, nevertheless to overthrow that ambition will cost Europe a ghastly price in blood and in treasure' ('How Long Will the War Last?', May 7, 1915). The fecklessly rapid changes of the grammatical subject— changes made without due regard to consecutiveness—are indefensible: and the effect is woolliness.

'We have just emerged from a great peril. We have emerged triumphantly. The greatness of the peril we can hardly conceive at the present moment. It will take time for us fully to appreciate its vastness. The greatness of the triumph we cannot fully estimate now. I met a man the other day who came to me and said, "This victory is so vast that I can only take it in in parts". I think that that was one of the truest things said of our triumph. He said, "I see one phase of it to-day, and to-morrow I see another, and the third day I see another". That is true about the danger we have averted and about the victory we have achieved' ('Reconstruction', Nov. 24, 1918).

But let us take an American statesman. Elihu Root. He is much less woolly, in fact, than Ramsay MacDonald. Yet the following passage creates a rather blurred impression.

'One accustomed to the administration of municipal law who turns his attention for the first time to the discussion of practical questions arising between nations and dependent upon the rules of international law, must be struck by a difference between the two systems which materially affects the intellectual processes involved in every discussion, and which is apparently fundamental.— The proofs and arguments adduced by the municipal lawyer are addressed to the object of setting in motion certain legal machinery which will result in a judicial judgment to be enforced by the entire power of the state over litigants subject to its jurisdiction and control' ('The Sanction of International Law', April 24, 1908).

Elihu Root, however, was generally lucid and direct, despite his tendency to verbiage. Compared with Hitler, he was almost indecently lucid. The Führer generated so much heat and smoke that, far too often, one *feels* what he meant but one cannot see clearly what it is he meant; far too often, indeed, he was expressing, not a precise meaning but an emotion, or an aspiration, or some grandiose ambition. Those who attempt to deduce a precise meaning from his fiery, vatidical speeches and writings are often baffled by the muzziness of his style and the woolliness of his oratory. One feels that he wrote as he spoke: at top shriek. This passage is taken from *My Struggle*, the abridged English translation (1933) of *Mein Kampf*.

'The *psyche* of the mass of the people is

not receptive of anything savouring of half-measures and weakness.—Like a woman whose sensibilities are influenced less by abstract reasoning than by an indefinable longing governed by feeling, for the strength which completes what is to be done, and who would rather bow to the strong man than dominate the weakling, the people love a ruler more than a suppliant and feel more inwardly satisfied by doctrines which suffer no rival, than by an admission of liberal freedom; they have very little idea how to use it and easily feel forsaken. They are as little conscious of the shame of being spiritually terrorized as of an abuse of their freedom as human beings, calculated to drive them into revolt; nor are they aware of any intrinsic wrongness in the teaching' (I, ii).

WORDINESS. See VERBOSITY.

working-man and **working man; workman.** A *working man* is vague, for it = 'a man that is or happens to be engaged in work', whereas *a working-man* is 'a man employed to work for a wage, especially in a manual or industrial occupation'; *working-man* includes *artisan, mechanic, labourer.* (The corresponding female is a *working-woman.*) A *workman* is 'a man engaged, on a wage, to do manual labour', especially if he is 'employed upon some particular piece of work' (an *operative*); often the context shows that 'a skilled worker' is meant; often *workman* is opposed to *employer* or to *capitalist*, though *worker* (especially in the plural) is more usual in this opposition. *Workman* has the further, more general sense, 'one who works—or practises his craft or his art—in some specified manner', e.g., in painting; thus, 'My health makes me a very slow workman'. *Workwoman* is 'a female worker or operative'. (*O.E.D.*)

world. See EARTH and SPHERE.

worse is misused in 'He was self-conceited, knew little, and wrote worse'.

worst, misused for *most*, as in 'What I need worst is a haircut'. An idiomatic usage of *worst* is that with verbs of liking or loving, allowing, pleasing, as in 'This pleased them worst of all', where *worst* = 'least'. (*O.E.D.*)

worst two is incorrect for *two worst* in, e.g., 'The worst two pupils were sent down to the class below'. Cf. FIRST TWO.

would, misused for *were*. See SUBJUNCTIVE. Here is a glaring example:— ' "Would it not be better," Pyke said very slowly, "if you *would* be quite frank with

me?" ', W. S. Masterman, *The Perjured Alibi.*

would, misused for *will*. See PAST SUBJUNCTIVE.

would and should. *The O.E.D.* quotes Mrs S. Pennington, 1766, 'I choose rather that you would carry it yourself', as misusing *would* for *should*.

Apart from its subjunctival use, *should* is the past tense of that *shall* which = 'to be obliged (to do something)', and *would* is the past tense of that *will* which = 'to be resolved (to do something)'. Thus 'He *would* go (= he was determined to go), say what I might'; 'I would not (= was unwilling to, did not wish to, refused to) answer him when he spoke to me yesterday'; 'It seemed to him that he could nowhere find in his heart the chords that *should* answer directly to that music'; 'As I was walking along the High Street, whom *should* I meet but my cousin Tom', where 'should I' = 'I was fated to'.

In conditional sentences of Group II (sentences in which 'the principal clause speaks of what would be or would have been and in which the *if*-clause states, or implies, a negative'), *should* and *would* are used in virtually the same way: 'Even if I knew, I *would* not tell' (= *should* not *be willing* to tell, or should not wish to tell); 'Wert thou creation's lord, thou *shouldst* not taunt me thus' (= *wouldst* not *be permitted* to taunt me thus): here, *should* and *would* are subjunctives.

Properly subjunctive, too, is *should* in 'You *should* do that', i.e., 'You *ought* to do that', i.e., 'You *would* be bound to do that', i.e., 'It *is* right for you to do that'; 'I know that I *should* do that, but I cannot bring myself to do it'. But what the practice amounts to is this: the past subjunctive *should* is not only used in all persons, but is employed as, virtually, a present indicative synonymous with *ought*.

Would as a past indicative is occasionally synonymous with 'used to', for past habitual action: 'He paid little attention to what was being said: he *would* constantly be looking at the window': this usage is now literary, not general.

So far we have considered *should* and *would* as words having independent meaning. Now we come to their employment as mere auxiliaries expressed in the past tense; *should* and *would* being used in dependence on verbs that are themselves in the past tense. 'I knew that if I stayed here, I *should* see him pass', 'I knew that if you stayed here, you *would* see him pass', and 'I feared that he *would* come to a bad end'.

Thence we pass to their employment as indications—and auxiliary verbs—of mood: as subjunctives and subjunctive-equivalents. In the principal clauses of conditional sentences of Group II (see CONDITIONAL CLAUSES), *should* is to be used for the 1st person, *would* for the 2nd and 3rd persons, as in 'Though you said it a thousand times, I *should* not believe it—no one *would* believe it'. But in certain subordinate clauses, *should* is used in all three persons, thus:—

(*a*) In such clauses as have an action stated or implied to be under consideration (in prospect, or a subject of contemplation), as in 'He refused to budge until he should receive a thousand dollars'.

(*b*) In conditional clauses of Group III (i.e., in conditional sentences in which the principal clause does not state, nor imply, what would be or would have been, but in which the *if*-clause not only indicates an action that is contemplated or planned but also connotes some degree of reserve on the part of the speaker),—i.e., in such conditional clauses as 'If the king *should* fall, he will fall in fair fight' and the disguised 'I am sorry that you *should* be so angry'.

(*c*) In certain dependent statements or commands, as in 'It is natural that I *should* visit my family', 'It was disgraceful that you *should* fail us in that way', 'I saw to it that he *should* not give me the slip', 'Providence furnishes materials, but expects that we *should* work them up by ourselves', 'It is right that you *should* be dismissed', 'He commanded that no one *should* leave the room'.

It is an odd fact that whereas *would* is colloquially shortened to '*d* (better '*ld*), *should* has no shortened form. In *The Observer*, 1938, Mr Conor O'Brien writes: 'Sir,—we think, and we say colloquially, "I'd like . . ." We are told that this can only be expanded to "I would like," and as half of us don't recast our thoughts when writing, we write down "I would" ', although the correct form is 'I should like (to do something)'. 'Why, in the name of common sense', Mr O'Brien continues, 'cannot this necessary abbreviation stand equally well for "I should"?'

The trouble is that '*d* already = *had* ('I'd done it already') and *would* (for which I prefer '*ld*). Yet '*ll* = *shall* or *will*, so why should not '*ld* represent *should* or *would*? [*Webster's* and certain American grammarians give authority for '*d* and '*ld* to represent both *should* and *would*.]

would best is unfortunate for *had best* in 'She would best avoid such a marriage'.

would better is incorrect for *had better* in 'I would better depart now'.

would have, in conditional sentences, is incorrect for *had*, as in 'If he would have wished, he could have spared you a troublesome journey'.

would rather and **had rather**. In the first person, *had rather* is almost obligatory ('I had rather die young than live to be a hundred'); in the third, *would rather* is perhaps the more usual ('He would rather sleep than eat'); in the second, 'You would perhaps rather wait here than at the house' is preferable to 'You had rather'.

wove and **woven**. *Wove* is the preterite of *weave*; *woven*, the usual past participle, *wove* being inferior except in such technicalities as *wove mould* and *wove paper*.

wrack is misused for *rack* in at least three senses. It should be a *rack* of clouds; *rack*, an instrument of torture; and the horse's gait should be *rack*. In the sense 'ruin', both forms are correct, as in go to (*w*)*rack and ruin*, but, except in that phrase and its variants (*bring to, put to, run to r. and r.*), *wrack*—a cognate of *wreck*—is the more general. (*O.E.D.*)

wrapt and **rapt**. In 'He was absorbed in wrapt meditation', *wrapt* is incorrect for *rapt*. *Wrapt* or *wrapped* is the past participle (and participial adjective) of *wrap*, 'to cover or swathe by enfolding in, e.g., a cloth', 'to cover or envelop (an object) by winding or folding something round or about it', etc. *Rapt* is the past participle (and participial adjective) of *rape*, 'to take and carry off by force', fig., 'to delight'. *Rapt* = 'taken and carried away', whether lit. or fig.; hence, 'transported with some emotion or thought', as in 'The book held me rapt', 'I stood gazing, rapt in admiration'. (*O.E.D.*)

wrath, 'anger', and **wroth**, 'angry' (a literarism), are sometimes confused.

wriggle. See WIGGLE.

wring—wrung—wrung are the current inflections. The preterite *wrang* is now dialectal. The past participle *wringed* is obsolete.

writ. The noun *writ* is obsolete except in the phrase *Holy* (or *Sacred*) *Writ*, the Bible or Holy Scriptures, and in Law (a *writ of certiorari, writ of venire facias,* etc.; 'a Parliamentary writ').—The past participle *writ* is archaic, as in 'The moving finger writes, and having writ, moves on'.

writer and **author.** See MAN OF LETTERS.

writer, the; the present writer. These are not wrong. But, in general, the honest *I* is preferable.

write upon impulse. See PREPOSITIONS WRONGLY USED.

wrong (adv.) is obsolescent for *wrongfully* (mistakenly, erroneously), as in 'You have been wrong informed *or* informed wrong'; for *wrongfully, wrongly,* in the sense 'unfairly, unjustly', as in 'to set right what one has done wrong' (morally); and for *amiss, improperly,* as in 'Every guest's uneasiness lest he drink his coffee wrong' (Owen Wister), except in *to go wrong* (to turn out badly, to err, etc.). Note that *a word pronounced wrong* is now less common than *a word wrongly pronounced. (O.E.D.)*

wroth. See WRATH . . .

X

Xmas, a contraction of *Christmas,* is allowable in letter-writing, but has no excuse in the pronunciation, *Exmas.*

Y

Yankee, loosely applied (in England) to all Americans (i.e., of the U.S.A.), means only a citizen of the New England states (Massachusetts, Connecticut, etc.), or by extension a citizen of any Northern state, as distinguished from a Southerner.

ye in such popular uses as 'Ye olde Englysshe Tea-Shoppe' is founded on a complete misconception of the old symbol þ, the letter 'thorn', which in Old English and Middle English represented the sound of *th*. In printing, the *y* was substituted for it and has come to be mispronounced.

yet cannot always, as an adverb, be used for *still* or *even.* 'Hilary's letter had been written on plain white paper, and the en-velope was probably yet less distinctive': 'still less' or 'even less' would be much better.

Yiddish is so often misused that the editor feels it incumbent on him to mention that, although the language is written in Hebrew characters, it is not Hebrew nor yet a dialect of Hebrew. Yiddish is the language used by Jews in Europe and America, consisting mainly of German with an admixture of Baltic-Slavic or Hebrew words. The word is simply the English form of German *jüdisch,* 'Jewish'.

Note that *Yiddisher* is not any Jew, but a Jew that speaks *Yiddish.* And *Yid* is a vulgar shortening of *Yiddisher.*

you aren't and **you're not.** Cf. WE AREN'T.

you both. See BOTH OF US.

young and **youthful.** The former is literal, with the emphasis on the mere fact of age; the latter stresses the fact that one is characterized by youth, or that one is still young; *youthful* also = 'juvenile; characteristic of or suitable for the young'; and especially, 'having the freshness and vigour of youth'. 'Though he is a young man, one does not think of him as being youthful', 'youthful impatience', 'The world was still at its youthful stage'. *(O.E.D.)*

youth and **youthfulness.** *Youth* corresponds to *young; youthfulness* to *youthful,* as in the preceding entry. 'The youthfulness of the old man was astounding'; 'Even in youth, he was like an old man'.

yourself; yourselves for *you.* See MYSELF.

Z

Zoilus (pron. *Zō'ĭlus*) and **Aristarchus** are not synonymous: only the former = 'carping critic'; *Aristarchus* may be safely used for 'a (very) good textual critic' and for 'an excellent grammarian and literary critic'. Aristarchus, 'the founder of scientific scholarship' (Sir J. C. Sandys), lived in the 2nd Century B.C. and was head of the famous Alexandrian Library. Zoilus, another Greek, lived in the 4th Century B.C. and rendered himself extremely unpopular with his hair-splitting animadversions upon Homer's invention and grammar.